W9-AFY-585

Striking a Balance

*A Guide to Enhancing the Effectiveness of
Non-Governmental Organisations in
International Development*

Alan Fowler

London • New York

For Wendy,
trusted friend, critical companion
and valued partner

First published in the UK in 1997 by Earthscan
Reprinted 2000, 2002
Moved to digital printing in 2006

Copyright © Alan Fowler 1997

All rights reserved

A catalogue record for this book is available from the British Library

ISBN-10: 1 85383 325 8
ISBN-13: 9 781853 833250

Typesetting and page design by Derbyshire Design Associates

For a full list of publications, please contact:
Earthscan
2 Park Square, Milton Park, Abingdon, Oxon OX14 4RN
Simultaneously published in the USA and Canada by Earthscan
711 Third Avenue, New York, NY 10017
Earthscan is an imprint of the Taylor & Francis Group, an informa business

Earthscan publishes in association with WWF-UK and the International Institute
for Environment and Development.

INTRAC: The International Non-governmental Organisation Training and Research Centre
INTRAC was set up in 1991 to provide specially designed management, training and research services for NGOs involved in relief and development in the South and dedicated to improving organisational effectiveness and programme performance of Northern NGOs and Southern partners where appropriate. Our goal is to serve NGOs in (i) the exploration of management, policy and human resource issues affecting their own organisational development, and (ii) the evolution of more effective programmes of institutional development and cooperation.

Contents

Part 1: NGDOs in International Development

Part 2: Making NGDOs Effective

Part 3: Improving and Moving On

List of Illustrations

Figures

Tables

Boxes

Glossary

ABONG — Association of Brazilian NGOs
ACBAR — Agency Co-ordinating Body for Afghan Relief
ACFOA — Australian Council for Overseas Aid
ADAB — Association of Development Agencies in Bangladesh
ADHOC — Cambodian Human Rights and Development Association
ADP — Area Development Programme
AKRSP — Aga Khan Rural Support Programme, India
ALIANCE — Alianza para al Desarrollo Juvenil Comunitario, Guatemala
ALOP — Latin American Association of Promotional Organisations
AMREF — African Medical and Research Foundation, Kenya
ANGOC — Asian NGO Coalition for Agrarian Reform and Rural Development
APRODEV — Association of Protestant Development Agencies, Brussels
ARP — Action-Research Programme
AWARE — Action for Welfare and Awakening in Rural Environment, India
BINGO — Big NGDO
BOND — British Overseas NGOs for Development
BRAC — Bangladesh Rural Advancement Committee
BRO — Bureacratic Reorientation
CAA — Community Aid Abroad, Australia
CAMPE — Campaign for Popular Education, Bangladesh
CAP — Consumers Association of Penang, Malaysia
CARE — Cooperative for American Relief Everywhere
CBO — Community - Based Organisation
CDRA — Community Development Resource Association, Cape Town
CDTF — Community Development Trust Fund, Tanzania
CDTP — Community Development Technical Programme
CEBEMO — Catholic Bureau For International Co-operation
CEDEP — Centro de Estudios Para el Desarrollo y la Participacio, Peru
CENDEC — Centro de Estudio de Desarrollo y Participacio, Brazil
CEPES — Centro de Promocion y Estudios Sociales, Peru
CHE — Complex Humanitarian Emergencies
CIDA — Canadian International Development Agency
CIDSE — Catholic International Development Centre, Brussels
CIED — Centro Internacional y Education y Desarrollo, Peru
CINDE — Centro Internacional de Desarrollo y Educacion, Colombia
CIVICUS — World Alliance for Citizen Participation
CODE-NGO — Caucus of Development NGO Networks, Philippines
CONVERGENCE — Convergence for Community-Centred Area Development, Philippines
CORAT — Christian Organisations Research Advisory Trust, Kenya
CRDA — Christian Relief and Development Association, Ethiopia
CRS — Catholic Relief Services, USA
CUSO — Canadian University Service Overseas
D-GAP — Development Group for Alternative Policy

DAC	Development Assistance Committee		Environment and Development,
DEC	Digital Equipment Corporation		London
DELTA	Development Education and	IMF	International Monetary Fund
	Leadership Training for Action	INTRAC	International NGO Training and
DESCO	Centro de Estudios Y Promocion del		Research Centre, Oxford, England
	Desarrollo, Peru	IRED	International Development
EASUN	East Africa NGO Support Unit,		Resources and Networks
	Tanzania	ITDG	Intermediate Technology
ECA	Economic Commission for Africa		Development Group, UK
FAVDO	Forum for African Voluntary	JICA	Japanese International Co-operation
	Development Organisations		Agency
FINCA	Campasino Financing Fund, Costa	KAACR	Kenya Alliance for Advancement of
	Rica		Children's Rights
FLO	Foundation Like Organisation	KENGO	Kenya Energy and Environment
FOCUS	Focus on the Global South, Thailand		Organisation
FS	Fundacion Social, Colombia	LFA	Logical Framework Analysis
FU	Functional Unit	LNF	Lebanese NGO Forum
GAAP	Generally Accepted Accounting	MA	Management Assistance
	Principles	M&E	Materials and Equipment
GAD	Gender and Development	MODE	Management and Organisational
GAPVOD	Ghana Association of Private		Development for Empowerment,
	Voluntary Organisations for		Philippines
	Development	MYRADA	Mysore Resettlement and
GATT	General Agreement on Tariffs and		Development Agency
	Trade	NCA	Norwegian Church Aid
GDP	Gross Domestic Product	NCSWS	National Council for Social Welfare
GEF	Global Environment Facility		Services, Tanzania
GRO	Grassroots Organisation	NET	North East Thailand Project,
GSO	Grassroots Support Organisation		Canadian University Service Overseas
GSS	Gonoshahajjo Sangstha, Bangladesh	NGDO	Non-Governmental Development
HACU	Humanitarian Assistance		Organisation
	Co-ordination Unit, Rwanda	NGLS	UN Non-Governmental Liaison
HASIK	Harnessing Self-Reliant Initiatives		Service, Geneva
	and Knowledge, Philippines	NGO	Non-Governmental Organisation
HIVOS	Humanitarian Institute for	NGORC	Non-Governmental Organisation
	Co-operation with Developing		Resource Centre, Pakistan
	Countries, Netherlands	NGOSO	NGO Support Organisation
HRD	Human Resource Development	NGRO	Non-Governmental Relief
HRM	Human Resource Management		Organisation
IBFAN	International Baby Food Action	NIPA	NGOs For Integrated Protected
	Network		Areas, Manila
ICCO	Interchurch Co-ordination Committee	NOVIB	Netherlands Organisation for
	for Development Projects		International Co-operation
ID	Institutional Development	OA	Organisational Assessment
IBFAN	International Baby Food Action	OD	Organisational Development
	Network	ODA	Overseas Development Assistance
IDR	Institute for Development Research,	ODA-UK	Overseas Development
	Boston, USA		Administration, United Kingdom
IFI	International Financial Institution	ODI	Overseas Development Institute, UK
IIED	International Institute for	OECD	Organisation for Economic

	Co-operation and Development	RD	Relational Development
OJT	On-the-Job Training	ROSA	PLAN Region for South Asia
ORAP	Organisation of Rural Associations for Progress, Zimbabwe	SCF-UK	Save the Children Fund, United Kingdom
Oxfam-UK/I	Oxfam, United Kingdom and Ireland	SIDA	Swedish International Development Agency
PA	Peasant Association		
P&A	Personnel and Administration	SORP	Statement of Recommended Practice on Accounting By Charities, UK
PACT	Private Agencies Collaborating Together, USA	SSM	Sarvadoya Shramadana Movement
PACT/PRIP	Project of a US NGO named PACT operating in Bangladesh	TA	Transactional Analysis
		TACOSODE	Tanzania Council for Social Development
PALM	Participatory Learning Methods		
PAs	Peasant Associations	TANGO	Tanzania NGO Council
PBS	Planning and Budgeting System	TBA	Traditional Birth Attendant
PBSP	Philippines Business for Social Progress	TC	Technical Co-operation
		TOE	Training for Efficiency/ Effectiveness
PER	Project for Environmental Recovery, Thailand		
		TQL	Total Quality Learning
PHILSSA	Partnership of Philippine Support Service Agencies and Urban Poor Associates	TQM	Total Quality Management
		TRRM	Thai Rural Reconstruction Movement
PID	Project Identification Document	UCL	Union for Civil Liberty, Thailand
PLAN International		UNDP	United Nations Development Programme
	Foster Parents Plan International		
POP	People's Organisation for Participation, Thailand	UNHCR	United Nations High Commission for Refugees
PPI	Philippine Peasant Institute	UNNATI	Organisation for Development Education, Ahmedabad
PRA	Participatory Rural Appraisal		
PRIA	Society for Participatory Research in Asia, India	UNTAC	United Nations Transitional Authority in Cambodia
PRIP	Private Rural Initiatives Project Trust, Bangladesh	USAID	United States Agency for International Development
PROSHIKA	Human Development Centre, Bangladesh	USK	Undugu Society of Kenya
		VITA	Volunteers in Technical Assistance, USA
PRRM	Philippine Rural Reconstruction Movement		
		WARF	West African Rural Foundation
QUANGO	Quasi Non-Governmental Organisation	WID	Women in Development
		WVE	World Vision Ethiopia
RAFAD	Research and Applications for Alternative Development, Switzerland	ZOPP	Objectives – Oriented Project Planning

Acknowledgements

With only an outline to go on, a number of people had the confidence to invest in an initiative to document the way in which non-governmental organisations (NGDOs) involved in international development function and to suggest how their effectiveness can be improved. Eleven NGDOs contributed the funds which made this book possible. They are ActionAid (UK/I), Aga Khan Foundation (Canada), Community Aid Abroad, DanChurchAid (Denmark), HIVOS, Norwegian Church Aid, NOVIB, Plan International/Childreach (South Asia/USA), Redd Barna (Norway), Save the Children Fund (UK), World Vision International, and an individual donation from Joel Joffe of the UK. My thanks for their trust and patience.

The request for support challenged NGDOs to show that they are prepared to invest in learning by indicating that finance would not be sought directly from the official aid system. In addition, so that the process did not appear to serve a particular organisation, a limit of 15 per cent was set for any one contribution. Finally, it was proposed that any author's income be donated to an NGDO and not come to me personally. In support of its work, all royalties from the sale of this book will be paid to the International NGO Training and Research Centre, based in Oxford, England.

Talking about NGDOs, rather than the people in and around them, gives the wrong impression about how this book came to be written. While responsibility for the content rests with me, I have enjoyed generous support from many individuals who have acted as critical readers, advisers, sources of information and organisers of my visits to NGDOs in Latin America and South East Asia. In addition, working on the principle that more experiences are better than one, there was an open invitation to provide contributions from personal experience; these have been edited and included in the text. Contributions have been provided by: Binoy Acharya, Héctor Béjar, Richard Holloway, Hans Hoyer, Tom Lent, Carmen Malena, Nicky May, Ezra Mbogori, Marion Nell, Peter Oakley, Juan Sanchez, Helen Shapiro, Ian Smillie, and Roy Trivedy.

In addition to those directly involved in the writing of this book, there are many others whose work, writing, attitude and encouragement have, over many years, inspired and shaped my ideas. Those whom I owe particular thanks are: John Batten, Dave Brown of IDR, Tom Carroll, Robert Chambers, John Clark, Sonia Corea, David Court, Mike Edwards, Katalin Ertsey, Liz Goold, Aroma Goon, John Hailey, Veronica Hope, Ad Hordijk, Mick Howes, Allan Kaplan, Gaim Kebreab, Kabiru Kinyanjui, Abigail Krystall, Kamal Maholtra, Boy Morales, Peter Oakley, Brian Pratt, Chris Roche, Salil Shetty, Rajesh Tandon, Sally Timpson and Aubrey Williams. In addition, there are countless people who – at conferences, during consultancy work or as participants in workshops and training courses – have contributed in one way or the other to my learning. If this book is a useful reflection of what they have helped me to understand about NGDOs, I hope it returns a little of what they were willing to share.

Nairobi/Manila
February 1997

Introduction

This book is written about and for voluntary, non-profit, non-governmental organisations working within the framework of international development co-operation – commonly, but misleadingly, referred to as non-governmental organisations (NGOs). To be clear about the type of non-profit organisations I am concerned with, the abbreviation used throughout is NGDOs – non-governmental development organisations.

The subject covers a wide range of organisations found throughout the world. Diversity is inevitable within the NGDO community, stemming from the contrasting values and goals of those who start and lead them, the different times and contexts in which they evolve, the many levels at which they operate in society, the varied scope of their activities, and the wide mix of resources they mobilise. Diversity, furthermore, is necessary in order to deal with the wide range of tasks and almost limitless settings in which international development takes place.

But diversity presents problems. First, because NGDOs are so varied, comparisons are difficult, while exceptions and alternative points of view will always exist. Therefore, while generalisations have to be made, they must be treated with caution; it is up to the reader to decide how well they correspond to their own experience. Second, it cannot be expected or assumed that a single, fail-safe set of rules or methods can be applied to make NGDOs more effective. There is no universal recipe for improving NGDO performance; instead, performance rests on the unique history, the characteristics of the people involved and the environment at any moment in time. Nevertheless, while there is no hidden formula, examining how NGDOs function and what they achieve is one way of identifying patterns of behaviour, general principles, best practices and 'tricks of an ambiguous trade' which leaders and managers regularly use. This book draws on the richness of their experience to identify where effectiveness might lie.

The information used to describe and understand NGDOs has been gathered over the past 20 years from the vantage points of project manager, consultant, trainer, donor programme officer, NGDO and World Bank policy adviser, analyst and writer. However, irrespective of how many roles one plays, more experiences are better than one. Therefore, a number of experienced individuals within the NGDO community have also contributed 'distillations' of their knowledge about specific topics. Yet, despite these comparative perspectives, it is still hard to get a firm fix on the way the 'better' NGDOs perform. This difficulty also exists for people working in NGDOs who find it easier to talk about what they do than how they do it. One reason for this is that the lives of NGDO people are dominated by daily events; they seldom have the time to reflect on their actions. Consequently, because the internal workings of NGDOs involved in international development are a relatively unexplored area, the pages which follow reflect an ongoing learning process. Their contents are not a conclusive account of effective NGDO management and organisation.

The Importance of Striking a Balance

Systematic analysis of the organisational functioning of NGDOs is in short supply. What emerges, however, from this review is that effectiveness is achieved by those NGDOs who find and maintain the right balance between the contradictory forces, expectations, demands and processes associated with performing complex tasks in collaboration with resource-poor, powerless people in unstable and often hostile environments. There are two significant factors in striking a suitable balance. First, the right systems inside an NGDO must be coupled in appropriate ways to external systems and organisations. Second, the NGDO's structure must reflect a consistent vision, adaptive capacity and culture of trust which motivates and facilitates staff responsiveness. A further characteristic of successful NGDOs is their ability to recognise, organise and manage the ambiguities and dilemmas which are built into the international aid system and are inherent in the role of civic – as opposed to state or market – actors managing social, economic and political change.

In the words of one person interviewed, managing NGDOs is 'a form of gymnastics', a balancing act requiring fitness and agility to keep going in the chosen direction while holding the organisation together as it comes under pressure from structural and unexpected internal and external forces. What pressures exist and how they can be balanced is a theme that recurs in this book.

The Audience

The primary audience are the leaders and managers of the many NGDOs who are seldom able to gain expert advice or support to improve their skills. NGDOs are often created and managed by people who have gained little formal exposure to the ideas, concepts and comparative experiences of non-profit management applied to development work. Committed to act against social ills, they learn about leading and organising by doing it. Although attitudes are changing, NGDOs have had a tendency to regard formal 'management' as inappropriate and anti-people. This stance implies that the poor and marginalised who justify an NGDO's existence should be satisfied with solidarity, commitment and good intentions rather than relevant professionalism as well. This position is not acceptable. NGDOs must actively seek to improve their competence. One way of doing so is to combine learning through personal action with learning from others within the community. This book focuses on sharing such comparative experiences with practically oriented analysis of what has been found to contribute to NGDO effectiveness around the world.

A second audience are the larger international NGDOs and official aid agencies, for instance donors. Both international NGDOs and donors prioritise and adopt strategies that help to build the organisational capacity of their 'partners'. Unfortunately, the equality of relationship implied is seldom achieved because of barriers in the aid system which stubbornly perpetuate power imbalances. Understanding factors that influence NGDO effectiveness can help to reduce these obstacles; in this way, donors are better able to constructively engage with NGDOs, and perhaps other organisations of civil society.

Another audience are existing and aspiring specialists in the field of NGDOs, development and non-profit management. To cater to such an audience, endnotes are used selectively to amplify or comment on issues, while topic-by-topic readings group the references used in each chapter. The readings and extensive bibliography are also intended as a resource for students and those with a more academic interest. Inclusion of this material does not intend to make this an academic work. Rather, the intention of pulling together and commenting on existing publications is to push forward thinking about NGDOs as a subset of the non-profit sector[1].

It is conventional wisdom that the end of the Cold War has led to uncertain times for NGDOs. Today, NGDOs are confronted with a new global policy agenda for international development assistance that presents opportunities, threats and instability as old assumptions become invalid and rules of the game change. Helping to better inform their responses to a new era is therefore one reason for investigating and writing about NGDO management and organisation.

The shifting policy framework has also brought with it a number of potentially negative trends that need to be countered. For example, one consequence of today's aid policies is a much more critical view of NGDO performance, which many recent studies on NGDO impact show to be justified. The solution to shortcomings is believed to be in making NGDOs more business-like. In short, to be more professional, NGDOs are being encouraged, if not forced, to take on practices and perspectives found in commercial enterprise. While often misplaced, this trend has gained hold because of the lack of study about non-profit management and organisation (especially in international development). In this sense, today's management science is incomplete. There is an urgent need to fill this gap by distilling NGDOs' own experiences, based on their perspectives. This will provide firmer grounds to assess what business has to offer to NGDOs and visa versa.

As Peter Drucker contends, business has perhaps more to learn from the management and organisation of non-profits than is customarily thought.[2] This book responds to his argument by describing how NGDOs behave as they struggle to provide a complex 'product-process' mix called people-centred sustainable development.

Second, the 1990s have seen a growing appreciation that NGDOs are only one of many civic actors that can, and must, feature in the international development effort. Documenting the functioning of NGDOs will help locate them within this wider perspective and, hopefully, highlight what can and cannot be reasonably expected in terms of their goals.

Third, NGDOs have long been reluctant to treat management as a priority concern. Good intentions were percieved as a means of achieving results; the moral high ground put NGDOs above criticism and continued funding meant that difficult choices were avoided. Such an attitude implies that people who are poor should be satisfied with, often, less than adequate performance. I believe that this stance is an affront to those providing legitimacy to an NGDO's existence. People who are poor or marginalised have the right to effective management and organisation. The challenge is to learn from NGDO experience so that professionalism is defined, understood and applied in an appropriate way, not simply imported from elsewhere.

Dilemmas, Trade-Offs and Biases

A book requires a meaningful flow of information with a start and finish. However, the story of NGDO effectiveness is one that is changing over time. There is no single beginning or end because effectiveness is not achieved through a standard sequence of events. Consequently, this book's flow is based on what has worked well in the organisational development of NGDOs across the world. In other words, the material has been put together on the basis of practical experience rather than theory.

NGDO effectiveness is both situation-specific and dynamic. It is impossible to describe all situations or every set of relationships within NGDOs and their interactions with the outside world. Two strategies have been employed to deal with this. One is to take a broad look at the NGDO world, selecting a few critical areas – such as resource mobilisation, performance assessment and capacity growth – for detailed treatment. Second, each chapter employs frameworks to highlight key relationships between specific factors. This approach should enable readers to apply their own experiences and interpret examples according to their own perspective.

Some biases run through the book. First, there is a primary focus on operational NGDOs – that is, organisations working directly with communities and groups, but not to the total exclusion of others involved in policy advocacy; in fact, more and more NGDOs are doing both. Second, as East Africa has been my home for many years, I may not have completely avoided African interpretations. Finally, there are my own limitations and prejudices which probably over-idealise what NGDOs can achieve. Please accept these ideals as criteria for critical reflection.

Structure

This book takes the reader from the 'what' of development, through basic features of developmental NGDOs, into areas of NGDO organisational capacity, the 'hows' of managing constraints to effectiveness, to speculations about their future.

Part I contains two foundation-laying chapters. The first answers the question: 'what tasks must NGDOs master in order to be effective in sustainable development?' The second answers the question: 'what are the characteristics of NGDOs?' Part II concentrates on five areas of competence that NGDOs need in order to be developmentally effective and organisationally viable. The areas are: an appropriate organisational set-up; leadership and human resources; external relationships; mobilising high quality financial resources; and managing through achievement. Part III looks to the future in two ways. First, by showing how NGDOs can develop effectiveness; second, looking beyond a 15-year time horizon to see what choices NGDOs must make to stay relevant and viable in a rapidly changing global context. Inevitably, this involves speculation rather than prediction.

My original intention was to cover the management features of NGDO humanitarian relief and emergency assistance, as well as churches involved in these activities and in development work. Limitations in terms of book length have stood in the way of incorporating these themes. Hopefully, additional publications will emerge to fill this gap. A compromise has been to include readings and references on these topics.

The Writer and the Reader's Role

To help internalise content, a well-known writer on management suggested that, after reading, his book be burnt and that readers rewrite their own, as this is 'the only way to really own the concepts'[3]. Such a suggestion is environmentally unsound; passing the book to someone else would be more useful. But the point is still valid – concepts and knowledge are of little use if they do not influence peoples' behaviour. Real understanding of this story will emerge through change in the actions of individuals and those who support and study NGDOs. My hope is that readers will retell this story in their own way because it has succeeded in contributing to their beliefs, insights and actions.

Part 1

NGDOs in International Development

Understanding International Development

The Changing Nature of International Development

A programme of international development assistance, commonly called the aid system, has existed for 30 years or more. Initially the system assumed that inputs of finance and expertise from Northern-donor countries could accelerate and direct change in poorer countries of the world – the South.[1] In later years it became clear that development could not be externally directed, but required local ownership and sufficient capacity to guide the process. Throughout, the primary public goal of international aid remained one of bringing about changes which reduce the proportion of poor or otherwise disadvantaged people in society. About 15 years ago an important condition was added to this goal, namely that change should be sustainable today and for future generations. Even more recently, under the label of reforms for 'good governance', the purpose of aid has expanded to include the promotion of a particular form of politics based on democratic representation, social justice, the rule of law, and adherence to international agreements on human rights.

However, some 30 years of providing aid involving hundreds of billions of dollars, millions of staff and countless projects, together with major shifts in priorities, strategies and approaches, have not made a substantial impact on the scale of poverty in the countries of the South. Transition to market economics in countries of the East, furthermore, is leading to increased human deprivation and criminality, with increasing pollution and the unsustainable exploitation of natural resources.[2] This disappointing reality has added extra fuel to long-running debates, from across the political spectrum, about whether the principles of the aid system are correct and whether present priorities and practices will ever lead to solutions. Disappointment also re-enforces the arguments of those who question the validity of the market-based growth model of development which underpins aid strategies, or if poverty reduction is the real purpose of international assistance.[3]

A more critical appraisal of the aid system is one sign of the post Cold-War context, which has also brought a new agenda for government aid. Recognising this shift, some agencies are trying to change themselves and the aid system overall; unfortunately, too many others believe that with modest adjustments they can carry on as before.

Suggesting how to enhance NGDO effectiveness calls for an approach which is both critical and pragmatic, starting from an analysis of what NGDOs have to be effective at. This chapter therefore explains what is currently known about the various tasks NGDOs must master in order to be an effective force for change within the aid system and within society at large.

Changing insights about the nature of poverty

Today, poverty is seen as a complicated condition, but this has not always been the case. Initially, poverty was simply treated as a lack of the minimum nutritional intake needed to sustain life; calorie counts became the key measure and feeding programmes the response. The poor were then identified as those who fell below the minimum.[4] Subsequently, this limited definition expanded to incorporate a basic set of human needs, including calorie intake, shelter and clothing; it was argued that without these basic needs people could not lead a human existence. Consequently, consumption became the common poverty measure, with a threshold set for the proportion of income that should be spent on basic requirements. The response of the aid system was to provide technical assistance and investment in primary health care, water supply and income generation.

Another shift in argument broadened the understanding of poverty to incorporate quality of life; this acknowledged people's capability to fulfil valuable functions within society. This capability is determined by a person's access to and control over 'commodities', which include tangibles such as food, income, and natural resources, but also cover less tangible, but nevertheless important, items such as education, good health, social standing and security. From this point it is a small step to link 'control over commodities' to the ability to influence decisions on how commodities are both generated and distributed. In other words, powerlessness in society is an additional poverty dimension.[5] Programmes, therefore, sought to organise people around common concerns and to help attain greater voice in matters affecting them. Today poverty can be seen as a human condition where people are unable to achieve essential functions in life, which in turn is due to their lack of access to and control over the commodities they require.[6]

In this way, poverty reduction can be seen as a process through which people progressively gain control over commodities in a rough sequence related to:

- *survival*, such as food, shelter and warmth;
- *well-being*, health, literacy, security; and
- *empowerment*, in the psychological sense of self-esteem and status, and in the political sense of exerting influence over decisions which affect their lives.

People, then, become increasingly entitled to commodities which are environmental, economic, social, cultural and political in nature. The question is: what stands in the way

of people getting their entitlements? In other words, why, in today's world, do people remain in a state of deprivation?

There are doubtless as many explanations of continuing poverty in the world as there are political and moral positions. It might be agreed that poverty arises from an individual's inability to gain access to life's essentials. In terms of selecting appropriate action, however, it is necessary to identify the reason(s) for this inability, as well as to determine who is responsible for altering the situation: the individual, civil society, the market, the state? It is here that ideas diverge and disagreements arise. The following list summarises positions taken on this critical issue. If effective development is to ensue, a decision has to be made on whether or not inaccess to commodities is:

- part of the natural or divine order of things;
- due to cultural norms which act as constraints on the generation or distribution of wealth;
- intrinsic to (international) market capitalism as an economic system;
- a consequence of international power relations and protection of Northern interests in a process of inter-dependent global modernisation;
- an expression of inadequate institutions and inappropriate public policies, or their management, which makes society unable to use existing resources well;
- a product of undemocratic politics and exploitation by unaccountable regimes through self-serving public policies backed up by force, threat and abuse of human rights, using the state's instruments of coercion;
- part and parcel of the historical trajectory of a country's growth and the world's development which, with technological advance, savings and capital accumulation, will eventually be eradicated;
- due to rapid population growth;
- due to market forces and behaviour rapidly eroding proven coping strategies;
- a result of the incapacity of human kind to comprehend and manage complex international relations;
- or a mixture of the above.

It is vitally important for all aid agencies to reach an organisational decision about such causes, otherwise only the symptoms of poverty will be treated. In the case of NGDOs, their impact will not be sustainable in the long term; if causes are not tackled, problems will persist. Second, treating symptoms can actually reinforce the causes of poverty by, for example, undermining people's motivation to act and to claim their entitlements or generate their own solutions. One sign of an effective NGDO, therefore, is an ability to explain the cause(s) of the issue it is trying to address. Surprisingly, very few NGDOs do.[7]

As to who is responsible for improving people's access to life's essentials, there is currently a pendulum swing away from the dominant Northern (welfare state) notion that society bears the ultimate responsibility for the well-being of its members. The responsibility for poverty reduction is no longer so clear cut and remains a highly contested issue.

Marginalisation and social exclusion

In addition to poverty, concern has extended to social justice, human rights and the problem of marginalisation of groups within society, especially women. By marginalisation is meant the exclusion of certain populations from the processes of decision-making that affect their well-being and prospects; this certainly applies to women in many countries. The 1995 UN Conference on Indigenous People has drawn attention to how groups with pre-colonial origins are systematically excluded, exploited and their rights abused due to the way countries continue to evolve economically and politically.

Exclusion in public decision-making is essentially a political issue closely linked to calls for better governance.[8] There are a number of governance definitions to choose from. One of the most straightforward is: governance is the application of political power in the management of public affairs. Governance has two elements of significance for reducing marginalisation. These are factors of inclusion and accountability. *Inclusion* is the active recruitment and involvement of people in ensuring that the regime in power is legitimate,

in the sense that it has an honest mandate to decide and act on public affairs. *Accountability* involves the ability of citizens to sanction the behaviour of those with political or administrative authority; with those in authority recognising that they are answerable to citizens. Reducing marginalisation and social exclusion, therefore, means enhancing poor people's participation in public affairs. This entails "real citizenship".[9]

The critical mix: complexity and power

For all development actors, reducing poverty and eradicating marginalisation are complicated undertakings. Complexity stems, first, from the fact that, as Robert Chambers argues, poverty is composed of an interlocking set of factors which trap people into and maintain their deprivation. Such factors incude:

- poverty itself;
- physical weakness;
- vulnerability;
- isolation; and
- powerlessness.[10]

Reducing poverty therefore requires appropriate change in the dynamic inter-relationship between these factors. Doing this well is difficult at the best of times, but even more so when the context is one of economic decline and instability as is found in many countries of the South and East.

A second area of complexity arises because the range of causes described above, most of which have a bearing at some stage in a country's evolution, operate simultaneously at many societal levels. While there are usually localised, situation-specific reasons for poverty and marginalisation among social groups, they are always linked to other factors. Correctly identifying key linkages and addressing them in the right order or at the same time is virtually impossible, in part because no single organisation controls the whole spectrum of necessary action. In addition, not all sectors of society are particularly interested in eradicating injustice and removing poverty from the face of the earth. For some, poverty has its place and role in the existing order of things. But, more commonly, it is a condition to be exploited – for example, by using child labour, paying below the minimum wage and maintaining a sense of insecurity amongst those fortunate enough to be earning a living. In short, one cannot assume a harmony or consensus model in addressing poverty as a local, national or global issue. Complexity, therefore, arises when dealing with, sometimes violent, opposition to changes in social relations. Opposition to structural change is, furthermore, not restricted to countries of the South or East; one has only to look at the resistance met in altering consumption patterns in the North. At the end of the day, the 'bottom line of strengthening the poor is clearly political'.[11]

In other words, it has to do with the generation and distribution of wealth, within and between groups, countries and continents.

In sum, all organisations involved in development work face a goal which is difficult to achieve and where surrounding forces and trends are likely to be inhospitable, if not actively hostile. In doing their work, however, NGDOs lack the status of the (inter-) governmental aid system, the legislative authority of governments or the 'clout' of capital. This calls for a distinctive NGDO approach to reaching development objectives and places specific demands on management and organisation. What these demands entail can be found by looking at the aid system in practice and seeing where NGDOs fit in.

Development Action in Practice

The practice of international development is more than 30 years' old. Figure 1.1 is a framework showing the major areas of action which make up development today and how they are meant to relate to each other. Explanation of the figure moves from right to left and bottom to top. In other words, we start with the reason for aid.

The different purposes of aid

There is often confusion about the overall purpose or goal of international development assistance. A source of uncertainty is the mix-up between means and ends, fed by multiple agendas and institutional rivalry.

Market capitalism is now the pre-eminent global economic model. This unrivalled position has pushed its major proponents – International Financial Institutions (IFIs), like the World Bank and the International Monetary Fund (IMF) – to the forefront in setting the agenda in terms of the purpose and content of international assistance. These influential institutions create the impression that efficient markets producing broad-based growth can be equated with development itself.[12] This is both dangerous and misleading. Danger stems from the implicit assumption that

economic growth is always good, it is also misleading in that higher growth becomes equated with a better human condition.

In opposition to this view, and competing for the acknowledged pre-eminent position in the aid system, the United Nations Development Programme (UNDP) has, for the past five years, been emphasising human well-being as the purpose of markets and development. NGDOs would, I believe, assert that people and their values are both the means, ends and judges of development and that markets are in the service of humankind. In other words, NGDOs can, and many do, take a more holistic, people-centred view, unimpeded by the blinkering made necessary by IFI's limited economic mandates.

Notwithstanding the debate between means and ends, there is probably a reasonable consensus about the overall long-term goal to be achieved by development assistance. This is the creation of societies without poverty and injustice. Put another way, the functional purpose of development is to nationally, and internationally, foster socially just, sustainable economies with accountable, inclusive systems of governance. How, then, does the aid system pursue this ultimate goal?

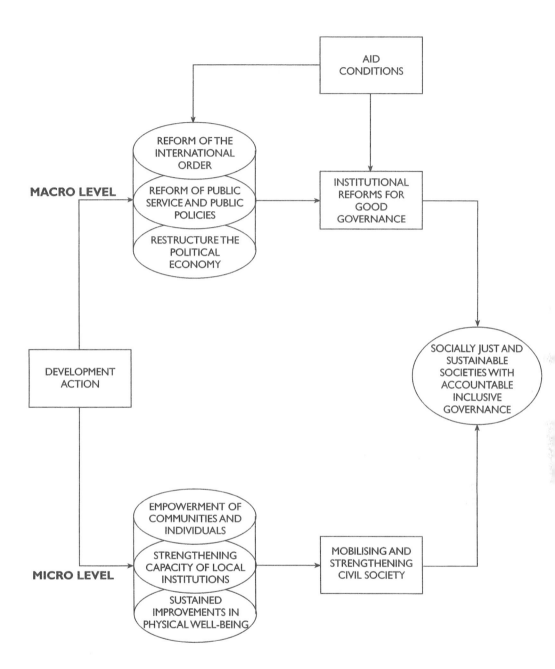

Figure 1.1 Framework of development action

Tasks at the micro-level

There are two stages to development action at the micro-level. The first involves poverty reduction in ways which are sustainable and which lead to the growth and functioning of strong, autonomous organisations. These organisations represent people who were poor but who have gained the ability to engage with other social actors on their own terms. The second stage is a process through which these disparate groupings collaborate, associate and form other social structures within which they exert themselves and pursue their interests. This arena of civic action influences the way society functions and impacts directly on governance. I therefore start with this dimension of micro-development.

The civic dimension

The box labelled 'strengthening civil society' in Figure 1.1 would probably not have featured in this framework five years ago. The end of the Cold War has brought with it a new concern for something called the institutions of civil society. While impossible to define satisfactorily, the aid system understands civil society to be the array of people's organisations, voluntary assoc-iations, clubs, self-help or interest groups, religious bodies, representative organs, NGDOs, foundations and social movements which may be formal or informal in nature, and which are not part of government or political parties, and are not established to make profits for their owners. In other words, civil society is often visualised as the arena of association and information between the family and the state. How this arena exists in practice varies enormously between countries.[13]

The critical point is that today civil society is expected to play a key role in the way that a country's system of governance evolves. It is here that citizens relate to each other and give collective expression to their demands and judgements on public affairs. In the process of making governance more inclusive and just, civil society is believed to play the following significant functions:

- provide space for the mobilisation, articulation and pursuit of interests by individuals and groups;
- provide the institutional means for mediating between conflicting interests and social values;

- give expression and direction to social, religious and cultural needs;
- limit the inherent tendency of governments to expand their control;
- nurture the values of citizenship required for democracy in a modern nation-state.

Listening to supposedly knowledgeable people talking about civil society at conferences and other fora, it is easy to fall into the trap of thinking that civil society is a level playing field and the new salvation for development. Too seldom is the point made that civil society is a messy arena of competing claims and interests between groups that do not necessarily like each other, as well as a place for mediation and collaboration. In the short run, strengthening civil society is as likely to increase social tensions as to reduce them because more voices are better able to stake their claim to public resources and policies.

Nevertheless, the new task at the micro-level is to stimulate and facilitate the forming of some civic institutions, as well as strengthening their capacity to engage with each other, with the state and with the market.[14]

Micro-development

The review of poverty describes the sort of changes needed to move people from deprivation to a situation where they have sufficient access to and control over existing commodities or are able to generate new ones with more equal exchange. Experience shows that effective micro-development requires that people, rather than money, technology or materials, are the starting point for the approach and that the right inter-play is created between three types of actions which:

- improve people's livelihoods and physical well-being in sustainable ways;
- build up the capacities of people's organisations; and
- empower in the sense that, individually and collectively, people are able and willing to make claims on development processes, as well as instigating their own.

The readings review the wide range of micro-development activities which are intended to sustainably improve livelihood and physical well-being. An observation worth highlighting, however, is the increasing concentration of development work around credit-based productive activity, particularly for women. This shift has serious organisational implications. It calls for a different mode of operation when compared with the more typical activities of investing in water supplies, health care, environmental protection, education, agriculture, and so on. Agencies wishing to move in this direction by combining credit with non-commercial initiatives risk introducing organisational tensions, not least because many are themselves not commercially oriented or skilled.[15] For many agencies, and especially NGDOs, the commercialisation of micro-development is a new challenge.

If externally supported development initiatives are to be rooted and woven into the fabric of rural or (peri-)urban life, a local 'host' of some sort is required. Grassroots or community-based organisations (GROs or CBOs) are terms commonly used for the local entities made up of the people whose lives are to be enhanced by development efforts. The task facing the aid system, however, is to adopt strategies and methods which build up the capabilities of these organisations, because it is their membership – the primary stakeholders, clients, beneficiaries, target group – which actually 'produce' development, not the agency. This point needs to be repeated and stressed : it is the poor and marginalised who produce their own development, not NGDOs or other aid agencies. Indeed, development is a process where people individually and collectively realise their potentials and in doing so become active protagonists in creating their own history.[16]

This fact should not suggest that governments and aid agencies have no role as providers of new resources, supporters or guides. Simply, it must be people who embody what development is about, since they are both its means and ends. A critical balance, therefore, has to be achieved to ensure that with external aid local institutions become self-sustaining and effective. Getting this right is probably the most vital element in the long term.

Fostering empowerment has two principal dimensions: psycho-social and relational.[17] The first is a shift in the way people who are poor or marginalised look at themselves. Low self-worth, a sense of negation and an attitude of resignation to circumstances and events must alter so that people can better their situation. Freire's principles of popular education, 'conscientization' and mobilisation are often used to foster this sort of change.[18] The second dimension, derived from the first, is an individual's capability and willingness to exert influence on existing power structures or to build new ones – particularly to increase the resources and choices available to them. This holds true for women in households as it does for groups in society. Without empowerment in the micro-development process, there is every likelihood that material, economic or social gains will simply be lost to or exploited by the better placed, meaning that structurally nothing will have changed.[19]

Controversy arose during the 1980s over whether consciousness raising for empowerment was always a necessary starting point for development, or whether it was in itself sufficient, since people would begin claiming what they were entitled to from government and land owners. Accumulated practice indicates that empowering approaches in development are usually more effective if they relate to peoples' concrete actions to solve identified problems. Success in overcoming a problem reinforces motivation, which is itself empowering, it contributes to organisational capacity and can initiate a positive spiral of further action without external support. In other words, the issue is not really about sequence but about combining and balancing the three elements of micro-development in the right way over time.

From micro-development we turn to the macro-level to review how actions here are intended to advance change.

Tasks at the macro-level

Taking a nation-state as the macro-level, the aid system tries to influence what happens in three distinct ways, all of which contribute to the manner in which society evolves and government functions.[20] The overall aim is to alter institutions, by which is meant the pattern of relationships between the important social actors and organisations which society values and supports.[21] Three types of reform in Figure 1.1 feed into and are intended to alter the conditions responsible for poverty, while creating better governance; this is our starting point for explaining macro-development action.

Improving governance

Establishing a system of good governance as envisaged by the official aid community involves a shift in four factors. These are:

- social justice: democratic rights, an independent judiciary and freedom of speech and press, greater political and economic equity between classes, genders, races and ages;
- economic liberalism: private ownership is protected, private investment is encouraged and greater equity is sought;
- political pluralism: public participation, bureaucratic decentralisation and a functioning democracy;
- administrative accountability: responsiveness and transparency in decision-making, reduced corruption and greater government efficiency.

One item missing is the need to establish ways in which a 'growing' civil society can negotiate within itself and with government.[22] In other words, there need to be recognised and respected mechanisms to increase the range of organised social, political and economic actors, that engage with each other and with public bodies. If these mediating institutions do not arise, the result is more likely to be chaos and strife than more broader-based, consensual development. Aware of this fact, South Africa, for example, consciously attempted to create such institutions, called forums, as part of the new arrangements for local government. Here, elected officials, civil servants, business interest and civic leaders meet to debate issues of common concern.

Arriving at a better governance situation should have a number of positive effects for people who are poor and marginalised. There should be greater opportunity for involvement in public policy-making; a higher likelihood of being treated equally by the law; more room to associate and pursue interests; and a better chance of bureaucrats behaving responsibly towards them. For voluntary organisations it should mean greater autonomy and more 'space' for their work. In short, good governance entails a more enabling environment with greater inclusion and reduced marginalisation.

The governance agenda points in a direction which has potential advantages for poor people. The problem is, of course, that it amounts to an imposition of the Western institutional framework on other countries: a set of political and economic conditions for aid which have long been a source of dispute and discomfort. That these conditions are now being applied inconsistently is exemplified in the cases of Uganda and Kenya. The selective and at times hypocritical application of aid conditions have not lessened since the end of the Cold War, when pro-Western despots were left in peace, shaded under the umbrella of East-West rivalry.

Restructuring the political economy

One way to alter the macro-situation for the poor is by uncoupling political and economic interests, while enabling a broader range of groups to engage in both, through better governance.[23] This can involve: altering internal terms of trade in favour of small-scale producers; removing regulations which act against the informal sector; changing the way foreign exchange resources are allocated; exposing corrupt practices; providing public information on issues, such as the inter-linked monopoly ownership of businesses; opening up dialogue with national organisations and networks representing civic and economic associations of the poor, such as federations of small-scale producers; encouraging voter registration; and progressive, redistributive taxation. The key is to employ strategies which reduce the links between political and economic power, that tend to centralise in favour of the haves rather than the have nots.[24]

One product of a strong interrelationship between political and economic interests is found in the formulation of public policies and the functioning of the civil service. These factors are the second target of macro-development action.

Reforming government

There are two main aspects to reforming government in 'pro-poor' ways. The first relates to how public policies are arrived at and applied, the second to how a state behaves towards its citizens, particularly in terms of attitudes and practices of government agents. The area of public policy is probably one of the most vital for the poor, because policies are the product of competing interests where the debate is usually framed as win-lose; the stronger usually win.

Public policies are basically a set of decisions which justify government actions. The idea that policy decisions are the result of a rational and open process of consultation, negotiation and trade-offs that seek to find the optimum balance between contending perspectives and needs is a myth. Supposedly neutral civil servants are guardians of this process. This description is so far from everyday reality in most countries that it is not very useful. More often than not, one person's policy gain is another's loss and potential winners and losers actively try and steer the outcome in their favour informally behind closed office doors, in (male) bars, restaurants, clubs and golf courses. These informal processes are usually discriminatory and reinforce marginalisation of the poor.

Public servants have interests too, in survival, in promotion, in supplementing meagre or unpaid salaries. It is unrealistic to expect them not to push or pull for a particular decision based on less than the public interest.[25] However, a truly professional public service inculcates an ethos that rises above these built-in difficulties and does not succumb to corruption. Those who are supposed to decide on public policy, furthermore, are politicians; this is their specialist trade and role in society. The strength of their mandate, in other words the legitimacy they enjoy with citizens, is determined by the quality of the electoral or other systems of selection, together with the ability of the public to sanction what they do not like – riots, rebellion, revolution and civil disobedience are sanctions of last resort. The tendancy of politicians to be subject to varying pressures is a major factor in what gets decided. Where electoral politics are meaningful, mass expression of popular disapproval by means of the post-bag can have effect.[26] Where this condition does not apply, more personalised pressures and publicity become necessary. The point of development agencies engaging in policy processes is to add the voice of the poor and marginalised into the policy equation. In short, policy-making is a jungle that is very difficult to penetrate, requiring detailed insights and connections.

To be effective in the policy arena one must be clear about:

- the content of the policy agenda;
- the nature of the policy jungle (who are the policy-making elite involved) and;
- the room for manoeuvre given the political and economic context of the country and the specific policy changes aimed at.

How this can be done effectively by NGDOs is explained in the readings and in Chapter 5.

Reforming how governments work in terms of their attitudes towards the poor and the practices they employ has been termed bureaucratic reorientation (BRO). It involves getting the civil service to change its stance towards society's bottom layers, most importantly by reducing the thresholds for inclusion of poor people in development initiatives and taking seriously what they say, what they think, what they know, what they need and their capabilities. Until now, the common way of changing the relationship between bureaucrats and people has been to bring them closer together. In practice this has entailed decentralising government functions by establishing intermediary levels of development action and decision-making, such as local development committees and local authorities. Without sufficient care, decentralisation can simply bring top-down government-dominated development projects closer to the people rather than increase people's influence. A development task is to ensure this does not happen.

The decentralisation approach to reform faces many obstacles. However, there is little doubt that the move to establish stronger intermediary levels in systems for local government and national bureaucracy is here to stay and will increasingly have to be a focus. In fact, decentralisation offers many new opportunities to improve NGDO and popular development action.

Another strategy for reorienting governments is to make sure they implement and conform to international agreements, protocols and conventions. Monitoring behaviour and publishing information about compliance can induce desired change. This approach is becoming an important part of development action, for example in monitoring national implementation of the International Convention on the Rights of the Child.

Reforming the international order

Some would regard the idea of changing the way the world works as an impossible mission. But the intention of this area of macro-development is indeed to alter the balance of international economic and political power in favour of poorer countries, or at least to make the relationship less one-sided. For a start, this can be done by reducing the debt burden of the poor, but also by changing unfair terms of trade and the extractive practices of multinational corporations, for example, their propensity for under- and over-invoicing.

Promoting this type of reform can focus on fora where international agreements are negotiated or where important international organisations meet. Examples include: negotiations for the Lomé convention; the establishment of the World Trade Organisation (WTO) to replace the General Agreement on Tariffs and Trade (GATT); and UN conferences on the environment at Rio, on population in Cairo, on social development in Copenhagen, on the rights of indigenous people in Vienna, and on woman in Beijing. Involvement with these gatherings does not, however, necessarily influence what is decided.[27] Be that as it may, changing the international order is firmly on the development agenda. The issue is to find ways and means of including the dimensions of injustice and inequity in international decision-making.

NGDOs in International Development

With broad sweeps, we have a picture of what the international development community is up to. The question is now: where do NGDOs fit in? What role are they playing in achieving the goals which the aid system has set itself? Figure 1.2 expands on Figure 1.1 by bringing NGDOs into the scene and showing what actions typically impact on the micro- and macro- levels of development.

Typical micro-level actions

At the micro-level, the interface between NGDOs and communities can vary enormously. Seven types of typical activity are shown in Figure 1.2, the last related to emergency and relief work. Material services cover the provision of an array of items: hardware for water supplies, school or road construction and fencing; inputs for agriculture and animal husbandry, such as seeds and medicines; and food during times of drought or other reasons for shortage. Social services can be health or legal advice centres, counselling, or special education for people with disabilities. Finance, normally now in the form of credit, and often following a model pioneered by the Grameen Bank, is becoming a more significant part of the NGDO package, usually lent to individuals through groups.[28]

Paralleling these essentially tangible transactions, NGDOs must also be able to engender change in human behaviour and capabilities. One specific area of human change is the capacity to organise. Literacy and training are the common ways of going about this, but changing human behaviour is more complicated than bestowing skills and knowledge; it requires experiential learning. This type of learning process is one way at looking at the role of field staff (generically called change agents) in interaction with groups and communities. In the long run, sustainability depends on the process followed, not just on what is achieved materially. Facilitation is a critical aspect of the participation process.

Fostering links is a significant part of moving the poor from a state of isolation to engagement with those in a similar situation. Horizontal lines between CBOs and vertical links with higher levels of association, with the market and with systems of governance are all vital for sustainability. Otherwise, external

intervention does not become rooted into the fabric of life. Links are also important for people moving into the arena of civic action.

The professionalism and effectiveness of NGDOs is critically dependent on achieving the right balance between these various types of interaction, not just once but over the whole course of the relationship. This constitutes a significant organisational and management challenge which we will come back to again and again.

Typical macro-level tasks

Typical NGDO tasks at the micro-level differ from those at the macro-level, where the focus is on influencing power-holders and structures, in order to consolidate social change.[29] The distinctive repertoire of activities and methods needed to realise macro-objectives also calls for people with different capabilities.

Policy advocacy (found within the macro-tasks box) requires good knowledge of the area, backed up by sound analysis and an ability to argue with technocrats and specialists who have their own interpretation of affairs. Advocacy normally focuses on influencing the general public as well as a small number of the policy-

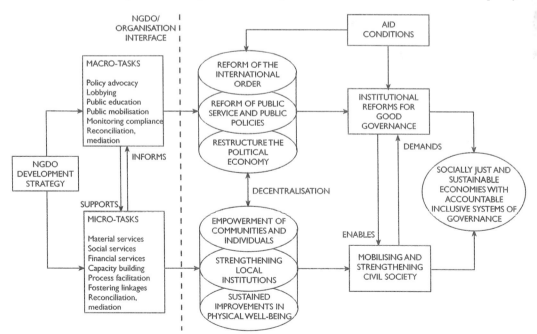

Figure 1.2 NGDOs and development action

making technical elite; lobbying takes advocacy messages into the political realm. Here the challenge is to identify and put pressure on specific actors. Campaigns, which can be seen as a type of public education with mobilising purpose and effect, can be used to support both advocacy and lobbying efforts.

Public education, more broadly, through school curricula, television programmes and newspaper articles, is intended to raise the population's awareness of development as a problem and challenge.[30] In other words, the objective is to build knowledge, understanding and a motivation within the public at large to actively engage with issues of poverty, marginalisation, risk, and sustainable development.

Lastly, monitoring compliance, which can be seen as the source of advocacy initiatives and other macro-action, calls for access to information about the implementation and effects of the policies and agreements the government has undertaken.[31] For NGDOs, sources of information are critical for the strength of their case. To be both effective and distinctive from research or policy institutes – which could point out the same shortcomings – NGDOs must derive their positions from ongoing experience of their, or other NGDOs micro-level work. In other words, there needs to be a coupling between the two. Achieving complementarity between different levels and types of action, and their effects, constitutes a set of critical balances. Success in sustainable poverty reduction is tied to linking these two spheres.

Development Principles, Tools and Proportionality

So far we have given a structure to the content of the international aid system and NGDOs within it. What the framework does not show are some of its key principles and the methods being used. It also does not say anything about NGDOs in relation to the wider context of global development. All of these factors are significant parameters for effective NGDO management and organisation. Two key principles are complementarity and people-centred participation; the most important method is the use of projects, while the significant contextual feature is the proportion of NGDO input compared to others.

Complementarity in development action

Achieving appropriate synergy between activities and the intended effects of the aid system has a significant influence on effective development. In other words, we are talking about a fusion not a fixed division of labour between different levels of action.

Complementarity in governance

Moving from right to left in Figure 1.2, the first important complementarity is mutual re-enforcement between civic strengthening and good governance. The theory and practical intention is that as civic institutions become stronger they are better able to make demands on government in terms of services, rights, access to resources, behaviour of state agents, desired priorities, and public policies. Simultaneously, reforms for good governance should enable and provide greater freedom of action for forming and operating civic associations; this pluralises the civic fabric of society. People can freely take initiatives or get together. In sum, there is greater room for choice, negotiation and pursuit of interests.

While these two dynamics are supposed to be, ideally, in harmony, they are usually out of step, because popular pressure for change can build up more quickly than power holders can tolerate or bureaucracies can adapt to. Common results are civic unrest, government repression and a slipping back to old authoritarian habits. This dynamic is an inherent part of the ebb and flow between civil society and states. But the challenge is to ensure that the swings of the pendulum are aligned with the concerns of the poor and marginalised so that they have their rightful place, say and influence on society.[32]

Complementarity in micro-action and micro-macro links

Two further complementarities are needed within and between different types of micro- and macro-action. First, the three elements or layers of micro-development have to be properly mixed with each other, the balance between them shifting over the different phases or stages of an NGDO's interaction with communities. In addition, the mix needs to be tailored to the specific context of the community. In this sense there is no standard 'product' which NGDOs deliver; at best we can talk of a consistent, adaptive approach to stimulating change. Effective NGDOs get this right, ineffective NGDOs do not.

The second interplay to get right is between restructuring the political economy, reforming policies and bureaucracies and effecting changes in international relations. This interaction is messy and very difficult to orchestrate. In essence, coherence between the three comes from coherence in linking and balancing national, regional and international action. For good or ill, throughout the world, with few exceptions, the dominant setting for complementarity is one of free trade, competitive, market-based economics with liberal-style democratic pluralism shaping the national institutional set-up required to make 'wealth creation with justice' effective.

The structural adaptations required in terms of policies, size and role of the state and the autonomy of other actors are sometimes willingly adopted as in the Tiger economies of South East Asia; in other cases as in Central Asia, India and much of Sub-Saharan Africa they are unwillingly accommodated. Whatever, the case, the context for macro-reform is a globalising market.

For international NGDOs, impacting on this level inevitably involves linking actions in different countries, so communication and a common agenda or framework of understanding becomes important. Therefore a proper interplay must be created between the source of advocacy activity and evidence, lobbying approach and campaigning which may now straddle the globe. This calls for a globalisation

of NGDO strategies and a mind-set which transcends existing organisational and national boundaries. This aspect is explored in more detail in subsequent chapters, which look at the factors affecting NGDO alliances, partnerships and networks. Ultimately, because power over the international agenda for change presently lies with the North, this is where much policy advocacy still has to be directed.

In Figure 1.2, the two arrows pointing upwards and downwards to the left of the organisational interface show the final complementarity. This is the proper coupling between micro- and macro-action. As suggested above, the quality and distinctiveness of NGDO advocacy work stems from the fact that it is informed by the real life experiences of poor people and their struggles. In other words, their testimony is brought to the table with a voice, presence and legitimacy of perspective which is commonly silent. Similarly, if properly selected, advocacy, lobbying and other macro-actions should alter the policy environment and other contextual factors in ways which support an NGDO's micro-actions, making them more effective. In other words, organisation and management establish mutually supportive relations between the various levels of NGDO action, which will increasingly include the intermediary level as decentralisation progresses.

The need for mutuality between micro- and macro-levels to enhance effectiveness does not imply that every NGDO has to do both. Alliances between specialist NGDOs operating at different levels are an attractive and useful option. The point, however, is that any NGDO worth its salt will be aware of, if not contributing to or co-ordinating with, other actors and levels of action which have a direct bearing on its work. For example, NGDOs providing AIDS counselling should be aware of what policy change would benefit their clients, such as obtaining state support and stopping compulsory AIDS testing for insurance or travel purposes. If nothing is done to create a better policy environment, initiatives should fill the gap. The reasons for this are discussed below in relation to leverage.

Historically, the 'natural' focus for NGDO activity has been at the micro-level of people, where small was considered beautiful, while official aid agencies concentrated on working through governments from the national level. In retrospect, equally 'natural' is the incompleteness of this division of labour and the serious need to re-think how poverty is created and maintained. Fortunately, over the last decade, this crude division of labour has altered substantially, but much remains to be done. Increasingly, governmental agencies wish to reach down and work more directly with specific groups within the population, while NGDOs are more interested in the macro-level. These moves have modified what used to be a big distance, with much mistrust and antipathy, between NGDOs, governments and official aid agencies, leading to far greater interaction. However, these changes contain tensions. What can be said, overall, is that there is now more, rather than less, complementarity between the various actors involved in international development work, and this trend is set to continue.

Authentic participation

Despite remnants of doubt lurking in corners of the official aid system, particularly in development banks, there is a common understanding that participation is crucial to the success of development work at all levels of action.[33] There is such a vast amount of writing on this topic that in my view there is little left to be said about the concept, except to stress that this book's concern is with participation which is 'authentic', (a process of engagement which is not simply treated as a co-opted input, and means for making externally supported development happen more effectively, but is regarded as a foundation for any development strategy).[34] What has to be addressed is why authentic participation is so seldom happening in practice.

Any definition of participation which takes into account the multi-level nature of development must acknowledge, first, that there is more than one party involved; someone wants someone else to engage in something. In today's parlance, there are various stakeholders: parties or actors interested in a development initiative;

they do not necessarily enjoy equal relationships. Second, power imbalances are often involved. Third, participation is ongoing. A working definition, therefore may be: *participation is a process through which stakeholders influence and share control over decisions and resources that affect their lives.* One feature of this definition is that it does not limit participation to the narrow sense of involvement in development initiatives and projects, but covers citizenship participation as well.

The crux of participation in practice then becomes: how are activities agreed upon and arranged so that influence is shared throughout the process? A good test to determine who 'counts' most, is to ask: whose capacity to solve problems has primacy in this development initiative? Experiences of, and techniques for, achieving authentic participation are to be found in the readings and in Chapter 7. This book's concern is to identify factors of internal organisation and management which get in the way of NGDOs doing this well. Equally, it is to identify where NGDO participation may not be as impressive and consistent as conventional wisdom would suggest.[35]

If NGDOs cannot organise and manage participation properly, lack of effectiveness is virtually guaranteed. The one thing commonly standing in the way of authentic participation is the mechanism used to interact with communities: development projects. Because projects dominate development organisation and management, their key features require critical analysis.

Development projects: a case of cutting paper with a hammer

A visitor lost in a foreign country approaches a local person on a remote rural road and asks, 'Could you please tell me the way to Tinaheally?' The local person responds, 'Well, indeed I could sir, but if I were you I wouldn't be starting from here.'

This joke reflects the present position of sustainable development. After 30 years of learning that effective development must be people-centred – be they farmers, peasants, workers, bureaucrats or politicians – projects are no longer the place where we should be starting from; but they are. Simply put, as a tool, projects are not appropriate for all but the most technical types of development initiative, such as building roads. Where altering human behaviour is concerned, the less appropriate projects become. Many limitations to NGDO effectiveness stem from this fact. Projects serve the bureaucracy of the aid system more than the micro- or macro-tasks described so far. They are time-bound, pre-defined sets of objectives, assumptions, activities and resources which should lead to measurable, beneficial impacts. They are most suitable when development means building physical infrastructure, and least appropriate for complex change involving human beings. With some variations, logical framework analysis (LFA) has become the standardised format for defining projects.

The central assumption of the project approach is that it is possible to construct a defined future, but this does not reflect how societies change. Chapter 7 examines this dilemma in relation to assessing performance. For now, it is sufficient to make clear that incompatibilities between projects and people-centred development create difficult conditions which NGDOs must organise for and manage, because the project mode is unlikely to be replaced by something more suitable.

The following items are common drawbacks of projects and their effects when it comes to undertaking authentic participatory development.

At their worst, projects:

- impose a linear way of thinking on cultures which may have other and richer modes of understanding;
- assume that the future can be accurately foreseen and constructed imposing a rigidity on processes (such as schedules) which should be adaptive and flexible;
- introduce financial time frames which usually have no bearing on the (seasonal) cycle, cosmology or time availability of rural people;
- induce false optimism and negate assumptions which might be significant enough to mitigate against taking the initiative while imposing optimistic goals to attract finance;
- do not recognise the consequences of unintended effects;
- place effective power in the (literate) hands of those who finally define the project;
- call for extensive data gathering, creating false expectations;
- introduce an imbalance between tangible outputs and human processes, with a bias towards the former because of donor expectations;
- recognise, but then ignore, necessary links to other (project) activities so that its own deadlines can be met;
- restrict free choice during the process, claiming ownership of participants, even to the extent of removing their freedom to relate to other initiatives or services;
- introduce a mind-set that is predisposed towards an authoritarian style of interaction, which equates progress with disbursement and accountability with accounting for financial or material resources;
- lead to an abrupt termination rather than a phased withdrawal as appropriate conditions are created;
- keep all participants, but especially the NGDO, in a constant state of insecurity, inducing them to aquire projects for self-sustainability, over-riding community perspectives;
- work against organisational continuity and consistency (due to changes in staff, ideas and priorities);
- are too short-term in relation to the ultimate goal and confuse means with ends, so inputs are equated with impact;
- force relationships into a contractual mode as opposed to other styles;
- do not allow learning through trail and error while ignoring learning from post-project effects.

These factors are not always present and do not carry equal weight in terms of how they affect micro- and macro-development work. In addition, a number have as much to do with cultural differences as with the project mode of action. However at their best, good projects recognise and take all these factors into account.

There are two crucial limitations of projects for effective development. First, they stand in the way of obtaining the critical balance between *products* (tangible activities and outcomes) and human behavioural and relational *processes*. Second, when there is a disparity between primary stakeholders and donors' views, project-based assistance deflects NGDO attention, behaviour and interests away from those they are meant to serve towards satisfying donor requirements.

A serious organisational drawback of projects is that they are used by NGDOs as an alternate measure for achieving the overall mission. This is wrong. For instance, it is as if by looking at one brick you can tell what a wall is going to resemble and judge whether or not it serves the intended purpose. Obviously, if the brick is poorly made the wall is unlikely to be strong. But, unfortunately, a strong brick doesn't guarantee a strong or suitable wall. Not much sense can be made of organisational goals by simply adding up all the development projects. Projects can make sense in terms of a manager's tasks, but not in terms of an organisation's overall mission.

Despite all these limitations, projects remain the standard mode of operation because they cut complexity into bite-sized, manageable and fundable chunks. Furthermore, despite many calls for reform, and some limited experimentation, the project system still dominates because it suits the administrative needs of financiers. Indeed, it is difficult to imagine any commercial enterprise of this scale which would maintain for so long a tool known to be inadequate. Nevertheless, it remains because of the way public accountability is understood and applied; the bureaucratic need to keep up levels of aid allocations untied from performance; the inadequacy of existing performance measures; and a basic lack of trust between agencies, which alternatives require.

Projects dictate the NGDO landscape. To be effective, therefore, NGDOs must manage and organise in ways which either neutralise or compensate for the developmental limitations of the basic tool they have to work with. Much of this book is about how they do so. And, if this reality isn't disturbing enough, the last factor which has to be taken into account is the relatively limited scale of NGDOs in relation to the problem they are tackling.

Recognising proportionality: NGDO humility and leverage

Poverty is to be found in every country of the world, but international development assistance is directed at the third of the world's poor who live in the South and East, some 1.6 billion people. Therefore, to gain a perspective on its likely impact, aid funds can be seen as a form of investment, which may have short-, medium- and long-term benefits, often one being at the expense of the other. To get some realistic feel for what aid can achieve, this type of investment needs to be set against other financial flows directed at the South and East.

In 1993, total foreign direct investment worldwide amounted to some US$180 billion, which includes intra-company investments, the majority being applied within the Organisation for Economic Co-operation and Development (OECD). Private flows of finance to the South and East (excluding Russia) amounted to US$87.6 billion, corresponding to 58.7 per cent of the global total of US$149.2. Of this, overseas development assistance (ODA) contributed some US$ 55.2 billion, or 37 per cent, while NGDOs accounted for US$6.3 billion ($4 dollars per poor person), or 4.2 per cent.[36] These figures hide significant variations between countries of the South and East in terms of the relative proportion of private and official investment.

So when it comes to investment in development, in financial terms NGDOs are very minor players and will remain so.[37] This reality calls for three responses: humility, leverage and deflection. To remain credible, NGDOs need to be more modest about what they are able to achieve. While this stance may not be good for fund-raising and market share, it will protect NGDOs from the charge of misleading supporters, as more and more assessments show that there is a large gap between public statements and what is realised in practice. The distance between NGDO claims and their achievements is already coming to light with implications for credibility and legitimacy.

The second challenge is to expand the organisational focus from poverty alleviation, through direct development projects, to gaining leverage on the larger forces which keep poor people poor. Leverage is detailed in Chapter 9; action, for example, where small amounts of resources influence how far larger amounts are applied. By regarding the ultimate objective of the organisation to be learning for leverage, the new NGDO strategy will be to gain purchase on and re-direct official aid and other flows, not simply to tap into them in order to run more and larger projects. One tool for leverage is proven alternatives, not slogans and exhortations.

The third challenge is to use characteristics of markets in favour of the poor, rather than to look for countervailing power to push markets back. In other words, it is to deflect the built-in, profit-seeking force and contradictions of market economies in ways which generate poverty-focused benefits, in terms of reduced extraction and creation of non-exploitative alternative commercialism. Together, deflecting investment and gaining leverage make up the last set of conditions and criteria which NGDOs have to manage in order to be effective. This chapter closes with a brief summary of the factors and tasks NGDOs must organise in order to achieve effective, people-centred, sustainable development. After finding out more about NGDOs as a type of organisation, the rest of the book looks at how these tasks can and are being done effectively, ending with speculations about what the future holds in terms of new choices.

Summary of Critical Balances and Tasks for NGDOs in People-Centred Development

The following are major critical balances and tasks which must be organised and managed in NGDO development work, not just momentarily but over the course of relationships. Striking the right balance does not mean equalising efforts in a static way. It means creating the right mix between what an NGDO gains from and brings into the outside world and continually adapting this mix as processes move along and learning is gained. To be effective, NGDOs individually, in alliances and collectively must have the capacity to:

- balance the knowledge, experience, motivation and values of people who are poor or marginalized, especially women and powerless minorities, against the expertise, links, resources and relative power of outsiders;
- balance external inputs with local mobilisation of resources and links;
- balance tangible products with human processes over time;
- balance the time perspectives, interests and power relations between stakeholders while tilting them in favour of the powerless;

- balance and adapt the material, organisational capacity and empowerment dimensions of micro-development;
- balance and maintain coherence between pushes for change in the political-economy, government system, public policy reforms and reforms in the international order;
- balance micro-, macro- and increasingly intermediate levels of development, coupling direct action at the grassroots with learning for leverage to gain structural change;
- balance tangible impacts which reduce poverty while strengthening civil society.

With reasonable confidence, it can be said that NGDOs which successfully organise and manage these factors will be more effective in producing sustainable impacts in terms of reducing poverty and increasing social justice. The task in the next chapter is to explain the organisational peculiarities of NGDOs and how these characteristics should equip them to achieve the balances demanded by sustainable development.

2

Understanding Development NGOs

Characterising NGDOs

Writers on organisations define what they are dealing with in different ways. In this book, the simplest method would be to declare that the organisations of concern are the non-governmental, non-profits involved in the aid system. Unfortunately, two negative (non this and that) and one positive criteria (part of the aid system) tell us nothing useful about NGDO characteristics. An alternative approach is to look widely at a variety of relevant organisations and search for common features. A drawback is that subsequent results can be strongly biased by the initial selection.[1] A further option is to begin with more general, abstract understandings of organisations and then narrow down the selection by progressively identifying features which correspond most closely to those being analysed.

This last method has been chosen for four main reasons. First, characteristics of NGDOs must include their function in society compared to other organisations. Second, the nature and roles of non-profits are so varied that without a preliminary framework for analysis, it is difficult to make sense of what is to be found across the world. Third, there is already a substantial amount of study on organisations in society, albeit biased towards business and public administration. It is therefore more sensible to take this work as a resource to build upon. Finally, managers will run their NGDOs more effectively if they have some basic principles to refer back to.

Working Definitions

Much of today's international development effort is directed at a variety of organisations and institutions - social change is seldom achieved by an individual acting alone. Understanding NGDOs therefore requires working definitions of these two terms.

Organisations and institutions

Probably the most basic definition of organisations is that they are purposeful, role-bound social units. In other words, they are groups of individuals who allocate tasks between themselves to contribute to a common goal. This simple definition gets very muddled

in practice because, for example, not everyone may share the goal to the same degree, or they may be in the organisation for personal reasons which have little or nothing to do with what the organisation wants to achieve. Despite these complications, the two items to bear in mind are: to exist an organisation needs a purpose; and an organisation is made up of people who know what their role is (what is expected of them in relation to each other, in order to reach the purpose). The significance of purpose, or mission, in organisational life makes this a common starting point for subdivision or classification. A more difficult classification is between organisation and institution, terms which are, incorrectly, used interchangeably in today's development jargon.

Where organisations themselves, or where principles or norms of people's behaviour, become a stable, accepted and collectively valued basis on which society works, we can talk of social institutions. However, not all organisations become institutions and not all institutions are made up of organisations, which can be confusing. For example, marriage is a valued social institution which is not made up of organisations. Similarly, money is a valued social institution, but it cannot be equated to the behaviour of all banks, insurance companies or the Treasury. Corruption can also become institutionalised in some societies as the only way of getting things done, but this pattern of behaviour is not typical of one place or one organisation.

Some organisations can become institutionalised in the sense that they are a recognised and valued part of society. In the context of Great Britain, Oxfam has become such a household name that it is itself institutionalised. The same can probably be said for the Fundaçion Sociale in Colombia, United Way in the USA, the Bangladesh Rural Advancement Committee (BRAC) and the Red Cross. By and large, NGDOs seldom make an adequate distinction between development of organisations and social institutions, which means that their strategies and methods are often not optimal. While there is no water tight distinction, an NGDO needs to be clear about these two terms, because they are not interchangeable and affect the way things have to be done. Nevertheless, even if the intended impact is institutional, organisations are the most common operational focus of development

work and therefore remain the primary subject of this book.

Formal and informal organising

Before identifying specific characteristics of NGDOs, it is necessary to highlight a common short-sightedness in much Western analysis of organisations and institutions; this is the tendency to overlook what is not formally organised and legally recognised by governments. While informal organisations are found across the world, a significant feature of organisational life in countries of the South and East is that they rely on interpersonal networks. These networks are familial and customary rather than enshrined in organisational constitutions, and can be very powerful in shaping how both organisations and institutions work in practice.

There is a rich array of non-legalised forms of organised co-operation that people create to achieve shared goals; these may be formal for those belonging inside them, even if outsiders see them as informal. Age sets are an example common throughout sub-Saharan Africa, as are the *pakikisama* affiliations in the Philippines. As governments retreat, opening space for civic initiatives, the number and density of both informal and legally formal ways of collaborating is growing rapidly. While the merits of non-formalised organising should not be over-idealised, it would be very wrong, especially in the work of people-centred development, to remain unaware of the resource significance and demands which this type of growth makes on the work of all development agencies.

Organisational Sectors and their Principles

Purpose is a common way of differentiating between types of organisations. Past study indicates that the evolution of societies as modern nation-states gives rise to institutions and organisations established for three relatively

distinct purposes:

- to protect, secure and regulate the lives and actions of citizens; for example, to manage how society is defended as well as how it

functions and progresses;
- to make a livelihood and create and accumulate wealth; and
- to purse individual interests or tackle personal or social concerns which are separate from gaining a livelihood.

The first set of purposes typically belongs to governments, the second to business and the market, and the third to the self-willed association of citizens. Organisational science uses a shorthand of first, second and third sectors as labels for these purposes.[2]

The sectors themselves can be divided into whether the purpose they serve is private or public. The first sector is concerned with what is called the public realm, that is the common area affecting all citizens in which they have rights and obligations, both of which are enforced by state agencies. The second sector makes up the private realm of people's initiatives to survive and improve economically; the third makes up the private realm for the pursuit of recreational, spiritual, social, cultural, and other personal or collective interests.

In reality, the three -way spilt is confused by the fact that private organisations can play a similar role to governments when they are established for public purposes. For example, this occurs when a voluntary organisation is set up to serve some common good – such as, helping the aged, or assisting people whose rights have been abused. In addition, establishing a business or a non-profit is an act of free will: society does not expect or require any one private organisation to exist or be around for ever; this is not the case with government. Choosing to gain social recognition by formal registration means accepting society's right to oversee that you do what you say you will. In other words, registration is accepting obligations of public accountability which society determines and regulates.

An important division within third sector purposes, therefore, is whether the organisation is established to serve others or to benefit those within it.[3] This distinguishes between third-party public service providers and self-help or mutual-benefit organisations. The former delivers something to others, the latter is there

for the benefit of its own members. A charity can be created to provide clean water to poor households (third parties), while an amateur football team or choir provides mutual benefits for the players or singers. Being either a service or mutual benefit organisation affects how they work.

The size and content of the three sectors varies from country to country and each is usually distinguished and regulated by specific legislation.[4] Relative size is primarily determined by the political ideology dominating society, or the regime in power, and is expressed through policy preferences, legislation, and public versus private investment choices. Figure 2.1 compares two examples of different sectoral set-ups. The left-hand side of the figure corresponds to a society which, like the USA, actively limits the role of government while encouraging private enterprise and voluntary initiative. Western Europe would probably exhibit a larger state sector, with other circles being of a more similar size. The right-hand side is more typical of societies where governments dominate; this is often the case in the countries of the South and East, such as Tanzania, Kazakstan and India, where an ideology of public ownership and central planning has made the state the primary force for economic and social development. It should come as no surprise that the intentions and funding conditions of the international aid system are designed to make the organisational pattern of countries of the South and East look more like those of the left.

In reality, there are many overlaps between each sector, which are important when understanding NGDOs today; these are explained below.

Comparing operating principles

To understand the organisational dimensions of NGDOs, it is helpful to compare the basic operating principles of these three sectors. This will enable us to identify features which are supposed to make voluntary organisations particularly suited to people-centred development work. Differences of particular interest have to do with:

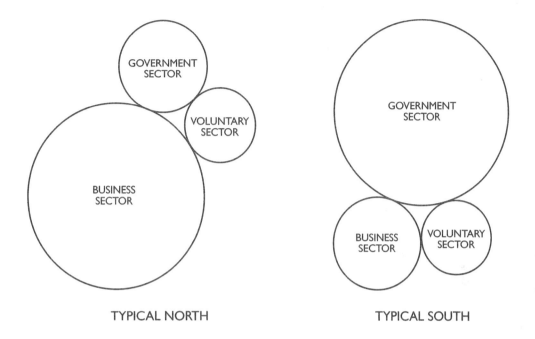

Figure 2.1 Comparison of formally organised sectors

- obtaining required behaviour of people in the organisation;
- the nature of the relationship between the organisation and the outside world, particularly towards those it serves;
- the way of mobilising resources; and
- feedback on and assessment of performance.

People in organisations

How do you get people to behave well in their organisational roles? Studies suggest that people behave the way they need to in organisations either: because they have to, that is, they are coerced; because they have incentives to do so, they are induced; or they are driven to do so by their own internal beliefs and values.[5] At the risk of gross generalisation, each of the three sectors is found to adopt a different way of ensuring that people behave effectively in their roles: governments tend to rely on hierarchy,

command and enforcement; businesses provide (or deny) monetary and other rewards as incentives; voluntary organisations rely on personal values, commitment and self-motivation.

While elements of each type of motivation can surely be found in all organisations, an important consequence of self-motivation in third-sector organisations is that individuals feel empowered to behave like co-owners, with a corresponding expectation to be treated in such a way by management; this impacts on organisational culture and decision-making processes.[6] Of course, a person's technical competence, experience, aptitudes, personal situation, and aspirations are also important for fulfilling a role effectively. But the basic way an organisation goes about motivating all these elements within an individual is distinct for each sector.[7]

Relating to the outside world

Organisations in each sector tend to differ in how they relate to the outside world, particularly towards those they are supposed to serve. Governments, because of their public role and unique position of power, are inclined to be authoritative in their dealings with citizens; this may be tempered by setting standards for and soliciting feedback on the performance of public services. Further, the state-citizen relationship is effectively tied within a permanent set of mutual obligations which are, or should be, negotiated through the political process. Governments are also empowered to legislate and enforce; in this way they create much of the environment in which they operate.

Private businesses seldom have permanent relationships with their owners or customers from birth to death, although banks and insurance companies may get close to it. The relationship between business and their customers is overwhelmingly based on momentary transactions called purchases – the universal process of buying, selling, or bartering. Lacking formal coercive power, businesses try to condition the external world through advertising, by building monopolies and by, occasionally, employing corrupt practices or attempting to coerce customers into buying from them. Without legislative power to construct the environment in which they operate, enterprises try to protect their internal functioning from external disruption – such 'insulation' is particularly necessary for mass production lines and processes which transform physical resources into products.[8] In addition, businesses are concerned to maintain their image of reliability, quality and corporate social responsibility, where advertising and media events play an important role.[9] However, left to their own devices without public controls or incentives, competition naturally inclines businesses to minimise the internal costs and externalise the public costs of their activity – such as environmental degradation or pollution – to tax payers.

Voluntary sector organisations do not have the legislative capability and coercive force of the state, nor the economic clout of commercial capital and enterprise. What they have, instead, is the dynamism and power of self-willed human action, which can encompass very large numbers of people and exert significant influence in society, as seen in civic protests or consumer boycotts. In as far as voluntary organisations are set up by value-driven, self-motivated people to serve a segment of the population unreached by the state or market, there is a strong identification between the organisation and those it is set up for. In NGDO jargon, this is termed solidarity. Groups or classes with particular interests can go so far as to set up non-profit organisations to gain political power – for example, establishing themselves as political parties.

The duration of relationships between voluntary organisations and the individuals they serve differs widely. For member-based institutions, such as organised religion, the relationship is usually permanent. For others, such as social and recreational organisations, membership is unlikely to be permanent but may span a number of years. For historical and legal reasons, non-membership voluntary organisations are usually most active in providing public goods with a social benefit, such as education, health and welfare. Interactions with clients, therefore, tend, on balance, to be more than momentary but seldom permanent, which orients third-sector organisations towards transactions which could last from days to years, but where the idea of eventual separation is understood from the start.

Looking back to the goals and tasks of development, it is clear that NGDOs can hardly be in the business of selling services to those in poverty. If the poor could pay the full cost, the market, in theory, would respond to satisfy their demand. Moreover, the actual process of 'producing' development is rooted within communities themselves, which means that NGDOs must negotiate in order to integrate their work with ongoing external processes. How they can do this well is the subject of other chapters, where we will see that an NGDO's ability to negotiate is related to its attitude or stance, as expressed through the staff who do the negotiating. In its turn, organisational stance depends on the degree to which the voluntary sector has a vibrant presence. It also depends on the ability to mobilise appropriate financial resources, and here again there are sectoral differences.

Resource mobilisation

Each organisational sector mobilises resources in different ways. Figure 2.2 illustrates what they are. Governments function from taxes paid by citizens who should receive adequate public services in exchange. While shareholders and banks provide capital, a business stands or falls on its ability to sell goods and services to customers for an amount sufficiently greater than their cost; if not, bankruptcy results. By and large, non-membership voluntary organisations do not recover the full cost of what they provide to their clients or beneficiaries;[10] and this is certainly the case for NGDOs who, on an ongoing basis, have to raise finances from other sources, loosely termed donors.

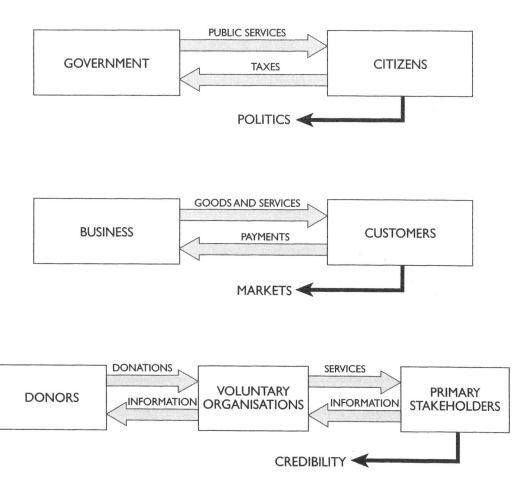

Figure 2.2 Mobilising financial resources

In the case of international development, most NGDOs fulfil an intermediary role in a chain which generates and transfers resources: knowledge, technology, money, information. The NGDO task is to add value to the transfer process. Figure 2.3 illustrates this position. For the present, it is sufficient to point out that being located between donors in one continent and stakeholders in another, or between affluent urban-based financiers and geographically remote, impoverished and socially marginalised beneficiaries, presents particular difficulties for management; these difficulties are further aggravated by the fact that performance is not easy to measure.[11]

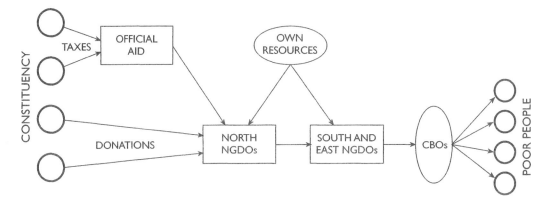

Figure 2.3 NGDOs in the aid chain

Feedback and performance

What constitutes a 'bottom line' for each sector? How can an organisation find out how well it is doing? What feedback provides such information? For governments, or better said the regime in power, the bottom line is political – the level of citizen satisfaction expressed through the ballot box or through civil disobedience, unrest and riots. For example, refusal to pay local government service charges in South Africa was one way that disenfranchised citizens could express dissatisfaction with services to their townships. Imperfect as they may be, existing democratic systems and public feedback – expressed through civic action, constituents' letters, petitions and percentages of the vote – do periodically focus politicians' minds and call them to account.

While arguments are raised to include corporate social responsibility as an element of performance, the bottom line for businesses remains that of profitability. Market indicators, such as share value, price/earnings ratios and market share, while obviously open to differences in interpretation, provide effective and immediate feedback to managers.

In the voluntary sector, when it comes to performance measures and feedback, there is a significant difference between the two kinds of organisation – mutual benefit and service – we identified earlier. In the former, performance measures and feedback can be readily gained from those who should be reaping the benefits. In formal set-ups, this process is usually built into the governance system of annual meetings and members' voting rights, while informal organisations select their own ways to provide information on whether or not members are getting what they want.

For most third-sector service-providing organisations, on the other hand, no straightforward, uncontested performance measures present themselves. The nearest we can come to a bottom line is credibility and legitimacy, measures which must to be 'constructed' from the combined social judgement of the organisation's many 'users', including intended beneficiaries, governors, volunteers and staff. This is a complicated way of going about things, lacks the immediacy of the market, is open to dispute because users are seldom of equal weight, and makes comparisons or 'benchmarking' very difficult. . What can be done about it is described in Chapter 7. The lack of clear performance indicators makes the management of non-profits more complex and difficult than other sectors

For third-sector service providers in general, and for NGDOs specifically, the most critical line of feedback and measure must come from the primary stakeholder (this term is increasingly used instead of clients, beneficiary or target group), because it is their poverty or deprivation which is used to justify the organisation's existence. Changes in the well being of the primary stakeholders must be reported back to donors. Unfortunately, this line of feedback is usually very weak and is seldom able to influence an NGDO's overall performance; all too often, NGDOs prefer to fulfill pre-defined project activities which qualify for further financing. Relative inattention to long-term impact means that feedback on working with communities does not gain equal weight with pressures coming down the aid chain from constituents and donors.

Summary

So far we have identified, at a very general level, some basic principles that the three sectors of organised society apply in their functioning. Again, these are not mutually exclusive, but one type tends to dominate in each sector. This is summarised in Table 2.1.

Table 2.1 Sector comparisons

Characteristic	Sector		
	Government	Business	Voluntary*
Relationship to those served based on:	mutual obligation	financial transaction	personal commitment
duration:	permanent	momentary	temporary
Approach to external environment:	control and authority	conditioning and isolation	negotiation and integration
Resources from:	citizens	customers	donors
Feedback on performance:	(in)direct politics	direct from market indicators	'constructed' from multiple users

* service providers, not mutual benefit

Comparative advantages of the third sector in people-centred development

It is commonly assumed, and argued strongly by NGDOs, that their place within the voluntary (third) sector, and the principles which go with it, give them comparative advantages.[12] What are the arguments supporting this view? First, value-driven, committed and self-motivated staff should more readily identify with and be able to adopt an appropriate stance towards their clients, engendering trust and enhancing authentic participation. In comparison, and irrespective of the individual or their technical function, government staff always carry with them the status of power, limiting their ability to identify with the poor or to be accepted by them. It certainly confines their ability to support empowerment processes when such processes are directed against government itself.

Second, NGDOs do not need the uniformity or standardisation of practices which state bureaucracies apply; as a result, they can adapt more readily to local contexts and meet the demands of people-centred development. They can organise themselves to provide tailored support to a particular disadvantaged group – unmarried mothers, the landless, people with AIDS, the non-credit worthy, or the disabled. In other words, they are better able to target their assistance, which should improve efficiency and effectiveness. Third, while commercial organisations can adapt themselves to their clients' needs, they are not particularly interested in, and cannot reach, the really poor in the way NGDOs can because of donor support (which could be called a form of subsidy); such support is only forthcoming because of the trust in their non-profit principles.[13] Fourth, NGDOs are not a public body, giving them the flexibility to stay long enough to help make a difference, but not so long that dependency results. Governments, on the other hand, are there for ever. Fifth, in not seeking profits, NGDOs can be less costly than business, while staff self-motivation enables them to function at less than market rates because part of the employee's

reward comes from self-fulfilment. Finally, NGDOs can undertake necessary development functions and supporting processes which are not 'services' as such. These functions can entail, for example, providing a channel for information and other types of 'bridges' between different types of organisation, facilitating links, acting as a catalyst and temporarily filling gaps; such activities are effectively impossible to measure and difficult to classify as a service, but important none the less. Because of their principles, NGDOs are less likely to face the accusation of creating work simply to profit owners, a common complaint made against service-contracting companies, such as consultancy firms, which are driven to sell staff time.

While the validity of these arguments may be questioned, in theory at least, applying voluntary sector principles should be positive in terms of development effectiveness. The next step is to trace what happens when organisational theory moves into today's development practice.

Understanding NGDOs

The three sectors described above are imaginary; they are unlikely to be found exactly like this in the real world. But this framework helps to describe NGDOs and why they behave as they do, identifying underlying forces which must be dealt with in practical organisation and management. When the different principles of each sector overlap within an organisation, however, problems can result.

Overlapping sectors: tensions within NGDOs

Chapter 1 describes the overall purpose of NGDOs and the typical tasks and critical balances involved in being effective. Attention should now be focused on what happens to people-centred development in an increasingly contract-oriented aid system. In other words,

what challenges arise to NGDO management and organisation when they have to operate in the more complicated areas of overlapping principles? This is examined in Figure 2.4.

Rather than dealing with mutual benefits and other types of organisations within the voluntary sector, this discussion concentrates on service-providing NGDOs. One observation is that organisations located firmly within the third sector, and consistently applying its principles, are most likely to be supplying welfare-type services. Like the Lions and Rotary clubs, they may be composed of unpaid volunteers, occasionally raising donations from well-wishers, or they may have evolved into more stable charitable institutions, providing homes for destitute children or people with disabilities. While beneficial, this type of activity is not what today's empowering people-

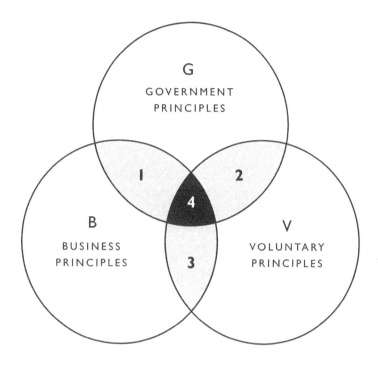

Figure 2.4 Overlapping principles affecting NGDOs

centred development is thought to be about and, consequently, such voluntary organisations, although sometimes recipients of aid, are not the focus of this book.

Instead, the third-sector organisations of primary interest are those operating within the framework of objectives and tasks set out in Figure 1.2 that is, NGDOs. Today, evidence suggests that these voluntary organisations are more likely to be found in areas of overlap *2, 3* and *4* than in 'voluntary principles'. Why? The answer is as follows: over a period of 30 years the aid system has become an aid business demanding a high degree of professionalism from NGDOs, displacing moral motivations with more functional concerns of effective delivery. International assistance, furthermore, is increasingly assigned on the basis of project-based competitive contracts. Aid priorities are

shifting away from governments, reallocating what were once state responsibilities for public services into the other two sectors; this has lead to more NGDO tax-based funding. Structural adjustment policies have decreased spending on public services, creating a 'moral' pressure on NGDOs to fill the gap and a dilemma on whether or not they should do so. There is a stagnation in the growth of private donations to development work, and the proportion of NGDO funds derived from official aid donors is rapidly increasing.[14] To appreciate what all this means in terms of effects and challenges, we must look at what is likely to happen to the comparative advantages of voluntary development as the different sectoral principles overlap.[15]

Overlapping sectors: consequences for NGDOs in development

Overlaps between sectors can work in two directions. For example, business can combine its principles with those of the voluntary sector by, for example, creating non-monetary incentives as a motivation for staff. Conversely, in the voluntary sector values of participation and empowerment can be combined with the material rewards common to business in how staff want to be rewarded. Current trends are towards the latter rather than the former, so our concentration is on how government and business principles overlap and affect the management and organisation of NGDOs.

The government overlap

What might occur within NGDOs when they provide public services similar to the state (area 2), which many do? For a start, staff may be inclined to behave in directive ways, treating those they serve simply as recipients who should be happy with whatever level of service they get. Put another way, solidarity is an unlikely attitude. The NGDO may start to believe that it has a right to an everlasting place in society, putting its own interests above the continual need to demonstrate its credibility, with staff expecting permanent employment. Arguing that it is doing the government's job, NGDOs will make claims on public funds which – without sufficient care – bring with them conditions and expectations that the organisation will operate in accordance with government standards, practices and political needs. In short, the NGDO functions as a parastatal agency in all but name. This behaviour is observed in India, where the government has allocated large sums of money for NGDOs to assist in implementing the National Development Plan.[16]

The business overlap

Where NGDO functions are overlapped by businesses principles, NGDOs may adopt the ethos of entrepreneurs and contractors. Poverty alleviation and humanitarian relief may change from being a moral response to a social problem,

turning poor people into a 'product' to be marketed and sold. Market position, in terms of the organisation's share in private and public aid donations, becomes a dominant concern, leading to fund-raising practices which overstate achievements or which, in pursuit of a sympathetic response from donors, distort information or present images which may do an injustice to those for whom the NGDO operates.

Growth and the ability to spend, rather than the profitability of a company, become criteria for measuring success; the legitimate difficulties of performance measurement may be used to hide shortcomings in development impact. Transparency in operations also suffers because failures or set-backs are treated as potentially bad publicity and therefore unwelcome news, instead of a source of learning. As a consequence, internal systems which seek to monitor or evaluate performance are viewed as a contract imposition and their outputs are not made available to the public, which undermines accountability. Increasing market profile and income share is a now a common concern of Northern NGDOs' fund-raising; overstating impact is wide-spread; distortions in fund-raising images are a frequent complaint of NGDOs from the South and East; and the lack of transparency is a source of growing disquiet in development circles and the media.[17]

Commercial companies continually search for ways to reduce costs, especially by applying economies of scale. NGDOs may do the same in order to save donor funds, but at the cost of dis-economies of development processes and wilful ignoring of indirect effects. For example, an NGDO involved in supporting school construction throughout a country in East Africa negotiated with communities that when they had built the walls, the NGDO would provide the roofing materials. To save money, materials were bought in bulk from one supplier. But the centralised purchasing arrangements bore no relationship to the varied stages of interaction with communities. The rains came before materials arrived, and in some cases substantial damage occurred to the new classrooms. Result? Community demotivation and economic waste. Simply put, economies of scale come at the cost of choice and flexibility. NGDOs must therefore be able to make difficult trade-offs setting desirable economic optimisation against effectiveness in complex development processes.

What the business overlap also brings is a greater concern to control costs and ensure sound financial management. As long as these aspects are applied in ways which do not undermine or limit the application of best development practice, they constitute a significant benefit to NGDOs who are often lax in these areas, partly because business approaches have not been seen as consistent with a culture of solidarity. Part of appropriate NGDO professionalism must include attention to costs and benefits and ensuring proper use of financial resources; business can offer useful experience and guidance, but not necessarily as pre-packaged methods.

Financial incentives are needed to gain professional staff; however, this runs counter to the spirit of voluntarism and self-motivation and the organisational culture which goes with it. The introduction of a competitive culture creates organisational tensions, conflicts of conscience and personal stress, especially for middle managers. For example, it is argued that hierarchy, which is accepted as normal in government and business, increases effective decision-making, while committed staff, who are prepared to forego a market rate for their labour in NGDOs expect democratic decision processes as well as the right to influence policy and practice; this expectation can lead to a 'paralysis of participation'.[18] How are the two to be balanced? Finally, pressure to compete can sway NGDOs' attentions towards donors as primary stakeholders, rather than towards those who provide their legitimacy. Put another way, the service given to the donor becomes more important than the benefit to those who justify the NGDO's existence.

The three-tiered overlap

Going back to Figure 2.2, it is easy to see that area 4 is a position of great complexity, calling for NGDOs to juggle with and balance three different sets of principles at once. They must contribute to sustained poverty alleviation and

social justice using their voluntary attributes, while functioning as businesses to provide public services. This is obviously not a desirable position, but sometimes it cannot be avoided, particularly in conditions of severe economic decline, ineffectual governments and high levels of national dependency on aid as, for example, in Burundi, Malawi, Mozambique, Mauritania, Nepal and Sierra Leone. In these settings, NGDOs must operate as very complicated hybrids, with the potential to suffer from all the tensions and unwelcome effects described above. NGDO organisation and management must actively counter the problems arising from multiple operating principles at the risk of otherwise becoming completely ineffective. Governments and businesses are seldom confronted with such situations and therefore have little to offer in terms of proven solutions.

Overall, while varying in degree between and within continents, opportunistic business and government behaviour continues to confuse the voluntary sector. An entrepreneurial shift in the aid market place leads to the NGDO label being appropriated by a variety of participants. Lip service is paid to voluntarism and solidarity. The overriding concern becomes survival at all costs.

Box 2.1 shows the – often less than flattering – acronyms used across the world for organisations which claim to be NGDOs but are not inspired by the principles and values of voluntarism. One long-term observer asserts that NGDOs are, in fact, no longer part of the third sector, but belong in the second because their practices show that market, rather than voluntary, values dominate.[19] The question this poses, and a concern of this book, is how can NGDOs reposition themselves to regain and apply the principles of development voluntarism in a commercial world?

Re-establishing NGDOs within the voluntary sector

The past five years have seen significant tensions and upheavals occurring within NGDOs as the tectonic plates of voluntary, government and business principles collide with each other. In geology, such collisions result in

---

Box 2.1
Acronyms for NGDO pretenders[20]

BRINGO Briefcase NGO	An NGO which is no more than a briefcase carrying a well written proposal
ComeN'GO Come and go NGO	An NGO that appears spasmodically; only used by the owners when the NGO pasture looks greener
CONGO Commercial NGO	NGOs set up by businesses in order to participate in bids, help win contracts, and reduce taxation
CRINGO Criminal NGO	Organisation established for illegal purposes, especially import-export (i.e. smuggling); common in transition economies
DONGO Donor NGO	Created and owned by donors to do their job while shifting overhead costs outside
FANGO Fake NGO	NGO used as a front for something else; not uncommon in Eastern Europe
GONGO Government-Owned NGO	Type of GRINGO used to capture or redirect non-profit funds allocated by the official aid system
GRINGO Government-Run and Initiated NGO	Variation of a Quango, but with the function of countering the actions of real NGDOs; common in Africa
MANGO Mafia NGO	A criminal NGO providing services of the money laundering, enforcement and protection variety; prevalent in Eastern Europe
MONGO My Own NGO	An NGO which is the personal property of an individual, often dominated by his or her ego
NGI Non-Governmental Individual	A person who operates as if he or she is an NGO but without an organisational affiliation
PANGO Party NGO	An aspiring, defeated or banned political party or politician dressed as an NGO; species of Central Asia and Indo-China
PHANGO Phantom NGO	NGO existing only in the mind of the speaker; used to bolster an argument
PONGO Politician's NGO	Established to capture or direct NGO funding to the home constituency as a defence against incursion by opponents
QUANGO Quasi NGO	Para-state body set up by government as an NGO, often to enable better conditions of service or create political distance

a new landscape or, in some cases, ongoing instability with occasional earthquakes and eruptions. The NGDO landscape is still far from stable, but there are signs that without conscious counter measures it will settle, Uphoff has argued, outside the third sector. This would be a misfortune.

Northern NGDOs have tended to adopt two distinct strategies in the struggle to introduce and somehow reconcile different sets of organisational principles. Some have embarked on massive and painful organisation-wide processes of reorientation, commonly labelled restructuring. Others have tried to change organisational culture and practices from above by importing chief executives and senior managers from the business world. Some have done both. There has been a common trend to redirect, streamline and increase the impact of operations by embarking on strategic planning, a still ongoing process for many NGDOs which has seldom been part of their management repertoire. What this activity entails in practice is an important topic of the next chapter.

In the South, NGDOs have also been facing the dual challenge of repositioning themselves in a new aid context, as well as adjusting to the installation of democracy, especially in Latin America, sub-Saharan Africa and the old Communist block. The responses have been steered by ideology, donor pressure and local opportunities. Soul-searching internal reviews, accompanied by difficult dialogues with Northern counterparts, have been undertaken by many of the larger organisations, such as IBASE in Brazil, DESCO in Peru and, by the sound of it, almost all within the NGDO community in Chile. Repositioning through strategic planning is becoming a preoccupation with Southern NGOs, partly as a consequence of the strategic choices made by Northern supporters; these will be examined later.

In the East, local NGDOs are a recent organisational arrival; there is often confusion about their legal standing, especially if the regimes in power are unsure of what autonomy they can or want to tolerate. An example is Kazakstan, where recent constitutional amendments have curtailed possible areas of NGDO activity. The major challenge to NGDOs

in finding a social position in Eastern countries is not the pressure that arises from overlapping sectors. Rather, difficulties arise in forming a socially recognised, stable third sector in post-authoritarian states – in a context where long-term support from the North is uncertain and inadequate. However, despite differences within and between continents, one agenda that is emerging for some NGDOs of the South and East which rely on aid is to look for long-term strategies which tie NGDOs more firmly to their own economies. This is described in Chapter 6.

All in all, NGDOs are in the midst of a severe identity crisis. The issue is to determine how NGDOs can emerge from this period so that voluntary values, principles and development advantages co-exist with, but are not made subordinate to, those of business and the market. Some would argue that it is too late; NGDOs as we knew them have already lost their soul. The immediate task is to examine what, in organisational and management terms, can be done to re-establish a position which embodies voluntarism in practice as well as in name.

Regaining identity within voluntarism

Retaining a position somewhere within the voluntary sector means ensuring that voluntary values and principles remain dominant in the context of a non-profit market place. Making this happen will depend on the nature and strength of an NGDO's identity, which in its turn is determined by consistency in the beliefs of those who govern its organisational values. Simply put, identity is determined by power over organisational philosophy and its translation into action.

The importance of values, beliefs and development philosophy

Examining values and power in NGDOs is not straightforward because the first is highly abstract and the second seldom transparent. We will start with the most fundamental element of NGDO identity, its beliefs. Beliefs are the foundation for organisational values and philosophy of action. Together, beliefs, values and development philosophy form the reference point for what an NGDO is and stands for. They are the measure against which the organisation must judge itself and be judged by others.

Surprisingly, and unfortunately for the security of NGDO positioning, values and beliefs are seldom if ever explicitly talked about or clearly stated.[21] A handful of NGDOs have recently attempted to do just this (see examples in Box 2.2), but in the vast majority of cases we can only deduce what an NGDO believes in from its statements of purpose and the methods it employs.

Box 2.2
An example of NGDO beliefs

We believe that all people are of equal value and have the same rights, but are born into inequality of circumstance and opportunity; this can be changed.

We believe in the fundamental equality of human dignity which goes beyond the essential inequality of possessions, skills and circumstances.

We believe that poverty is an injustice which is caused, and can be changed by, human action.

A few NGDOs express their beliefs through statements about their analysis of development – for instance, their views on the causes of poverty and strategies for change. A sample of NGDO statements about development analysis are shown in Box 2.3.

Box 2.3
NGDO development analysis

Poverty is a result of inequity in the structure of national and international economic systems.

Neglect and abuse of children's rights results from a breakdown in national and family values.

Global environmental degradation is due to overconsumption in the North and the necessary survival strategies of poor people in the Third World.

The positive point about making beliefs and analysis more explicit is that it enables staff to better decide whether or not they belong in the organisation and to identify with the views which underlie its culture. In other cases, clues about what NGDOs might believe in or the values they hold are to be found in their statements of vision, purpose, mission and actions (see Box 2.4).

Box 2.4
NGDO vision, purpose and action

We envision a world without hunger and injustice.

Our organisation works for the eradication of poverty in the world through direct community development action.

We are committed to working together with our partners to address the social, economic, political and spiritual concerns of our constituencies.

We are an organisation development consultancy which aims to contribute to the building of organisational effectiveness amongst those organisations working towards social transformation.

Our purpose is to relieve distress, poverty and avoidable suffering throughout the world.

Formulating these types of (mission) statements is also a relatively new endeavour for the majority of NGDOs. Consequently, the most frequent source of information about NGDO identity are simply the statements they make in fliers and information sheets about either the problem being addressed or the activities they are carrying out. A few examples are show in Box 2.5.

Box 2.5
Statements by NGDOs about themselves

Our organisation works with communities to improve their livelihoods.

With our help, street children are rehabilitated so that they can play a full part in society.

Through public awareness raising, our organisation works to protect the environment.

Here, the lowest common denominator is that some individuals cared enough about some aspect of society to form an organisation to change things. For NGDOs which think no further than what they do, identity is equal to activity. In the aid system, this means that an organisation is no more than the project it runs. In other words, what the NGDO does equals what it is. In organisational and management terms, clear values and a philosophy are essential for effectiveness because they link an NGDO's purpose, policies, strategic aims and operational choices (discussed in the next chapter). Beliefs, vision and values are at the top of a hierarchy of organisational features which need to be in place if lower levels of organisational activity are to be done well. Without these 'foundations', serious inconsistencies between policies and real-life practices can and do arise. For example, while an NGDO believes that war veterans have a right to national respect and adequate economic support, their actual activities amount to little more than distributing hand outs, such as food and blankets. The inconsistency between the two is not seen or is simply accepted for reasons of organisational survival.

Is it chance that so few NGDOs have clear statements of the beliefs which inform their values and purpose? Not really. Most NGDOs are adverse to reaching this level of agreement; if such a statement is made, it appears that a creed must be followed. Better to leave things implicit than face contention and futile debate. This pragmatic view has, however, the drawback of avoiding issues which are critical to interpreting events and making consistent choices in unpredicted circumstances. One of the most important negative consequences is that a lack of shared beliefs and values reduces internal trust, leading to a top-down, control-orientation which lessens an NGDO's ability to respond rapidly, to adapt to diversity or to adopt the truly participatory practices needed in interaction with primary stakeholders.

Other sources of NGDO identity

In addition to beliefs, the origins of NGDOs are important to their identity and approach with similarities and differences between North, South and East.[22] Northern NGDOs have arisen:

- from political affiliations;
- from the motivations of social groupings;
- for the promotion of national values;
- to tackle specific issues, such as the environment;
- to advance technological solutions to problems;
- to promote particular ideologies;
- to support similar organisations;
- from personal inspiration.

In their many combinations, these different origins lead to a wide diversity in organisations, giving each a unique identity as well as a tendency to ensure that their individuality is maintained.

A similar list of origins applies to Southern NGDOs, but with added historical and social dimensions. For Southern NGDOs, an important additional feature contributing to their identity is

a past domination by foreign powers, which is still to be found in new guises. Hussein Adam has identified three common identity-shaping responses of Southern NGDOs to their colonial histories which he terms, 'return to the past', 'seize the future' and 'transmission belt'.[23] The first, exemplified by the Six-S movement in West Africa and the Savadoya movement in Sri Lanka, seeks to rehabilitate and build upon the cultural or religious norms which were negated by colonisers and to use them as the well-spring of people-centred development action. Identity is closely associated with indigenous values. 'Seize the future' NGDOs react against past and present exploitation within and between countries. NGDOs within the anti-*dependencia* movement of Latin America, such as IBASE in Brazil, and others associated with communist movements in Asia, such as the People's Organisation for Participation (POP) in Thailand, find identity, amongst others, from their structural analysis of continuing domination, exploitation and denial of fundamental rights within their society and beyond. Identity is essentially defined in terms of an ideological position. As the name implies, 'transmission belts', provide that function through the transfer of aid resources. Identity derives from their role somewhere in the aid chain and the services they deliver. In other words, who they are is what they do.

In addition to colonial exploitation and injustice; NGDOs in the South and East can arise from struggles against internal oppression such as military or civilian dictators. Often informed by ideologies from the left (including theological interpretations of the Catholic church) and allied to revolt by peasants and farmers, NGDOs have been established by individuals and groups who may have been driven underground, or adopted other forms of resistance. Examples may be readily found in South East Asia and Latin America. But in response to such threats, in order to show that they are concerned about the plight of the poor, dictatorial regimes have been known to form, allow or promote certain NGDOs too. In either case, NGDO origins arise from, and mirror, a context of indigenous oppression. All in all it is not safe to look at the identity of NGDOs devoid of context or history.

Power over identity: NGDO governance

The mix of values, philosophy and origins described above all contribute to the content of NGDO identity, but not necessarily to its strength or stability under pressure. Resilience in identity depends on how widely and consistently beliefs, values, development philosophy and organisational principles are shared between key groups.

A crude division governing identity can be made between an NGDO's formal 'owners': those recognised as accountable in law; its constituency: the organisation's social base; the leadership: the chief executive and senior management; and the staff at different levels. All groups exert power in their own way and to a different degree. Where significantly different perceptions about beliefs, purpose or principles arise, identity can become fragmented. For example, splits within the NGDO community and within an NGDO like the Philippines Peasant Institute can partly be attributed to widening differences in the political interpretation of the function and identity of NGDOs in the post-Marcos, post-Cold War era. Whether or not splits occur depends on the balance of power between the groups, the type of governing structure, and personalities and communication – where the chief executive's role is often pivotal.

There are three common governing structures: self-regulated, with or without membership; self-selected oligarchy; and constituent based. Much of Latin America conforms to the first type. The civic code under which NGDOs register creates a governing body composed of staff representatives, which can be expanded to include outsiders but this does not have to occur. In this sense, the staff who make up the organisation also own it; in effect, they own themselves and lack a social constituency with formal power. While differences in opinion can exist, in this set-up communication between owners and staff should not pose a problem. Organisational identity is likely to be strong and coherent, unless confidence is lost in the leadership. The drawbacks of this circular or incestuous set-up for public accountability and for dealing with contentious organisational change, such as reducing staff, are examined later.

In the rest of the world, a more common structure is a governing board which is self-selected in perpetuity – an oligarchy. Staff and volunteers can be allocated places, but the majority of power rests with outsiders chosen by each other for their social position, political links, expertise, representative status or other beneficial attributes.[24] In these circumstances, significant differences arising between board, leadership and staff on how to respond to pressures on voluntary principles can lead to public wrangling, long-term instability, demotivation and seriously reduced effectiveness. Less frequent, but not uncommon, are constituency-governed NGDOs. Constituency is an umbrella term for identifiable political and economic group(s) in society which the organisation stems from and relates to strongly. In the North, secular NGDOs with constituent assemblies are MS in Denmark and NOVIB in the Netherlands, the overseas development arms of trade unions to be found in Canada, and Amnesty International. NGDOs funded through child sponsorship, such as Plan International, ACTIONAID, World Vision, Christian Children's Funds and the Save the Children Funds, can readily point to a constituency or social base, but are not governed by them. With slight variations, these NGDOs have self-selected boards and only one includes representatives from countries of operation, which means the South and East are not formally represented; this can give an imbalance in interests served towards funders.

If the system of governance allows them to do so, NGDOs with a broadly-based, clearly definable constituency are more likely to be held to their founding principles and voluntary values than those which do not; members will have to be persuaded that the convictions they adhere to no longer hold. However, constituents' ability to exercise control in practice is largely determined by the information made available to inform their position. And here, leadership and staff usually have the upper hand, which can, and often does, reduce any governing body to a rubber stamp. What one commonly observes is NGDO leaders and staff shaping and shifting identity. Too frequently, boards end up taking remedial rather than preventive action.

How NGDOs go about re-establishing organisational identity when it becomes confused, contested or lost is dealt with in the next chapter. The point to conclude with here is that irrespective of the formal systems of governance, identity boils down to the integrity and honesty with which leaders and staff adhere to voluntary values and founding principles.

What Characterises NGDOs on Today's Development Scene?

The previous pages have been a long route to characterising the sort of organisations which are the subject of this book. What the approach illustrates is that it is possible to describe these organisations in positive ways without having to resort to the double negatives of non-profit and non-governmental. But what does this tell us about the essential characteristics of third-sector organisations and of the organisational and management features of development-oriented agencies?

Non-governmental organisations

The formal organisations making up the third sector differ from governments and businesses in that:

- They are not established for and cannot distribute any surplus they generate as a profit to owners or staff.
- They are not required nor prevented from existing by law, but result from people's self-chosen voluntary initiative to pursue a shared interest or concern.
- Formed by private initiative, they are independent, in that they are not part of government nor controlled by a public body.
- Within the terms of whatever legislation they choose to register themselves, they also govern themselves.
- Registration means that the founders wish to have social recognition; this calls for some degree of formalisation and acceptance of the principle of social accountability.

Obviously, these basic criteria cover a vast array of organisations in any society, ranging from the Ku Klux Klan, through churches, amateur football teams, societies for the blind and physically handicapped, foundations for cancer research, ethnic welfare associations, the Ramblers Association, and the Salvation Army. In addition, there is a socially significant set of third-sector organisations which do not seek recognition in a formal sense, but may nevertheless be developmentally important.

Within this definition, how do NGOs dedicated to international development, distinguish themselves?

Non-governmental development organisations

NGDOs are a subset of organisations within the five voluntary sector criteria listed above, but do not necessarily operate solely on the basis of voluntary sector principles. In terms of their particular characteristics:

- Within the framework of international co-operation, NGDOs are legitimised by the existence of the world's poor and powerless and by the circumstances and injustices they experience.
- By and large, NGDOs act as intermediaries, providing support to those who legitimise them; they are not mutual benefit organisations or associations.
- NGDOs are predominantly hybrid in nature, operating on the basis of multiple, partially conflicting, partially re-enforcing organisational principles.
- Realising effective sustainable development is critically dependent on NGDOs retaining

voluntary values and principles as the primary force in their way of working.

In today's aid system, NGDOs face a particular set of challenges which require appropriate organisation and skilled management if they are to be competent agents of development. What are they?

Organisational and management balances faced by NGDOs

The organisational trade-offs and balances which NGDOs must achieve to be effective can be grouped under three main headings: the nature of voluntarism; the dynamics of the development scene; and the nature of social change in a world becoming dominated by market-driven economics and liberal political systems. As with development work, balancing does not mean equalising, but continually adjusting and managing the mix of internal and external forces to ensure that, overall, voluntarism overlaps government and business principles (rather than the other way round).

The nature of voluntarism

When maintaining voluntary principles, NGDOs will have to:

- Balance and ensure consistency between potentially conflicting claims on organisational ownership and values.
- Balance a third-sector governance style with market-oriented standards.
- Balance an organisational culture of voluntarism with that of competitive contracting and public service.
- Balance volunteer and staff self-motivation and commitment with market-related incentives and expectations.
- Balance staff participation and empowerment with directive decision-

making.
- Balance between trust versus control in the allocation and application of authority.

The development scene

When operating in the system of international development co-operation, NGDOs will need to:

- Balance individual identity with NGDO collective interests and collaboration with other sectors.
- Balance accountability to primary stakeholders with credibility towards constituency and contributors.
- Balance the resource mix to ensure retention of autonomy in decision-making.
- Balance market-related and development-related performance criteria and demands.
- Balance the needs and standards of participatory development processes with for-profit approaches to cost-effectiveness and accounting.

Social change

When pursuing processes of social change, NGDOs will have to:

- Balance competencies in service provision with competencies which cause structural change in society.
- Balance operating within market forces with changing how the market operates.

It is always easier to state what NGDOs should do than how they can do what is needed. Part II take this practical step by focusing on five major areas of organisational capacity that NGDOs need in order to balance the demands listed above, as well as those summarised in the first chapter.

Part 2

Making NGDOs Effective

3

Organising Non-Profits for Development

The Capacities Framework

There are almost as many ways of describing organisations as there are writers about them. The model applied here, shown in Figure 3.1, has evolved from the concerns of NGDOs themselves. While not pretending to be 'the' model, the framework reflects NGDOs' key characteristics: it concentrates on areas which are critical to their work and their role in society. To do development well, NGDOs must have adequate capacity in five areas; each must be consistent with the other. The first two relate to an organisational design and systems which link vision to action through appropriate development strategies, programmes and projects; these are carried out by competent and well-managed people. The next three capacities link the NGDO to the outside world by mobilising necessary resources; maintaining a variety of external relationships; and producing results consistent with the mission. This chapter looks at the first type of capacity, which is the ability to define activities and create the right organisational set-up to do them effectively. To begin, both capacity and effectiveness require a short explanation.

Organisational capacity

What is organisational capacity? The simplest definition of capacity is the capability of an organisation to achieve what it sets out to do: to realise its mission. In this sense, capacity measures an organisation's performance in relation to those it is set up to benefit[1]. While we can look at the many factors which contribute to capacity – people, finances, physical facilities,

procedures and so on – these ingredients are not the same as seeing capacity itself; this must be viewed according to an organisation's results. Therefore, as we will see in Chapter 8, efforts at capacity building must not be separated from assessing external change.

The problem for NGDOs is that results are seldom clear cut. Moreover, as we saw in Chapter 1, the role of NGDOs must be to 'dissatisfy' some stakeholders, such as governments or development banks, when exerting policy influence in favour of people who are poor or disadvantaged. Whatever the mix of specific goals and stakeholders an NGDO has, it is vitally important to be consistent about which one is the most significant – who is the NGDO's primary stakeholder – because the values and expectations in relation to this group provide the most important standards against which to assess capacity. The dualism between satisfying some and dissatisfying others leads to the following definition of NGDO capacity: *capacity is the measure of an NGDO's capability to satisfy or influence stakeholders consistent with its mission.* This type of definition has consequences for how to approach and evaluate capacity building efforts, because it requires asking the question: capacity-building for what?

What is organisational effectiveness?

If capacity is the ability to achieve an impact in terms of satisfying or influencing stakeholders, effectiveness means achieving this impact at an appropriate level of effort and cost. It means

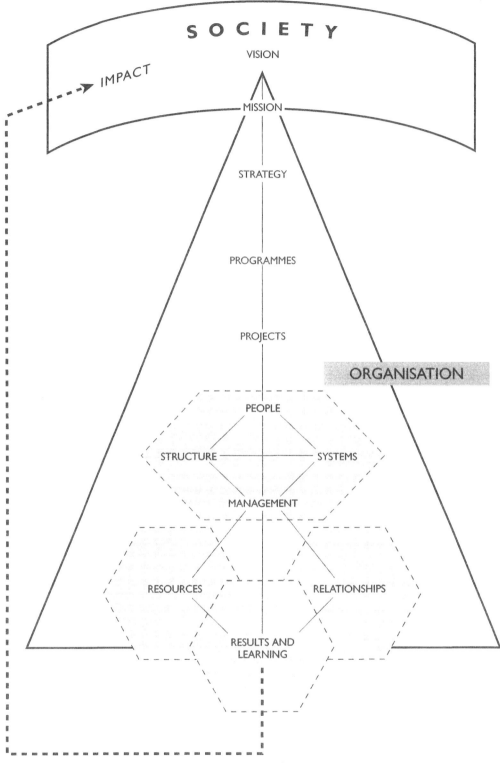

Figure 3.1 NGDO capacity framework

only doing the things that are necessary and doing them well within available resources. The starting point for effectiveness therefore, is knowing what tasks to do, why, and how they must relate to each other. This involves a reasonably logical set of steps that move from the organisation's vision of a changed society to the actions or activities needed to reach it. In technical terms, this is moving from reaffirmation of mission to ensure it is still relevant, through strategic analysis, into operational planning and then development activities. The immediate limitation of this approach is that the planet is not a readily ordered place and development is too complex a process to anticipate every eventuality.

Nevertheless, you have to start somewhere, but with the understanding that action based on (shaky) prediction must be balanced with an ability to continuously learn and adapt. Building an organisation which can do this is a prerequisite for an NGDO's effectiveness.

Moving from vision to action calls for two types of consistency: first, between vision and concrete development activities with stakeholders; second, between the chosen activities, the organisational structure and the principles of participation and empowerment described in Chapter 1. How this looks in practice for development NGDOs is the subject of the next two sections.

Moving From Vision to Action in Development Work[2]

Inconsistency between an NGDO's vision of the world, what it says it wants to be and what it does is a common source of ineffectiveness. Staff, supporters and the outside world get confused, actions do not combine and support each other in optimal ways, there is a loss of focus and energies become dissipated. It is therefore important that the path from vision to action hangs together. Achieving this condition has three essential stages:

- re-examination and confirmation of what the organisation stands for in terms of coherence between vision, mission, identity and role in society;
- linking these to longer-term strategic choices that give it overall direction and maximise impact on society; and
- translating choices into tangible actions and tasks to be carried out by staff, volunteers and others in collaboration, or perhaps in opposition, to some stakeholders.

Going through each stage properly should ensure consistency throughout the organisation.

What makes the whole affair complicated is the knowledge that, to be relevant and sustainable, this cannot be worked out by the organisation on its own. This top-down approach must be matched by a bottom-up process of dialogue and negotiation with the external stakeholders that eventually determines if there are lasting social changes and benefits from the NGDO's efforts. Matching these two directions is one of the most difficult problems facing NGDOs. It crops up in virtually everything they do and is a constant tension which must be managed. Managing the tension is made easier if there is consistency between what an NGDO says it wants to be and what it does.

Ensuring coherence between vision, mission, identity and role

Vision and mission are concepts and statements which tie NGDOs to processes of desired social change. But they are not enough to 'position' an organisation and give it a clear identity and role which is understood both by insiders and outsiders. The degree of clarity and shared ownership of vision, mission and identity differs widely between NGDOs; however, as a rule of thumb, this is likely to be clearer and stronger for organisations founded on ideological motivations and activist roots, as in much of Latin America and parts of South and East Asia. But the post-Cold War era continues to challenge the founding ideologies of existing NGDOs – so how are they redefining their identity and role in society?

The following examples suggest that there is no single answer, but a variety of options are available depending on the system of governance and mechanisms existing for internal dialogue. For example, DESCO in Peru has been a think tank for the political Left. With over 100 staff, most located in field programmes, mechanisms for extensive dialogue were not in place. DESCO therefore utilised a strategic planning process to redefine what it stood for – a method also chosen to engage the whole organisation in debate and to 'objectify' the findings. This latter dimension was necessary because staff representatives formed a majority in the governing assembly and were effectively being asked to put aside personal interests to adjudicate on the organisation's, and hence their own, future.[3]

For CEPES, a Peruvian NGDO known for its activism on behalf of peasants, the search for new values based on the original principle of solidarity has taken place in a weekly meeting of all (16) professionals and a tradition of working lunches where issues affecting the organisation are discussed. This tradition provided a recognised forum for debate; no new mechanism was needed to address the fundamental issue of 'who do we want to be in the new context'. Overall, without recognised fora for wide internal dialogue and a mediating input by independent outsiders, the path to redefining position and values in ideological NGDOs is likely to be rocky. The departure of staff who cannot reconcile themselves with new perspectives is not uncommon.

A different situation arises when an NGDO without any particular ideological position sets out to (re)define identity by clarifying beliefs and values. One operational Northern NGDO organised a workshop for staff at various levels from all countries of operation with the aim of defining organisational beliefs and values and making them explicit. An immediate difficulty in this exercise was to move through cultural differences, particularly regarding gender. The deliberations eventually focused on basic human aspirations, such as mutual respect, appreciation

of the equal value of individual lives and the rights that reflect this belief [4].

A common bottleneck with defining organisational values as a way of clarifying identity is that the task is not taken seriously enough because it is not recognised as building the foundations for effectiveness. Instead, it is perceived to be an abstract, academic luxury which unnecessarily depletes hard won overheads. A lesson when defining values that underpin vision, mission and identity is therefore that:

- it must be seen and treated as an organisation-wide priority endeavour; and
- allocating time and resources to dissemination must be built in; the human process of grappling with values is more important in the long run than the actual wording of value statements.

Value statements are not an optional extra for professional NGDO's; together with beliefs, they are the most fundamental expression of what the organisation stands for – its identity. Clarifying vision and mission, which are usually framed as broad aspirations, provide the necessary initial orientation for choosing paths and goals for action.

Using strategic planning to move from a social role to development goals

A consistent vision, mission, identity and social role are preconditions for effective actions; however, they only reside in people's minds, hearts and on paper. Linking these aspirations and intentions to the right activities means understanding what is going on in the outside world and then 'fitting' the organisation's work into the environment in a way which maximises impact. This task is sometimes called 'positioning' the organisation. A common way of working out the best fit or position is through strategic planning.

The objective of strategic planning is to make long-term choices in terms of concrete goals and resource allocations that are likely to maximise impact without compromising identity, autonomy and viability. Strategic planning has been relatively neglected by NGDOs during the period when resources were expanding with few questions being asked about effectiveness. Those days are over, and strategic planning is now a common way of rationalising and prioritising resource allocations. But this process can only be carried out properly if vision, mission and identity are in place, consistent with each other, widely understood and internalised by staff.[5] A strategic planning process can also help in creating and spreading consistency.

Many NGDOs have grown haphazardly or opportunistically. Strategic planning is a useful way to sort themselves out and focus their skills and energies on what they can do best and where. However, one problem in the way NGDOs are going about this is that they confuse strategic planning with strategic management.[6] Some NGDOs believe that through strategic planning they have laid out a railway track which will then carry them smoothly along for five years or so. But

people-centred development is not a known track. Given the high degree of uncertainty, complexity and open-endedness involved, the assumptions which underlie planning systems make them a risky tool to rely on. Their principal benefit is the rigour of thinking and argument they introduce.

Nevertheless, strategic planning can benefit NGDOs in adapting to the new world order if it helps them get their house in order, ensures a (re)orientation towards what they are good at, establishes a common framework for responding to the unexpected, and ensures that third-sector principles inspire people to move in the same direction. But a plan is not a substitute for managers who must manage with a strategic perspective; managers must have an ability to correctly judge the long-term implications of short-term events, in relation to the strategic direction, and respond accordingly. Hopefully, NGDOs will move quickly through the phase of investing in strategic planning to concentrating on building

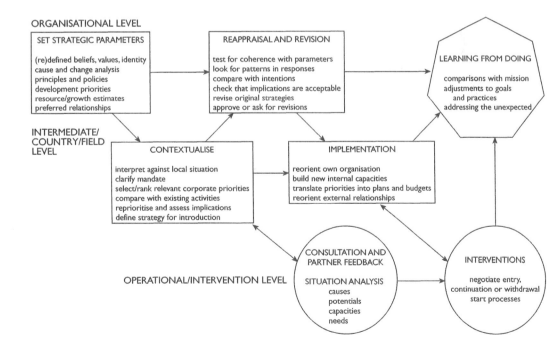

Figure 3.2 Strategic planning flow

competencies in strategic management.[7] For the moment, strategic planning in NGDOs is a necessary 'waste' of time, which still needs to be done well; but how?

Figure 3.2 describes a strategic planning process framework for large or international NGOs. This flow together with reflections on an exercise carried out by an international NGO provided by Hans Hoyer, and my own experience, are drawn on to offer pointers about how this activity can contribute to better organisational functioning, as well as making programme and project choices.

Starting points for carrying out a strategic planning exercise

Strategic planning is commonly assumed to be a linear process which starts at the apex of the organisation and then moves logically out to the periphery. This is not the case. Why? Because the nature of sustainable development processes means that they cannot impose and have to be negotiated. So, for NGDOs, any plan has to be arrived at through a process of consultation. If done properly, strategic planning is a down-up-down-up, inside-outside-inside process between the organisation and its key stakeholders. Figure 3.2 illustrates this process, which eventually leads to choices about direction, priorities for action and indications for expected resource allocations that can be applied throughout the organisation, but then tailored to context.

The balancing act in strategic planning is to create sufficient firmness to ensure organisational coherence and maximum impact, and then match this with sufficient flexibility to allow for local interpretation and application. It is not just the technical content of planning in terms of analysis, activities and budgets which must give this balance, but also the method used, which should include as many different perspectives as possible. The starting point for strategy formulation must, however, be at the top, because this is the only place able to generate an overview of the whole organisation and its surroundings. For example, this is the vantage point for seeing trends in financing which determine possibilities for growth. In addition, it is where the final accountability for legitimacy rests. And, assuming

that internal systems are generating the right information, this is the place where an assessment can and must be made of how well the organisation performs in terms of its mission, as opposed to individual activities or projects. For small NGDOs, these functions may all be within two or three people; for large NGDOs they can involve dozens.

The importance of first setting strategic parameters

In addition to a restatement of identity and desired position, strategic planning must start with decisions about a few basic parameters; these may carry the heavy name of 'corporate policies': principles and choices that are the governors' responsibility and which should be adhered to throughout the organisation. One key policy is about financial growth and mobilisation. Other corporate policies could deal with gender, relations with other organisations, mandates to different levels of authority and decision-making.

There is no universal name for the framework of organisational policies and priorities which an NGDO's leadership must set at the beginning of a strategic planning exercise. The term 'strategic intent' was used by Oxfam UK/I for this step in its process; other NGDOs call the same thing a vision statement, or a corporate vision. Whatever the title, the formulation process tends to be similar in that necessary background materials and preliminary ideas are gathered by staff, either as part of their normal work or as members of a task force. To incorporate governors' perspectives, board members or constituency representatives are commonly involved.

The degree to which field staff are asked to submit their ideas, situation analyses and preliminary priorities, or other inputs to strategic planning, varies between NGDOs. However, experience indicates, that if no basic parameters are made available when such requests for input are sent out, responses may be incoherent. In drafting their inputs, field staff may have consulted with their key stakeholders. Unless they do this with extreme care, unwarranted expectations can be created which have to be renegotiated later, causing frustration all round.

TIPS **Experience with introducing a strategic planning exercise suggests the following tips**

Initial data collection should draw on existing internal and external sources, rather than soliciting draft plans from field staff unless there is an initial orienting framework. The starting point should be a board-approved framework which includes:

➤ a restatement of organisational identity: beliefs, values, vision and mission;
➤ a restatement of the cause and change analysis which justifies the overall approach to development work and provides the basis for interpretation of events;
➤ a restatement of key principles to be applied throughout the organisation – for example, on relations with government, participation, gender, organisational and individual accountability;
➤ a statement of intentions with respect to qualitative and quantitative growth;
➤ a statement of organisation-wide thematic priorities for development – for example, environment or income generation or human rights;
➤ an indication of any desired changes in relationships that significantly affect the organisation's position in society – for example, working more (or less) with civic actors, such as trade unions, informal sector organisation, or with governmens and official aid agencies.

Lessons from strategic planning in practice

A successful strategic planning exercise will ensure consistency between the NGDO's vision and the practical directions it will take in the environment in which it lives. There are, however, a number of reasons why strategic planning may not go well. Box 3.1 provides one example of what happens when corporate intentions are translated into strategic plans. As the lessons indicate, where strategic planning is introduced for the first time, leaders and managers have a pivotal role to play in creating the conditions necessary for staff (and outsiders) to critically question existing ways of working and to re-evaluate the organisation's role. In this situation, the attitude, styles and competencies of those guiding strategic planning has a strong influence on the degree to which the planning process becomes a form of staff development.

The origin of a strategic planning initiative influences how the process runs and its impact on the relationship with partner NGDOs. Occasionally, strategic planning is prompted by internal reflection, but more frequently results from external pressure as the aid system shifts into a post-Cold War mode. Today, in pursuit of greater accountability, a concern for cost effectiveness, and demonstration of impact, donors are calling for a better specification of what NGDOs intend to do with their funds, why, and the measures they will use to prove their performance. Strategic planning is the tool usually chosen by Northern NGDOs to come up with a response. As the next link in the aid chain, Southern and Eastern partners are on the receiving end of this process. They must decide how to respond.

All too often weak, dependent Southern NGDOs respond by embarking on a strategic planning exercise which simply reorients their priorities towards those of their Northern partners. In other words, they do not look for options which will make them less dependent and then negotiate an uncoupling from the existing relationship based on a well-thought through strategy. This is an important issue because three lessons from strategic planning by Northern NGDOs give cause for concern:

- Strategic plans, particularly at the country level, seldom include an analysis of their consequences, especially for existing partner relationships and staff competencies. A rough calculation for those I know about suggest that some 15 to 30 per cent of partners and 10 to 15 per cent of staff would no longer fit into the strategic priorities being chosen by Northern NGOs.[9]
- Strategic plans must themselves make provision for resource allocations for the plan's implementation, including a process for withdrawal from existing relations and entry into new ones.
- A third shortcoming is the highly unlikely idea that a strategic plan is operational in its first year. A more realistic assumption is that it will take the duration of a new strategic plan to introduce it. In other words, the pattern of priorities envisaged in the plan will only be in place by the end.

Box 3.1
Lessons from strategic planning in a transnational NGDO

Background
PLAN International is an NGDO founded in 1937. Using funds raised from some 800,000 child sponsors in the North, it carries out development work in 35 countries, managed through six regional offices. A corporate strategic planning task force – composed of seconded field managers, a board member and headquarters staff – was established in 1993. The task force respecified vision and mission, indicated preferred levels and locations for growth, and initiated a further process which subsequently identified five priority 'domains' for PLAN's work: child learning; economic participation and well-being; growing up healthy; child protection and participation; and habitat.

The Regional Strategic Planning Process
PLAN Region for South Asia (ROSA) comprises Bangladesh, India, Nepal, Pakistan, and Sri Lanka. Like other regions, ROSA was engaged in the corporate planning process, providing senior level responses to draft plans and other documents and approving of the final board submission. Translation of corporate intent to regional action was the task of a special group drawn from a cross-section of regional and country staff. The drawback of so many levels was balanced by the multiple perspectives which enriched data selection, collection and interpretation. The approach involved a down-up-down process between the group and country staff, with time built in for sharing and feed back. The steps adopted were:

- undoing the historical conditioning of group members to create a common understanding, bolstered by a spirit of enquiry, entrepreneurship and risk-taking;
- redefining vision and values from a regional perspective, by awakening, sharing and exploring innermost feelings;
- defining mission, particularly by sorting out the contending stakeholders and defining a model of sustainable development which calls for cause analysis and provides progress measures;
- formulating strategic questions which guide the collection of information;
- undertaking analysis which answers the strategic questions and leads to specific actions;
- converting mission into objectives in each of the themes, which correspond to priority areas within PLAN's corporate domains;
- assessing organisational implications and strategising implementation.

Lessons: blockages and how to deal with them
Strategic planning was a new process for staff which also demanded reflection. The following lessons emerged about blockages and how to deal with them.

- *Functional myopia:* staff prioritise their own functions and underplay the significance of the work and links to other units. A solution is patience, placing stress on shared values, creating a common vocabulary and criticising ideas which are myopic.
- *Command-and-control orientation:* staff are regarded as hands to be directed, rather than heads to be tapped and hearts to be engaged, leading to their passivity and risk avoidance. A solution is to actively foster and guide dissatisfaction by exploiting the difference between the actual and the desired organisational culture.
- *Preoccupation with daily routines:* people cannot balance their work with plans for the future. A solution is to create space, not to underplay the magnitude of the task, and to stress that crafting a strategy is an exercise in entrepreneurship which entails a degree of risk.
- *Excessive formalisation:* too strict adherence to systems constrains innovation, induces a fear of straying over the line, and produces apathy which is not conducive to the inquisitiveness and exploration that strategic planning calls for. A solution is to agree that mistakes are a natural and valuable source of human learning and create space to do so by allowing selective relaxation of rules and procedures.
- *Insufficient external orientation:* internal preoccupations filter out signs of external changes which have a direct bearing on relevance and effectiveness. Paying attention to what is outside, however, requires a capacity to absorb and process what is seen and heard. A solution is to build up and retain an analytic capacity, because sheer effort and creativity are not sufficient for correct organisational positioning, which must be grounded in an assessment of the external environment.
- *Lack of will to change:* conforming with authority, limited mobility across functional areas, and excessive job security all conspire to make any change seem threatening. A solution is to create triggers against the status quo which link external forces for change with internal dissatisfactions – for example, by raising questions about staff perception and assumptions.

Source: adapted from contribution by Dr Hans J Hoyer, Regional Director, PLAN International South Asia

---

Translating strategy into programmes and projects: ensuring consistency and quality

Outputs of strategic planning are statements about the NGDO's future efforts and resource allocations. For example, with an organisational mission to increase food security, an NGDO could chose to do research on the drought resilience of traditional crops, or introduce new high-yielding varieties, or propagate the use of fertilisers, or introduce better grain storage facilities, or improve farming practices, or any combination of these. Whatever strategic choice is made needs to be accompanied by specific measures of achievement, for example, the uptake of new varieties by a target number of farmers. Each of these goals can be attained through a narrow or broad array of activities for which resources and relationships are required. Where the scale of activity is wide and multifaceted, development jargon talks of a development programme, which is split into discrete fundable projects.[10]

Many publications detail how to move from strategic choices through programme definition to the design of specific development initiatives. The issue of importance is to question how NGDOs ensure that choices of action are consistent with their values and mission and that the outcome is of high quality in terms of capitalising on NGDO advantages and past experience. The next sections answer these two questions.

Moving from strategy to development initiatives

Assuming that an NGDO's strategy is well understood, there are a number of reasons why inconsistencies can appear when projects are defined. Typical factors are poor information, miscommunication, opportunism, lack of internal discipline, inadequate professionalism and a mismatch between demand and supply – for example, empowerment initiatives are more difficult to 'sell' than water supplies and health care. One frequent cause is the difference in understanding and imbalance in power between those doing the work of negotiating 'in the field' with stakeholders and those providing or mobilising financial resources. Bridging this gap is important and the ability to do so is influenced, in part, by the size of the NGDO, where bigger organisations often split tasks over different people or even locations.

For small NGDOs, where the people involved in negotiating and planning are likely to be the same as those raising funds, there should be little gap in internal information. But inconsistency can still occur if the NGDO tailors its proposals to funders' expected or stated preferences at the cost of inputs from primary stakeholders, whose influence is also weakened by a lack of upfront funds for the NGDO to get out and consult with people first. For large NGDOs, lack of upfront pre-planning funds can exist as well. But an additional difficulty comes from the separation of tasks within the organisation between those who consult with communities, those who write proposals, and

those who raise money. For international NGDOs, the centre is likely to be in its headquarters or home country, which poses an even greater communication problem, worsened by competitive pressure to 'bring in' grants as a measure of performance. Unless countered, using grants as indicator of effectiveness works against basic participatory principles.

There are various ways NGDOs can guard against inconsistency creeping in and authentic participation being pushed out. Oxfam UK has moved away from fund-raisers trawling through files in Oxford and looking for projects around which fund-raising messages can be constructed. It now employs a system where communications officers work in programme departments, helping to prepare materials which fit identified projects. This has helped to bridge the culture gap between fund-raising and programme staff, where the merits of being able to present tangible benefits is now common currency and a shared concern. Secondly, 'prime projects' are identified by programme managers as likely candidates for communication material and an agreement is made with the marketing department to provide a regular flow of information. The focus of communication and message initiative has shifted more to the South and East, which reduces the likelihood of distortions appearing when resources are mobilised.[11]

Nevertheless, this positive shift does not deal with a more basic problem. Namely, what may be a strong vision at the centre of the organisation weakens when the priorities and expectations of primary stakeholders, and the preferences and priorities of donors, must be accommodated. NGDOs face a real problem of juggling their strategic priorities with the expectations and priorities of diverse communities and the conditions attached to available funds. Chapter 5 focuses on how structured negotiation between key stakeholders can help reconcile these differences. The point to remember is that the periphery of the organisation is the place where consistency is most likely to be weakened as the NGDO's own choices are confronted by those of others. The risk of creating inconsistency is greatly reduced when the strategic planning process has already drawn on inputs from stakeholders. In addition, NGDOs can introduce control mechanisms to ensure both consistency and application of existing experience. This is where we turn to next.

Checks and balances for ensuring consistency and quality of development initiatives

Given the self-interest and horse-trading which goes on in designing projects, at some stage there must be a way of ensuring that what is defined is consistent with the NGDO's values, principles, strategies and standards. For small NGDOs, consistency can be built into the design process but will only occur if the staff involved stay true to the organisation's identity and have not been significantly deflected by funding factors. However, the weak identity of many NGDOs discussed earlier does not inspire confidence. Bigger NGDOs have to construct more complicated ways of safeguarding consistency, and these are normally combined with ensuring quality, such as the sustained benefits of development initiatives. How is this done?

Quality is a word not often found in NGDOs. This is a serious lapse, because quality is a useful concept as it combines both objective and subjective elements which are part and parcel of the balancing act. The closest NGDOs come to worrying about quality is a concern to identify and apply best practices. Big NGDOs employ two principal methods to ensure that best practices are followed when defining programmes and projects. The first relies on in-house technical specialists, for example in health care, gender, participation and water supply, who assess and judge what is proposed. The second is a review process involving knowledgeable outside volunteers who may function as an advisory committee. Some NGDOs employ both. The perverse outcome of such mechanisms is that they can dilute ultimate responsibility for decisions to such an extent that no one is accountable. Why does this occur and what can be done about it?

Intended development investments and activities, hopefully negotiated with primary and other stakeholders, are enshrined on paper as projects or programmes; in big NGDOs they enter a formal system of review and decision-making. The process, using specialists and/or professional volunteers, is meant to vet a project proposal for consistency against stated organisational principles, policies and priorities. The commonsense merits of this approach to assuring quality and consistency, however, rely on a basic delusion and have unfortunate organisational effects. Moreover the process is both disempowering and semi- or nontransparent. The basic fallacy lies in the idea that the documents can ever describe the situation or its dynamics sufficiently to pass judgement without a final leap of faith. Project proposals are sales documents anyway, and are obviously biased against including controversial information.[12]

There are two perverse organisational effects. First, reviews diffuse decision-making, resulting in a situation where everyone and no one is accountable. The further away from the project site the deliberations occur, the worse it all becomes. I do not know of any case where NGDO staff have been censured for a shoddy or ill-designed project because it has passed through so many hands. Second, operational staff perceive specialists as a nuisance, imposing additional burdens, and view committees as ritual obstacles to be overcome rather than valued sources of knowledge. Further, because advisers usually hold staff functions, and are not involved with daily operations, a struggle emerges as to who has ultimate power: the specialist or the line staff doing the negotiating. Resolution of these tussles for control is usually determined by personal chemistry between protagonists than by hard and fast rules defining relative turf. Meanwhile, communities – or others with whom negotiations may have been held – wait in limbo for a decision. The whole set-up is a cumbersome way of obtaining quality, is disempowering and lacks field transparency.

The stress on review and vetting as a way of guaranteeing quality stems from an historical lack of NGDO performance criteria. Specialists and advisers are supposed to compensate for this fact by making sure that the design is as right as possible, relying on the project's logic to do the rest – the well-known blue-print syndrome. Today, a big NGDO who believes it needs such central bodies and processes is likely to be a long way from the internal conditions required for authentic participation; here responsibility, authority and accountability for negotiation, design quality and subsequent performance belong to those doing the work. The specialist's role is to encourage learning through experience across the organisation as well as from outside, promote internal and external sharing of new insights, and facilitate the setting of standards.

Gaining development consistency and quality in any NGDO calls for processes of critical review where everyone is involved. While organisational structures and systems are important in making this happen, it is the strength of shared understanding about the NGDO's beliefs, vision and mission which is the first safeguard against inconsistency. Where this exists, a threshold is created which acts against adopting activities which don't fit. Whatever methods are chosen to move from vision to strategy to programme to project, at a certain moment activities are defined, together with their timings and resources; these should be in harmony with each other. Such activities contain the concrete tasks to be carried out by people who can now be identified, organised and managed.

Matching Organisation to People-Centred Development Tasks[13]

How can NGDOs design themselves to do effective people-centred development work? This section answers this question by drawing on both management science and the real life of NGDOs to identify preferred ways of organisation. However, doing this requires skating on thin ice. Why? Because systematic comparisons of NGDOs' performance are lacking due to the fact that: project evaluations have seldom, if ever, included organisational assessments of the NGDOs which ran them; and the concern with the ability of NGDOs to satisfy or influence stakeholders is relatively new, which means there are few instruments and agreed measures to judge whether one way of organising is better than another. For the time being, what we have to draw on is haphazard, relying on a growing accumulation of case studies, experiences of practitioners, conference presentations, and elements of comparative management.

A word of caution is that there is a tendency to stress structure as the primary factor influencing NGDO effectiveness.[14] This is dangerous. Structure cannot and should not be uncoupled from the systems which relate people internally and link them to the outside world. An NGDO is not a closed entity with walls around it that can be structured without regard to its transactions. So, while structure and systems are discussed separately here, this is only for clarity.

Building an effective NGDO for development work involves five major elements. First, the right trade-offs must be made in key areas of: skill integration, balancing development with administration, creating the optimum degree of organisational flexibility, and allocating authority at appropriate levels. Second, structure must be created to divide tasks and relative power, especially between the centre and operational areas. Third, structure must be matched by systems which ensure authentic participation, specifically when it comes to decision-making, planning and budgeting. The fourth and fifth are particular combinations of structure and systems which assess achievements, learn and adapt, and which couple micro-to-macro perspectives in order to gain leverage and create a positive context.

Important trade-offs in deciding about an effective organisational set-up

Trade-offs in organisational design determine if an NGDO will tilt towards or against the first, second or third sector principles explained earlier. Here, the link between structure and system is crucial because this is what makes trade-offs operational. For example, one NGDO splits water engineers, community development workers and government liaison staff into different departments based on their expertise and then gets them to work together through a system of mutual work scheduling. The community development worker starts the mobilisation, the water engineer follows with technical advice, and the liaison officer looks for government approval once the technical solution is known. Another NGDO focuses on communities within a geographic area and puts together teams with a mix of these three skills. The three start by negotiating mobilisation, technical and governmental aspects with communities and then sequence their involvement. The first approach optimises the input of expertise across the organisation; the second optimises a system of community engagement, but at the probable cost of making full use of each professional area. One organisational approach to allocating expertise appears to be more effective – this is being adopted by more and more NGDOs.

Integration or specialisation of skills

The previous example highlights one area of choice in making organisational divisions, namely the segregation of skills into specialised units or their integration into individuals or teams of people working together. Sustainable people-centred development calls for an integration of three change factors: material, organisational and psycho-social. For example, within a technical sector, such as water provision, technology is accompanied by building local management capacity and by behavioural change of users to ensure that potable water translates into improved health status. The bias in NGDO work should therefore be towards skill integration and sharing which can be achieved through structure, systems or both.

The focal point for integration lies with the primary stakeholder, who should provide the agenda around which external expertise is applied. For example, an NGDO involved with community development work in the slums of

Nairobi structured its expertise in health, social counselling and income-generation around each individual client. The 'intake' process was a case assessment which looked at the person's circumstances in order to identify appropriate responses by the NGDO, or others, including a joint course of action.

Balancing development and its administration: harmony rather than friction

It is not uncommon to find friction between NGDO development and administrative staff. Why is this? To ensure financial probity, NGDOs must employ personnel skilled in finance and administration. However, commercialisation of aid and fear of public exposure introduces an overriding concern to minimise and strictly account for expenditures. In this setting, financial optimisation and administrative procedures can end up dictating what is, or is not, developmentally possible or acceptable; the administrative tail wags the development dog. A second source of tension arises from the fact that finance and administration bring a professional culture which emphasises adherence to a uniform set of rules, this culture is uncomfortable with the discretion, flexibility and continual variation which must be second nature to operational staff. In the worst case, conflict of culture leads to a 'them and us' mentality between development staff and administrators, accountants and auditors – at the cost of working for a common goal.

What can be done to alleviate this friction ? Polarisation between development and administration is more likely to occur if they are separated at each level of the hierarchy, only coming together when the chief executive must negotiate between the two.[16] To avoid this occurring, some larger NGDOs use a method of partial integration which locates administrative staff within development teams who are accountable to development managers. These staff follow systems and procedures within norms which are negotiated between development and administrative management. Compliance is monitored by a central administrator. Failure to comply is the responsibility of the development manager, who is held responsible for all aspects of quality, including administration, and cannot shift the blame for shortcomings.

An additional step to reduce friction is the use of internal auditors; auditors can help development managers to carry out their financial functions, rather than simply controlling and looking for fault. A further strategy is to systematically include finance and administrative staff in discussions about values and development strategies in order to better understand what the organisation is about. Too often, especially at lower levels in NGDOs, developmental discussions exclude supporting staff, who therefore do not comprehend or strongly identify with the organisation's purpose. Involving support staff in developmental discussion is one way of ensuring that structure and system balance out.

In the Philippines, HASIK adopt the *zangera* principles used by farmers on small-scale irrigation schemes. Here land is parcelled and shared along the canals from intake to tail so that no farmer has privileged access to the headwater. Similarly, all activities – including domestic affairs – are approached on a team basis. For example, the 25 staff all spend one a day month on office cleaning, with the director responsible for the toilets. Teams include clerical and administrative staff supported by team-based budgeting. This far-reaching approach not only brings administrators and development staff together 'culturally', it also works against undue specialisation.

Appreciating the context: standardised or tailor made, static or dynamic

People-centred development is tailored around NGDO interaction with communities, groups or individuals. Staff must therefore be actively encouraged to use judgement and discretion along strategically chosen themes, bounded by shared values, agreed principles, known policies and negotiated performance standards. In other words, NGOs must be designed and staffed to give self-regulated adaptability. Induction of personnel and monitoring systems are important ways of supporting this behaviour.

Further, the environments where NGDOs work lack the stability which would allow for strict routines and schedules. Poor people often live from hand to mouth, grab opportunities when they present themselves, may be harassed by authority, live in areas where resources are non-existent or must be accessed illegally, face violence if they assert themselves beyond an arbitrary or culturally defined limit, and are vulnerable to variations in seasonal cycles and climatic change. There is no particular reason why they should trust and commit themselves to outsiders who cannot accommodate their reality. This means that there can be few, if any, very strict organisational rituals. At best there can only be rhythms, most commonly around planning, budgeting and learning, which focus staff energies and direction over time, but do not attempt to dictate how work goes from day to day, season to season. Attempts to do so, such as strict time scheduling for field staff, are usually ineffective; rather they give a sense of security to an insecure, control-oriented management instead of improving effectiveness.

True people-centred development is, in fact, a form of action-research adapted to each setting within each community, group or individual. In other words, it is a learning process for all concerned. Organisational trade-offs must therefore deliver sufficient structure for coherence and sufficient flexibility to adaptively interact. Experience and theory show that this combination – structured flexibility – is best achieved through a type of decentralised organisational set-up.[17]

Allocating authority: centralisation or decentralisation?

A critical factor influencing NGDO effectiveness is the power of authority to make decisions.[18] And the degree of centralisation or decentralisation of NGDOs is determined by whether decision-making authority is concentrated at the top or spread downwards and outwards. There are three basic ways to decentralise: deconcentrate, delegate and devolve. NGDOs use all of them but are generally moving towards one – delegation.

Deconcentration is the most limited form of

decentralisation where responsibility for decisions is shifted downwards and outwards within the organisation; however, authority, that is the actual power to decide, remains at or near the top.[19] For example, responsibility for scheduling and allocating transport is given to a transport officer, but the authority to actually use a vehicle has to be obtained from the chief executive. Or, a manager is responsible for overseeing daily operations, but not for deciding what they will be. Or, field offices of international donors are made responsible for negotiating grants, but cannot decide about approval. Deconcentration tends to: limit flexibility as requests for decisions go up the chain and answers come down; create a layer of delay and reduce transparency; and add costs which do not necessarily translate into significant development benefits.

As the name implies, delegation is one way that management assigns power to a lower level. This process, in fact, begins with the board or governors who delegate their powers to the chief executive – who remains accountable to them for how such power is used. Delegation occurs when authority is spread downwards and outwards. Typical examples are the maximum expenditure that can be approved by different levels of management.

Devolution is the most far-reaching approach to decentralisation as it involves placing decision-making powers outside of the organisation. It is similar to franchising.[20] Examples are not that frequent. NOVIB, a Netherlands co-financing NGDO, negotiated a devolution-type arrangement with a number of Latin American NGDOs, who would act as local funders within an agreed framework. Problems arose for the Latin American NGDOs when their role, and hence identity, became confused.[21] Some local financing relationships used by international NGDOs in India come close to devolution, but are made complicated by structural dependency.

An important point with any form of decentralisation is to ensure that power does not become associated with abdication. In other words, *performance-based checks and balances must complement shifts in power downwards and outwards.* The level of safeguards required depends on the degree of trust that can be permitted, which in turn depends on many factors. Important amongst these are the strength of shared identity, leadership style and the nature of activity. In other words, a mix of ingredients dictate how firm or relaxed controls have to be if power is to be spread around. And, generally speaking, more controls mean less flexibility, which is bad for participatory development. Table 3.1 summarises this relationship.

Table 3.1 Important relationships in power distribution and participation

Shared Identity	Leadership	Trust	Authority	Controls	Flexibility	Effect on Participation
strong	consultative	high	decentralised	relaxed	high	positive
weak	autocratic	low	centralised	firm	low	negative

Unfortunately for many NGDOs, centralisation is the rule rather than the exception. This is because:

- leadership tends to be highly personalised and autocratic;
- trust is not created and valued as part of organisational culture;
- identity is weak and not widely shared; and
- reasonable, practical performance measures are lacking.

Delegation of authority is preferred when allocating power within NGDOs because it can best provide the structured flexibility needed to satisfy the principles involved in people-centred development. Deconcentration offers little gain in terms of effectiveness, but can cause additional costs if a layer of responsibility is introduced but can decide nothing. Slowly delegation is the path being followed by many NGDOs (and official aid agencies). For example, the major child-sponsorship funded Northern NGDOs have moved to an area-based development approach where field directors have significant levels of authority, together with a full complement of expertise – effectively functioning as a self-contained unit. Any NGDO which believes that it can directly manage truly participatory development from the home office or a capital city is ignoring both theory and best practice.

Devolution of authority to other organisations is an alternative which can work well and is a necessary strategy for the future withdrawal of Northern NGDOs from the South and East; however this needs to be approached with caution. Devolution is common between international and local NGDOs in India, but such NGDOs can simply become an extension of their foreign counerpart in all but name when the local organisation has ineffective governance, weak identity and no means to maintain some degree of financial autonomy.[22] A strategy which moves from delegation to devolution needs to be thought through as the implications are significant for all the NGDOs involved.

A common obstacle to delegation is the supposed cost. Local structures with the power and expertise to run things are perceived to duplicate tasks, creating unnecessary overheads. This stance reflects an economies-of-scale thinking, measured in dollars and cents, which has not been balanced by calculations of the dis-economy effects on sustainable change processes, discussed in Chapter 2. So, unless the leadership fully appreciates the nature of participatory development, the balance is likely to tilt away from the principle of people-first to organisation-first. Leaders brought in from business may contribute useful experience and insights but may lack the experiential 'feel' needed to 'calculate' the costs of non-delegation.

A further barrier to delegation, which crops up everywhere, but more noticeably in the South and East, is a cultural block to power-sharing, especially between genders. Cultural limits to power-sharing, together with how the chief executive is expected to express his or her status, tend to favour hierarchy and male centralisation, a dimension explored later. The final point to repeat in terms of organisational trade-offs is that, for authentic participation, evidence suggests that authority should be delegated as far down and out as possible, consistent with the principle that the NGDO periphery is the centre of development action. But such delegation must be complemented by performance standards negotiated with stakeholders.

Characteristics of a preferred organisational structure for operational NGDOs

For all organisations, structure is created by dividing tasks and authority amongst staff and perhaps volunteers. For NGDOs, a critical factor that determines their structure is the division of labour between them and the communities, groups or individuals who actually 'produce' sustainable development. This choice lies at the heart of what is called an NGDO's 'development approach', which is a product of founding principles and theory of how sustainable change is best brought about. For example, do communities manage and account for project funds and undertake any necessary purchasing, or is this done by NGDO staff? Do write proposals or build the capacity of communities until they are able to do so? Does the NGDO raise funds for activities negotiated with communities or help the community to find resources for itself? Does the NGDO facilitate social processes to mobilise material inputs and expertise from elsewhere, or provide all this itself?

These, and many similar developmental questions can be (partially) answered by the way an NGDO structures itself. The guiding principle of solving dilemmas in NGDO design is to start from the connection with primary stakeholders and build up from there. All functions and tasks above this interface must be be justified by what

is done to support this central interaction. Typically, in ineffective NGDOs, points of contact with communities serve the organisation, rather than the other way around.

Figure 3.3 illustrates the sort of organisational set-up which can produce structured flexibility in an NGDO. It shows the type and location of functions needed to produce a delegated authority design, which should give the necessary people-centred tilt in development initiatives. How it works is described in terms of positioning, functions at the centre and the operational interface with communities.

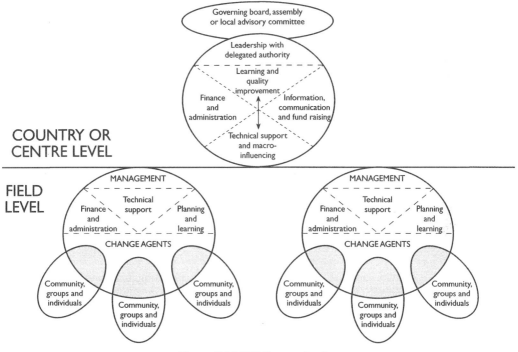

Figure 3.3 NGDO organisation

Local positioning and accountability

NGDOs must be recognised by society and be held accountable for what they do. NGDOs originating in the South and East can satisfy these requirements through a governing structure which is consistent with local laws (where they exist). This is not necessarily the case for international NGDOs, where the issue of being locally embedded and accountable can

be contentious. The point of friction is about relative role and the power of local governing bodies *vis à vis* the international governing structure.

Some Northern, operational NGDOs tackle this problem by having an international governing structure which includes representatives from countries of operation. Others aim, at some stage, to 'spin off' their operational work in the South and East as a local

NGDO and create a local advisory body as a first step. Whatever the intention, how an NGDO is governed influences its position in society in terms of who it belongs to and which interests it serves. Sorting out local governance is an increasingly important issue for international NGDOs in a climate where it is less acceptable for foreigners to do things for others; this is perceived as contrary to the principle of encouraging societies in the South and East to do things for themselves.

Functions at the centre

The centre of an NGDO could be located anywhere, depending on whether it works locally, nationally, or regionally. In a delegated set-up, the centre would:

- provide formal accountability to governors;
- provide strategic assessments and direction through policy development;
- learn from across field activities, guide the application of learning into practice and share experience with others;[23]
- ensure that there is sufficient coherence of approach between field operations, while overseeing and guiding improvement in the quality of work;
- raise finance;
- consolidate plans and budgets, together with reporting on activities and their financing and generating management information;
- support field operations in areas of common concern, such as technical innovations and human resource development;
- influence public policies;
- ensure organisational viability through resource mobilisation; and
- provide communication and public information.

Some functions, such as learning, quality improvement and innovation cluster together because they call for similar expertise.

Another important function which should receive greater attention is to develop and apply strategies that root operations in the local economy away from the aid system and – for international NGDOs – to embed their operations in society, sometimes called localisation or indigenisation.

Regionalisation

Larger international NGDOs often create an intermediary level of management, commonly called a region. The guiding principle in doing so is that it should generate something of use in development terms. For example, lumping all French-speaking African countries together may help with staff recruitment but has little to offer in terms of development strategies. The added value of regional management is within the fields of ecology, trading relations, migration, formal economic relations in customs unions, and preferential trade areas. The point is that amalgamating areas on the basis of administrative convenience is not always beneficial – a development benefit should always be sought and underpin regional set-ups.

The operational interface with communities

In effective NGDO set-ups, field operations are almost semi-autonomous units – self-contained, self-directed and self-regulating within boundaries set by organisational strategies, policies and norms together with result and performance criteria negotiated with stakeholders and agreed with the centre, usually through a planning and budgetary process. Many functions are similar to the centre, where again the primary point of reference is the change agents' interaction with communities and external transactions with other stakeholders.

Defining the role and competencies of change agents is vital for effective development. Get this wrong and no matter how much else is done well, sustainable development will not be likely. A group of like-minded NGDOs in the Philippines, forming a network called CONVERGENCE, have moved to team-oriented interactions with communities in geographically defined areas. Multi-skilled teams enjoy a substantial delegation of authority, including negotiating agreements with local governments and alliances with other NGDOs operating in the same area. In my view, the trend in NGDOs is towards seeing change agents less as individuals and more as teams with a mix of competencies, which can be applied in flexible ways. There is evidence that, while 'context is crucial [it] is not determinant; therefore, organisational choice always provides some room for manoeuvre'.[24] In other words, much affects effective performance externally, while NGDOs must still make a difference through their organisational design.

Characteristics of key organisational systems

Complementing structure, NGDOs have two major overlapping sets of systems: procedures, processes and recognised ways of working, which need to function properly. One set relates NGDOs to the outside world and is the subject of Chapter 5. The other set has an internal orientation, the most significant being: decision-making; operational planning and budgeting; reflection, learning and quality improvement; micro-macro links for leverage; human resource development; information and communication; and accountability. The last three are dealt with in other chapters.

The design and operation of internal systems influences the externally-oriented set and the two combine to tilt an NGDO towards or against poor people sharing control and influence, and towards or against structured flexibility. Internally, an NGDO needs to install participatory decision-making and then apply this outside with primary stakeholders. Decisions often relate to plans about activities and budgetary resources, therefore the planning and budgeting system must support a participatory approach. How this works is described in the following sections.

Participation and power in decision-making

NGDO decision-making must be consultative enough for shared ownership of the outcomes and directive enough to be timely, while ensuring accountability. The reason for opting for a consultative process (internally and externally) is that people more willingly modify their behaviour when they participate in problem analysis. The task for managers is to treat their role in decision-making as one of facilitating a group process with the right people and then discharging their final authority in a transparent way. The NGDO approach to consultative decision-making typically relies upon committees and meetings – often to the detriment of effectiveness.

TIPS **Experience suggests that effective decision making requires:**

➤ only involving those who directly control a situation – the 'gatekeepers' – and those most affected;
➤ mediation and guiding the process rather than directing it;
➤ a culture of openness and self-criticism;
➤ clear allocation and mutual understanding of who is responsible for what.

Decision-making in NGDOs with a delegated set-up often takes place within management teams constructed for just this purpose; these operate at different levels and combinations of authority in the centre and the field. Common limitations on their effectiveness occur when:

● a team has too many tasks to perform;
● insufficient distinction is made between policy and operational issues, leading to

overloaded agendas and discussions about items which should be dealt with elsewhere;
- deliberations require information which must be specially generated, but where there is no extra capacity to do so, which either displaces other work and/or causes delays;
- participants find it difficult to stand above their areas of responsibility and decide on the basis of the interest of the organisation as a whole, even if it is disadvantageous;
- lack of self-discipline leads to repetition, avoidance of difficult topics and informal decision-making behind the scenes by sub-groups, which reduces transparency and leads to factions and discontent;
- individuals lack skills in decision-making or accurately framing questions.

Approaches to human-resource development and team building need to help staff work through such limitations.

The role of operational planning and budgeting systems in tilting the balance

A planning and budgeting system (PBS) serves three vital roles. One is to function as an important cycle holding the NGDO together, especially big organisations with a wide geographic spread. Second, for the vast majority of NGDOs, planning and budgeting provides an impetus and framework for negotiation with primary and other stakeholders. Third, it presents a regular opportunity to introduce changes from organisational learning. The PBS lies at the heart of spreading internal authority and sharing power with outsiders and (co)determines the degree of flexibility an NGDO possesses. Not getting the PBS right is one common reason why authentic participation and true people-centred development does not occur.

A common shortcoming of NGO planning is that it is tailored to the negative aspects of project-type demands. In other words, too often plans are overspecified, try to predetermine too much and are biased towards accounting as a proxy for accountability. This problem is well documented, and the characteristics of alternatives are summarised below and in

Chapter 5. By comparison, the contribution of budgeting to ineffectiveness is less well documented or understood, but is critical: it can limit as well as enable power-sharing and flexibility.

The quality of funds – described in Chapter 6 – can work for or against maintaining voluntary principles and authentic participation. Typically, NGDO funding works against these principles in three ways. First, budgets are directly related to plans which specify the level and timing of resources required to carry out a predetermined sequence of activities. Because impact indicators are seldom around, expenditures against budgets are used as an indirect measure of both project and organisational performance. Consequently, management attention becomes fixed on time-expenditure relationships, where deviance from planned versus actual resource use becomes the sign of progress rather than measures of change which development initiatives bring to people's lives.

Second, budgets are an important instrument for the daily exercise of power and control. Where budgets are constructed around organisational structure and their outputs – such as departments and their products – rather than processes, systems, relationships, external transactions, and impact, internal empires are too easily built, bureaucratisation sets in and the necessary integration of development activity suffers. Where budgets are built around negotiated changes for stakeholders and controlled by staff, management energy is steered towards the organisation's goals, rather than towards its 'products'. For example, gender or training budgets may be allocated on the basis of the intended effects rather than allocated to a gender or training department for scheduled courses. In this way, budgeting re-enforces desired behaviour. Too frequently the NGDO set-up serves top-down control rather than relying on performance-related discretion from the bottom up.

Third, the most creative area of NGDO budgeting is usually found in the way overheads are defined in order to make them appear minimal. We look at this in more detail in later chapters, but the point to be made at this stage is that an NGDO's definition of overheads is, in effect, its understanding about development. Many years ago (but not any more), CARE had two major budget categories, materials and equipment (M&E) and personnel and administration (P&A). Everything in the former was taken to be a direct cost, the latter was treated as indirect and hence an overhead. Today, no NGDO aware of the links between material and behavioural change would treat all staff as overheads.

In fact, what is classed as an overhead sends out a strong signal about the organisation in terms of its professional understanding as well as its identity – for example, the theory of change it subscribes to. In an age of economic hardships, negotiation on overhead levels becomes, at a deeper level, a struggle about market or voluntary values – a significant component of NGDO identity.

Defining overheads is not just about cost-effective development. Looking at what an NGDO classes as overheads is an important message to both staff and outsiders and must be consistent with what the organisation believes in. For example, it is no good stressing macro-influencing or organisational learning as a policy while allowing funders to treat staff time for these activities as an indirect cost because the work is not direct 'project' work with communities.

In sum, budgeting is a grey, but critical, area influencing the way difficult balances are tilted by allocating power, by steering relationships between parts of the organisation, and by bringing into day to day work many of the hidden assumptions and tensions inherent to development. What, then, are the preferred practices in planning and budgeting? They may be described as follows.

- The plan and budget cycle begins with the change agent being told about the availability of resources, usually within a (perhaps revised) long-term strategic plan which specifies specific commitments and reconfirms the agent's authority.
- Dialogue with stakeholders about budgets is a useful tool to evaluate the relationship because it takes previously negotiated

measures of performance as the point of departure for future joint action.
- The PBS process does not generate false expectations with an unprioritised shopping list of needs.
- Agreements with primary stakeholders do not disappear only to reappear after an obscure internal selection process; rather, internal decisions confirm that the NGDO is committed to the relationship for a future period, for example by showing that the CBO's own learning and adaptations have been accommodated.
- Tests for consistency with organisational policies, strategies and best practices take place at the lowest level possible, ideally by the change agent or one level above – an aura of total flexibility is not created by the change agent.
- While occurring perhaps only once a year, planning and budgeting is not an 'add-on' but forms an integral part of the development approach by providing an agreed moment for critical reflection, evaluation, learning and renegotiation.

In terms of internal process and content:

- The basic building blocks for planning and budgeting are mutual performance agreements – in terms of ultimate development impact as well as NGDO outputs – and are negotiated with communities and other stakeholders. For example, there is a line item for increased local organisational capacity (as an outcome), rather than for training or trainers, visits and exchanges which are inputs.[25]
- Budgets are structured to encourage and enable team-oriented, integrated activity around external transactions rather than to support top-down management control.
- Horizontal planning between parts of the organisation is as important as vertical planning.
- Budgets at each level have a low maximum in terms of the number of approved line items, (for example, grants from the Ford Foundation seldom have more than eight),

and ideally match authority levels for approving expenditures.

- Reallocation of budgets is not treated as a sin, but as a learning opportunity.

There is much that stands in the way of small, project-dependent NGDOs adopting these best practices, because funders want plans and budgets before they are prepared to commit themselves. So, at best, what takes place is a chicken and egg game of uncertain funding. If the planning system for the organisation becomes *de facto* that of the projects it implements there is little more than contracting going on.[26] This situation has negative consequences. No matter how small, it is vitally important that an NGDO has its own organisational planning and budgeting system based on its specific requirements. With this foundation, it can respond to and incorporate the project demands of funders; without it identity will be lost. In short, project plans and budgets should never become the same as NGDO organisational plans and budgets.

Reflection, learning and quality improvement: moving from rhetoric to practice

An almost universal weakness of NGDOs is found within their often limited capacity to learn, adapt and continuously improve the quality of what they do. This a serious concern because, for reasons set out in Chapter 9, the future usefulness of NGDOs for the world's poor will depend on their ability to overcome their learning disabilities.[27] Crudely put, if NGDOs do not learn from experience, they are destined for insignificance and will atrophy as agents of social change. NGDOs urgently need to put in place systems which ensure that they know and learn from what they are achieving – as opposed to what they are doing – and then apply what they learn.

This inability to learn is deeply rooted. It may arise from an ethos which cannot relate to failure in a positive way; this means that error is not embraced as a source of learning but is denied. Other obstacles to learning also exist. First, critical reflection is insufficiently done because it is not prioritised, and it is not prioritised because it is not adequately valued within a culture of commitment to action. Second, in a competitive funding environment, it requires a lot of organisational capacity, strength and skill to see lessons learned from failure as an asset. Third, the costs of learning put upward pressure on overhead levels, which always meet with resistance.

Today, therefore, NGDOs buy into organisational learning as a (fashionable) principle, but do not make sufficient investments in learning capacity, systems and practices. At best, the odd consultant is hired to review reports, or there may be an annual retreat to discuss issues, or a burst of interest in a hoped for magic bullet like total quality management (TQM). Only on the odd occasion is systematic reflection built into NGDO culture and development as part of the work itself.

Two examples of systematic reflection and learning show what can be done. CENDEC in Recife, Brazil, provides judicial services in defence of human rights and uses cases to take up public issues, especially those related to government abuse of power. With support from Save the Children Fund (UK), this NGDO has the benefit of a periodic, critical review of its work by a knowledgeable outsider – a form of quality audit. For two days every three months, CENDEC's staff present and discuss their work and achievements and are challenged to explain how it furthers its objectives. This encounter serves as a periodic opportunity for learning and adaptation. It also provides an ongoing check that the organisation is staying true to its founding principles, which acts as a form of identity re-examination and re-enforcement. Box 3.2 contains another example of NGDO reflection for CDRA in South Africa.

Box 3.2
The content and process of organisational reflection

The Community Development Resource Association (CDRA), is a small NGDO comprising seven professionals based in Cape Town but working throughout southern Africa. CDRA assists the organisational change and capacity building of other NGDOs, a process which usually involves a series of engagements often spanning several months. In the context of South Africa, organisational change has meant fundamental transformations of NGDOs from anti-apartheid goals to those of promoting sustained development with a newly enfranchised black majority.

To improve the quality of their work with NGDOs, CDRA staff are called upon to participate in a monthly reflection which lasts one day. In addition, a process of practice guidance ties together pairs of staff as counterparts to share critical dialogue. The monthly review normally contains:

- a round-up summary of work each consultant is doing to bring each other up to date;
- presentation of a case study in progress to highlight key features;
- cross-organisational comparisons which draw out similarities and differences in organisational problems, and accordingly change strategies being considered or adopted;
- reflection on the state of NGDOs in the region and the forces they are dealing with;
- testing of CDRA's work profile against its own strategies and goals.

Distillations of experience are shared through CDRA Annual Reports, as well as contributions to journals and other publications. CDRA is currently acknowledged to be a leading resource for not just doing but understanding organisational change in the region.[28]

Three preconditions enable CDRA to put reflection and sharing into practice. First is the stance of the leadership, which believes in action-reflection learning as a key to NGDO effectiveness and contribution to development. This also provides the self-discipline necessary to ensure that staff are in Cape Town on the dates scheduled. Second, is the type of financial support it receives. As well as charging, at a subsidised rate, for its services, CDRA receives programme, not project by project, support. This has permitted long-term scheduling of reviews so that they have now simply become part and parcel of what CDRA is. Third, is the commitment to be a thinking as well as a direct professional resource to the NGDO community; this is a specific organisational goal, also reached through a publications centre.

Source: interview with Allan Kaplan, Director of CDRA

However, these are both relatively small organisations. So, while parts of larger NGDOs, such as international NGDO field offices, could employ such methods, something extra is needed to make reflection a valued, organisation-wide way of working. What this might be is listed below.[29]

Whatever methods are chosen, they all require adequate capacity, which has costs. Be that as it may, action-reflection-learning is a legitimate and necessary part of what NGDOs must do if they are to exploit their comparative advantages and be relevant to the world's poor in the next century.

TIPS *Increasing NGDOs' ability to learn from reflection on experience can be achieved by:*

➤ a management which practices what it preaches, allocating time to reflection and actually enjoying it;
➤ a management information system that is fed from processed primary data;
➤ a designated fund which staff can draw on for specific learning activities;
➤ team-building finance to bring together different (horizontal) perspectives on the same issue, project, relationship, or evaluation;
➤ mandatory post-mortems on all projects closed in a particular period;
➤ planned thematic studies to be carried out each year;
➤ annual review of progress on a selected organisational objective.

Complementarity in linking macro and micro action

To be effective agents of poverty reduction, operational NGDOs need to cast their eyes not just towards communities but also towards the structures in which their micro-work takes place. What an NGDO needs to be concerned about is the link between its own micro- and/or macro- initiatives, and its own engagement to other organisations working at complementary levels. Despite many efforts, few NGDOs link micro to macro very well, even those where it is a central objective. Why is this so and what can be done about it?

There appear to be three organisational obstacles standing in the way of effectively translating micro-experience into macro-action. In terms of causes, there are similarities and differences between international and national NGDOs. For both types of NGDOs, the rhythm of micro-development work and its financing does not readily match that of winning macro-impact. Micro-work with people who are poor and marginalised is situation specific and often has a seasonal element. On the other hand, macro-work is driven more by short-term political opportunity as well as by the domestic concerns of the elite and middle class; both require access to key personalities and decision-makers.

Second, the skills needed to deal with the poor and disadvantaged are not the same as those needed to interact with the elite,

sometimes in co-operation other times in confrontation. A consequence of doing both types of development work is to introduce cultural tensions within the organisation, partly because macro-work at conferences and in the corridors of power is more glamorous and appealing than slogging away at development in tough physical conditions with the potential for local harassment. Staff functioning at grassroots levels may feel exploited when their work, and the information and insights which it brings, elevates their colleagues into the limelight of the national or international arena.

Third, and this is particularly the case for Northern NGDOs, topics which are alive and worthy of attention in the domestic context may have little resonance with communities in the South. For example, corruption may be a priority Northern concern, while issues of enforcing land redistribution laws may dominate the lives of the poor. A process must be put in place to determine which advocacy agenda is selected and how its content – that is the position to be adopted and methods to be employed – is defined. In other words, internal systems must decide whose reality – South or North – counts most.

There is also an opportunistic element to macro-initiatives, such as advocacy, which creates peaks and troughs of work and makes significant demands on communication resources. In responding to an ecological crisis in Kankoen, staff of the Project for Environmental Recovery (PER) in Thailand sat by a fax for days on end interpreting and relaying information to Northern counterpart NGOs. This demanded sufficient sharing of knowledge between staff so that anyone could deal with what was coming through. Teamwork was essential.

What can NGDOs do to bring macro and micro together, rather than fragment or pull them apart? Box 3.3 brings out the experience of a Peruvian NGDO, CEDEP, which has been dedicated to policy influencing based on its micro development work.

International NGDOs concerned with macro-influencing typically recruit people with specialist skills and locate them in a part of the organisation which interfaces with policy-makers. They may even locate these individuals close to a target agency, as the Oxfam family have recently done by opening a Washington office to interface with the World Bank, IMF and UN bodies in New York.[30] More typically,

---

Box 3.3

Micro – macro linkages: the CEDEP experience

For almost 20 years, the Centro de Estudios para el Desarrollo y la Participacion (CEDEP) has been working on grassroots projects with communities, currently in the geographic areas of Ancash and Ica in Peru. Initially, CEDEP focused on the promotion of agrarian cooperatives and land reform; today its work is directed at improving the situation of agricultural producers, specifically to counter the negative effects of market-oriented (adjustment) reforms on their productivity and livelihoods.

In Lima, CEDEP has a unit of five staff whose primary task is documenting micro-experience and lobbying on issues arising from their analysis. Detailed agreement is reached at a monthly meeting of field and central managers, but this occurs within a strategic and operational planning framework where likely areas for policy influencing are identified based on analysis of domestic reality and existing micro-experience. Location within approved plans means that micro-activities are already budgeted for within the field and macro-work is budgeted separately in the Lima unit. Co-ordination and monitoring of progress is done monthly through the management committee. Irresolvable problems in terms of, say, interpretation of the grassroots situation can be addressed to the governing council, which meets every two months.

For example, in 1992-93 the Peruvian government put forward proposals for constitutional reform which did not consider decentralisation or regionalisation. As part of a reform group of NGDOs, CEDEP organised meeting with mayors in its areas of operation, which eventually led to them drafting an alternative chapter on decentralisation (supported by the association of local governments) – elements of which were eventually included in the final constitutional proposal which was voted on in a referendum.

CEDEP's later contribution was to assist in the decentralisation of government functions to local authorities by identifying preferred institutional arrangements. Operational offices in Ancash and Ica made initial contact with the local authorities; this has now become a regular exchange. CEDEP gathers information on what is happening as decentralisation takes place in these two areas; identifies problems and possible solutions; documents this in a format suitable for senior government officials responsible for implementing decentralisation and then pushes for change directly and through other publications targeted at the general public. To give added weight to proposals, specialists in local government form an advisory group to provide independent judgement and opinions on the policy and implementation options which CEDEP comes up with.

Source: adapted from a contribution by Héctor Béjar Rivera, CEDEP

---

however, lobbying and advocacy have a domestic focus.

The perpetual difficulty is to link advocacy specialists with those involved in managing and doing the operational side of things, which is usually organised on geographical lines of, for example, Africa, Asia, Latin America, or Eastern Europe. Here the choice between specialisation and integration of expertise becomes vital.[31] One organisational variation is to centrally finance and keep lobbyists together, allocating either regional and/or thematic (debt, gender, environment) responsibilities between them.[32] Lobby and advocacy agendas are then negotiated with relevant operational and technical staff. An alternative is to place lobbyists within operational departments where they 'live' the action and are financed as part of the geographic staff.

NGDOs in the South and East are more inclined and able to tackle lobbying with local and national government – a role foreign NGDOs can play less well because they risk the accusation of meddling in internal affairs. But here a polarisation between lobby and operational NGDOs is not uncommon. In Latin America one usually finds lobby NGDOs to be intellectual think tanks without a coupling with grass roots levels – CEDEP is more the exception than the rule. In Asia, by contrast, local NGDOs with operational programmes have shown success at lobbying with district and state governments and banks to change regulations in support of the communities they work with. By and large, a major limitation on micro-macro coupling in NGDOs is the conditions attached to donor financing which undervalues this link.[33]

The advantages of the first arrangement are: a pooling of expertise; cross-fertilisation of ideas and methods; and keeping the NGDO's overall policy and goals as primary focus, while ensuring coherence in approach. The drawbacks are: a too peripheral engagement with and understanding of micro-action; limited personal exposure to micro-reality; third- or fourth-hand experiences, so understandings remain superficial; no real relationship of trust and empathy; and, finally, domestic concerns dominate agendas for action. The alternative set-up, integrating advocacy staff within operations, essentially reverses these strengths and weaknesses.

One way of minimising the negative aspects of both set-ups is through budgeting. If the purpose of policy advocacy is to act for the interests of the South and East then funding should be controlled by those operationally involved with these areas. In the jargon of internal markets, the user of the advocacy service pays for it. Lobbying and advocacy funds should therefore, in principle, be allocated to each (sub) regional part of the Northern NGDO. In this way, Southern and Eastern agendas, which should be negotiated with partners, get priority attention. In sum, the dilemma of integration or specialisation in micro-macro linking can be partially resolved by a strategic approach using budgeting.

TIPS **Effective systems for micro–macro linking:**

➤ have expertise and capacity for policy action at both levels, either internally or as part of an alliance;

➤ use agendas for policy issues, policy positions and influencing methods which have been negotiated with partners or negotiated internally;

➤ allocate finance to advocacy and lobbying activities as part of operational budgets based on agreed agendas.

In the final analysis, the effectiveness of systems and structure is determined by the most essential element of any organisation – people. With the tasks of sustainable development, the nature of NGDOs and organisational trade-offs in mind, we can now turn to the human dimensions of capacity.

4

Enabling and Empowering NGDO People

The Changing Nature of International Development

All organisations are made up of people, but the complex nature of many development tasks makes NGDOs especially dependent on the attitudes and competencies of staff and volunteers. In addition to the availability of other resources, four key factors enable staff and volunteers to work effectively. These are: organisational culture, the qualities of leadership, sensitivity to gender, and suitable approaches to human resource management, particularly getting incentives right and 'forming' and empowering staff. This chapter focuses on these factors and answers the question: what can NGDOs do to ensure that the capabilities of the organisation's individuals and groups are adequate and motivated towards its mission?

The Cultural Dimension of NGDOs: Overlays and How to Manage Them

Culture has never been static; it continues to evolve under the influence of many factors.[1] After defining culture, this section identifies its key dimensions, how NGDO culture gets built up from two or three overlays, the forces which shape its evolution and what this means for staff and international relations.

Technically, organisations are defined as purposeful, role-bound social units. Viewed another way, organisations can be seen as self-selected communities which develop their own norms and social structures. In the words of one definition: 'Culture is the complex whole of solutions that a given community inherits, adopts or invents to face the challenges of its natural and social environment'.[2] In other words, based on the society they grow up in, people enter NGDOs with expectations of how it should function and also how it should be led and managed. In addition, individuals bring psychological and material needs which leaders and managers have a role in satisfying. When the organisation does not measure up to people's expectations, it is more difficult for them to comply with what is required, and their effectiveness lessens. Appropriate leadership and management in NGDOs calls, therefore, for an understanding of what sort of expectations and needs staff and volunteers bring with them. Cultural analysis is one way of gaining such an understanding.

Dimensions of national culture in relation to organisations

Cultures differ because human interaction with its environment has also differed over time. Cultures differ, furthermore, because struggles in human relations have created categories of people within cultural groups; aggregations of these groups have then evolved into larger geographic assemblies, sometimes culminating in nation-states. Through these processes a mosaic of (national) cultural identity is constructed and differentiated by, for example, ethnicity, region, country, language, gender, generation, class, status, occupation, and organisational affiliation. The result is a mix of cultural attributes which each individual brings into his or her work setting.

A study carried out by Geert Hofstede, then complemented by others, identified five dimensions of national cultural orientation which influence how people behave within organisations.[3] The five provide a framework for understanding differences in people's expectations of management and leadership. Figure 4.1 shows spectrums of possible positions relative to each other. There are no absolute measures in Hofstede's system only a comparative ranking. In other words, there is no right or wrong, but differences which can be recognised.

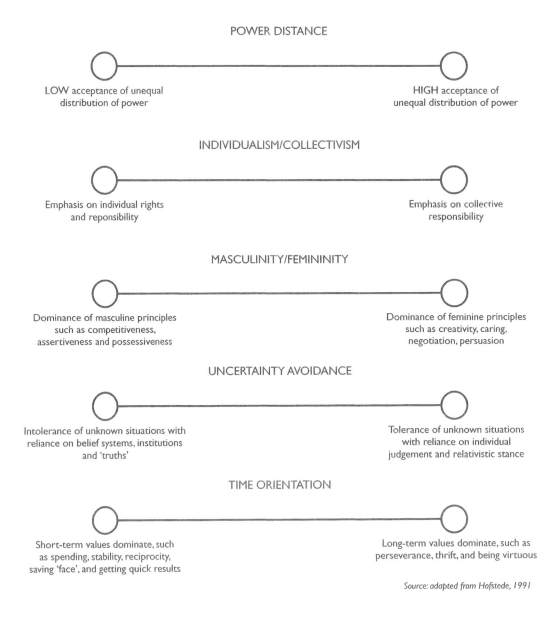

POWER DISTANCE

LOW acceptance of unequal distribution of power

HIGH acceptance of unequal distribution of power

INDIVIDUALISM/COLLECTIVISM

Emphasis on individual rights and reponsibility

Emphasis on collective responsibility

MASCULINITY/FEMININITY

Dominance of masculine principles such as competitiveness, assertiveness and possessiveness

Dominance of feminine principles such as creativity, caring, negotiation, persuasion

UNCERTAINTY AVOIDANCE

Intolerance of unknown situations with reliance on belief systems, institutions and 'truths'

Tolerance of unknown situations with reliance on individual judgement and relativistic stance

TIME ORIENTATION

Short-term values dominate, such as spending, stability, reciprocity, saving 'face', and getting quick results

Long-term values dominate, such as perseverance, thrift, and being virtuous

Source: adapted from Hofstede, 1991

Figure 4.1 Hofstede's five cultural dimensions

Hofstede compared nations in the light of these five dimensions. A few examples illustrate what he and others found. Western countries cluster in an area of relatively low power distance, together with relatively high individualism. In other words, people generally do not tolerate a big spread in power and tend to look to their own interests first and others afterwards. Conversely, countries of South East Asia and Central America cluster in an area of high power difference together with greater valuing of collectiveness.[4] Here, dominant leaders and wide gaps in power are more readily accepted by those at the bottom, but those in power are respected by the degree to which their power is used for the common good.

Although biased towards individualism, in terms of masculine and feminine values, the North, excluding Japan, shows a wide variation with Scandinavian countries and the Netherlands exhibiting a bias towards femininity, while the rest of Europe and North America remains relatively masculine. Japan is biased towards a masculine collectivity, as are Equador, Venezuela and Colombia. East and West Africa slant towards collective feminine orientations.[5] Here, mutual support, reciprocity, clan and family are valued more highly, and organisations would be expected to reflect this fact.[6]

These general dimensions about national culture are just that. They are not statements about any one citizen. But they do provide pointers for understanding differences between countries or groups; this has implications for what people expect about organisational life, together with norms about the role and behaviour of leaders and managers. While a starting point, national cultural characteristics do not dictate an organisation's own culture because this is created by the unique set of its members.

Organisational culture: how is it built and what does it affect?

Organisational culture evolves from two major sources for Northern NGDOs, and three for Southern and Eastern NGDOs because they are further down the aid chain. The sources can be thought of as layers which mingle and mix with each other, but are seldom in complete harmony; this can lead to confusion, friction and stress. Staff expect an NGDO's culture to be consistent with its vision and mission. Where these are out of step, motivation can be negatively affected. What this means in practice is discussed below.

Recognising distinct cultural layers

A mix of the five dimensions identified by Hofstede are initially brought into an NGDO by all its members. This can be called the culture within the NGDO. But by working together over time, individuals implicitly create a unique organisation in terms of ways of thinking, using language, beliefs in myths and symbols, and ways of doing things. These become part of the natural life of an NGDO and codefines its identity in addition to formal written statements about governance, vision and mission. This is the living culture of the NGDO itself, and it can be distinct from the general culture of society. In fact, it is likely to be very different because the organisation tries to change the way society works, part of which is cultural.[7]

In addition, the tasks and processes of people-centred sustainable development call for an organisational culture which values internal equity and solidarity – values which Hofstede associates with feminine culture.[8] In many cases in the North, South and East, this would conflict with surroundings where very large power differences and competitiveness are an accepted norm. So NGDO leaders, managers and staff are often called upon not to replicate the general pattern of national culture but to be consciously different from it. Doing so without being seen as subversive by power holders is a balancing act in itself.

Cultural motivation

People work in NGDOs for a number of reasons. In theory people who join an NGDO located within the third sector do so to satisfy a personal commitment and expect an organisational culture founded on trust: one which listens to people, respects their opinions, values personal judgement and shares responsibility and authority. For 'service delivery' NGDOs, staff expectations would probably be slanted towards recognition, valuing and rewarding of their expertise and personal efforts consistent with market standards and rewards. Many NGDOs, however, have a mix of the two which needs to be balanced; here the personal model set by leaders and managers strongly influences the culture which dominates.

For example, where chief executives argue that their remuneration should be determined by comparably sized commercial 'caring' organisations, the message is clear to everyone else that business is their bench-mark; organisational culture and incentives will be shaped accordingly.[9] Where leaders and managers use norms of responsible behaviour towards the poor and tailor their remuneration and life styles accordingly, a different signal is sent and staff respond accordingly. A crude way of assessing the degree to which third sector values live in an NGDO's culture is, therefore, to measure the difference between the level of remuneration professional staff receive and that which they could gain if working in the commercial sector.[10] For some transnational NGDOs, the difference is negligible.

The third layer: whose culture counts?

We have identified two types of culture operating within NGDOs throughout the world: culture coming 'within' and culture 'of' the organisation. But NGDOs of the South and East have to deal with a third culture, that of their donors or Northern supporters. This fact often leads to North-South relational strife and choices between whose culture counts most. Typical cultural differences in North-South NGDO relationships are given below to illustrate points of friction. Often developmental reasons exist to give priority to the cultures of Southern and Eastern NGDOs. Reasons why are explained below, together with practical ways of approaching cultural dialogue.

Struggling with the third layer for NGDOs of the South and East

Located in an aid chain which transfers and translates resources into sustainable development places South and Eastern NGDOs on the receiving end of Northern culture. There are often significant disparities, which include:

- *Individual versus collective.* The North's individualism does not match Southern collectivism; this causes a lot of trouble in dealing with reciprocity and mutual support which is readily labelled as corruption or nepotism.
- *Time.* The North favours short-term results while other cultures take a more long-term stance. This often results in a schedule which negates social processes, such as consensus building.
- *Power distance.* The North expects low power distance in internal consultations, which may be inappropriate, while simultaneously requiring speedy decision-making which high power difference can give. This is both contradictory and destabilising.
- *Masculine/Feminine.* Generally speaking, the North prioritises effective delivery over caring, the South caring over effective delivery; the East is still working this out. In other words, there is a mismatch in emphasis between masculine and feminine behaviour, which sends mixed messages internally and externally (an example of the overlap problem described in Chapter 2).
- *Uncertainty avoidance.* Northern NGDOs may pay lip service to cultural orientations which value institutional rituals and conventions, such as taking the time to pay homage or showing respect; however, they often cannot take these cultural orientations on board.

A recent example of what can happen when these differences accumulate is found with the Savodaya Shramadana Movement (SSM) in Sri Lanka. During the 1970s, major donors expressed solidarity with the movement's calling, which was not simply to improve living standards but to 'create a spiritual, moral, cultural, social, economic and political environment in which the individual personality can awaken ... based on the values of participation justice and peace'.[11] Following Buddhist teaching, human awakening is SSM's driving concept and goal; material change is a means to this end.

The 1980s saw significant organisational expansion with: growing dependency despite initiatives to generate local incomes; a consortium of donors providing funding, accompanied by a more critical attitude towards performance, together with concerns about financial probity. There was also harassment by the regime in power because of a perception that Savodaya provided a political launching pad for its leader. By the early 1990s, dialogue between Savodaya and its supporters about performance had become fraught to the extent that a director of the oldest donor asserted that SSM's spiritual values and objectives were of no consequence; a contractual relationship to deliver benefits was what they wanted.[12] Savodaya is a salutary lesson in NGDO relations when values eventually collide.[13]

Whose culture counts most?

This crude list of cultural differences implies that Northern NGDOs have more of an obligation to shift towards the South and East than vice versa. Is this the case and why should it be so? While the cultural mix and practices of Southern and Eastern NGDOs should always be open for discussion, on balance effective sustainable development calls for greater cultural adaptation by Northern NGDOs. Why? The simplest answer is that to be sustainable, development has ultimately to be controlled by those most concerned and affected, that is primary stakeholders and Southern and Eastern

NGDOs. Their culture counts for them, so this must be the reference point.[14] But in addition, adapting Southern NGDOs to the organisational cultures of their Northern counterparts introduces three distortions, namely 'mirrors', 'echoes' and 'hats'.

The predominant task of most Southern NGDOs' is to work with communities, that of the North to support these efforts; this calls for a different organisational set-up. Southern NGDOs who take on Northern cultural traits end up as 'mirrors' – this may lead to inappropriate organisation for the job they are meant to do. Second, echoing the language of the North detracts from indigenous ways of thinking about Southern and Eastern reality. Engaging in dialogue, rather than listening to an echo, only occurs when both parties adapt their way of speaking. Again, because change must be valued as development by people in the South, their expression should carry most weight. Finally, the hat a Southern NGO wears, that is the identity it portrays, becomes ill-fitting when the organisation's cultural shape bends towards the North. Contention about which values count becomes internalised and identity is consequently weakened or confused. Southern and Eastern NGDOs becomes less of themselves. What, then, can be done about gaining authentic organisational culture in NGDOs?

Meeting the challenge of cultural difference between NGDOs

There are strategies and mechanisms for making NGDO organisational culture appropriate, strong and authentic in the sense of self-chosen and not imposed. NGDO leaders play a critical role in all of them. Tips are summarised below, but a common precondition is cultural self-awareness.

TIPS **For all NGDOs it is important to:**
ensure that organisational culture reflects development values and approach. Achieving this goal requires:

➤ that beliefs and values are understood and actively shared;
➤ that structure and systems reflect principles derived from organisational values;

➤ that treatment of personnel is similar to primary stakeholders, so that staff experience what the NGDO preaches in terms of its desired relationship with those it serves.

As an organisational task, organisational values should be set against those of society at large. This will help focus on the dimensions which need to be re-enforced and identify areas of potential difficulty with staff expectations and needs. For example, in Eastern Europe and Central Asia, autocratic leadership, and the historical centralisation of decision-making power in Moscow and the Communist Party, may lead NGDO staff to expect that they will be told what to do rather take responsibility for their own decisions.

For Southern and Eastern NGDOs, cultural pattern(s) coming down the aid chain should be compared with what the NGDO and its stakeholders aspire to. NGDOs should:

➤ signal where significant differences lie;
➤ set up dialogues on both sides of the chain to negotiate who is going to adapt and how;
➤ be explicit with the North about cultural imperatives.

International NGDOs should acknowledge that the onus of cultural adaptation to Southern and Eastern NGDO organisational culture lies with them. Adaptation should not be done uncritically, and on occasion not at all, but the principle of respect for local cultural preferences is the starting point for dialogue.[15]

NGDO Leaders and Investing in the Next Generation

Of all the factors which make up an organisation, leadership and management are often considered to be the most important for effectiveness and viability. In NGDOs, this point of view could probably be widened to all staff. Why? The answer lies in the fact that people-centred development work cannot be regimented; every individual brings their own character to the job in hand. What this means for NGDO leadership and management is dealt with in the first part of this section; the question is asked: can leaders be nurtured? Put another way, where is the next generation of NGDO leadership coming from and can this be influenced?

NGDO leadership and management: today's generation

Traditional Western management theory struggles with opposing views about leaders and managers. The first area of disagreement has been over semantics. Are leadership and management really different? A second debate

centres on authority; does it rest with the individual or with the organisation?[16] My experience of effective NGDOs suggests that good leaders have many management qualities and good managers have many leadership qualities. In an ideal situation, the overlap between the two is complete.

The second issue rests on the assumption that authority within an organisation can be uncoupled from outside. In many cultures, this assumption is just not the right starting point because authority is codetermined by the logic and need of the (cultural) situation, rather than an enduring organisational principle. Consequently, in many countries of the South and East, NGDOs are known by who is leading them, rather than by their proper name. This is not a function of charisma as such – an aspect of NGDO leadership which is more myth than reality – but of who the individual is seen to be in wider society.

In NGDOs, leadership and management are highly personalised.[17] No matter what the formal position and job description may specify, the individual occupying it is expected to make a qualitative difference to how things get done. This is a natural outcome of voluntary commitment and co-ownership – each person counts as a person not simply as a functionary occupying a chair. Where NGDO leadership differs from management is the degree to which a leader is responsible for two key tasks: to set and maintain the overall organisational agenda – the vision; and to mobilise followers behind the agenda.[18] But in delegated set-ups, NGDO managers are leaders too and need to set agendas and mobilise followers by appealing to their inner convictions; often other instruments of guidance – coercion or incentives – are less available, nor culturally appropriate.

A study in Brazil, and my own observations, suggest that the fundamental trait of effective NGDO leaders is their adherence to moral principle.[19] It is an enduring, consistent drive, rather than charismatic personality or style *per se*, which inspires, leads and mobilises. The quiet strength, vision and commitment of many long-term NGDO leaders, such as the Bangladesh Rural Advancement Committee (BRAC), the Philippines Rural Reconstruction Movement (PRRM), the Organisation of Rural Associations for Progress (DORAP) in Zimbabwe, or DESCO in Peru testify to the importance of an individual leader's personal ethos, rather than their abilities in public expression. In fact, as the situation of a Colombian NGDO – Nino de les Andes – shows, too charismatic leadership can set off adverse reactions in governments which try to impede the organisation's work.[20]

Based on the discussions so far, we can sum up the distinctive, critical tasks of NGDO leader/managers:

- to provide a consistent guiding image and moral ethos;
- to retain and promote sensitivity to deprivation and injustice experienced by the poor;
- to build a culture of association within the organisation which encourages sharing, and promotes reflection for learning;
- to bring coherence between members' interests and organisational objectives;

- to act as a 'holder' for the psychological needs and frustrations of staff and volunteers;
- to reconcile individuals' values and contributions with collective needs;
- to put the process of personal relations into sustainable development;
- to enable followers to become leaders themselves.

The question is: can the personal qualities needed to perform these tasks be nurtured, or will new leadership be a natural event where investment makes little real difference?

NGDO leadership and management: tomorrow's generation

The inner conviction and drive of NGDO leaders is a product of their individual potential, socio-political exposure and personal circumstances. For example, leadership of the big NGDOs in Bangladesh was a product of natural disasters and the independence struggle against West Pakistan, and an appreciation that the scale of the problems facing the newly independent state needed large scale solutions. The notion of big scale was there from the outset, as was the belief that the new state should be secular.[21] Countering military dictatorships and applications of Marxist ideology shaped the thinking and drives of the individuals who formed the leadership of Latin American NGDOs in the 1960s and 1970s. NGDO leaders in much of post-colonial sub-Saharan Africa took over organisations from departing expatriates as part of the new regime, or established new organisations within the collective process of nation-building; an oppositional role was unthought of and consequently uncommon.

Times have changed. Consequently, potential leaders of NGDOs will be shaped differently in terms of their experience, interpretations and motivations. In addition, concerns for greater justice and greater equity will be expressed differently, as will the tools needed to pursue these goals. In short, new generations of NGDO leadership will be formed by different experiences and processes, which may make existing leaders inappropriate role models. Be that as it may, existing experiences are best built on rather than discarded and there is no reason why the forming process of new leaders should be left to chance. Instead, given the projected demands on NGDOs and the dilemmas they face, it is strategically necessary to invest in leadership development which draws on but does not simply try to reproduce, accumulated experience. The following are a few ideas in this direction.

● Existing NGDO leaders should come together to agree on the strategy and content of global, regional and national programmes of leadership development. El Taller, located in Tunisia, was an initiative in this direction but has been hampered by the untimely death of Sjef Theunis, its champion. There is no reason why regional and national NGDO collaborative bodies and some of the management training centres and programmes being established by NGDOs cannot carry this idea forward.[22] The crucial point is that any such

initiative should have the firm backing of existing leaders, who are prepared to put in time and effort to share what they have learned.

● Leaders of NGDOs in the Philippines have started a dialogue with younger generations to identify ideas and differences as inputs to strategies for a leadership development strategy.[23] Similar initiatives would be useful for other countries.

● Consistent with the way NGDO leaders have emerged, a forming process should be founded on the principles of experience-based learning, interposed with structured reflection.[24]

In order to influence, if not set, the new policy agenda for international development, there is an urgent need to be ahead of, rather than behind, the rapidly changing demands and opportunities NGDOs face. Putting time, energy and financial resources into NGDO leadership development is a matter of urgency, which should include gaining a better gender-balance than presently exists.

The Role of Gender in NGDOs.[25]

As in any community, gender is a dimension of NGDOs. First, it can be found in the way roles and power are divided along gender lines. Second, it is expressed in the degree to which male and female principles are reflected and valued in organisational culture. The two are related, but are not the same and hence are frequently confused. A third aspect of gender is in an NGDO's development approach. The focus of this book is on organising and managing; therefore, incorporating aspects of gender in development activity does not feature in detail. Nevertheless, gender awareness within NGDOs affects their sensitivity to work relationships, and there is a link between the ways in which gender expresses itself and how NGDOs ultimately perform in development. For this reason, important aspects of gender and NGDOs will be dealt with here.

Gender as an NGDO issue:

Gender dimensions of development have been around a long time, originally framed as WID: women in development. However, the growth of gender awareness is out of step with its translation into practice, which lags a long way behind. One reason for this gap is to do with organisation. Our task, therefore, is to focus on the organisational obstacles to gender sensitive development, which means looking at how they are being overcome within NGDOs.

Recognising gender as an organisational issue within NGDOs has been best documented by Northern agencies; this has introduced an element of bias. Moreover, in addition to pressures from local women, Southern and Eastern NGDOs' appreciation of gender has been influenced by Northern demands and sometimes negative reactions to them. Put another way, whatever their merits, Northern initatives towards better gender relations have provoked the feeling that this type of sensitivity is a Northern cultural imposition, especially among men. Whatever the justification for this response, putting gender-sensitive rhetoric into practice is tough because it requires getting into the 'deep structure' of organisational psychology and stereotyping, which are culturally determined.

The journey we make in this section begins with a restatement of why gender is a crucial issue in NGDO development work. Then, to see the historical trajectory, we look briefly at how the appreciation of gender has evolved in the aid system, leading to today's concern with gender in organisations as well as in development initiatives. Altering gender aspects of NGDOs usually meets with resistance. Why, and what can be done about it, are therefore the next topics to address. Finally, we look at the way gender issues shape North-South relationships between NGDOs and how this aspect of their interaction can be made more constructive.

Why is gender an issue for NGDOs?

Why should gender be at the forefront of NGDO concerns? First, social justice as a moral imperative calls for direct attention to who wins and who loses in society. While varying by degree, place and time, women systematically lose out to men in terms of access to society's resources and power over decisions. Further, as producers, women are usually responsible for providing the subsistence foodstuffs and informal 'off-farm' incomes which determine family survival. Consequently, their efforts, abilities and incentives are vital factors in determining the profile and scale of poverty. An additional developmental reason is that investments in women have a greater tendency to translate into increased household well-being than into consumption. Socially, women are central in maintaining cohesion, stability and local organisational capacity. All are important conditions for ensuring the sustainability of benefits which result from development interventions. Women's fertility determines long-term population growth rates. Their control over reproduction translates into the threshold above which economic growth can mean per capita improvements. In short, for an NGDO to be blind to the position and concerns of women is to choose ineffectiveness. Some observers would say it is an inexcusable sign of deep-lying organisational prejudice.

The trajectory: from WID to GAD

For most of the 1970s and 1980s, the appreciation of gender was framed in terms of the position and development needs of women. In keeping with its standard mode of operation, the aid system and NGDOs defined projects specifically for women, and established women's units to promote their interests. Generally speaking, women in development (WID) became an add-on, something parallel to what was already being done out there, or set up as an entity with responsibility for women, the rest of the organisation carrying on as before. Women's issues became a ghetto.[26]

While WID is still around, a more recent trend is gender in development (GAD). This takes as its starting point the definition of gender: sexual specificity in culturally determined perspectives on the roles and relationships between men and women, rather than the position of women *per se*. GAD acknowledges gender differences and disaggregates development work and impacts in terms of men and women as complementary actors. While the GAD approach aims to improve quality of life for all, gender analysis concentrates on how existing patterns and structures in gender relations can be modified in favour of greater balance and equity.[27]

The shift to GAD from WID stemmed, amongst others, from the way in which governments had taken women's concerns on board. In the South, the response was initially due to donor pressure. Establishing specialist women's units, which is what governments and NGDOs did, may have provided a focal point but also marginalised their impact. In response to this experience, greater attention is now being paid not just to GAD, as opposed to WID thinking, but also to mainstreaming gender

---

Box 4.1
Obstacles to a gender-fair NGDO culture

A gender-fair organisational culture is one which recognises and draws on the complementary potential of men and women's life experiences and competencies in all aspects of organisational life.

Covert obstacles
Covert obstacles arise from deep-lying but dimly understood attitudes of the organisation's power holders, usually imported from patriarchal cultural surroundings. Typical attitudes are:

- assuming that women are best suited to support roles;
- applying male norms to everyone's behaviour;
- repressed anxiety about female rejection, which translates into keeping women in their place, including overt disrespect, control, violence and sexual harassment;
- treating female authority as something to be countered, contained or marginalised;
- disrespect for femininity and hence feminine principles in organisational behaviour, often signalled by sexist humour;
- inability to accommodate different communication styles: non-assertive women are ignored, while forcefulness is criticised as unfeminine.

Overt obstacles
Overt obstacles result from covert feelings and prevent women from making their full contribution to organisational functioning. They include:

- too few women in positions of authority;
- tokenism, which allocates professional women to stereotyped functions, such as secretaries and personnel officers, rather than line managers;
- assessments which are used to subvert change;
- defensive action which argues that biases against women are an inviolable part of existing culture rather than a failure to be remedied;
- an over-proportion of women in non-professional positions, creating low expectations for and about women's value;
- working hours and lack of facilities which act as barriers to women who are mothers;
- downplaying the importance of gender as a legitimate organisation-wide issue.

Source: adapted from a contribution by Nicky May

---

awareness throughout organisations. In other words, there is now a realisation that a major impediment to applying gender principles in development work is within organisations themselves – the problem is not just out there with projects. But, to be effective, strategies need to be underpinned by an analysis of obstacles which stand in the way of gender awareness. What does this mean for NGDOs?

The gender of NGDOs

As organisations, NGDOs are not gender neutral.[28] By and large, NGDO organisations reflect rather than contradict wider society with its stereotypical views of women; here, women act as servers of men; seldom function as decision- or policy-makers; and are seen as women first and workers second.[29] Judgement on performance differs, with women having to prove themselves by being twice as good as men. Norms of behaviour, rules, physical structures, organisational divisions of power and tasks, and functional categories naturally tend to reflect and favour men rather than women. And, importantly, informal communication, decision-making and negotiation take place in male preserves.[30]

Patriarchal bias in organisational culture does not mean that NGDOs are not feminine in their development work, far from it. NGDOs are essentially caring institutions, concerned enough about an aspect of society to do something about it. This difference implies either a discontinuity or tension between a feminine development approach and masculine organisational culture – an inconsistency which contributes to frustration, reduced effectiveness and, on occasion, wholesale questioning of the sincerity of leaders/managers. Reaching effective gender-fair development work would, therefore, be aided by gender, fair NGDO culture and practice. What commonly stands in the way of this happening is summarised in Box 4.1.

Making NGDO culture more gender-balanced and fair

What do you do if your NGDO believes that gender must feature more strongly in its culture? Existing experience suggest the following items for NGDOs interested in becoming more gender-sensitive and fair.

TIPS **Firstly have a holistic view of what needs to be changed organisationally. This would include:**

Identity:
➤ ensure gender features in belief and value statements;
➤ establish policies about gender in the organisation and in development;
➤ ensure the governance system is gender fair.

Structure and systems:
➤ set targets for women at different staffing levels;
➤ create job structures which recognise gender features and their relative contributions, such as female communications officers for issues affecting women's rights;
➤ arrange provision for child care;
➤ have gender specialists with systems which clarify their contribution and degree of influence;
➤ build alliances to learn about and promote gender sensitive approaches;
➤ collect gender disaggregated data for all planning activities and for assessment of organisational performance.

People:
➤ provide gender training for managers;
➤ include gender awareness in recruitment and selection;
➤ include gender as an item in staff development;
➤ have gender training scheduled for all employees, including women;
➤ create mixed gender teams whenever appropriate.

Secondly, specialist gender skills (in a unit) should be complimented with mainstreaming; both are necessary. Avoid compartmentalising or tokenism. Thirdly, avoid deflection through endless studies or dilution of policy to a lowest common denominator.

Box 4.2
Strategies for creating a gender-balanced NGDO culture

Altering organisational culture is the most difficult and time-consuming type of organisational change. It is a long-term process which requires commitment and perseverance. People are loath to address, let alone give up, ingrained, subconscious beliefs and attitudes in which they are secure. This must be respected. To change culture, go carefully, but with conviction.

Preconditions:
A number of pre-conditions must be in place if change strategies are going to be meaningful. The following are important:

- The leadership, even if not convinced, should not be actively opposed to gender fairness (forcing it on partners is counter-productive).
- Resources for change, including time, should be overtly allocated; activities must not be treated as an add-on to business as usual.
- Change management should be a recognised responsibility with agreed progress indicators.

Strategies and steps:

Strategies:
- Change should be incremental, comprehensive and iterative – that is, continually going back to check on responses, problems and achievements.
- Getting and keeping people on board is vital.
- Deal with people's reservations; do not disregard the value of resistance.

Steps:
- Start a process of diagnosis analysis.
- Introduce frameworks and tools for gender analysis, linking external cultural dimensions to what is happening internally.
- Identify the myths and prejudices existing within and between men and women in the organisation.
- Place organisational culture in the context of life cycle; identify where forces for and against change are likely to lie.
- Build consensus on what sort of change is needed over what time scale. Do not give up. Cultural change is an iterative and incremental process, especially when management is not ready.
- Diagnose the personal reorientation needs in terms of individual knowledge, attitude and working relations with others.
- Introduce training, counselling and team-building.
- Identify outside allies, such as women's organisations, who can support the direction of change by providing information, experience and advice.
- Periodically monitor progress and provide organisation-wide feedback on what is being achieved.
- Gradually reduce the intensity of change activities, but do not stop, because organisational change is a constant process.

Source: adapted from a contribution by Nick May

If these are things which need to be done, how can they be implemented? Experience from Northern agencies provides the pointers and strategies to be found in Box 4.2.

Gender fairness is also a common subject of dialogue between partner NGDOs who may be at different stages in appreciating its importance. How can this, often cross-cultural, dialogue be made effective?

Gender in NGDO partnerships

Initially, acknowledgement of the gender dimensions of development was not equally shared or valued between NGDOs. An old complaint from the South was that gender issues were an imposition and conditionality. However, the women's movement in the South and the Beijing NGDO Conference have shown that gender issues are not simply Northern priorities pushed along the aid chain, but exist within the lives of women everywhere. But, while the hurdle of imposition has been pushed aside, there are still differences in perception between North, South and East in how gender issues can best be understood and addressed within organisations. In striving for partnership, how can such differences be addressed between NGDOs from different cultures?

Difficulties arising from dialogues about gender in NGDO partnerships are related to other issues as well. However, because gender gets to the heart of social relations, there is little doubt that this topic is one of the most difficult to deal with; doing so calls for gender to be an integral part of a human resource strategy.

TIPS *A seminar organised by a confederation of European NGDOs came to the following advice when placing gender within the context of partnership.[31] As with all approaches to the dimensions of culture, the first step is to be aware of cultural history and organisational values.*

Changes should be identified and summarised in order to encourage gender fairness. Dialogue should be used to:

➤ explore and prioritise respective positions;
➤ create a consensus wherever possible and acknowledge differences where they occur;
➤ look for likely internal and external resistance to proposed changes.

It is helpful, furthermore, to do a disaggregated stakeholder analysis in order to look for those actors who are likely to accept or reject change. Clarify the required personal attitudes of those who may function as change agents.

➤ Be clear about how organisationally deep change should go, and then sort out differences according to time frames.
➤ Make an assessment of the other forces and factors in play, arriving at a reasoned guess of the chances of success.
➤ Agree on an ongoing participative process for monitoring.
➤ Encourage donor sensitivity about the links between gender and funding conditions.

Recipients should also be clear about limits to change and use this as a reference point for dialogue, to ensure that their own identity is not compromised.

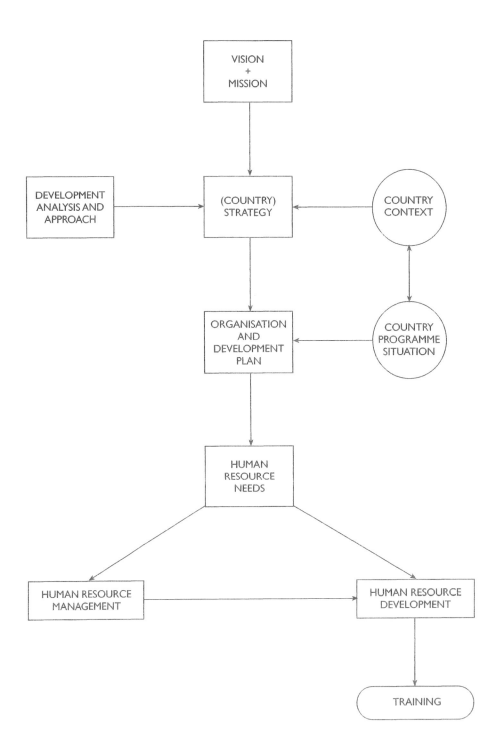

Figure 4.2 Human resource management in the context of NGDO work

Human Resource Management

Human resource management (HRM) is an important function of NGDOs. It should not be located in one place – the personnel department – but instead be part and parcel of recognising and utilising people's competencies: a task of managers everywhere.[32] HRM is not just about the technical functions of personnel management. It is an approach that sees people as a key resource rather than as a unit of production.[33] Our first concern is to set a framework linking personnel management with NGDOs' overall aims, and to look at some of the key things HRM has to get right in order for people to be effective. This focuses on: motivation and incentives; the competencies and formation of front-line staff who provide the interface to primary stakeholders; the role of expatriate technical assistance and processes of bringing the right people into the organisation and helping to build their personal capabilities.

Linking human resource management to NGDO work

The requirements for human resource management flow out of an NGDO's overall mission. Figure 4.2 is the 'flow' used by an international NGDO to work out what human resources it needs to implement a new country strategy, recognising that the existing situation already provides a foundation for human resources. The top part of the diagram is similar to the elements in the strategic planning process outlined in the previous chapter.

Human resource needs are defined in terms of competencies – that is, the skills, knowledge, attitudes and values not available to do the various tasks of translating vision into action. It is the gap between what is available and what is required. While strategic planning assesses longer-term needs, any learning organisation is constantly making this assessment and investing in individual improvements. Human resource management is fed by and responds to this ongoing identification of needs, and the performance and potential of existing staff and

volunteers. While leaders/managers are involved in this process and can set the motivational tone, they face particular problems in getting the mix of incentives right. Why is this so?

Managing the mix of motivation and incentives

In NGDOs, the leaders/managers have tasks to fulfil beyond those of internal routines – sometimes called the bureaucratic hygiene – and project management.[34] In terms of motivation, it is most important to satisfy the psychological needs of staff, helping them to constructively relate to others inside and outside the organisation. NGDOs predominantly 'relate' to communities rather than produce products, and the abiding stress on partnerships, and now on alliances, coalitions and networks, signals the deep-lying significance of relationships to NGDOs' subconscious life and needs.[35]

The style that leaders/managers employ in going about maintaining their own relationships – through consultation, dialogue, listening, and joint reflection – are an important source of motivation for others. However, psychological motivation doese not put bread on the table – material incentives and working conditions also play their part in people's attitudes to doing what is expected of them. In the early years of NGDO activity, financial incentives were supposed to be offset by the moral reward of contributing to social change. The extent to which this really reflected the situation throughout the world is open to question, especially in the resource-poor South where cultural norms express service to others in different ways. Whatever the case, things are different today.

Becoming more business-like and market-oriented in the 1990s affects NGDO incentives by making financial rewards more significant for retaining and motivating staff. In addition, the predatory behaviour of official aid agencies is also altering the incentive pattern of NGDOs.

The pro-NGDO policies of the inter-governmental aid system are leading to an escalation in the market value of experienced NGDO staff. The situation is especially acute in heavily aid-dependent countries with a small NGDO community, such as Tanzania and Nepal.[36] With political pressure to disburse more funds through the second and third sectors, official aid agencies offering relatively high salaries and sometimes hard-currency, tax-free payments, are absorbing some of the most capable NGDO people.[37] In this way the thinking and implementation capacity of the sector may be weakened; as a result, a serious imbalance may emerge when it comes to civic-policy influencing, interfacing with government in general, and in collaborative undertakings where NGDOs end up the weakest partner.

In addition to contracting their services, donor absorption of NGDO personnel tilts the NGDO ethos away from moral commitment towards material reward, which may in the long run throw the developmental child away with the aid bath water. Leaders/managers face serious dilemmas in striking the appropriate balance between tangible and intangible incentives in their organisations. While trends are similar across the world, I have not come across any rules of thumb to help with solutions; the choices being made are situation-specific. It is worthwhile highlighting, however, the requirements of community change agents (CA), as this is a central issue in human resource management for NGDOs.

Human resource management and the crucial role of change agents

NGDO leaders/managers have little effect without followers. In operational NGDOs, the most important followers are those furthest away, who are out on the organisational periphery and working as community change agents. What can leaders/managers do so that these followers become the centre of the organisation rather than remain on its edge? The answers are: select properly; 'form' appropriately; and then empower organisationally. What does this mean in practice?

Recruiting insiders or outsiders?

Change agents (CAs) are catalysts of peoples' development action; this often requires comparative experience. But an effective catalyst also requires deep insight into the community in question, as well as trust and acceptance by them. Do you therefore recruit from within the community or bring someone from outside? Opinions differ. Outsiders must climb steep learning curves and go through a usually long process of gaining local acceptance, which can be helped or hindered by existing cultural prejudices. In addition, working away from home ties external CAs more to the NGDO and its intentions than to the community. Insiders obviously have local insight but may find local credibility difficult if they take on a new role, especially if linked to external resources where personal commitment to the common good may be overridden by personal reward.[38] Furthermore, because insiders remain within their group, sharing the NGDO vision, mission and identity is likely to be weaker. On balance, it seems that change agents coming from outside the community are probably more appropriate.[39] Though not without its dangers, community members who are potential change agents have more to contribute through their actions in community-based organisations than on the NGDO payroll. As Umtali[40] point out: 'We need a new breed of change agents who, first and foremost, care for people as human beings, who treat them as subjects and not objects or recipients of change, who steep themselves in the aspirations, problems and wisdom of the people.'

If a change agent's stance towards poor people is wrong, their technical skill and knowledge will seldom be sufficient compensation. Key personality traits which make up the needed stance include: patience, a habit of listening rather than talking, inter-personal sensitivity, team work, self-confidence without arrogance, empathy, commitment, respectfulness, diplomacy, and perseverance. Skills in communication are vital, as is an ability to analyse and diagnose events. Gender, age and socio-economic standing are additional criteria to be applied, all directed at gaining community trust and fulfilling two roles, initially as facilitator of group awareness and then as adviser or consultant on the changes people want for themselves.

The 'forming' of change agents

A crucial task of human resource development (HRD) is to form change agents. The word 'forming' is used instead of training in order to stress that change agents become effective by learning through experience – that is, reflecting on what they have been through, rather than by classroom instruction. Too often, NGDOs place change agents on courses which do not engage them in real-life situations. How this can be done differently is covered in detail in a book by Stan Burkey.[41] Transactional analysis (TA), DELTA Training,[42] and participatory rural appraisal (PRA), are types of orientation for CAs which lend themselves to action-based learning. The preferred approach is, however, not to treat these simply as techniques, but to sequence them as different practical engagements which, together, cover the whole process of sustainable development. Each exposure should be followed by opportunities for dialogue, reflection and self-criticism. It is important that after initial forming, or after learning new skills, the organisation matches up to what has been acquired.

Depending on individual motivation, mismatches between participatory methods and non-participatory organisational culture can lead to frustration, cynicism or apathy, which undermine commitment and reduce the moral reward. A feeling of voicelessness in NGDOs will become apparent in a change agent's work with communities. In the words of one change agent, 'If you are not being heard, why listen?' The life of a CA then becomes one of earning a living first. Effective NGDOs take steps to stop this happening. One step is organisational empowerment, described below. In addition, time is created for CAs, staff and volunteers to discuss their situation and concerns within a team setting; new ideas are sought or introduced through a bottom-up approach; staff are systematically included in organisational consultations and invited to come up with

proposals; income differentials between authority levels are modest, reflecting a CA's comparative value to the organisation; and, there is a system which gives everyone a formal input – though not necessarily formal control – over organisational policy and practice. Committees are one frequent approach, representation in the governance structure common in Latin America, is another.

The third step: organisational empowerment

The crux of empowerment for change agents is having the authority to make decisions with communities. This should not be in a strategic vacuum, of course, and not without negotiated performance criteria, but the necessary power and trust must be present.[43] Systems for making this happen appear in the previous chapter, planning and budgeting being very significant. However, systems are a necessary but not sufficient condition. A more important, subtle element of empowerment lies in a leader's/manager's conviction that the NGDO values social justice, not just for its primary stakeholders but also for its staff. The more confidence that change agents have in the way management reaches and implements decisions affecting them, the less likely they are to misuse the trust they are given, which in turn strengthens management confidence in sharing authority. This is where internal transparency is vital. Promises made are seen to be kept, consultation is treated seriously, and moral principles are consistently applied.

The element of staff confidence in management is, in fact, important for all staff and takes on added dimensions when expatriates are involved. Human resource management must therefore be sensitive to this dimension too.

HRM and NGDO expatriates: yes or no; where and when?

The official aid system has reached the conclusion that expatriate technical cooperation has been a very expensive failure; however, it seems unable to kick the habit.[44] Are NGDO expatriates appropriate? Expatriates are still commonly recruited to work in foreign countries for Northern NGDOs, or for local NGDOs who request expertise they cannot find or afford. The circumstances under which this happens are often far from straightforward, with implicit as well as explicit agendas in play. This section looks at expatriates as a human resource and the dilemmas this poses for the giver, the recipient and expatriates themselves.

When to use expatriates

'The justification for employing expatriates in [supporting] operational work is mostly unconvincing. Northerners' skills, knowledge, and ability to represent the poor have been over-rated, while Southerners' incompetence, vulnerability to corruption, and lack of concern for the poor are usually exaggerated'.[45]

This is the first paragraph in Emma Crewe's analysis of factors associated with NGDO expatriates. Her conclusion is to choose insiders, that is country nationals, whenever possible. This principle is consistent with development goals of building and using local capacity and reduces time and costs associated with gaining local knowledge and local acceptance. Given the short-term contract nature of expatriate appointments local people can also provide greater continuity and greater investment in the South as their remuneration is not repatriated. What situations can therefore justify an expatriate from the North or from the South?

● Skills are not available and a gap needs to be filled while training is provided by a local person.
● There is a need for confidence building and communication with the donor in the short term.
● An exchange of mutual learning and breaking down of stereotypical views between North, South and East are required.
● If comparative experience is needed, expatriates may contribute to reduced learning time and capitalisation on investments in outside knowledge.
● There is a recognised, valid need for the

challenging inputs that expatriates can bring.

To these reasons can be added less valid, but nevertheless more common, justifications for expatriates being chosen, especially for management positions. These are to:

● act as 'impartial' gatekeepers for resources;
● ensure that donor concerns are fully respected and taken care of;
● ensure cross-country consistency with interpretations of organisational mission and policies;
● promote the organisation's national identity (fulfilling a tacit expectation, if not formal condition, of bilateral donors).

Underlying the first three of these justifications is the notion that because expatriates are in a foreign setting and externally dependent, their primary allegiance will be to the international NGDO, and thereafter to the country of work and its people. In other words, it boils down to a higher probability that in unpredictable situations the individual can be trusted to act consistently with the NGDO's best interests.

A number of international NGDOs are fully conscious of the inconsistency in development principles which this belief introduces. HRM strategies have therefore been adopted by some NGDOs to reduce this often unspoken, but nonetheless common, preference for expatriates in the South and East. Their laudable objective is to reach a situation where degree of trust has nothing to do with country of origin. This is, however, a tall order given that trust is culturally preconditioned; differences are usually trusted less.

While certainly no panacea for establishing trust, acknowledging the importance of building personal affinity with the organisational culture is a step in the right direction.

Personal allegiance: expatriate moral dilemmas

Expatriates are not always imposed upon an NGDO. Often Southern and Eastern NGDOs see the merits of an outsider who will bring useful skills, insights on how the North works, contacts for fund-raising, and who, importantly, are free – someone else pays. This is usually the case with volunteers. But even though the expatriate is requested, problems can still arise. Typical of such problems are: dual allegiance to the NGDO and to the sending organisation, especially if financial resources are involved as well; and value differences which may be of an unconscious racial nature.

In North Tanzania, a local NGDO had been struggling to raise funds for work with poor urban communities. Every dialogue with donors led to adjustments away from what was originally intended and closer to donor priorities. To assist in fund-raising, the NGDO applied for and obtained a Danish volunteer. So successful were her efforts in helping to draft and send out proposals that eventually two donors approved assistance for the same project. For the NGDO's management, this was a windfall which could be used for what it saw to be really necessary, the 'donor' project being implemented as well. For the volunteer, this stance was dishonest and after repeatedly asking the NGDO's director to be open about dual funding, which he refused to do, she informed donors of the duplication, and was promptly sacked. What went wrong?

The past ten years have seen a growing trend to couple funds to volunteers and other NGDO expatriates, which can only increase the moral dilemmas they face. The expatriates' induction process can partly address this problem by analysing typical situations which call for moral choices.

Yet again, these steps do not guarantee that no friction will occur, only that the 'rules of the game' are established from the outset.

Expatriate appointments in local NGDOs are usually accompanied by a plan to build local 'counterpart' capacity. There are other ways of doing so, and this is where HRM moves to human resource development – that is, specific initiatives to improve the competencies of staff and volunteers.

Human resource development

Human resource development is a label covering a wide range of activities which should lead to better capabilities and hence effectiveness of staff.[47] This section summarises the types of HRD leaders/managers can chose from, then

TIPS **Existing strategies to best utilise and trust expatriates are:**

➤ making a clear distinction between national and international posts;
➤ employing conditions of service which are equitable for Northern and Southern expatriates and which do not penalise a national who applies for an international post in his own country;
➤ paying significant attention to selection on the basis of personal values and beliefs, as well as professional competencies, including an assessment of ability to deal with moral dilemmas;
➤ putting a lot of effort into induction, not simply concentrating on operational procedures and manuals, but also exposing and exploring organisational culture.
This is done by;
➤ integrating strategies with internal policy discussions, where dilemmas are laid on the table and critical trade-offs made;
➤ interacting with Northern constituencies in order to understand their socio-economic profile and expectations;

➤ meeting with some board members to understand their perspectives and thinking;
➤ talking through likely practical issues that require on-the-spot personal judgement, such as dealing with political pressures and irresponsible staff behaviour;
➤ mapping and comparing individual and organisational cultural norms and mores.[46]

relates them to different types of staff commonly found in operational NGDOs.

Types of HRD

There are eight distinctive types of HRD available to NGDOs. They can all be considered as forms of training understood as a time-bound process which results in individuals acquiring the appropriate values, attitudes, skills and knowledge required to improve their performancc in rclation to the organisation's mission. They involve the following:

● *Internally designed courses:* training events designed specifically for the NGDO and therefore tailored to its needs. They are cost-effective when a large number of people need to learn the same things.
● *Pre-packaged courses* (local and foreign): pre-packaged events whose content is sufficiently similar to the needs of the individual, though per capita costs remain high.

● *Workshops:* 'output-oriented' gatherings, which are useful for solving a particular problem, especially where joint ownership is needed.
● *Seminars/conferences:* provide an exposure to issues or people, network information, create relationships, and facilitate individual broadening or insights.
● *On-the job training* (OJT): a method of practically exchanging expertise between one person and another. It is suitable where it is difficult to release staff, the tasks involved are technical or routine, or where detailed observation is needed to ensure that competence has been gained.
● *Exchanges:* tend to be short-term visits to gain an understanding of other ways of doing things, to see innovations, to gain new ideas and horizons, and to introduce new staff.
● *Secondment:* normally involves someone taking on a known role in a different setting, with training in mind. Secondments can help people to do old things in new ways as

$TIPS$ *In addition, agencies can and are doing the following:*

➤ Before recruitment, be up front with the collaborating organisation about whether or not the volunteer is under an obligation to report to the agency; in other words, are they expected to have a direct line of communication? The preferred situation is one of primary allegiance to the host organisation.
➤ Agree from the outset how any irreconcilable differences will be signalled and arbitrated, preferably bringing in a mutually respected third party.
➤ Indicate the degree to which financial resources are or are not coupled to the presence of an expatriate.

they adapt to other circumstances.

- *Self-study/correspondence courses:* systematic ways of gathering knowledge for an individual, sometimes accompanied by group work with others doing the same study. They are often chosen where access is difficult, the topic specialised, there is no urgency and where a recognised qualification is required but course attendance is not an option.

Each of these methods has different costs and benefits and are more suited to some types of staff than others, depending on their personal career trajectory.

Categories of NGDO staff

There are no standardised job types or cadres in NGDOs to use as a point of reference. Therefore, the following five types of staff are used (see Table 4.1); they would need to be translated into categories which make sense to each organisation.

Table 4.2 brings together the eight types of human resource development and the five cadres of NGDO staff, and assesses the relative merits of the relationship between each in relation to costs and benefits and strengths and weaknesses. Where internal HRD is not an option, human resource management needs to competently deal with the process of finding and bringing new personnel into the organisation. What this involves comprises our concluding topic.

Recruiting new staff

There are four stages to bringing new staff on board so that they find their place and function effectively. The stages of new recruitment are: specifying the job, notifying the pool of people available, selecting an individual, and induction into the NGDO's processes.

Person specifications

In order to begin a recruitment process a specification needs to be checked to see if it is consistent with the requirements of the organisational plan. The specification sets out the primary tasks, authority and responsibility associated with the job; the minimum specifications in terms of skill, knowledge, attitude and values; the position in the organisation; cultural requirements; religious requirements; any trends/growth/changes envisaged in the future; the expected duration of contract; formal education; budget/salary scales and applicable limits; the location of work; and, any salient points to be born in mind during advertising and selection – for example, if a particular gender, nationality, age or experience is sought. The specification is the basis for the advertisement and recruitment exercise.

Notification and Identification

The conditions affecting recruitment vary from country to country as does the (NGO) pool in which recruitment is to take place. The first assessment to be made is whether the person specification is likely to be satisfied locally. If this is thought unlikely, advertising abroad can be considered. If both local and foreign advertising takes place, it is important to ensure consistency and not, for example, demand more years of experience in local than in international advertisements, which does occur.

Advertisements can also test the arena, to determine if local recruitment is likely or if the specification is realistic. Comparisons can also be made with other similar organisations to check on the appropriateness of salary levels versus qualifications. Identification of potential candidates is also frequently done by informal networking, poaching and direct head-hunting. Personnel recruitment bureaus can also be used if the NGDO wishes to avoid some of the pressures normally associated with recruiting in politicised environments where there is mass unemployment.

Selection

The selection process is likely to vary with the cadre concerned. Only some general pointers can therefore be given. These are:
- the selection process should identify a candidate's *potential* as well as their ability

Table 4.1 Types of NGDO staff

Category	Sample description
Change Agent: (community development worker, community organiser, extension officer)	Task is to work directly with the primary stakeholders as catalyst, facilitator, information source, adviser.
Technical Specialist: (sector specialist, technical officer, communications/information officer, fund-raiser; HRM, HRD staff)	Provide technical support to change agents, learning from field operations; problem solver, trouble shooter; technical liaison to similar people in other agencies; lobby and advocacy work in area of expertise.
Administrative/Support Staff: (accounting, purchasing, transport, audit, documentation)	Provide non-programme/project services to CAs, specialist staff and all management levels.
First-Line Manager: (field supervisor, field co-ordinator)	Provide direct functional support and guidance to the work of CAs; dealing with daily problems.
Middle Manager: (branch manager, zone manager, area manager)	Carry direct responsibility and authority for staff and costs in all programme operations and performance.
Senior Managers: (chief executive, executive director programme, finance, research, marketing directors)	Carry authority and responsibility for strategy, performance and learning in programmes and across the organisation as a whole, with accountability to the governing body.

to satisfy the specification;

- fairness is more apparent if the process is transparent, requiring good public communication;
- interviewing should be both structured and open-ended and can involve both group and individual encounters;
- testing should be both job-specific and generic; for example, to assess judgement, discretion, decision-making capability, values and attitudes;
- references, when sought, should be both verbal and written;
- (early) life histories can be important sources for indicating potential;
- independent assessors can offer a beneficial comparative view of candidates.

Induction into the organisation

Like selection, the induction process will usually differ between cadres. When designing induction, background information should be provided, such as:

- documentation on the NGDO as a whole;
- details on the strategy and programme being run;
- personnel policies and conditions of service;
- a collation of any policies that have been approved by the board;
- a document explaining the NGDO's development approach.

For international NGDOs, some of the documents can best be produced to serve the

Table 4.2 Applying HRD methods to NGO cadres

Method Cadre	Internal courses	Packaged courses	Workshops	Seminars/ conferences	On-the-job training	Exchanges (visits)	Secondment	Self-study
Change agents (CAs)	cost effective; relevant; highly recommended; proven utility; relevance may be a problem	suited for specialist technical areas;	team building; for experienced staff; skilled facilitator vital; good to generate knowledge from experience	good for local level inter agency sharing	practical orientation; suited to induction and orientation; good for special skill development	suited to local level inter agency		requires motivation and commitment; may help identify high performer; requires an agency policy
Junior and intermediate managers	good for specific organisational systems; high cost if numbers low or irregular; adaptation of external courses recommended	ditto	good for problem-solving; good to develop horizontal linkages; good for cadre strengthening	provides exposure and broadening; less suited for junior management except local-level interagency		usually relevant and useful; recommended	use only very selectively	ditto
Senior/top managers	ditto	ditto	ditto highly recommended	builds networking; provides exposure and broadening; important for policy development and conceptual issues	limited application	useful for policy exchange and strategic development	recommended where suitable opportunities exist	
Technical specialists	suited for specialist team development	ditto	as for junior and intermediate managers	ditto highly recommended	ditto	useful and relevant; recommended	ditto	ditto helps keep abreast with specialist knowledge
Administration and programme support	relevant but normally of limited application	relevant to professional development	useful within departments	important for internal information sharing	ditto	useful within country programmes	limited application	as for CAs
All cadres	good for addressing specific issues	suited to specialist technical areas	encourages reflection and participation; good for organisation building; skilled facilitator vital	information sharing	suited to orientation and induction	good for developing ideas and learning techniques	case-by-case decision	requires individual motivation; needs a country policy on support

whole organisation; others need to be tailor-made by each country. In addition, induction could involve:

- a meeting with key staff;
- training in participatory planning and resource-appraisal methods;
- assigning a mentor for two to three months;
- visiting selected programmes or development initiatives;

- specific upgrading in specialised skills or procedures.

An important outcome of the induction period is that the new staff member understands the NGDO as a development agency, identifies with what the organisation stands for and is trying to achieve, and can explain this when relating to the outside world, which is the focus of the next chapter.

5

NGDOs Are Not Islands: Making Relationships Effective

The Art of Relating

The world of NGDOs is dominated by choosing relations with others, making them work well and combining their effects towards their own vision and mission. Located in an aid chain, NGDOs are challenged to manage relationships in two primary directions – with primary stakeholders and with funders – and in many secondary directions, for example with other NGDOs, governments, the general public and so on. NGDOs must be skilled in balancing a variety of unsteady and often unpredictable relational pushes and pulls. For example, the move towards multi-party democracy in many countries, the retreat of governments from social development responsibilities, the negative effects of economic adjustment policies on the scope and depth of poverty, and pressures from fashion-driven funding, all change the situation and the demands of those whom NGDOs relate to. Selecting responses and modifying relationships is a continual occupation of NGDO leaders/ managers and staff. Getting this right can make the difference between success and failure in development work.

This chapter looks at managing and organising external relationships common to NGDOs, starting at operational relations with primary stakeholders. The discussion then proceeds to different ways NGDOs relate to each other, including partnerships, networks, alliances, consortia and collective bodies. NGDO relationships with governments concentrate on situations where there may be hostility and mistrust; in these cases strategies must keep open 'development space'. Finally, the chapter ends with a practical review of increasingly significant type of NGDO interactions with governments, which are aimed at influencing public policy-making and modifying state behaviour. Because of its importance and complexity, relationships with governments and the official aid system on mobilising financial resources are the subject of a separate chapter.

The Primary Relationship: Interfacing with Primary Stakeholders in People-Centred Development Initiatives

Previous chapters indicated the many ways in which project-based micro-development can work against NGDO effectiveness. What, then, is a possible alternative and how might it work in practice? Drawing on NGO experience, this section offers an answer in two steps. The first step examines a critical choice operational NGDOs must make in terms of identifying whom they work with. The second step uses an alternative 'intervention' framework for understanding the relationship between external development agents and those whose situation NGDOs wish to improve. Interventions offer a potentially more effective way of thinking about and doing micro-development, which is beginning to show itself in NGDO work.

Indigenous local organisations: choosing who to work with

When translating vision into action, an NGDO must select the local community, group, organisation or set of individuals it is going to work with. This involves a principal choice of searching for an existing local organisation – which may itself have been created by other outsiders – or activating a new one. The decision depends on a combination of organisational factors including: a development philosophy which values indigenous societies; an ability to recognise, respect and (where suitable) engage with informal associations; and the type of activity intended.[1] The following table summarises the advantages and drawbacks involved when choosing whether to set up a new local organisation or to work with one that already exists and is historically and culturally indigenous.

Table 5.1 Setting up or working with an existing community-based organisation

	Existing	**Set up by the NGDO**
Strengths	familiar and legitimate; trusted and understood; already institutionalised in society; already sustained	more efficient for new social tasks; dedicated to change; can reduce biases, enhancing equity; can operate more democratically
Weaknesses	biased towards *status quo;* may be controlled by elites; may exclude or marginalise key groups, eg, women and children; may be inappropriate to intervention or technology; can sustain anti-developmental attitudes or practices;	unfamiliar; must be sustained; establishment must be accepted, trusted, institutionalised and embedded; may replace local with external control; can introduce exclusiveness which can threaten cohesion and be divisive

Indigenous forms of association are often very resilient, able to withstand governmental and outside pressures to disband. But resilience does not mean that they are static and not open to taking on new tasks. For example, in Ethiopia traditional associations were repressed by the Mengistu regime and supplanted by peasant associations (PAs) and official co-operatives. This forced NGDOs to work with state-sanctioned organisations, ignoring other associations which had been formed and were trusted by the populace. However, after almost a century of active state repression, numerous types of indigenous association continue to exist. A pertinent example is the Timbaro people of Omosheleko in South West Showa Region in Ethiopia. Despite many years of systematic marginalisation and repression by successive regimes, the Timbaro retained forms of association fulfilling social, economic and leadership tasks. Six distinctive forms of Timbaro informal association were still active when the Mengistu regime was overthrown and enforced PAs abandoned.

At the local level, NGDOs commonly deal with a complex mix of state-sanctioned, aid-imposed and otherwise induced development organisations existing alongside indigenous bodies. As a general rule, before trying to induce a new one NGDOs should be sure that an existing CBO, co-operative group, or other member-based entity is not capable of evolving incrementally with new tasks, practices and more equitable divisions of power.[2] Why? Because there is an inevitable danger that a new local organisation, induced by an NGDO and relying on external resources, defines itself by taking on aspects of the NGDO's identity and mission. Such identification brings higher risk of patronage relations, external dependency and potential for unsustainability, especially if the new entity does not become respected and supported in its own right as an integral part of local society – which in turn calls for greater efforts and costs to localise control.

The modest and uneven NGDO track record in inducing sustainable CBOs confirms how difficult it is. One reason is the double bind of buying into the existing elite structure in order to get started and facing resistance as new leaders start to arise. Another is the emergence of leaders who behave in the same ways as the role models around them, while the local organisation does not (yet) have the capacity to do anything about it. Members therefore either rely on the NGDO to use its leverage on resources to exert pressure, or call on the existing elites to use traditional sanctions, which makes members dependent on the very system from which they are trying to break away.

The principle of working with indigenous elements calls for NGDOs to find out what local institutions exist, who uses them for what purposes and who is excluded – a process which can take can take from weeks to years.[3] Today, a common way of doing so is through participatory (rural or urban) appraisal and social mapping techniques. And this takes us to a different way of approaching and improving development work, which I call 'process interventions'.

Engaging with communities: from packaged projects to process interventions

A feeling exists in aid circles that intervention is not an appropriate word to describe development work; it sounds like an imposition. Using the term 'projects' to define external influences aimed at reorienting what is going on in society sounds innocuous, but it is not. Projects are heavily loaded ways of thinking and behaving; they are not neutral. Seeing development initiatives for what they are – selected interventions into complex, ongoing processes – is a potentially powerful antidote to the drawbacks of project thinking and practice described earlier.

Adopting an intervention approach is not necessarily as radical as it sounds; it can incorporate many positive aspects of current micro-practice. What differs is the framework of thinking and action which better meets the requirements for people-centred sustainable development. This section explores what intervention means in micro-development and the reorientation it requires.

The intervention framework

Figure 5.1 illustrates what is meant by an intervention approach.[4] The concept has four characteristics which NGDOs can use to work effectively.

- *Position:* interventions remind NGDOs that they are outsiders; their reality is different from those of primary or other stakeholders.
- *Context:* implicit to the intervention approach is the recognition that processes are going on which outsiders must take time to understand.
- *Purpose:* interventions are undertaken for a reason; NGDOs must be clear about why they are there and what they want to achieve. Agendas must be explicit and a starting point for negotiation.
- *Duration:* in interventions, saying 'goodbye' is an acknowledged part of saying 'hello'. This implies that conditions and criteria for withdrawal are, from the

outset, given the same attention as methods and criteria for entry.

While the overall period of an intervention will vary, people-centredness calls for time scales which respect individual and collective human change. PRRM in the Philippines and ACTIONAID take 10 to 12 years as the likely duration for intervention; PROSHIKA in Bangladesh and ALIANCE in Guatemala, operate on the basis of five-year agreements with people's organisations and local governments.

Interventions have three stages: entry, consolidation and withdrawal, illustrated in the next figure.

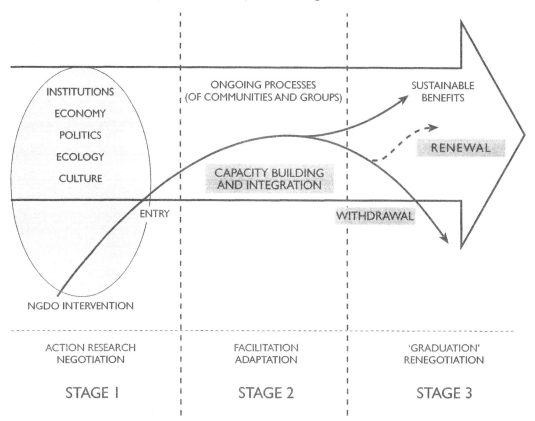

Figure 5.1   Intervention in development

Unlike the typical project approach – with a clearly defined cycle of identification, appraisal, implementation and evaluation – transition from one intervention stage to the next is seldom clear-cut. However, the move from negotiating an agreement to joint action can be taken as a threshold of transition from stage 1 to stage 2. The move from stage 2 to stage 3 occurs when agreed objectives have been met or when there is a necessity for renegotiation, described below, in the withdrawal stage.

Stage 1 – entry as the critical process

Correct entry within an ongoing complex social situation is the key to effectiveness. Various preconditions must be satisfied to ensure that entry goes well. First are organisational factors, and second are the processes NGDOs use to identify and negotiate with primary stakeholders. In both cases, the source of funding can help or hinder things right from the start. Finally, moving into the next stage calls for all parties to agree on measures of performance. Proper entry, therefore, has at least four elements: organisation, process, funding and performance.

Organisational preconditions for effective entry

The way an NGDO organises itself creates preconditions which affect the quality of community entry. Table 5.2 lists factors identified by a group of South Asian participants on a management course, tabulated according to: what an NGDO could typically control; what it could influence; and what it could only appreciate and take into account at its entry.[5] Some of these potential limitations have been dealt with and others are tackled in chapters to come. The crux is that, at entry, an NGDO's change agents must have the capability of undertaking real negotiations about: mutually agreed goals and the measures to be used in assessing achievement; and how power will be shared and applied over time.

Table 5.2 Organisational factors affecting entry

Issue	Factors affecting best practice
What NGDOs can control	distribution of decision-making power (calling for decentralisation);
	layering of the organisation (less levels is better);
	organisational psychology (conditioning the degree of self-interest with willingness to share and eventually forego power);
	staff skills (knowledge, attitudes, philosophy, internalisation of values and awareness of biases);
	organisational culture (that empowers staff);
	(local) resources (which allow flexibility and adaptation);
	the development approach (overcoming the limitations of projects);
	incentives for staff;
	learning systems (which recognise and guide adaptation to local circumstances);
	transparency (especially towards primary stakeholders);
	planning and budgeting;
	accountability to primary stakeholders and funders.
What NGDOs can influence	donor culture;
	type of external resources;
	planning and budgeting of others, e g, donors;
	legal situation and conditions.
What NGDOs can only appreciate	national (religious) culture;
	indigenous resources, including knowledge;
	legal situation and conditions.

Another precondition is to ensure that people understand what the organisation is all about in terms of its vision, mission, funding sources, and limitations. When this does not occur, false expectations can arise, while uncritical acceptance of people's goals may create a gap between agreed activities and the NGDO's own strategic priorities. (For international NGDOs, this leads to lack of coherence across its world-wide operations.) The crucial element at entry is to negotiate within parameters already determined by the NGDO, but with outcomes which reflect people's priorities.[6] Finding goals which correspond to people's real aspirations – as opposed to opportunistic or ill-informed responses to the availability of external resources – and which match an NGDO's development strategies and capabilities is probably the most difficult entry task. (When there is no perfect match between an NGDO's and people's priorities, it is often worthwhile to begin with what motivates people in order to build up confidence in the relationship, moving later to initiatives which people may not have thought of, and which are closer to the NGDO's core skills).

The next critical factor is that the organisation must deal with authentic participation. Box 5.1 is a checklist, together with advice for NGDOs wanting to assess or increase internal participation.

Box 5.1
Organising for authentic participation: a checklist

Participation preconditions
1. Does the NGDO have a recognisable vision of what it is doing, and where it is going?
2. Does the NGDO have minimum competencies and resources to translate vision into action with the optimum mix of trust and control?
3. Does the NGDO have a clear working understanding of the concept of participation which does not lead to different or inconsistent interpretations?
4. Is participation recognised throughout the organisation as an operating principle, not a set of techniques to be selectively applied?
5. Is the NGDO resource base of staff skills, literature and time allocations adequate?
6. Are there personnel in the centre and in the field with a watching brief, keeping an eye on what is happening in practice, signalling when a gap between rhetoric and practice appears?
7. Has training in participation/facilitation been part of the forming for all staff?
8. Are the necessary organisational factors listed in Table 5.2 in place?

Main tasks in building up capacity in authentic participation
1. Undertake exercises to ensure that the concept of participation is mainstreamed; do not allow it to become a preserve of the few .
2. Maintain an organisational culture consistent with participation principles.
3. In assessing resources for participation ask:
   ● what organisational experience of participation can be drawn on?
   ● what is the direct experience of staff in how many different settings?
   ● what level and kind of human resources are required to be effective?
   ● is there access to relevant publications on the subject?
4. Ask an outsider to assess whether the strategies, organisational mechanisms and methodologies chosen are consistent with each other and show that they are in place.
5. Negotiate with stakeholders about the type of participation that will suit their circumstances in terms of who is involved, how frequently, the information they need and when.

6. Test to see if the practical work situation, administrative and other demands on staff are in harmony with each other and with the method through which participation will occur.
7. Create a resource base of materials on participation, similar to what is often done for gender, or the environment.
8. Ensure that staff training in participation includes practical experience (see Chapter 4).
9. Be prepared to evaluate the extent to which authentic participation is occurring, using an internal participatory process to define criteria.

Typical difficulties and pitfalls
1. Participation can mean so many things to so many people that coherent action is sometimes not possible; what is done is therefore sometimes ineffective and perhaps counter-productive.
2. Because participation is an art, it calls for judgement based on extensive experience, which is an investment too seldom made.
3. Participation does not fit neatly into project cycles; be prepared to deal with the frustration and impatience this causes.
4. Embarking on true participation without full awareness and acceptance of the consequences, such as sharing and eventually relinquishing control, leads to organisational pain and reduced effectiveness.

Words of advice and caution
1. Do not treat participation as another input to be managed.
2. Participation does not occur by proclamation; it only flourishes if there is institutional commitment backed up by an investment in organisational capacity.
3. The answer to the question 'why do we want to promote participation?' must be clear enough to lay the institutional foundation for putting words into practice.
4. Do not cut corners for quick results; be prepared to take the time needed. If you cannot do this from the outset it is better not to begin – be an effective contractor instead.
5. Use participatory evaluation as both a capacity-building tool and as a source of knowing what is really going on.

Source: adapted from a contribution by Peter Oakley

Entry process: the use of participatory planning

Over the past 15 years or so, aid agencies have paid greater attention to the process side of entry. Participatory tools for local self-assessment are now so common that donors expect to see them employed in formulating proposals for assistance. Participatory resource and situation analysis is now a typical starting point, usually creating a baseline which defines the context and serves as a reference for assessing future change. But a major obstacle to the effectiveness of participatory techniques is that they seldom become organisationally embedded, for example in PBS and finance procedures. Consequently, there is an encouraging participatory build-up, but reduced or token participatory organisational behaviour in subsequent stages.

Correct entry is also less likely to occur if participatory techniques are simply used to engage local people in collecting data so that outsiders can go off and design a better project – useful as this is. Sound entry occurs when an NGDO is in a position to negotiate with communities and groups about what each may or may not have to offer in an intended relationship and, then, together determine how the whole process will be controlled.

Box 5.2
Participatory entry

Tackling the fundamental dilemma

As intervening agencies, NGDOs face a core dilemma. On the one hand, they already have a mission, policies and agenda, while on the other authentic participation calls for starting with the situation and priorities of people themselves. Two approaches are usually used to resolve this paradox. In one the NGDO treats its agenda as short term and the people's unaddressed aspirations as medium term, but usually only the former is tackled. In the second, the NGDO begins by explaining its situation, mission and development principles; this approach is recommended.

The entry process and elements

1. *Building collective consensus on a shared mission.* The starting point, before any planning, is a mutual educational process where community and agency learn about each other's reality, vision and limitations. This is not brainwashing, but an honest explanation by the agency of the parameters which guide it. The purpose is to identify any common ground and shared principles; it is not a discussion about needs.

2. *Clarifying roles.* The NGDO's primary role must be the promotion of civic action and capability, which is not bounded by its own area of interest. In other words, the task is to create an atmosphere beyond plans and budgets, for example by advising on how other things can be done and where assistance might be found.

3. *Maintaining participatory values.* Forming community groups must not be treated as an activity, but as a strategy for controlling agreed activities – outside of or after the intervention.

4. *Ongoing learning.* Prior ideas, learning and negotiated activities must be open for questioning based on experience as it arises. This calls for mutually understood ways of judging progress and process and bringing this into dialogue on a regular basis.

5. *Tools for sharing the burden.* It is unlikely that an NGDO can cope with all of the aspects raised through a participatory planning exercise. This calls for prior knowledge of who else is doing what and where, and a preliminary exploration of possible collaboration, which is followed up in the planning exercise itself.

6. *Strategic links.* The NGDO must be in a position to form strategic links with others without losing its own values and orientation – for example, joining with local government in complementing local actions, interfacing with other agencies and so on.

7. *Asking the most difficult questions about performance.* Not defining what will be achieved is common but self-defeating. Clarity about the outcomes resulting from intervention is a necessity, as is identification and agreement on what will be monitored to guide and assess the process. Without such measures, mutual accountability will remain a contentious issue leading, eventually, to no accountability. For example, in planning to strengthen Panchayati Raj institutions in Gujarat, people were challenged to say what an ideal institution would look like and the measures they would use to assess it. They identified four sets of indicators related to characteristics of: effective membership, effective Gram Sabbas, ability to develop their own micro-plans, and well-functioning committees. Attributes for each set were elaborated as progress measures.

Source: adapted from a contribution by Binoy Acharya, UNNATI, Ahmedabad

Participation will also be difficult if the NGDO has not empowered its change agents by enabling them to use their best judgement in negotiation and decision-making. The need to continually seek permission for decisions also weakens change agents in the eyes of those they are working with, as well as being more costly.

Participatory planning is an entry method which NGDOs often use. Box 5.2 describes joint planning-based entry employed by UNNATI, an Indian NGDO. UNNATI's emphasis on beginning by 'collectivising' the mission is born out by a comparative study, where a shared understanding was found to be the most significant promoting factor in effective participation.[7] Reaching a joint guiding image is often cited when NGDOs specify the critical criteria for a successful entry process; this means change agents must be clear about what the organisations stands for as well as the limits to what it can do.[8]

It is unusual for an NGDO to obtain an ideal participatory situation where the poor are readily identifiable, homogenous and have sufficient capacity to participate and negotiate; where development priorities are not in dispute and correspond fully to the NGDOs competencies, strategies and ideal choices; and where the elite are not involved or do not interfere. More common is a situation where the NGDO must adopt steps to map and address these situations in incremental ways.

Funding which aids or constrains effective entry

Typically, donors want projects to contain information gained from participation before they will consider support, leading to a chicken and egg situation of either engaging with communities and provoking expectations, or not engaging and designing the project from best guesses. In either case, authentic participation is the loser, resulting in a greater need for compensatory measures in the next stage of the intervention, such as more attention to confidence building, adapting to local realities, dealing with elites and generating commitment for community ownership. The outcome is reduced effectiveness overall.

A dislocation between the entry process and subsequent flow is frequently caused by the way aid is allocated. NGDOs have to do a lot of preliminary work – which creates local expectations – without the assurance of funds being available later. So expectations often remain unfulfilled. And, let us be clear, expectations and ground rules come into existence at the first encounter between an NGDO and a community or group. Local effects of the entry process start then, not when a project has been approved. In short, if funding conditions are not appropriate, a crucial precondition for sound entry is not in place.[9]

Negotiating performance criteria: a foundation for effective management

NGDOs must be able to take on board and prioritise performance criteria which are meaningful for local people and their experiences. Negotiating local measures of success determines to a substantial degree whether interactions in the two subsequent stages are going to be fully effective or not. Projects using logical frameworks, unless jointly negotiated with all parties – including funders and primary stakeholders (which seldom occurs) – tilt the balance towards 'old-professional' definitions of poverty and criteria of positive change.[10] Mutually agreed performance criteria are also a prerequisite for effective management; amongst others, they are needed for delegating authority and for learning. This second issue is discussed further in Chapter 7, but it is useful here to illustrate what participant-based criteria might look like.[11]

ACTIONAID UK operates with a significant degree of delegated authority to its country programmes. In India, ACTIONAID supports local NGDOs in development work with communities, adopting up to a ten-year time frame for its assistance in an area. The entry process may itself take up to two years, as the local NGDO progressively negotiates with primary stakeholders on how it will engage with them, what will be achieved and how control will be allocated. Because of sponsorship funding, they are able to do so with the knowledge of what resources will probably be available over the whole period. The negotiation is meant to arrive at an agreement on mutual outcomes and indicators.[12] In addition to the usual indicators, such as an increase in immunisation and literacy rates, more locally applicable measures are agreed upon. For example, in Malarchi, Tamil Nadu, the amount of government funds accessed was considered important, as was an increase in earnings from collective farms and the retention of children within primary schools. In Mudhol, Andrah Pradesh, communities determined that a reduction in indebtedness to less than 2000 rupees per family would be a measure of positive change, in addition to a 20 per cent decrease in the days water was unavailable from locally maintained hand pumps. These criteria form the content of periodic review between the NGDO and communities, providing a basis for the monitoring and management information system. Without such measures, spending against budget and reaching target outputs would become the focus for management: an inadequate substitute for finding achievements and impacts.

Looking towards withdrawal

A final element in entry is to anticipate withdrawal. Negotiating performance criteria already sets markers for the conditions under which NGDOs will disengage. When this is not taken into account as part of the entry process – for example, in order to keep things open-ended, flexible or holistic – seeds of dependency can be sown, measures of performance do not set parameters for learning, and continuity of resources becomes the guide for action and progress.

Gaining a shared perspective on withdrawal corresponds to real life; external resources will not be available forever to every community. For NGDOs to ignore this fact is plainly unrealistic. It also works against empowerment because it can lead to the creation of a new patronage system which justifies sustaining the NGDO. Further, it can constrain an NGDO's ability to increase its coverage by moving into new areas. This creates pressure for continual expansion, which is difficult to achieve without losing

comparative advantages of flexibility. In short, saying 'goodbye' needs to be part of saying 'hello'.

Stage 2: reverse intervention: 'partnering', integration and consolidation

Progress and effectiveness in stage 2 has three main features. First is an action process – achieving the right mix of development-oriented interaction, which brings an organisational demand called 'reverse-participation'. Second is the building of local capacity to sustain benefits, enabling a shift of control to the local organisation. Third is reaching agreed objectives and benefits which initiate stage 3: withdrawal or renegotiation.

The action process

Development action is guided by the processes, objectives and performance measures agreed during entry. Micro-development objectives can best be reached by an incremental process of shared learning from experience produced through the successive cycles illustrated in Figure 5.2.

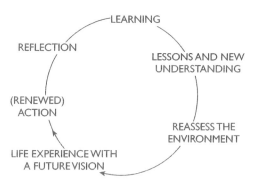

Figure 5.2 The cycle of micro-development action

Here, the sequential cycles of action-reflection can be viewed as a positive spiral running along the intervention curve. Each cycle is a step which shifts peoples' material situation with additional learning, increased organisational capacity and greater intrinsic power to deal with the wider world – the three elements of micro-development described in Chapter 1. For those tied to a project perspective, each cycle could be defined in mini-project terms, where each successive project is located within a wider intervention framework of entry, flow and withdrawal. At each step, time is allocated to look at what happened, learn lessons from it, reassess the external environment in relation to strategy and then define and execute the next action. The importance of environmental scanning is often insufficiently stressed and hence seldom built into logically framed approaches to development; however, it is vital for steering new steps towards the overall goal. Rescanning is an essential component of the strategic management stressed earlier. Experience suggests that with each step, people progressively take control and NGDO input lessens. Furthermore, through other aspects of their lives, local people make the link to processes outside the NGDO's control; this is critical for sustainability. For example, an NGDO intervention may have the goal of reducing infant mortality through expanding parents' nutritional knowledge. The same parents are also involved in making choices with their resources – for instance, which food they buy. Their altered preference for more nutritious foods will create a demand which may stimulate a new supply (as well as putting upward pressure on the price) and create a link to the market.

Consolidation occurs when people have improved their life situation, have increased their self-sufficiency, and when NGDO-related activity is integrated with other ongoing processes. At this stage the NGDO's external input has become firmly embedded in the lives of the local populace.

The organisational response: reverse participation

Organisationally, something distinctive happens if authentic participation occurs at the start of an NGDO intervention: the community or group intervenes themselves. In this way, the community's voice is heard within the NGDO system and, if all goes well, remains heard and acted upon with appropriate strength until the stage of withdrawal.

The principle of 'reverse participation' applies to the interaction between operational NGDOs and primary stakeholders as well as between donor NGDOs and their partners. This chapter concentrates on the first, Chapter 8 on the second. Figure 5.3 illustrates the mirroring of an intervention which should take place in operational settings. A 'mirror' occurs where the NGDO's 'extension' into communities is reflected internally by community influence on processes within the organisation. At each stage, it should be possible to trace how an NGDO reacts to what the community is saying and doing – as well as to other factors and inputs. Any effective NGDO should be able to explain an intervention in terms of the people's 'voice' within it. The 'all going well' noted above largely depends on systems within the NGDO, from change agents through PBS and management to the funding sources: the whole chain. In a typical large NGDO, funding uncertainty means that tentative agreements made between a CA and communities (often as shopping lists – prioritised if you are lucky) are weighed against other demands and the (sub)total calculated. The aggregation can go on for two or three levels – for example, community to region to country. The final demand is then set against available funding with other factors – such as political pressures, inflation, exchange-rate fluctuations, macro-economic conditions – coming into play. Cuts in demands are finalised and information passed down the chain to the CA, who has the task of informing the community of their luck in the draw and of any new conditions which may be attached.

The degree of authority delegated downwards and outwards dictates how hard primary stakeholders have to shout in order to be heard and to have real influence and control over the intervention, which is what authentic participation requires. Achieving shifts in relative power over decisions is the critical factor in the second stage of an intervention, complemented by mutually negotiated performance benchmarks. More often than not, however, monitoring is limited to NGDOs'

COMPARE THIS:

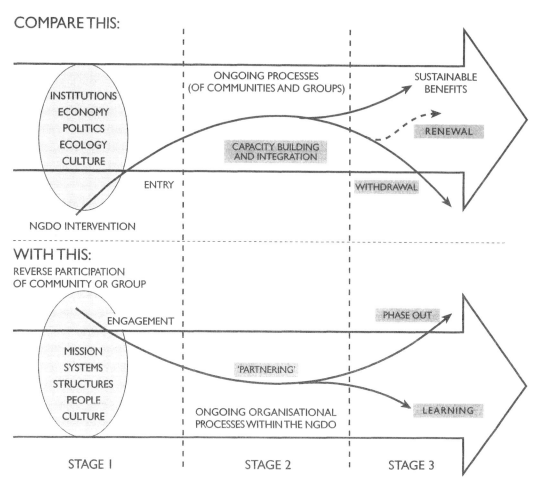

Figure 5.3   Reverse intervention

outputs and levels of expenditure against budgets, not to behavioural outcomes or impacts on well-being. Observation suggests that if the four types of entry preconditions detailed above have not been incorporated, the voices of primary stakeholders are weakened at each stage. People may participate initially, but their specific control or influence is progressively diluted.

The issue of 'ownership': shifting control to the local organisation

Stage 2 is the period of integration, consolidation and sustainable benefits that arise from a development initiative. The critical issue in this stage is to ensure that control over choices, decisions and resources made available by the NGDO becomes firmly rooted within the

community. In other words, the community or group 'own' the development process. If this does not occur, NGDO withdrawal will, as likely as not, mean stagnation, collapse, and non-sustainability of tangible benefits and other gains.

In technical terms, the challenge is to move the locus of decision-making and resource generation further and further out of the NGDO into community dynamics. When entry has been carried out with care, it ensures that those who should have most control within the community gain it, while minimising the risk of take-over or appropriation by the already powerful. Change agents are the key figures in estimating an appropriate pace and amount of movement for an NGDO in stage 2, guided by performance indicators negotiated during entry.

Three common trajectories of process

ownership can be found in development work. In the first, participatory processes and negotiation place control in the hands of the community with the NGDO having a modest say. The likelihood of this happening increases when the NGDO's agenda corresponds with people's real, rather than mirrored, priorities, and when capacity building is the primary objective. Paradoxically, starting with high community control may be easier to achieve for NGDOs, such as Njera Kori in Bangladesh, which concentrates exclusively on mobilisation, not providing any technical or financial inputs. The community is not, in order to improve its chance of support, seduced into reflecting the NGDO's agenda as its own. This type of NGDO is not tied to a specific type of intervention. In principle it can support any goal a local organisation sets itself, helping it to identify and access the resources needed.[13] Majority control starts and stays with the local people.

The second trajectory is more common where the external agency initially has most influence; this occurs when communities 'buy in' the NGDO's priorities. This does not mean that the intervention is not wanted or useful, only that it may not figure as highly in terms of local motivation, or it introduces choices which did not exist or were not valued before. A similar NGDO-controlled bias also arises when a new local organisation is created. The fact that it did not exist before, and must find its feet with an outsider's help, makes the trajectory to local capacity and ownership that much longer and harder. For the NGDO, this means more staff time, energy, patience and skill, as well as the strategic ability to let go – a process of self chosen disempowerment.

The third trajectory is the least desirable scenario, not uncommon in the official aid system, where an external agency dominates from the outset and is unable to shift power to those who must carry on whatever process has been initiated.[14] Reduced or no sustainable benefits is a very likely outcome.[15] NGDOs which have tight funding-dictated targets face the situation of starting with their majority ownership, which must be transferred. The shorter the time frame for this to happen – typically a one- to three- year project grant – the

less likely that transition will occur. Impact studies indicate that too often aid agencies are not skilled or around long enough to make the needed transfer, and no one feels responsible for continuity once the inputs stop. This is another reason why negotiated signs of community ownership are needed to guide and monitor the intervention process. Ensuring that ownership is where it should be, within the right people in communities and groups, is an important threshold for entering the withdrawal stage.

Stage 3: withdrawal with sustainable impact

Withdrawal is one of the least understood and documented aspects of development work and needs urgent attention. This lack of understanding occurs possibly because, too often, disengagement is not thought through but results from funds running out, donor fatigue, transfer of staff, or tiredness of the NGDO (which may have lacked clear objectives in the first place). Activities are also stopped because of aid cut-backs and for political reasons.

External elements create a more or less positive context for withdrawal to take place. Where government policies are supportive, for example in tax incentives and subsidies, thresholds to self-sustainability can be lowered. Similarly, where laws exist or state services are operating against which claims can be made opportunities for continuity increase. Where alternative economic niches have been found and have been exploited, new sources of surplus can ensure the continuation of benefits. Conversely, when the surrounding economic environment is in decline, primary stakeholders will be hard put to hold their own let alone improve their situation, which may mean renegotiating the original criteria for withdrawal.

While there is not much written experience to go on, observation suggests that two key factors play a role in a community's disentanglement from NGDO support. First is a demonstration of people's individual and organisational capacity to act autonomously, with the needed contextual links in place. Second is an NGDO's ability to strategically reduce its engagement and leave in the right way.

Links and community graduation

The few NGDOs which have adopted an intervention approach look at withdrawal as a process of 'graduation'.[16] What they mean is that mutually agreed objectives and performance standards have been reached, and the local organisation or community or group is increasingly capable of pursuing other interests beyond the intervention – shown, for example, by solving new problems and making claims on public and other resources without the NGDO's assistance. Indicators of this capability are:

- new initiatives undertaken without support;
- evidence of positive government responsiveness to legitimate demands;
- involvement in the development of local policies and input into the translation of higher-level policies locally;
- market engagement without being exploited;
- sustainable generation of benefits without NGDO inputs;
- continuity of membership with equitable distribution of benefits.

When this condition is near or reached, the NGDO begins to phase out and adopts a strategy of progressive redundancy or 'incremental disengagement'[17]. It moves from active involvement to being a trusted friend: there to be consulted when needed, a channel for information when necessary, a conduit to other actors when appropriate.

In practice, NGDOs seldom try to phase out by shrinking themselves; rather, when resources permit, they try to phase over into another area or community. This is typically achieved by change agents reducing the frequency and duration of contact while building up new relationships elsewhere. When potential relationships are too far away, staff transfer to new locations and their tasks are spread among those who remain – less difficult when a team approach has been in operation.

This sketchy story of withdrawal points to the urgent need for studies on how operational NGDOs leave their primary stakeholders. We need to better answer questions such as what strategies and steps for withdrawal work under what conditions? How far do prenegotiated objectives

and criteria assist in establishing future-oriented, *predictive indicators* of sustainability which can be used to manage a withdrawal process? It is time to make up for the lack of investment in learning about withdrawal as a critical part of externally supported development initiatives.

Saying goodbye

A common alternative to withdrawal is for NGDOs to renegotiate and start new initiatives with the same groups. This can occur so frequently that NGDOs never actually leave an area; this may result in dependency, operating in a rut, or having to help people 'unlearn' old behaviours and expectations as NGDOs try to introduce different and better practices. A difficult 'unlearning' must occur when NGDOs, which have initially given hand-outs or acted with too much largess during entry, begin asking people to contribute more. In other words, the NGDO tries to change an established, comfortable, patronage relationship which resembles parent-child patterns.[18] Moving to more equitable transactions is difficult for both parties, leading to accusations of changing the rules, thereby exposing the shallow rhetoric of partnership and the reality that people are not the centre of decision-making. Continuation becomes a bitter process, effectiveness drops and sustainability suffers.

Undesirable as this scenario might seem, it happens all too frequently. Why? Because an extended period of growth in NGDO funding has made it possible for agencies to stay on. Expansion and growth are simply achieved by intervening in new locations without leaving old ones. There is always a case to be made for continuity in development work, especially when there are no real performance criteria other than the ability to disburse according to budget, which has been the case up to now. Chapter 6 explains why an open-ended work agreement is less likely to be viable in the future. Increasingly, an NGDO's own continuity will be tied to its ability to phase in, demonstrate impact and then phase over. Staying for an unspecified time, usually until funding stops, is not good development practice, nor is it the way ahead.

Organising and Managing Relationships Between NGDOs

NGDOs maintain diverse interactions with each other, either because they want to or because they have to. A medley of names are used to describe different types of relationships between NGDOs and the mechanisms used to bring them about. Common are: partnerships, networks, alliances, coalitions, consortia and coordination (bodies). This variety suggests that relationships are a necessary and significant feature of NGDO life, which is rooted deep in the psychology of the sector and those who choose to work within it. The task is to find the key differences, if any, between these types of relationships in order to identify their consequences for NGDO organisation and management. We start with an important type of inter-NGDO relationship, called a 'partnership', usually between Northern and Southern organisations.[19]

Closing the rhetoric–reality gap in partnership

The notion of partnership between Northern and Southern NGDOs stems from the 1970s, when it expressed an ideological aspiration of international solidarity in the development cause. In the 25 years since then, the term has been used and abused as a blanket covering all sorts of relationships between all sorts of development agencies. Not only has this eroded the usefulness of the term, current trends towards contracting in the aid system are turning NGDOs away from the concept, especially in the South, where Northern counterparts are seen to have moved away from this principle. In the words of one European NGDO manager, 'the age of solidarity has come to an end, and the age of pragmatism and efficiency has begun.' Or, as put by John Slanger of IBASE Brazil, Northern NGDOs are 'swinging from solidarity to neo-realism'.[20]

The need for authentic NGDO partnerships

Overuse and the apparent abandonment of the premise of solidarity makes non-contract partnerships appear to be a waste of time. But this is not the case, for authentic partnership 'new-style', understood as mutually enabling, interdependent interaction with shared intentions, is still very much needed for two reasons. First, politically, this quality of national and international NGDO relations contributes to the 'social capital', which enables civil society to better deal with states and markets at all levels of their operation. Social capital is a recent term used to identify the self-willed webs which connect individuals, groups, communities, societies and other forms of human association. It is created from the networks of relationships and affinities people rely and call upon in times of joy or sorrow, surplus or need. It is the sum of trusted, reciprocal relationships between citizens and their associations at all levels of politics and economy. Evidence suggests that richer and thicker civic relationships generate greater social capital, enhancing society's ability to democratically regulate its affairs and increase prosperity, partly because acceptable ways of negotiating differences emerge and form a part of cultural heritage.[21]

Social capital is built up when people solve shared problems and satisfy economic, spiritual, recreational and other needs to levels which change over time. It is eroded when social trust and a sense of fairness is undermined by, for example, cut-throat economic competition, and worker exploitation; when personal interaction is lessened or destabilised by technology or forced migration; through ill-designed, dehumanising urban dwellings; and when politics is used as a divisive instrument. For those that can afford it, loss of trust is made good by insurance, legal contracts and sheltering in enclaves protected by armed guards. For those that cannot afford it, life becomes more insecure, weakening a commitment to legal non-violent norms of behaviour. The glue holding these extremes together is shared capital in society together with civic strength – understood as citizens' ability to engage as first among equals with the state and market institutions which are there to serve them. As social capital and civic strength are depleted, society falls apart in riots, in unregulated pollution and environmental exploitation, in unchecked sale of inferior or dangerous products, in state abuse of citizens' rights in the name of public security, and so on. From an NGDO perspective, building and countering the erosion of social capital must be a larger part of a future agenda.

But the ability of NGDOs to build social capital and civic strength will depend not just on their work but also on their own local, national and international capital. Relegating NGDO partnerships to willing-buyer, willing-seller of aid contracts reduces interpersonal and organisational trust and empowers the market at the cost of people's capacity for oversight and control of the society they live in. For NGDOs serious about contributing to better governance nationally and internationally, new-style partnerships based on a more mature understanding of solidarity are the way ahead, not contracts.

A second reason for being serious about partnerships and building social capital within the NGDO community is economic. In the language of economists, authentic partnerships can reduce transaction costs within the NGDO system which leads to greater cost-effectiveness.[22] When there is sufficient similarity and trust between parties, tasks can be achieved more smoothly, problems are dealt with more quickly because frameworks of interpretation are similar, understandings can be reached with less effort, and coordinated action is achieved more readily. Crudely put, reducing friction in relationships saves energy, improving efficiency and the NGDO's ability to 'heat up' funds (described in the next chapter). Formal agreements may define transactions on paper, but the self-protection, and lack of respect and confidence which a North-South NGDO contract culture implies calls for mechanisms of guidance, control and enforcement, which all bring added costs.[23]

Ironically, the present corporate search for alliances (which also use the label 'partnership'), rather than contractual relationships with suppliers and distributors, occurs at a time when NGDOs are induced to move in the opposite direction. This irony is bad for participatory socio-economic and civic development because a spirit of mutual trust between primary stakeholders and NGDOs is of more significance for effectiveness than letters of agreement. Forcing contracts down the aid chain inevitably impacts on the NGDO interface with those it assists. The next logical step will be for NGDOs, in negotiating with poor people, to include penalty clauses should they not sustainably develop their way out of poverty and injustice!

The long and short of the argument is that authentic partnership can deliver both political and performance benefits which NGDOs should not ignore. The quality of partnership is more crucial than ever if NGDOs are to remain part of the third sector and relevant to the global challenges set out in Chapter 9. How, therefore, can 'authentic' partnerships be achieved?

Past experience suggests that key organisational features between NGDOs influence the probability of attaining authentic partnership. Table 5.3 summarises these factors in approximate order of importance. When sufficient congruence and grounds for compromise exist, partnerships can arise which are authentic – for instance, premised on solidarity rather than on contracting. An important contextual factor is the degree to which NGDOs have a similar, recognised position and function in society. In the newly independent states of Central Asia, for example, NGDOs are not yet socially credible institutions. They are readily assumed to be fronts for the Mafia or businesses in all but name. Foreign NGDOs are also interpreted in this light – being seen as self-serving and exploitive.

Table 5.3 does not imply a cloning of NGDOs with each other. For the reasons given in Chapter 2, no two NGDOs are identical. Rather, Table 5.3 is a checklist which NGDOs can use together to critically look at their relationships; do the conditions for authentic partnership actually exist, or can they be established? The modest performance of NGDOs in realising authentic partnerships old-style makes such an exercise necessary. Again and again, Southern NGDOs observe that there is seldom an ethos of mutuality and reciprocity

Table 5.3 Organisational features influencing authentic NGDO partnerships

Rank	Organisational Feature	Explanation
1	Constituency	Owners and supporters are more likely to understand and endorse relationships formed with others having similar socio-economic characteristics.[24] For example, workers, professionals, and school children can more readily identify with their counterparts in other areas of the world than an affluent middle class does with the poor.
2	Beliefs, values and culture	Beliefs, values and culture determine organisational behaviour; the more these are shared the better the grounds for mutual respect and confidence, with less likelihood of major incompatibilities in other areas and processes.
3	Theory	Shared understandings of the cause of problems and of the way societies can be changed lead to consistent, mutually supported choices on issues of public policy.
4	Strategic choices and time scales	Shared strategies imply compatible views of the operating environment, with common goals and understandings about how long intentional change will take to occur.
5	Complementary strengths	Shared appreciation of what each has to bring to the relationship, in terms of competencies and comparative advantages, should work against disagreements on roles and divisions of labour – in addition to creating consistency between the rights and expectations of both parties, which reduces competition or duplication.
6	Development policies	Significant differences in understandings of best practice, usually translated as development or technical policies, can be the source of significant friction, especially amongst specialists, which leads to time-consuming arguments and mistrust.
7	Approach to gender	Compatability in the way gender is approached internally and in external activities reduces the likelihood of insensitivity.
8	Distribution of authority	Negotiation proceeds most speedily if those involved carry similar authority; referrals and consultations lead to delays and added costs.
9	Human-resource policies	Disparity between staff motivation, incentives and treatment can give rise to frustration, jealousy or envy, leading to negative attitudes which interfere with communication and sound understanding.
10	Adaptability	The ability to adjust to changing circumstances is important for development effectiveness; mismatches in this area create out-of-stepness, leading to a sense of agreements being taken for granted or ignored.
11	Fund-raising	Similarity in the way funds are viewed and mobilised leads to shared perspectives on accountability; this reduces friction and misunderstanding in a sensitive area.
12	Standards for legitimacy and accountability	A shared concern for, and combined ability to demonstrate, legitimacy should lead to higher donor confidence, giving improved continuity in funding and contributing significantly to joint effectiveness and accountability.

TIPS Each relationship needs to set out mutual rights and expectations as perceived by the parties involved. This is a simple exercise where each NGDO writes down the rights it believes the other to have and the rights it expects to receive itself. Where the rights of one party match the expectations of the other, problems should not arise. The areas of difference are likely sources of partnership conflict. For example, a Southern NGDO expects to be involved in the selection and veto of external evaluators, while the Northern NGDO does not see this as its right. Or, a Northern NGDO expects to have access to all information about the Southern NGDO, including areas it is not financing, while this is not seen by the Southern NGDO as a right. Listing and comparing rights against expectations is a quick way of identifying areas of agreement or where negotiation is possible and, if not possible, burying the partnership rhetoric and getting on with honest contracting.

Any Northern policy towards Southern or Eastern NGDOs should arise from a process of real, not token, consultation. Areas of disagreement should be recorded and published, as well as the policy itself. Such inclusion respects the input of those without the final power of decision-making and indicates where tensions are likely to occur.

Every evaluation, assessment or impact study should include appraisal of the interface between the Southern or Eastern NGDO and those further up the aid chain. The whole system must be included, not just the project or programme out there in the field. Adopting the principle that all transactions contributing to the project must be subject to independent scrutiny will reduce the present tendency to place the burden of performance on NGDOs in the South and East, neglecting preconditions set up by the North in the beginning. Knowing that such an appraisal will occur may help share responsibility, instead of contracts being used as shields or cut-off points against the critical review of everyone involved.

A fourth, perhaps too optimistic, step is for Southern NGDOs to emphasise that in the last analysis it is their work which holds the key to the legitimacy of Northern aid agencies. Northern legitimacy is what effective Southern NGDOs place in the scale of partnership as counterweight to Northern resources. It is a seller's market for aid in the sense of demand exceeding supply. However, Southern NGDOs which have demonstrated their competence, such as the BRACs, DESCOs, and AMREFs of this world, can and do exact compliance from Northern agencies which cannot afford to be rejected, in part because of disbursement pressures and in part because of the questioning which would arise about the merits of the conditions they are imposing. Interviews with leaders of NGDOs which are considered to be successful bring out the following criteria for Southern NGDOs in reaching real partnership:

➤ be sure of yourself, who you are and what you stand for, because 'good donors do not like you to be donor driven';[26]
➤ be credible by being competent – show results;
➤ have information at your fingertips;
➤ be transparent in your internal and external dealings – don't hide failure when it occurs;
➤ demonstrate that you are learning from what you are doing, then challenge donors to show the same.

The hardest challenge for Northern NGDOs who dare to use the term partnership will be to:

➤ move to measures of joint performance;
➤ exercise trust within performance agreements;
➤ move to partner-based, impact-oriented financing;
➤ share aspects of governance which affect both parties;
➤ seek partner concurrence with messages and positions adopted on their behalf;
➤ open up decision-making processes to partner scrutiny (an element of reverse-intervention).

within Northern NGDOs – differences in resources almost inevitably lead to donor-recipient, parent-child ground rules. How this structural difference can be changed is a topic central to the next chapter, but even a balance in resources will not lead to partnership if there are serious disparities in other areas too, such as the capacity to 'be yourself' and to act autonomously. The present concern with NGDO capacity building suggests that there are indeed significant differences in the level of organisational competence between North and South; these must be redressed if equity is to be achieved.

The point to be made is that the intervention principles for micro-development described above can also be applied to a reciprocal process of capacity building for mutually enabling, authentic partnership. It is not just Southern or Eastern NGDOs that need to improve; so do NGDOs in the North. Northern NGDOs must acknowledge what they get out of the South and East because 'to give without expecting anything in return becomes [another] means of expressing superiority'.[25] Furthermore, an intervention approach takes a holistic view of NGDOs in their socio-economic context. Instead of treating them simply as project carriers, NGDOs are valued for their civic features as well as their competence at providing development services. Finally, interventions should also lead to complementary self-reflection, the process needed for new-style partnerships. How an intervention framework can be applied to NGDO capacity building is described in Chapter 8.

With the above checklist in mind, NGDOs serious about partnership can decide if there are enough grounds to approach another NGDO to explore a reciprocal relationship. This may involve both making attempts to reduce areas of difference; trying to learn why a difference exists; and learning when to avoid partnerships altogether.

Renegotiating the present: matching NGDO rights and expectations

The notes and readings cite a growing number of studies on Southern NGDOs' perceptions of

the behaviour of Northern agencies, both non-governmental and governmental. After 30 years of effort, findings about the equality of North-South, and now Eastern, relationships show how deficient, if not scandalous, things still are. The gap between the rhetoric and practice of North-South interdependence has never been closed and appears to be widening as the balance in aid tilts towards second-sector values and practices. And it is not as if practical suggestions for improvement have not been made often enough – the 1995 study by Muchunguzi and Milne is but one of the latest to do so.

The tips (opposite page) reflect my own experience at tackling the relational issue and suggest ways of pushing forward a renegotiation of the existing, generally unhappy situation.

Other modes of collaboration between NGDOs

There is a virtual jungle of terms used to describe the ways NGDOs collaborate with each other. Cutting through the jungle, therefore, calls for organisational distinctions between networks, alliances, consortia, coalitions and coordination. While not water-tight, I have chosen to distinguish differences along a spectrum of 'costs' to NGDO autonomy – from complete sovereignty of decision-making and action at one extreme to (self-)enforced constraint at the other.[27] This scale can then be set against the organisational benefits made in return for limitations on freedom. In other words, the greater the perceived benefit, the more likely an NGDO will be to give up autonomy of action and/or take on additional responsibility for its action with others. The management trade-off is to reach the best balance between the two for any given situation. Figure 5.4 sets out the two scales. Horizontally, autonomy decreases from left to right, while benefits increase from bottom to top. In the area above the sloping line, benefits outweigh costs; below the line it is the opposite, costs involved in collaboration outweigh the benefit to an individual NGDO. The discussion follows the line from bottom left to top right.[28] Finally, it is necessary to know if collaboration is pursued with self-motivation or out of necessity.

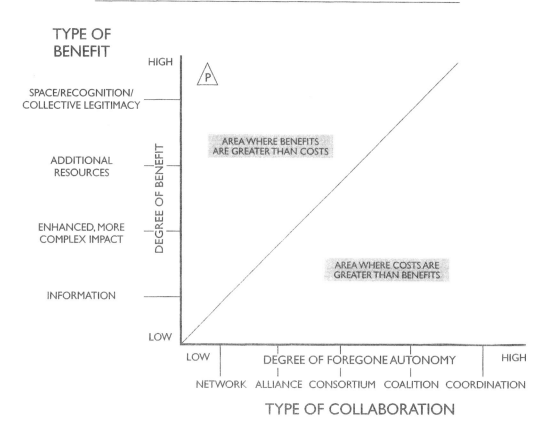

TYPE OF BENEFIT

SPACE/RECOGNITION/
COLLECTIVE LEGITIMACY

ADDITIONAL
RESOURCES

ENHANCED, MORE
COMPLEX IMPACT

INFORMATION

HIGH

LOW

DEGREE OF BENEFIT

AREA WHERE BENEFITS
ARE GREATER THAN COSTS

AREA WHERE COSTS ARE
GREATER THAN BENEFITS

LOW   DEGREE OF FOREGONE AUTONOMY   HIGH

NETWORK ALLIANCE CONSORTIUM COALITION COORDINATION

TYPE OF COLLABORATION

Figure 5.4   Trade-offs in NGDO collaboration

For example, the stimulus could be to counter a threat, as opposed to achieving an organisational gain – a situation arising when governments adopt a hostile stance to NGDOs.

The most common reason for weakness in NGDO collaboration is the inherent preference for everyone to be at point 'P', obtaining the highest degree of benefit with the lowest cost in terms of resources or reduced autonomy. The work of Jon Bennett on NGDO coordination (see Box 5.4) shows that NGDOs want the advantages this can bring but are seldom willing (and only able in special circumstances, such as emergency relief) to reach the compromises needed to make this happen.[29]

NGDO networks

Networks are the loosest form of collaboration in the sense that they function primarily on the basis of information exchanged between organisations, which is their primary benefit.

Members of a network can be quite dissimilar. For example, a logging company could and did sign up as member of an agro-forestry network alongside Friends of the Trees, an NGDO campaigning against logging.

A key feature of effective networks is the quality of their 'node': the point of network management.[30] Often this is an NGDO or small group critically involved with an aspect of development – AIDS, pesticides, large dams, children in difficult circumstances – who wants to take the lead in propagating its concern. The initiator(s) are not mandated by the membership which is essentially 'self-selected' and can come and go.[31] A network's value and utility stands or falls on members as sources of useful information to be shared. If the node manager brings together acknowledged leading actors in relevant areas, others are attracted, spreading the benefits of newly evolving knowledge and links, leading to improved action of all concerned. Networks become more effective as membership extends beyond an individual into their organisation as a whole. When this is not the case, there is little continuity in NGDO commitment as the person leaves. Organisational networking requires an NGDO to have awareness of the value of networking as one input to organisational action or learning, and internal systems with the capacity to give, take and employ information. Awareness stems, in part, from the importance of real-time information for the NGDO's work. For campaign and policy-oriented NGDOs – such as D-GAP in the USA, the Consumers Association of Penang (CAP) in Malaysia, PER in Thailand or special policy units in large international NGDOs, such as the various Save the Children Organisations and Oxfam – dependency on external information links is high. For most others, networking is one of the many tasks of a technical specialist, manager or leader. Consequently, because of time pressure, the tendency for many network members is to be recipients and translators of information, rather than active providers.

Networks are not, in principle, equal relationships. NGDOs may put more in than they get out and vice versa. In the words of Martha Arengo of CINDE, Colombia: 'Some people do the netting, others do the working'. Consequently, equitable participation can be hampered through jealousy or fear that ideas will be appropriated. North-South NGDO networks can also be a disguise for exploitive interactions, for example when Southern experience is appropriated to give added legitimacy to statements made by Northern NGDOs.

Network management has direct and indirect costs, as does membership. For reasons of administrative simplicity, donors have an inevitable tendency to fund one central point for network management. Where nodal costs are met by donors instead of members, as is usually the case, viability depends on the funder's perception that value is being added.[32] Member surveys are one way of ascertaining if this is the case. Less formal or decentralised networks operating as webs and clusters of interactions between interested parties – orchestrated but not resourced by a focal point – are more likely to be viable when donor interest inevitably moves on.

Membership in many networks can be an NGDO's way of gaining a high profile, which over time can erode each network's value.[33] During an organisational self-appraisal, when pushed hard, a South African NGDO concluded that it only really needed to be a member of five networks, not the 19 that it was part of.[34] Maintaining membership of a large number of networks can also be used for a false portrayal of an NGDO's status and legitimacy. My own observation is that NGDOs are not rigorous enough in restricting their energies to a small but optimum number of critical networks. As a result, their relational capacity is spread too thin but, more importantly, the organisation cannot properly process, apply and respond to the information and demands flooding in. Therefore, too many things are tackled ineffectively or tardily. A simple calculation of the anticipated number of hours required to properly engage in a network, together with internal dissemination and other actions set against the number of hours available to the responsible staff member(s) each year, may help sharpen the choice.

NGDO alliances

Networks can, and often do, lead to alliances between members. Alliances are essentially functional relationships where participants synchronise their efforts and resources. There is normally no question of compromising or modifying individual identity, even though synchronisation involves the loss of a certain amount of freedom of action. The benefit is broader, more complex and of deeper impact as a combination of forces and resources are brought into play in a more coherent way. Successful alliances depend on adapting and tailoring activities to the pace and style of others. UN Conferences have often provided a stimulus for this type of collaborative action.

Alliances in micro-development are becoming more common as NGDOs reduce their insularity, realise that they cannot do (or be) everything, and accept that a holistic view calls for complementary action with others. This appreciation is being re-enforced by the move towards an area-based micro-development approach. For example, in the Philippines, PRRM is forming an alliance with PLAN International to work jointly in an island province. On another level, the Kenya Alliance for Advancement of Children's Rights, (KAACR) is spearheading NGDO collaboration aimed at amending the Children's Bill submitted to, but subsequently withdrawn from, parliament in a barrage of criticism.

Looking back, observations were made about the rapid growth of credit provision by NGDOs. Given the specialist nature, skills and organisational culture needed to run credit programmes effectively, NGDOs with little history or expertise in this area appear to be forming alliances with micro-credit agencies so that communities can gain access to credit. The initial capital required to set up credit services may be provided by the NGDO or come from the credit agency's own resources. This relationship could be classed as subcontracting were it not for the fact that allies are essentially seeking complementarity, based on a mutual approach to development. Moreover, this initial goal can lead to a more complicated 'credit plus' collaboration where income generation is complemented by activities aimed at improved well-being through health education, access to family planning services and so on. Whatever the case, in alliances individual NGDO autonomy is only minimally constrained in terms of agreeing on mutuality within existing goals, timing and methods.

Other, more strategically oriented alliances occur to achieve micro-macro complementarity through NGDOs operating in these two areas. In this situation, organisational features of shared theory and mutual competencies become very significant for effectiveness. If potential allies are not like-minded on why, for example, poor people are poor, or why the environment is being degraded, together with a shared understanding of the role of macro-micro links in each case, there will be little foundation for effective cooperation.

While increasing impact through concerted action, alliances do not necessarily give rise to anything new in organisational terms, which is what starts to happen with the next type of collaboration: consortia and coalitions.

NGDO coalitions and consortia

With no general agreement on the use of collaborative terms, it is necessary to adopt a logical organisational distinction between coalitions and consortia which does not fully reflect current usage. Hopefully, this procedure is justified if it helps identify factors influencing effectiveness in each case. The similar feature of both coalitions and consortia is that they produce an organisational entity which is constituted by and is the legal responsibility of the founding NGDOs but does not have authority over them. This structure is common to federations. What differentiates coalitions from consortia are benefits more than costs. The principle benefits of consortia are increased access to, and better application of, (usually financial) resources which might otherwise not be available. In coalitions the principal benefits are increased presence, profile and leverage.

A shared limitation on NGDO autonomy is that consortia and coalitions demand acceptance of mutual accountability in two areas. First, the NGDO's behaviour must not come into conflict with the agreed purpose of the coalition or consortium. Once a position has been adopted on an issue, an NGDO must not act to undermine it by what it does or says elsewhere. Second, the NGDO is obliged to deliver on commitments entered into and shares the blame or costs when a member fails to do so. In other words, there is a joint liability for performance. Crudely put, consortia often have a grass-roots operational focus that seeks to move away from separated, small NGDO projects in a physical area or sector to a more comprehensive, joint approach for higher impact on an increased scale. In the words of consortium founder Juan Sanchez of CIED, Peru, consortia are 'closed inter-institutional spaces formed to design and carry out programmes, channelling [greater] funds from international cooperation.'[35] Box 5.3 summarises the place of CIED in a Peruvian consortium established to access funds for an integrated development programme.

> **Box 5.3**
> *Making consortia work: an experience in Peru*
>
> CIED in Peru is an NGDO founder member of a consortium carrying out a joint development programme with a focus on the environment. Forming and running the consortium brought to light the following organisational issues.
>
> 1. A significantly greater level of homogeneity is required of consortia members than is needed for networks; too little similarity in situation analysis, goals, styles and methods works against synergy.
> 2. In joint work, participating NGDOs have to modify their ways of working by:
>   - taking on shared planning norms and cycles;
>   - designing acceptable administrative methods and standards;
>   - agreeing on performance measures and ways of measuring;
>   - agreeing on personnel requirements and conditions of service which do not cause too much inconsistency with those already existing between participating NGDOs.
>
> Source: adapted from a contribution by Juan Sanchez B, CIED, Peru

---

Another consortium example comes from the Philippines, where 18 NGDOs and people's organisations formed NIPA (NGDOs for Integrated Protected Areas), with the express aim of accessing funds from the Global Environment Facility (GEF). With 14 staff, NIPA is responsible for identifying, financing and monitoring local NGDOs or other non-governmental bodies to initiate sustainable environmental programmes in ten vulnerable ecological areas. This takes place in collaboration with government and others agencies represented in protected area management boards.[36] In forming the governing body, NIPA's founders now carry collective responsibility for proper use and impact of US $27 million, allocated as start-up funds, as well as responsibility for mobilising the substantial additional funds needed for a full programme in each area.

A common drawback of consortia is that the constituent NGDOs seldom possess the extra internal capacity to carry and manage a new set of responsibilities. One reason is that the demands are just added on to the workload of the leader/managers of the founding NGDOs, without additional person power or finance included within their budgets. Consequently, the degree of active involvement in oversight is often weak, *ad hoc* and event/crisis driven.

Looking at consortia elsewhere, more often than not this type of load falls on the shoulders of the coalition's chief executive, with the governing board becoming less proactive once the start-up adrenaline has ebbed away. In short, uneven governance is a common factor inhibiting coalition effectiveness, with responsibilities which demand major capacity inputs not being shared amongst founders but shifted to the chief executive.

In distinction to consortia, coalitions can be seen as short- or long-term national, continental and global associations of NGDOs. They come together to promote mutual interests, creating a distinct entity for this purpose which may or may not formally register as a separate legal body. They tend to be established around specific development issues rather than concerns of the NGO sector. Coalitions do not necessarily have full-time staff. The required capacity can be provided by the membership, perhaps acting as a secretariat either permanently or on a rotational basis. Mandated by members, after consultation, to adopt and voice positions on their behalf, coalitions serve as platforms or fora for articulation of members' interests, but do not exercise any formal authority or sanction over them individually.

There is also no joint liability for operational performance beyond a shared loss of credibility.

A crucial organisational feature of coalitions is representation based on a governance system, which ensures active control by the members. The cost involved for members is the time, human capacity, information and investment in the processes needed to reach collective opinions on issues or on proposals, and then mandating the secretariat and office bearers accordingly. One benefit of a coalition is greater strength when voicing shared positions, together with enhanced informal access to information through trusted relations. However, benefits can sometimes be distant and diffuse – meetings and consultations do not lead to any immediate changes – while the costs remain real and seldom sufficiently financed; this leads to weak processes of consultation and consensus building, resulting in fragile mandates. Due to pressures of time and resource limitations, more often than not NGDO positions are glued together at the last moment by the few who are physically or financially able to attend meetings, which tends to exclude smaller organisations. Consequently, NGDO autonomy can be indirectly compromised if public statements are taken to be the prevailing opinion, when in fact not many NGDOs were actively involved in their formulation.

NGDO members of the World Bank-NGO Committee, which is not an elected body, face this problem by articulating what are often personal views, opinions, local knowledge and best guesses; these are then used to shape bank policy towards the sector overall or in specific areas, such as participation. Recognising this structural weakness, one of the biannual meetings was regionalised in 1996 in order to involve a wider spectrum of NGDOs. While an improvement, positions put forward during the other meeting with bank staff will not be binding on NGDOs transacting with the bank worldwide.[37]

NGDO co-ordination

Formal NGDO co-ordinating bodies usually operate along national lines. They offer significant potential benefits in terms of creating space and protection for NGDO work but may bring the strongest constraints on autonomy. The most far-reaching limitation on decision-making freedom occurs when NGO co-ordinating bodies can sanction and regulate NGDO behaviour by applying member-generated codes using moral pressure or the force of law. For example, CODE-NGO in the Philippines has a code of conduct for NGDOs which is voluntarily subscribed and must be adhered to through acceptance of membership. At the end of 1995, the National Council of NGOs in Kenya introduced a code of conduct, drafted by members and published in the government gazette. The code will be enforced by a special subcommittee of the council using statutory powers contained in the NGO Co-ordination Act. Other national NGDO co-ordinating bodies have or are drafting similar codes, which should ensure greater public accountability.[38] It is too early to know how well the principle of self-regulation will work in practice.

There are, however, positive counterweights to the constraining aspects of policing NGDO behaviour. For example, co-ordinating bodies are usually best placed to secure, protect and advance collective interests and help expand NGDO space – the freedom for civic development action. In some contexts this may be in opposition to governments, as occurred in Latin American countries during military dictatorships, or in competition with co-ordinating bodies set up by governments as instruments of control. Greatest impact and hence benefit to members occurs where a co-ordinating body enjoys an uncontested NGDO mandate and is recognised by government as the legitimate representatives of (part of) the community.[39] Further, NGDO co-ordinating bodies can help build and retain public confidence in NGDO integrity by showing transparency, concern and the ability to keep the NGDO house in order, from which everyone benefits. This can be particularly important where NGDOs are not a known feature of society, as in the states now independent of the former Soviet Union. A common additional benefit is fulfilling consortium functions described above: providing international links and voicing positions on behalf of members.

Virtually every country has an NGDO co-ordinating or umbrella body of one type or another. Exceptions occur in extreme situations where government is mistrustful of the NGDO community as a whole. An example comes from Rwanda where some 38 NGDOs were expelled and where the Humanitarian Assistance Co-ordination Unit (HACU), set up in 1995, is the only formal co-ordinating body in the country. NGDO co-ordinating bodies can also be quasi-governmental, set up, staffed and financed at arms length by ministries, a common situation in ex-British colonies. Others, such as ADAB in Bangladesh, ACBAR in Afghanistan, Ponleu Khmer in Cambodia, LNF in the Lebanon, CRDA in Ethiopia, GAPVOD in Ghana, the Colombian NGO Confederation, InterAction in the USA, and ACFOA in Australia, stem from and are backed by NGDOs without direct government involvement.[40]

At best NGDO co-ordinating bodies are able to minimise duplication and waste, mediate between contending forces and interests within the membership, articulate the community's needs and views on public issues, provide services which are widely needed but not suited to provision by one NGDO, and generally be an institution recognised, trusted, understood and respected by government, donors and the population at large. At their worst, they are instruments of coercion and control, used by regimes in power to ensure that NGDOs toe the line. Co-ordinating bodies may also be used as a platform by aspiring politicians or as a cover for political groupings or factions which misuse vague NGDO criteria or legislative vacuum to pursue their goals. For example, Cambodia and the newly independent states of Central Asia are both experiencing the registration of NGDOs by failed or aspiring politicians who then use all sorts of means to gain a prominent place in the co-ordinating body.[41] In the Lebanon, sectarian-based NGDOs have been co-ordinated along sectarian lines for many years. While in Afghanistan, Jordan and elsewhere, NGDO co-ordinating bodies have evolved through a process of internal struggle between ambitious individuals or groupings, sapping their strength and capacity to serve members.[42]

Organisational problems facing most NGDO co-ordinating bodies are: NGDOs do not want to be co-ordinated, in other words have their choices constrained or their conduct subject to sanction; different parties have contending demands or expectations which have to be balanced; funding is always insecure because members will not or cannot pay the full cost;[43] significant division between national and international NGDOs exists, making communication impossible; and factionalism may emerge in the absence of a shared external threat, which works against adopting common positions. Success in dealing with these difficulties is related to the quality of leadership; choosing the proper functions with the right mix of skills; the ability to talk different languages and address different needs; and the respect enjoyed by the staff as competent and non-partisan.[44] Box 5.4 summarises what is understood about effective NGDO co-ordination. Generally speaking, NGDO co-ordinating bodies are less effective if they do not enjoy support from the larger and stronger NGDOs in the country, which are often, but not always, international. However, bigger NGDOs can also highjack a co-ordinating body for self-promotion.

Box 5.4
Organising for effective NGDO co-ordination

Why co-ordinate?
Two fundamental reasons for co-ordination between NGDOs are:
- to minimise duplication and wastage through exchange of information and/or resources;
- to provide a mandated forum through which the collective consensus of NGDOs can be expressed to others, usually national governments, donors and UN agencies.

From this basis, co-ordination structures can also take on other tasks such as: facilitating divisions of labour with other development actors; playing a 'civic' role by pushing for greater space for NGDOs; guarding against encroachment; supporting small, new NGDOs by linking them to those with more experience; catalysing activities which may require a critical mass to get them off the ground; identifying NGDOs who may collaborate with donors; establishing guidelines for best practice and norms for proper conduct; acting as a reference point and analytical resource on sector-wide issues; and providing support services requested by the membership.

When does co-ordination work best?
While co-ordination is always a context-specific activity, the following items are commonly found where it is done well:
- NGDOs value co-ordination sufficiently to budget for it as a recognised activity.
- An agency is prepared to take the lead by investing in the required human capacity.
- There are complementary networks worldwide which re-enforce each other, particularly in emergency situations.
- A wholehearted approval and involvement in field co-ordination is reciprocated at headquarters, not overriding field directors' decisions.
- The individual leading the co-ordinating body has the right personality for the setting; sometimes a conciliatory figure is needed, other times a dynamic person to push things along and stand ground towards others actors.
- There is no perception of competition between a co-ordinating body and its members, in other words the co-ordinating body provides a value-added that only it can do, such as sector-wide information, analysis, publications and links to similar bodies elsewhere.
- The system of governance gives a mandate to act which is clear and widely supported.
- Co-ordination is treated as a learning process, moulding itself to emerging situations and member needs while looking around to see what is working well elsewhere and why.

Where NGDO co-ordination fails
NGDO co-ordination fails in the following cases:
- NGDOs only consider co-ordination from the perspective of self-interest – seeking benefits with no costs.
- There is rhetorical commitment to co-ordination at a policy level which does not translate down to mandates for field staff.
- There is insufficient delegation of authority with no agreed way of dealing with the internal NGDO demands resulting from co-ordination; everything is dealt with on an *ad hoc* basis demanding heavy communications traffic between the field and headquarters, frequently producing inconsistent, self-interested decisions.
- There is insufficient sensitivity by international NGDOs towards local NGDOs and the need for them to develop their own co-ordination dynamics in their own time frame.
- The demands of co-ordination in terms of resource inputs, especially staff time, outweigh the benefits.
- Junior staff are sent to meetings but cannot decide anything without top-level involvement; the process drags on and NGDOs who cannot wait go their own way.
- Collective decisions are not made (morally) binding; NGDOs can say 'yes' and do 'no' with impunity.
- Membership criteria is too broad and vetting is inadequate; this allows politically-aligned NGDOs to use the co-ordinating body for their own agendas, bringing neutrality or independence into dispute – this, in turn, provides an excuse for greater state control.
- Co-ordinating bodies become extensions of funders.

Source: adapted from a contribution by Jon Bennett

An example of a struggle to get coordination right occurs in Bangladesh, home to the largest secular, indigenous NGDOs in the South. Some 900 NGDOs link to the Association of Development Agencies in Bangladesh (ADAB) as the national co-ordinating body. Reaching this point has not been without its difficulties. While atypical in terms of an NGDO community, the ADAB experience offers pointers for dealing with internal tensions.[45] Smaller Bengali NGDOs, for instance, were feeling squeezed out by the indigenous giants, such as BRAC, PROSHIKA and GSS, whose expansion and insensitivity led to their projects overlapping, swamping smaller initiatives. An ADAB policy paper was drafted setting out a mechanism for prevention and agreeing on remedial action when a big NGDO interferes with the work of a smaller one. This is leading to a Memorandum of Understanding to be signed by all members. In countries where a small number of – often international – NGDOs dominate, this type of remedy could work against splitting and forming separate bodies (which occurred in Zimbabwe and Afghanistan). This may, in fact, be the best long-term solution, since the Northern NGDOs' role in the South is set to decline.

From 1985 to 1989 ADAB functioned as a funder to its members, which caused internal tensions because it became too powerful in terms of controlling the very members who should themselves be in control. A constitutional measure was introduced, preventing ADAB from channelling funds. However, because donors found it easier to deal with large sums, the perception arose within the small members that they were being cheated out of resources. A new initiative by ADAB to set up a legally separate channel is underway which would enable donors to fund credible smaller NGDOs in the country. During the past ten years, ADAB has relinquished support functions which could just as well be done by members, although training for smaller members is still continued. Guidelines for co-ordinating bodies are emerging, providing a bench-mark for preferred choices.[46] Some ADAB members have taken a more critical stance towards public policies which can be interpreted as leaning towards a more political, but not party-political, role. Other members have become uncomfortable with this move, preferring ADAB to return to its earlier, service-providing function. This tension was to some degree resolved when it was collectively agreed that ADAB should take a stance towards the gross abuse of human rights by the Ershad regime. A threshold was thus crossed in terms of acceptance of ADAB's role in linking development to rights and engagement with other issues of public policy. The governance of ADAB has moved from international NGDOs, to big national NGDOs, to small local NGDOs and then in a pendulum swing between them causing instability. The remedy was a constitutional amendment introduced in the early 1990s. Today, the constitution guarantees a maximum of four seats for big NGDOs, eight for small NGDOs, two for women's NGDOs and two for international NGDOs. In other words, ensuring fair representation with a highly differentiated membership may not be served by simple majority voting.

Co-ordination is notoriously difficult throughout the official aid system. It should therefore be no surprise that, with the far greater number of NGDOs affected and the imperative to preserve identity, NGDO co-ordination is a very difficult nut to crack. But, in my view, things are getting better. In most countries there are always a few NGDOs which recognise the great importance of co-ordinating bodies and are prepared to provide technical assistance and access resources for them. PACT in the USA is one example of an international NGDO concentrating on this area. Lessons are being learned, shared and applied. While a spur to competition, reduction in resources in some countries and more stringent criteria for access are pushing NGDOs together in search for common solutions and ways ahead. But, without external funding the viability of many co-ordinating bodies remains in doubt. Firmer support from members in cash and kind will be important for convincing donors that co-ordinating bodies are really rooted in local society and are adding civic and functional value to the NGDO community and its work.

Relating to governments

So far we have dealt with two types of NGDO relationships: to primary stakeholders and to each other. The third critical relationship for NGDOs is with governments, which often bring complicated conditions calling for complex organisation and management responses and development strategies.

There are many areas of significant interaction between NGDOs and governments other than funding. The scope for NGDO relationships with governments – both national and local – in the South and East is increasing by leaps and bounds. Collaboration, contracting and trilateral arrangements between NGDOs, governments and development financiers for project design and implementation are all gaining in significance for greater numbers of NGDOs. The basic trade-off for NGDOs in these relationships is balancing the dangers of co-optation, lessened autonomy and demands for conformity with approaches which may inhibit their comparative advantages with the benefits to be gained by influencing the way governments work and the increased scale and impact which state financing can give.

The principle concern of this section is not to explore what makes these relationships effective – the readings elaborate on this issue – but to focus on situations where governments are still averse to NGDOs as co-developers of society. In other words, what can NGDOs do to expand or make use of limited space for their work and to influence public policies where governments are not amenable to this type of activity? The following section is therefore about creating or making best use of limited 'development space' – for instance, enlarging the formal legal, political and administrative conditions which enable or constrain NGDO action, while simultaneously playing the informal rules of the game on which societies function.[47] The subsequent section concentrates on how an NGDO can impact on public policy and government behaviour in the South, East and North and on the international financial institutions which governments control.

NGDOs, governments and development space

Development space for all civic actors, including NGDOs, depends on the type and ideology of the regime in power. Rajesh Tandon identified three types of state distinguished by legitimacy and pluralism.[48] At one extreme are military regimes with no pretence to popular legitimacy or tolerance of non-sanctioned civic action. Then there are regimes with some form of public mandate gained through questionable means, with restricted choice of candidates (inherent to single-party systems common in Africa). Regimes also exist which enjoy popular support gained through a fair competitive or consensual process. Tandon points out the paradox that choosing a stance is easier towards autocratic and imposed rule than where the regime is legitimately mandated. The former calls for opposition, the latter for critical collaboration.[49] The competencies NGDOs require for each are quite different: a capacity for mass mobilisation, civic resistance and agitation in the former; innovation, technical expertise and demonstrable alternatives in the latter.

Where NGDOs are socially appreciated and legally recognised, explanations for government disapproval are seldom clear cut.[50] In part this can stem from the fact that governments are not monolithic, and a problem with one civil servant does not mean difficulty with the government as a whole. A common scenario is an ebb and flow of co-operation and tension within the high politics of state relations with civil society, punctuated by unpredictable events which trigger politicians, bureaucrats and other leaders into pro- or anti-NGDO attitudes. Man-made emergency and relief situations are particularly volatile, illustrated by government expulsion of NGDOs from Rwanda and Sudan. As as rule, governments everywhere are likely to be content and supportive when NGDOs substitute state services with their own funds. Discomfort grows in proportion to NGDO success in empowering people and in heightening popular demands for greater political accountability or transparency in public resource allocations.

A comparative study of NGDO-government relations in agricultural innovation identified five levels of government sensitivity to NGDO activities.[51] Governments become more discomforted as NGDOs move from 1 and 2 towards 4 and 5 in their development initiatives:

1. delivery of services and inputs;
2. developing new technologies and methods;
3. developing social innovations;
4. policy-level lobbying;
5. grassroots mobilisation and federation.

The level of discomfort with any NGDO activity depends on the characteristics of the regime in power. In Myanmar, for example, it does not take much for NGDOs to provoke regime hostility.

The previous chapters have assumed that space is available for NGDO activity. But what happens in situations where, for reasons of regime insecurity and/or ideology, autonomous action outside of the state is severely constrained or not tolerated? What can NGDOs do and what competencies do they need? The answer seems to be a leadership that can negotiate a *modus vivendi* with power holders; and an ability to 'layer' development work like an onion, with welfarist outer skins protecting inner strategies of sustained material improvement, community strengthening and empowerment.

Chapter 4 points out that, despite their best efforts (especially in the South and East) NGDOs are primarily identified by and with their leader(s). Old NGDOs which have passed through a number of leadership successions may escape association with an individual and his or her position with respect to the regime in power and in society at large. For the majority of Southern and Eastern NGDOs this is not the case. So, the ability to hold open space depends, in part, on whether the individual and his or her social group are perceived to be for or against the regime. Where politics is a function of clan and kinship, as in much of sub-Saharan Africa, the Philippines and other Asian countries, ethnicity may work for or against the NGDO. Where contending ideologies or mass action against dictators have shaped politics, as in Latin America and Asia, the individual's role within political factions and organised resistance may be more significant. Whatever the roots, the capacity of a leader to shield the NGDO's development work from active official harassment or passive administrative non-co-operation, is preconditioned by personal history. From this starting point, leadership calls for abilities to negotiate, to mobilise internal and external relationships as defence and to re-package explanations of what the NGDO is about.

As a development strategy, NGDOs can adopt 'layering', that is the promotion of welfare-oriented service provisioning covering empowerment-oriented activities and methods. In Kenya, after a failed attempted coup and government suspicion of any civic activity, the Undugu Society of Kenya (USK) had constructed six 'layers' of activity with corresponding levels of public promotion. The outer layer, given most publicity, was Undugu's work in care, shelter and rehabilitation of street children. This led into the next layer of an innovative approach to primary education, a three-year programme called 'education for life' which had won backing from the Ministry of Education. Counselling of slum-dwelling families in family life and health matters moved further inwards, away from individual street children into their social setting. Here, impoverishment was seen to be partially caused by endemic health problems due to poor shelter. People's ability to improve their living conditions was held back by insecurity of tenure and low income. Two further layers of activity, appropriate low cost building and business promotion and income generation were therefore added, but both built on a DELTA process of group mobilisation and conscientisation inspired by Friere. In sum, surrounding an inner core of DELTA-based group formation and capacity building were activities designed to: increase incomes, improve tenure and habitat, improve health status, provide education, and rehabilitate destitute urban children. Outsiders see welfare, insiders see a complex empowerment strategy.

In hostile political circumstances, autocratic regimes can attest their concern for social welfare by adopting and publicising NGDO work. Brian Smith, for example, argues that this was one reason why military dictators in Latin America tolerated an NGDO presence.[52] A decision against the NGDO, therefore, involves a loss which must be set against the perceived political gain which NGDOs can make use of without crossing an unknown tolerance borderline. This subtle, constant pushing against invisible boundaries can only be gained through professional experience.

Successful layering, however, makes a number of organisational demands. First, staff must fully understand each strategy and switch between them without feeling that they are being inconsistent. They must also work without confusing different stakeholders; in some cases groups receive welfare handouts, while others must contribute and mobilise their own resources. Third, staff must capitalise on the interest of local administrators or politicians in keeping welfare benefits flowing. Skilled management of donors is also required; the expectations of those financing welfare will be at odds with those expecting empowerment impacts. For example, welfare services can benefit from uniformity, economies of scale, application of standardised procedures and assessments against preplanned targets. These conditions are potentially in conflict with authentic participation and empowerment, which requires a responsive and flexible attitude. The result is an inbuilt tension which has to be consciously managed.

Another management consequence of the layered approach is that maintaining quality and evaluating impact can be complicated, as it becomes almost impossible to disentangle the effects of different layers. Finally, there is an inherent risk and tendency to slip into the 'safer' areas of welfare and technical delivery; this reduces the potential for friction with power-holders. USK's organisational solution was not to departmentalise its different skills and activities. Instead, teams with mixed capabilities worked together, taking the community setting as the reference point.

There are inevitable costs in efficiency when a development activity is carried out as part of a complex strategy versus implementation on its own. For example, a specialist NGDO running a credit programme for women is likely to have better credit/cost ratios than an NGDO which places credit provision within a mix of activities designed to improve the status of women by, for example, ensuring that increased female income does not simply lead to less male contribution. Similarly, family planning approached in terms of women's empowerment, as opposed to population control, will call for additional psycho-social processes that bring costs. The extra costs due to lessened efficiency can, however, be treated positively as the price of maintaining development space, which could be termed the 'civic value'. Donors not understanding or wanting to invest in this complex impact will push for higher cost-effectiveness, lessening the NGDO's room for manoeuvre and civic contribution.

Layering in response to government intolerance of NGDOs can also be found in an example from Thailand, a country which experienced a burst of NGDO registration in the short democratic period of the early 1970s. The Union for Civil Liberty (UCL) was formed in 1973 to provide protective support to families of people killed or being harassed after the October people's uprising. Its work expanded to providing preventive measures of civic and legal education to workers and peasants; however, it disbanded and its office was forcibly closed after the military coup of 1976. UCL restarted in 1979 with the same goals, but using the word 'humanitarian' assistance for its work, stressing cultural values and Buddhist religious teaching of love, fellowship and caring for others. Public attention was actively drawn to UCL volunteers accompanying monks on prison visits, cultural events, and fraternal exchanges with surrounding countries. Meanwhile, education on law, rights of association and training of leaders of mass organisations were set in motion. International events, such as the fortieth anniversary celebration of the UN Declaration on Human Rights in 1988, were used to get the notion of 'rights' accepted as a legitimate concern. Today, UCL's role is not just tolerated but accepted. It now plays a part in pushing for a local administration act which will decentralise authority to the *Tambol* level of administration; it also has been heavily engaged with setting up a house committee of human rights in the legislature.

Box 5.5
Creating NGDO space in difficult political environments: Malawi

Unless they simply provide relief or welfare services, there are many political environments where NGDO activity is treated with suspicion, if not direct suppression. This was the situation in Malawi from independence in 1964 until the early 1990s. Oxfam UK/I was therefore challenged to operate in ways which were tolerated and which created greater political space. The aim was to increase acceptance of non-governmental interpretations, perspectives and methods. Meeting this challenge called for analysis of where the political boundaries lay and strategies to expand them, without jeopardising the position of the Malawians involved. How was this achieved?

Assessment of political boundaries
The first step was to determine where political boundaries lay. This called for three levels of analysis: of Oxfam itself, of the regime in relation to society and community, and of the situation facing individuals. Oxfam staff reviewed where the organisation was competent and weak, its standing with the Banda regime and possible points of influence. The organisation was known for its support to health care through the Private Hospitals Association of Malawi – essentially a health education programme which provided legitimacy and potential for new initiatives. A review of the regime considered the political culture in terms of power base; looked at strained relations between traditional and modern authority structures; created a profile of insiders and excluded groups in the population; distinguished potential allies and opponents within government departments; and identified areas of sensitivity, one of which was the refusal to recognise the existence of poverty in the country. At the level of individuals, Oxfam examined party oversight on decision-making; the role of the Special Branch and Young Pioneers in ensuring loyalty and suppressing discontent; the influence of local women's league members; people's appreciation of limits to their expression; and male-female differences in representation. Based on the assessment, Oxfam proposed to push against the regime's denial of poverty by gathering and bringing firm evidence of rural deprivation into the public arena.

The strategy
Using previous experience, Oxfam's strategy centred on an action-research programme (ARP) in the Mulanje district involving a variety of tribal groups and agro-climatic zones. Six Malawian researchers were trained in a 'listening survey' approach to data gathering and then lived in villages for four months. Using flexible, question-based guidelines which included ways of recognising power, authority and status, their task was to observe, learn about and document daily life. From the outset, villagers' personal expectations were minimised by emphasising that findings were intended to help the government and other agencies in their planning for the district. Theatre was used for community problem analysis, as well as a method for feeding back and testing findings common to other villages.
Government staff were told about and approved the exercise, seeing it as an academic study by a small agency. By buying into the approach, civil servants (some of whom were sympathetic) were later less able to deny what was reported. Continual information from the study to the World Bank and UNICEF also made it difficult for the government to stop the activity or cover up its results, and these agencies brought leverage to bear when it came to accepting and implementing recommendations. While the Malawi government would not allow the word 'poverty' to appear in the title of the final report, it could not suppress or refute the findings because draft versions were already in the public domain.

Lessons learned

● It is important and useful to identify political, social and organisational boundaries for action.

● Governments are not homogenous. Some civil servants are seriously concerned about poverty and will say so in private. Their tacit support is a valuable asset which will not be available if a policy of non-engagement is adopted. Boundary assessments discover these hidden assets.

● Timely engagement with more powerful actors, such as multi and bilateral agencies, can offer significant multiplier effects and ongoing cover.

● Research methods which listen to and which share information between villagers can widen understanding about the mutuality of problems which cross perceived divides, such as ethnicity, raising awareness in the process. They also facilitate people's inputs into the development planning processes, which are blocked by other systems.

Source: adapted from a contribution by Hemansu-Roy Trivedy, SCF/UK, India

---

Box 5.5 describes another approach to working in a confined development space, this time by an international NGDO, Oxfam UK/I in Malawi.

Influencing government policy and behaviour: what competencies do NGDOs need?

In addition to expanding development space, another reason for NGDOs to engage with governments in the North, South and East is for leverage – influencing their behaviour and policies. This ability will be even more critical in years to come and is explored in detail in Chapter 9. The competencies and organisational requirements for exerting influence on public policies inevitably differ from those of micro-development, but it is necessary to link the two in order to bring people's 'testimony' into the process. In this way, NGDOs qualitatively differentiate themselves from others, such as paid think tanks or academic policy-studies centres, which also have policy opinions or agendas. This section identifies factors which contribute to successful influencing of public policies and which apply generally to all NGDOs.

An Indian administrative officer, Azeez Khan, on secondment to PRIA in New Delhi in 1996, studied cases of direct policy advocacy by NGOs in India, as well as experiences elsewhere, identifying factors which impact on their effectiveness. Box 5.6 summarises the findings from his study.

Box 5.6
Effective NGDO policy advocacy

Definitions

Azeez Khan defines policy broadly as 'the instrumentalities and actions which are deployed to define the framework within which social actors act or get things done'. From this perspective, direct policy advocacy is 'focused and deliberate efforts to influence the approach and instrumentalities by which major institutions and other actors impinge on public life.'

Requirements for effective NGDO advocacy

Using 'selling on the market place of ideas' as an analogy, NGDOs that are effective at influencing state institutions are those who:

● are credible as advocates, with equally credible products and packaging;
● have wider backing from other social actors; and
● adopt an appropriate sales strategy.

These factors define the competencies needed.

Credibility as an advocate: The seriousness with which NGDOs are treated as advocates depends on:

● the NGDO's standing in society;
● demonstrated experience, professionalism and work record relevant to the issue at hand;
● the 'usefulness' of what the NGDO has to offer in terms of analysis, expertise, on-the-ground information, access to relevant constituencies, and support from a particular party in a policy conflict;
● motives, is advocacy really for the public good?
● source of funds, with foreign finance a cause for suspicion;
● application of foreign funds (in as far as external support for campaigning will undermine legitimacy of the message);
● independence from political parties;
● size and/or visibility;
● reputation with other actors, easing access to bureaucrats or political power-holders/brokers.

Credible agenda: This is the policy change being pursued and its likely reception. Little or no conformity between the government's existing objectives and what is advocated offers scant common ground for dialogue; here public protest may be more apt. Where sufficiently similar goals exist, the government must be induced to believe that what is proposed by the NGDO:

● is capable of achieving objectives better than existing policies;
● has gained reputable independent validation of its merits;
● emerges from or clearly relates to a significant section of the affected constituency;
● is realistic and feasible, cost-effective and sustainable;
● is implementable in incremental rather than radical steps allowing adaptation, which often calls for the NGDO to be ready to compromise.

Credible packaging: In addition to coming from a credible NGDO, an advocacy strategy must project appropriately towards policy-makers, opinion-makers, own constituency, allies and even opponents. Presentations and projections should be designed to:

● make evident the depth of study and consideration of other interpretations and opinions;
● stress arguments and perspectives which would attract the greatest number of allies;
● project the issue rather than the organisation, including the use of other people's platforms;
● carefully involve and, where possible, direct or guide media attention.

Many 'backers': Breadth of support determines how many fronts and pressures policy-makers have to deal with at once; generally speaking the more the better. To this end:
- identify, develop and activate as many (personal) allies as appropriate;
- while focusing on the issue at hand, get others on board who push issues with the same policy-makers or institutions;
- recognise and use the heterogeneity of the state and competing opinions of groups within it;
- establish contacts while targeting key players.

Appropriate sales strategies and tactics: In as far as NGDOs have correctly analysed existing circumstances, significant policy-actors and emerging opportunities, on the one hand, and identified necessary policy changes on the other, how can this agenda best be put forward?
1. Make use of changes in key players or in other external forces within society.
2. Match the advocacy strategy to the organisational strength of the concerned interest groups:
- adopt mass constituency mobilisation when the groups are strong;
- adopt more informal pressures on key personalities and powerful decision-makers when interest groups are weak and the degree of harm is marginal.
3. Adopt or switch between a 'campaign' mode of short, intense activities versus a 'programme' mode of fewer, longer-term, measured pressures.
4. Investigate public interest litigation, which is a further advocacy path, but one which exerts high professional demands in terms of research and conformity with rules; it also contains potentially high risks in the event of negative judgements which may close off other legal possibilities, provide extra ammunition to opponents and encourage greater resistance amongst policy-makers.
5. Turn to the legislative arena, which offers a further advocacy potential; it elevate issues to a public platform which can involve presentations to parliamentary committees, prompting Private Member's Bills, letter-writing drives to pressure elected or prospective politicians and so on.

Making the right (combination of) strategic or tactical choices hinges on the mix of competencies an NGDO has or can mobilise, together with a sound assessment of opportunity costs – assessments which are hard to quantify.

Source: adapted from draft by Azeez Khan, 1996, Part V

From this analysis, at least six types of organisational factors can be identified for effective policy influencing. These are: untainted leadership, development legitimacy, corresponding analytical capability, relational capital, professional competence as advocates, and ability to document.

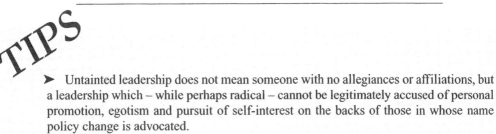

➤ Untainted leadership does not mean someone with no allegiances or affiliations, but a leadership which – while perhaps radical – cannot be legitimately accused of personal promotion, egotism and pursuit of self-interest on the backs of those in whose name policy change is advocated.

➤ Development legitimacy derives from the quality of the work being done, with practical alternatives to existing policies being one of the most powerful features for leverage.

➤ Analytical ability. To be heard by policy-makers, NGDO staff have to be able to use compelling arguments, which usually calls for high levels of abstraction and analytic powers often spanning more than one discipline; because professionals feel a natural affinity towards those with the same training, they are more likely to listen to and respect NGDOs who provide a professional match.

➤ Relational capital is built up from collaborative experience, generating the trust which can be drawn on when mobilising pressure on many fronts. Creating this capital requires previous investment in networks, coalitions and exchange of assistance. While opportunistic links are obviously useful, they cannot be relied on in the same way.

➤ Professional competence as advocates. Policy influencing is also a specialism where professional competence is vital. This includes: intellectual integrity, good interpersonal, verbal and written skills, links to a variety of organisations including the media, an ability to conceptualise complex processes, a sound grasp of technical details and evidence, good judgement of timing for actions, and a clear analytic framework. Also critical is respect for those at the periphery who are not in the public eye, but on the edge where the struggle to reach the organisation's mission is less glamorous, conditions are harsher and personal harassment is a real concern.

➤ Documentation ability. Often NGDOs need to prove what leaders and officials have said or committed themselves to, which calls for the ability to document information and retrieve it accurately.

A neglected element: influencing directors of development banks

There is a growing trilateral collaboration between governments, NGDOs and international financial institutions (IFIs), such as the World Bank and regional development banks. Influencing policy in IFIs must therefore become a part of the NGDO repertoire. The World Bank-NGDO committee is one example of a forum for policy dialogue about bank practices, but this has not (yet) been systematically complemented by applying pressure at the governing level.

Northern governments have a controlling interest in the boards of the World Bank group and IMF and also exert significant influence as minority shareholders, but major backers, of regional development banks in Africa, Asia and Latin America. For the global IFIs, Northern governments appoint individuals as directors to sanction policy, approve lending and, together with shareholders, hold IFIs accountable for their operations. At present, these key figures are virtually unknown to their national NGDO community; criteria for their selection are questionable, while appointment and monitoring is a closed administrative process. Instructions they receive are considered secret, yet the funds they oversee have been obtained from taxes, and legally they operate as public bodies which should be open to public scrutiny. Overall, mechanisms for supervising these guardians of public funds and policies are far from transparent or accessible. Such an important element in the official aid system should be as subject to public scrutiny and influence as are governments, donors, IFI managers and staff. This is not, yet, the case but could be.

Box 5.7
Accessing directors of IFIs

Tips for accessing directors of international financial institutions

To start, NGDOs should ask the appropriate ministry for written clarification of selection and appointment, followed by an explanation of the way in which instructions are arrived at and performance is assessed. Consultation with NGDOs in this process could then be negotiated. A myth is maintained that when they are appointed, IFI directors detach themselves from their status as national civil servants and employees of their home country. Consequently, there is no procedural requirement for public access to go via the nominating government. Nor are there barriers to lobbying and approaching the director directly, email is one simple method. A dual approach, involving contact through the home country government and direct communication, would probably be most effective.

Before embarking on this or any other approach, however, NGDOs in North, South and East, would be well advised to do their homework in terms of understanding the role, authority and working methods of directors in each of the IFIs. It is pointless starting with unrealistic expectations of the influence directors have in practice, for they are constrained by intergovernmental politics and the information staff make available to them. Directors can rightly question not just the legitimacy but also the accountability of those who take it upon themselves to exert influence. NGDOs who do not have a demonstrable domestic constituency, described in Chapter 2, must be prepared to provide good answers, in practice as well as on paper.

Whatever the target – governments in the North, South and East, bilateral donors, development banks, commercial enterprise – the effectiveness of NGDO efforts to influence will be affected by their sources of funding. Money can have a significant steering effect on NGDO behaviour and credibility. It is time, therefore, to detail the capacities NGDOs need to mobilise resources and manage the relationships and dilemmas which come with them in all aspects of development work.

6

Mobilising Financial Resources

NGDOs differ from government and business in the way they raise money for their work and for their own organisational viability. They must find ways of accessing an economic surplus produced elsewhere because development with poor people does not generate what they need. Northern and Southern or Eastern NGDOs differ in the number of potential sources they can tap. This chapter looks what the sources are, how NGDOs access them and trends affecting the fund-raising capacities they require. Money from different sources has different characteristics, or qualities, in relation to development work. In addition aid funds have different temperatures which influence NGDO effectiveness. These two characteristics are employed to assess the sources that an NGDO can access.

Unfortunately, Northern NGDOs have created a mine-field for themselves by convincing the public that sustainable development is quick, simple and cheap to achieve, which is not true. The public's perception that NGDOs operate at low cost leads to a permanent fear of being found-out. Suggestions are made about dealing with this anxiety. Aid sources can 'steer' NGDOs by tilting their priorities and worries away from voluntary people-centred principles in poverty reduction towards a concern for their own survival in a contracting market place. This chapter suggests how such a prospect can be avoided.

Characteristics of Financial Resources for Sustainable Development

In addition to quantity, aid for development has two other characteristics which influence NGDO effectiveness: quality and temperature. These features can show why NGDOs behave as they do, the dilemmas they face, the capacities they need for fund-raising and the risks they run in mixing funds as money supply changes.

The quality of aid

At its simplest, quality is the degree to which aid resources match the demands of best practices in participatory development. The greater the constraints on best practice, the lower its development quality. Six factors contribute to the quality of aid funds for NGDOs. These are:

- conditions and expectations of the giver (especially respect for NGDO autonomy);
- method of allocation;
- level of administrative burden;
- predictability and reliability;
- continuity and necessary duration;
- timeliness in disbursement.

This section looks at each. For ease, the term 'donors' will be used for professional funders within the aid system, 'contributors' for the general public who voluntarily support NGDO work.

Funding conditions and expectations

Most aid comes with conditions and

expectations. In technical terms, funds are 'tied' to requirements which can range from loose and open-ended to tight and stringent. Explicit conditions tend to be set by professional funders and are usually written into proposals and funding agreements. Expectations relate more to the general public who are motivated to support an NGDO's work, equivalent to moral rather then written contracts.

The positive impact of conditions is that, when right, they increase effectiveness. But when they are wrong, the opposite occurs. In both cases, donor conditions can cause unwanted organisational effects on NGDO autonomy, identity and capacity. For example, it is very unusual for donor conditions not to compromise independent organisational decision-making to some degree. Setting the right conditions is probably the most critical factor to a donor's professionalism. An ability to match funding conditions to the recipient organisation determines whether or not assistance leads to effective, sustained poverty reduction. When official aid agencies try to apply government-to-government conditional styles and practices to NGDOs, the results are generally disappointing.[1]

Appropriate funding conditions are equivalent to extra capacity in terms of creating a more professional NGDO approach and should be welcomed. However, inappropriate conditions undermine an NGDO's own knowledge and professional capacity. To stop this happening, NGDOs must be secure in, but not arrogant about, their own knowledge and understanding of what is best practice in their situation. This capability comes from a strong identity and an active learning from proven experience. Without these two, NGDOs are in a vulnerable position when negotiating conditions.

'Tying' assistance can have a negative effect when the problem an NGDO wants to address can only be seen in terms of the solutions and expertise known and available to the funder. This effectively disempowers the recipient and may result in poor-quality or expensive goods or services. When Southern NGDOs cannot shop around, tied aid acts as a constraint on best performance and typically increases costs.

Donors rightly set conditions on the authenticity and accuracy of financial and narrative reports. Unfortunately, by insisting on their own format, donors complicate an NGDO's system of financial management, making it more costly. Reporting on multiple formats, often over different time periods, is so common a problem for NGDOs that much of their management energy goes into this, at the cost of attention to development. A typical donor assumption is that its wider experience gives it an implicit right to influence, if not dictate, design. Comparative experience gets greater value than local knowledge. In Colombia, CINDE wished to adopt an indirect education-based approach to tackling the problem of empowerment under a military dictatorship. Their Dutch donor would only fund a direct activist, popular mobilisation approach. Only after activists were assassinated did the Northern agency come around to accepting the merits of a more subtle strategy.[2]

In short, finance which comes with strategic, operational, economic and political conditions and assumptions which do not match the situation, or respect the autonomy of local NGDOs, lowers the quality of donor resources.

Contributors' expectations differ from professional donor conditions because they are created by NGDOs as they go about fund-raising. Messages are sent and images are created which lead individual givers to expect certain achievements for their support, an implicit contract which an NGDO must satisfy. For example, in the late 1980s Catholic Relief Services (CRS) in the USA suffered major negative publicity when it was discovered that millions of dollars raised for humanitarian relief in Ethiopia had not yet been spent, but were sitting accruing interest. There were good reasons why CRS was not spending; adopting a development-oriented relief strategy calls for care and time. But this appeared contrary to the public appeal, which stressed the immediate dire need for money: 'give your gift today, tomorrow may be too late'.

As a result, NGDOs must have the ability to communicate in ways which generate a feeling of personal obligation without creating false expectations which the media might expose.

NGDOs which invest in development education have less to fear about, which increases the quality of the funds they raise.[3]

Funding Methods

Project-based finance can seriously reduce the quality of aid funds for people-centred sustainable development. Recognition of the drawbacks to project aid has initiated experimentation with other ways of allocating finance. The most common innovations are programme-funding agreements between governments and Northern donor NGDOs,[4] but less frequently between these NGDOs and their counterparts in the South and East.[5] This type of cooperation increases flexibility as well as an NGDO's control over decision-making.

Programme funding of NGDOs – a block of money allocated within an agreed framework for a known period – is a major step forward which should be expanded, especially North-South, but can also have quality limitations. First, the framework of a programme agreement can import donor-dominated priorities, such as gender, urban development and the environment. Second, an intermediary NGDO can act as a proxy for the donor by taking on responsibilities which do not belong to them. Third, an intermediary is added in the chain, introducing new costs and problems.[2] Fourth, when donors naturally ask for specific performance criteria at the end of the programme period, they impose a demand which they cannot usually satisfy if they do the work themselves. Moreover, in order to generate the necessary performance information, the intermediary must allocate finance on a project-by-project basis. In other words, the quality benefits of programme funding are lost as projects reappear further down the chain. Without doubt, greater attention must be paid to performance, but as the next chapter shows, care must be taken on how this is implemented.

Administrative burdens

Money causes paperwork. Logic would suggest that the better the paper definition at the beginning, the less need there is for further reporting. This does not occur in practice because a highly detailed design generates more items on which to report. Therefore, as a rule of thumb, the greater the amount of paper required to obtain a grant, the higher the administrative burden. High-quality donors recognise and make few extra demands on the administrative system already in place.[7] (An associated issue is that costs of donor-specific administration are seldom met in full because official aid is generally averse to financing organisational overheads.)

As the amount of paperwork and administrative energy per grant grows, the number of grants that can be given per staff member decreases. Consequently, disbursing the annual financial allocation calls for an increase in the average size of a grant or the introduction of a programme which shifts grant-making along the aid chain. In other words, the economics of grant or loan administration push towards big rather then small funding, which does not match most community-based needs. When donors are under pressure to disburse and staff turnover is high – which always seems to be the case – NGDOs face the burden of educating new incumbents. Although the situation is improving, too often official aid agency personnel have little if any exposure to NGDO culture or practices.[8] Satisfying administrative requirements and coping with inexperienced, transient donor staff can be an enormous quality-reducing burden on NGDOs. Moreover, this burden is seldom financed.

Predictability and reliability of funding

A precondition for effective development initiatives is that the resources needed during negotiation will be available over the long term. In other words, NGDOs must be able to operate on the firm assumption that predicted incomes will be raised. Guaranteeing incomes or resources years ahead is never easy. Official aid agencies with tax-based incomes can probably predict for the duration of an electoral cycle, but even that is less certain today.[9] Foundations raising income from prudent investments are probably in the best position in terms of predictability (Black Monday aside).

Predictions on public fund-raising are very difficult. For example, in 1996 Save the Children Fund UK and Oxfam announced income shortfalls of £9 and £5.6 million respectively. Internal solutions designed to increase reliability, such as reserves and contingency funds, are constrained by the fact that contributors expect the money they give will be spent soon and not invested. The financial management skills required by NGDOs dependent on public fund-raising and dealing with fluctuations with many currencies are awesome, and market rates for people with the necessary skills usually put them beyond reach.

Reliable funds are those which remain secure once they have been accessed, depending on where the donor gets them from. Northern NGDOs structurally funded by their governments enjoy pretty reliable funding. This is especially true in Scandinavia, the Benelux and Germany.[10] Child sponsor funds call for substantial initial effort, followed by attention to maintenance. Once the investment in mobilisation has hooked a sponsor, keeping them costs much less. In all cases, long-term reliability depends on NGDOs' capacity to continually satisfy donor needs through high performance and information.

In sum, high-quality incomes are those which can be predicted for many years to come, are generated in such a way that they can be accessed or paid out when needed, and are reliable. Endowments come close to high quality as do annual bequests from the estates of people who have died. Needless to say, there is not a lot of this type of money around. Unpredictable and unreliable funds are those which, for example, come from specific appeals and actions, donor fatigue setting in if they occur too often or are too similar. By and large, NGDOs work in the world of unreliable funding.

Continuity and necessary duration

Reliability, that is an assurance that donors will have always have access to the funds they give, is different from continuity. Continuity is the ability of the funder to ensure the support an NGDO requires as long as it demonstrates its merits while progressing along an uncertain road. Where decisions about funding are dominated more by internal donor considerations or domestic politics than by NGDO performance, continuity is threatened in a way that the recipient can do little about. Financial resources which are not allocated on the basis of performance but on fashion, self-interest or donor politics are lower in quality than those that have a long-term continuity tied to proven impact.

Project-based funds are typically one to four year grants. One reason for this convention is so that project performance can be evaluated towards the end while a new project is negotiated. This practice also builds in an exit possibility for unreliable donors. Stakeholders and staff are therefore in a state of insecurity from the word go, which can naturally lead to ambivalence in their commitment. Furthermore, evaluation becomes a threat or a ritual to justify donor decisions already made rather than a tool for learning. For most types of sustainable development work, short-term money without performance-assured continuity is low in quality.

Timeliness in disbursement

A common lament of NGDOs, especially in the South, is the poor time-keeping of their funders. Delayed disbursements usually have no penalty to the giver, but cause enormous headaches for recipients. Unless recipients have substantial flexible reserves or overdrafts – which is not likely – the solution is to cross-finance from other sources, which upsets auditors.[11] Cross-financing also means reduced transparency and increasing stress for managers who must keep staff motivation high. Donors who cannot deliver payments as agreed are responsible for reducing the quality of their resources.[12]

Temperatures in development funding: can NGDOs defy the laws of physics?

When mobilising finance, an NGDO leaders/manager's task is to arrive at the optimum mix of quantity and quality in relation to mission, culture, strategic goals and best practices. This is a difficult task made more complicated by the fact that the quantity/quality landscape is changing fast. In this uncertain situation, another way of working out fund-raising strategies and their likely consequences is to assess an additional characteristic of aid money: its temperature. Basic physics can show what lies ahead as leaders/managers hunt for the right mix.

Aid funds get their temperature from the process of giving.[13] An individual choosing to sponsor a child or responding to an appeal brings individual concern to the funds they give. This is hot money, loaded with personal warmth and expectations. Funds taken from taxes and distributed to an IFI, such as the World Bank, for disbursement – along with other countries' tax income as an official loan running into millions or billions of dollars – has lost personal human attachment. International bureaucrats and national politicians may talk to each other in governing bodies, but the individuals whose labours have generated funds from direct taxation or indirectly though company profits are not involved. Multilateral money is anonymous and impersonal, it is stone cold.[14] Bilateral aid may not be quite as cold because a discernible country and population is involved and must be accounted to, but warm it is not!

Hot money impacts both positively and negatively on quality. On the negative side, hot money has to be spent because contributors expect their support to solve an immediate problem. On the positive side, hot money keeps NGDOs in touch with their civic soul and non-governmental selves. It holds them to a constituency which must be convinced of their legitimacy, potentially enhancing quality by acting as a counter-weight to self-delusion, self-satisfaction, corruption and co-optation. Hot money is a double-edged sword that is much better to have than have not.[15]

The official aid system transfers mainly cold money, some US$ 55 billion per year, as soft loans and grants to governments for large-scale investment projects, sector support and rural and urban development programmes. Cold money is most cost-effectively applied to 'cold' purposes. For example, millions of dollars put into import or commodity support are cost-

effective paper transactions between treasuries. But community-level work which embodies highly differentiated primary stakeholders offers few economies of scale suited to large amounts of cold aid. Sustainable micro-development needs hot money: assistance which is humanised and personalised through authentic participation. So when donors want to apply cold money to sustainable human-development, costs increase because energy has to be applied to get the temperature up to a human level.

The official aid system has two primary strategies for heating funds. First are conditions to make cold money more human centred. Aid conditions have always been around, but today's insistence on stakeholder involvement, PRA techniques and emphasis on capacity-building of local people's organisations, are all requirements which should humanise official aid – hence increasing its temperature. Second is a priority to fund hotter organisations such as NGDOs. While aid levels are stagnating – dropping by 7.8 per cent between 1992 and 1993 alone – over the period 1990 to 1995, official aid to NGDOs has risen from US$ 2.3 to $4 billion. Unfortunately, this growing inflow brings drawbacks which have cooling effects on NGDOs.

NGDOs have an organisational temperature, determined by their ideology, constituency links, staff motivation, people-centred development approaches, and their resource base. Becoming and staying a hot organisation means making careful choices about the temperature of the resources mobilised and their proportion. Common values and approaches in authentic North-South/East partnerships 'insulate' hot money as it shifts across the globe and reaches primary stakeholders. Transnational NGDOs – organisations where funds are raised from individuals in the North for individuals in the South or East – also insulate the financial transfer by containing the whole process. These transnationals are 'horizontally integrated'.

When hot NGDOs mobilise proportionally larger inflows of cold (official) aid money, the laws of physics say that the organisation will get colder. This shows up in more bureaucracy, less flexibility, changing staff attitudes and reduction in NGDOs' comparative advantages. Stopping this happening requires an energy input from somewhere, but from where? One avenue is to raise more money from hot sources, but this is not easy because, globally, the proportion of hot, volunteered money is dropping and will be at or less than 50 per cent of NGDO income by the next decade.[16] Alternatively, the proportion of funds raised and allocated to internal heating processes can be increased. The difficulty here is that the resources needed for heating processes, such as community negotiation, staff development, more flexible systems, better monitoring, and learning are (mis)treated as overheads which must be kept low.

The low overheads myth works against allocating additional resources to counter the effects of taking cold funding. There is, however, a financially costless, but vital source of energy to stop an NGDO cooling off. This energy comes from owners and leaders/managers and staff who stay true to founding beliefs, values and voluntary principles. It is their ethos against convenient self-serving compromise that withstands buying into fashionable theories and cold aid interpretations of development. The heating power of personal principle and staff values has no monetary cost, but in today's *real-politick* is in danger of being marginalised.[17]

With luck, however, the aid system will not herald in a new ice age; instead, official agencies are slowly increasing the temperature of some of their funds, primarily by modifying their practices and conditions based on agency-wide learning. For example, the *Handbook on Social Development* published by the UK Overseas Development Agency, distils its experience in the form of best practice guidelines and checklists.[18] Previously, the problem of increasing the temperature of official aid agencies used to be one of not learning from experience. Today, evaluation and learning receives much more attention, which shifts the heating problem from a lack of knowledge to translating lessons into agency-wide procedures, practices and culture. The jury is still out on whether the official aid system will succeed in heating itself – without cooling NGDOs in the process.

The official aid system is also drawing more on proven NGDO practices, project negotiations and joint implementation. Learning from NGDOs by funding them has been called the 'reverse agenda' and needs further support.[19] Heat exchanged from NGDOs to the official aid system is a type of leverage that, in addition to policy advocacy, must become more central in NGDO strategic thinking.

TIPS **To assess the organisational implications of accessing and mixing funding sources, an NGDO leader/manager needs to do a temperature check as well as a quality check.**

What an NGDO manager/leader will look for are ideal funds which:

➤ are free from stringent, inflexible, imposed conditions;
➤ are allocated on programme or intervention terms (rather than as projects);
➤ are not constrained by accounting and administrative requirements which impede best practise;
➤ can fit into existing financial, administrative and other systems;
➤ are predictable in terms of where the donor obtains them and reliable in terms of flow;
➤ will, when based on demonstrated performance, be available throughout all stages of an intervention (continuity is not simply subject to donor interests or politics);
➤ arrive on time as agreed.

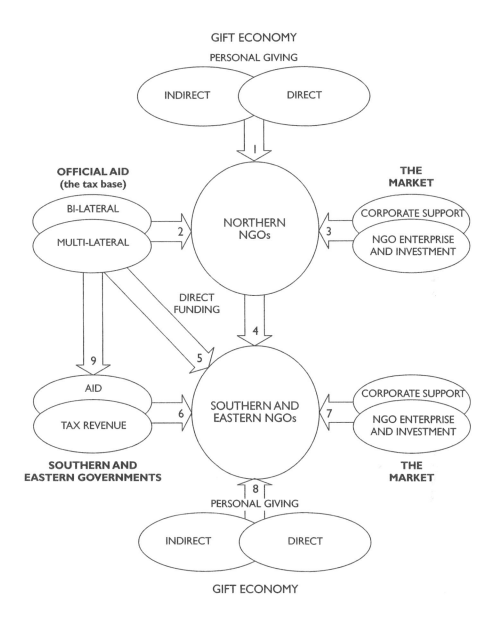

GIFT ECONOMY

PERSONAL GIVING

INDIRECT

DIRECT

1

OFFICIAL AID
(the tax base)

THE
MARKET

BI-LATERAL

NORTHERN
NGOs

CORPORATE SUPPORT

2

3

MULTI-LATERAL

NGO ENTERPRISE
AND INVESTMENT

DIRECT
FUNDING

4

9

5

AID

SOUTHERN AND
EASTERN NGOs

CORPORATE SUPPORT

6

7

TAX REVENUE

NGO ENTERPRISE
AND INVESTMENT

SOUTHERN AND
EASTERN GOVERNMENTS

THE
MARKET

8

PERSONAL GIVING

INDIRECT

DIRECT

GIFT ECONOMY

Figure 6.1 Global sources of NGDO finance

To fund their work, NGDOs can tap into three types of economic surplus: personal giving, the tax base and the market. Figure 6.1, shows that these types of surplus produce three main funding sources for Northern NGDOs and five for the South and East.[20] Each has distinctive qualities, temperatures and trends; each calls for different responses.

NGDO financing in the North

The gift economy

The gift economy (arrow 1) is the technical term used for funds given voluntarily by an individual, group, civic organisation or business. An economic surplus coming from people's pockets for development can, for example, be in direct response to an NGDO appeal, or a school collecting funds for another school somewhere in the South or East. Gift income can also be generated indirectly. Examples are regular wage deductions to create a development fund, a method employed by some Canadian trade unions, or allocations from national lotteries, which is happening in Britain. Indirect giving reduces personal engagement with development issues, but there is still a clear constituency concerned about what happens to their contributions.

Expectations generated by fund-raising messages can open or restrict freedom, and NGDOs have to decide how far this type of income is tied to a specific purpose or impact. If done properly, the quality can be high without being too hot. Data from the Netherlands indicates that the ability to mobilise gift funds is related to three key NGDO competencies.[21] These are:

- An ability to personalise the recipient. Child sponsorship organisations are obviously at an advantage here.
- An ability to communicate and use the media well. This means being as technically professional as commercial organisations which set the standard for the public's judgement of what they see and hear.
- Choosing the right issue – one that people relate to because they experience it. For example, leprosy is no longer a very strong message in the North; environmental pollution and child abuse are.

A common area of organisational struggle in Northern NGDOs is between fund-raisers and development professionals. Why? Because the messages needed to raise money in the North – appeals to pity and compassion – are inconsistent with the dignity of the poor and the slow, contextual nature of sustainable development work. False expectations are created which professional developers know cannot be realised. Effective NGDOs are those capable of internally reconciling the different realities of public fund-raising in the North and sustainable development in the South or East.

Another way of looking at this organisational difficulty is to recognise that, to be effective, staff must 'import' the interests, perspectives and values of the major external constituencies they deal with. This means the NGDO must reconcile the contradictions and tensions of poverty in a rich world, brought within the organisation. The task for leaders/managers is to organise and continually manage these tensions because they cannot be eradicated unless there is a major shift in contributors' understanding. Here is another place where the strength of shared beliefs, values, identity and confidence in the leadership are important. Why? Because they provide the emotional reference points which managers rely on to hold the NGDO together.

An overall decline in the Northern public's sense of personal social obligation,[22] is leading to stagnation in the growth of the Northern development gift economy.[23] In 1989, private giving generated some US$ 3.4 billion, constituting 65 per cent of total NGDO disbursements of US$ 5.2 billion. Tentative figures for 1995 suggest an unadjusted total NGDO disbursement of some US$8 billion with official aid now contributing almost 50 per cent of the total.[24] Unless Northern NGDOs do something about this, a highly competitive gift economy will not continue to grow for them.

The tax base

Northern governments take citizens' and corporate taxes and allocate them to international aid, mainly by using bilateral or multilateral channels.[25] Multilaterals can be divided between the UN grant-making agencies and the (soft-)loan development banks. While the level of difficulty varies, NGDOs in the North can access tax-derived funds from each of these sources (arrow 2).[26] Data above shows tax-based aid to be a fast-growing source of NGDO funding. It will probably continue to be so, given the aid policies of privatisation and civic strengthening which show little signs of abating. In other words, there will be more and more cold money around.

An OECD study describes the various ways Northern NGDOs access domestic tax-based funds.[27] The coldest funds are commonly allocated on the basis of logically framed projects with targets related to donor priorities and other interests in a particular country.[28] In countries where bilateral or mutlilateral relations are or were strained, official agencies use Northern NGDOs to gain a presence and potential foothold until times improve. Examples are Myanmar, Nicaragua under the Sandinistas, Cambodia, and South Africa under apartheid. When desired political change occurs, Northern NGDOs are pushed aside, ignored or their work sidelined.[29] NGDO policy-makers must be aware of and deal with the co-optation into foreign policy underlying all funding from official aid. Bilateral funds allocated on a block grant or programme basis – agreed amounts of money to be made available each year – are higher in quality to the extent that they provide the NGDO with flexibility and discretion. The danger of co-optation into foreign policy strategies is also reduced.

Accessing funds from the UN system is less coloured by bilateral interests, but NGDOs face complex administrative rituals; the politics associated with recipient governments' co-ownership of UN agencies; and the ambiguity of delegated authority with the UN system. Despite a shared development vocabulary, basic preconditions for collaboration between NGDOs and UN agencies do not exist – they must be constructed each step of the way. For example, theories of cause and change may differ; decision-making processes are not the same; personal motivations, incentives and rewards are incompatible; diplomatic protection and personal privileges set UN staff apart in the world; access to and relations with governments bear no similarity; organisational performance measures are not the same; and they are positioned and act differently in relation to power in society. Working through these differences calls for significant upfront investment in time and energy for NGDOs, which many lack. NGDOs who have this capacity are likely either to enjoy untied resources or are funded by the UN, which confuses relations from the outset. Both reasons can create an exclusive club of NGDOs able to interact with the multilateral systems to the exclusion of others. This is a potentially divisive effect.

Multilaterals also interact with NGDOs to have their funds heated up, while NGDOs interact with multilaterals to gain scale and leverage for their work.[30] This apparent mutuality of interest does not readily translate into equality of costs and benefits.[31] In fact, accessing multilateral funds creates costs and structural tensions which NGDOs must be ready and able to deal with.[32] The first is co-optation into strategies, plans and programmes already negotiated with recipient governments. Excluded on the grounds of sovereignty and national security, NGDOs are hired as implementers, having most influence over the least strategic aspects of development decisions.[33] Second, co-optation brings with it a reduction in autonomy and one-way accommodation of relatively small NGDOs compared to relatively massive donors. Third, multilaterals have a natural inclination to employ the instruments and terms they apply to governments or contractors. Modifying donor internal procedures is a major struggle requiring a long time. A slow pace of change calls for NGDO patience.

Fortunately, it is not all a one-way street with some NGDOs able to swim against the flow of cold aid, while others are swept away by the current. Although slow to change, the official aid system is adapting to the requirements of working with NGDOs in ways that do not diminish their comparative advantages. What this means for collaborating with an increasingly dominant actor on the NGDO scene, the World Bank, is summarised in Boxes 6.1 and 6.2.

The past five years have seen efforts within the World Bank to educate staff on what participation and constructive collaboration with NGDOs means in operational terms.[35] In addition, steps are being taken to amend bank procedures which work against best practice in sustainable micro-development.[36] Bilaterals are also amending their NGDO interface. For example, USAID has a New Partnerships Initiative which incorporates learning from past difficulties, and the Japanese are recognising the

Box 6.1
Collaboration with the World Bank (1)

The World Bank
The World Bank is a lending institution owned by governments and accountable to them. It raises funds from the official aid system, capital markets and income from loans. Unlike market lenders, the bank's fiduciary responsibilities keep it heavily involved with borrowers' policies and the implementation of the loans it makes. The bank has dual goals of reducing global poverty and maintaining triple-A status as a borrower. These are not always in harmony, which can lead outsiders to be confused about the bank's choices and methods.

The World Bank and NGDOs
Since the mid 1980s, the bank has opened up its relationships with NGDOs, and today some 40 per cent of bank-financed activity has some form of NGDO involvement. The NGO Group, located in the Poverty and Social Policy Department, is the focal point for supporting bank-NGDO collaboration. It provides information and maintains an NGO database with about 8000 entries. Approximately 35 NGDO liaison staff have recently been appointed to the bank's offices throughout the world. An internal Operational Directive (14.70) encourages staff to involve NGDOs. In its turn, the bank works with governments to promote an enabling environment for NGOs. An important interface is formed by the World Bank-NGO Committee that meets regularly to discuss issues of mutual concern and address obstacles to collaboration.

Forewarned is forearmed
As with other development funders, it is necessary for NGDOs to understand why and how the bank operates before deciding to collaborate. There are various sources of information about the bank itself and activities which NGDOs may be interested in. The most accessible are:

● World Bank Public Information Centres in Washington, D.C., London, Paris, Tokyo and Kingston, Jamaica;
● resident missions located in 70 countries;
● via the Internet at http://www.worldbank.org//;
● book stores, World Bank depository and libraries.

Bank Check
An NGDO quarterly bulletin provides critical commentary on bank activities and plans.[34]

Tips:
● World Bank missions do not always have full information about accessible documents. Make sure you obtain a copy of the Information Disclosure Policy and, when necessary, be persistent in asking for documents.
● Some NGDOs specialise in distributing information about the bank and its activities. Two in Washington, D.C., are: The Bank Information Centre and Bread for the World.
● Official bank publications are often translated into French and Spanish; project documents are sometimes available in local languages; make sure to check.

Source: adapted from a contribution by Carmen Malena

Box 6.2
Collaboration with the World Bank (2)

NGDOs interact with the World Bank through policy dialogue, involvement in lending operations, and accessing funds.

Engaging in policy dialogue
Jim Wolfensen's appointment as president has given renewed emphasis to the bank's dialogue with NGDOs. The forum for regular discussion provided by the World Bank-NGO Committee is complemented by consultations on sectoral issues with a growing emphasis on country-level meetings about policy, lending intentions and practice. These meetings are increasingly trilateral involving the borrowing government, although this can be a contentious issue.
The following tips will help NGDOs who wish to engage in policy dialogue with the bank:

● Contact the Secretariat of the World Bank-NGDO committee for up-to-date information.
● Contact the nearest Mission, or World Bank staff member in Washington (traceable through the NGO Group) to ask about local NGDO committees, consultations and opportunities for dialogue.
● Coordinate with other NGDOs who share your concern or interest, especially those who already have working experience with the bank.
● If you are worried about a potentially negative impact of a bank-financed activity, contact the World Bank Inspection Panel.

Working in bank-funded activities
The bank makes loans to governments. It does not generally fund NGDOs. Collaboration occurs primarily with NGDOs providing advice during design, information about local conditions, and while interfacing with communities. NGDOs are also hired, normally, by the borrowing government to identify local needs, conduct initial surveys and beneficiary assessments, implement pilot projects or project components, provide technical assistance, or carry out monitoring and evaluation work. Social funds, amongst others, sometimes provide grants for NGDOs or communities.

To get started:
● Register with the bank's electronic database.
● Request advice and information on collaboration from the NGO group.
● Obtain a list of upcoming bank-financed activities and current project identification documents (PIDs) for the country of interest from a public information centre or resident mission.
● Having identified a specific project or sector, gain contact with relevant government and bank staff.

To cope with bank-financed ways of working:
● It is important to work with the borrowing government according to their procedures and regulations *as well as* those of the bank.
● Study procedures to see if they are consistent with your philosophy and approach, paying particular attention to the time frame involved. A major stumbling block for NGDOs can be complex procurement procedures and disbursement delays that negatively impact on community development processes.

- Obtain advice from NGDOs experienced with the bank to learn ways around problems and to calculate if you can afford the effort.
- Insist on clearly defined terms of reference and lines of responsibility so that you are not caught between the government's ownership and the bank's supervisory role.
- Beware of taking on responsibilities you cannot deliver – there may be penalties for failure to perform according to agreements, including loss of reputation.
- Make use of innovative practices to deal with typical project difficulties (the NGO group has more information).
- Be realistic: when in doubt do not waste energy and time.

Source: adapted from a contribution by Carmen Malena

role of NGDOs in the analysis of how to achieve development goals.[37] But as in any two-way street, NGDOs must be capable of understanding and taking on board the modifications needed to work with official aid.

What can be said about the capabilities and characteristics NGDOs need if they want to tap tax-based, cold incomes without cooling off? The key capacities may be summarised as:

- a proven track record;
- clarity of identity and development analysis;
- sufficient untied funds or other sources of capacity to protect autonomy, and to cover the substantial staff time for negotiation and proposal writing;
- an ability to speak on a par with the often highly qualified staff who are not nec-essarily professionals in terms of micro-development and are often transient;
- an ability to write convincingly and argue through funding proposals;
- good communication and shared understanding between the proposal writer and the operational staff who must provide the real-life data;
- patience.

The third item – access to untied funds – is tricky. Using contributors' funds to obtain official aid can be the trigger to a mine-field which has exploded for more than one NGDO. The trip-wire is pulled when a Northern NGDO uses untied gift economy money to access cold funds, which is not what 'hot' funders were led

to expect. Save the Children Fund (SCF) USA were exposed by *Penthouse* for doing precisely this.[38] A substantial proportion of funds raised from the general public were used to cover costs of the SCF-USA office needed to mobilise and run projects funded by official aid agencies. This was not the implicit contract for donations.

Today, NGDOs need flexible resources to engage with the official aid system or to access official aid funds. The risk is diversion of hot gift money to gain cold income and leverage rather than to do direct development work. An alternative source without the drawback of donor expectations and unexploded mines are the high-quality, untied funds raised from the market.

The market

NGDOs can generate income from the market either by direct activity or indirectly through corporate support (arrow 3 in Figure 6.1). Direct fund generation is of two main types: commercial enterprise or market investment. There are some examples of Northern NGDOs running their own commercial operations. Oxfam UK/I is one of the oldest examples. In 1993, for example, Oxfam shops in the UK generated some £17 million on a turnover of £53 million.[39] Sales of Christmas cards is a seasonal, but insecure, way of tapping the market. Sales of handicrafts from Southern artisans, or publications about NGDO work, are not uncommon. NGDOs concerned about fair trade, such as Max Havelaar in Holland and TradeCraft in the UK, generate both their incomes and more equitable terms for primary producers.

Raising income from investment is exemplified by American philanthropic organisations, of which the Ford Foundation is the largest with investments amounting to some US$ 6.3 billion. However, unlike commercial activity, stock market investment offers little opportunity to create a positive public profile and 'capture' buyers in terms of promoting the NGDO development agenda. New market-based variations, such as a percentage of credit card transactions coming to the NGDO, are also starting to appear. But on a global scale, the proportion of funds raised by Northern NGDOs through these means is small, amounting to little more than 2 to 4 per cent of the total. While small in volume, this type of money is probably the highest in terms of quality and development value. Why? Because profits come without strings, they are unconditional. An NGDO is only constrained in using this type of income by its registration as a non-profit organisation – not by the income itself. The temperature of market income can vary. Volunteers in shops, workers in fair trade NGDOs, and others who express a similar commitment give human warmth to these funds, with expectations about how they will be applied. They form one key group which the NGDO must be accountable to if it is to rely on their efforts in the future. Funds generated by market investment are not warmed at their source, it is the NGDO leaders/managers and staff who must add this element, which leaves significant freedom, together with strong challenges of probity and accountability. Market-based incomes are going to play a critical role in the future NGDO balancing act.

Aside from moral dilemmas, the organisational challenge for NGDOs directly engaged in generating market income is how to legally deal with two distinct sets of operating principles and taxation requirements.[40] A common solution is to establish the for-profit business as a separate legal entity, but under the sole ownership of the non-profit board, trustees or whatever the law has designated. Where staff are predominantly volunteers, it may be possible to locate the business arm under the same management as the development organisation.

This is the case with Oxfam UK/I.

Where staff are not volunteers and competition demands a market rate, it is difficult to bring business and non-profit development under one management as opposed to under one owner. Terms of service, incentives, culture, management style, reinvestment needs, and tax concerns can all differ too much from the value-orientation and work styles of development to make a happy marriage between the two. Without separation, transparency suffers; subsidising poorly functioning business operations can too easily occur, threatening the viability of both operations.

Collaboration with businesses in support of development work is receiving a boost from two directions. One is from NGDOs themselves, who see benefits from teaming up with companies and are actively hunting for opportunities. The second push comes from the growing, but disputed, political impetus for corporations to demonstrate greater social responsibility and take sustainability seriously.[41] The hoped-for win-win dimension in corporate fund-raising lies in a positive public image for the business with income for the NGDO. In other words, it can make good business sense to engage with and support social development – tax incentives included. The word partnership is also being applied to this sort of cross-sector relationship.[42]

From an NGDO perspective, a threshold choice is the type of business, the products it sells, the level of trust it enjoys with the general public, and the image it wishes to promote. A company manufacturing electric cattle prods, also sold as instruments of torture, may want to improve its image by sponsoring an NGDO's work. Would this be appropriate? Is Shell in Europe today a good company for NGDOs to be associated with? In terms of competencies and organisational issues, an NGDO seeking to access corporate funding needs:

● an ability to carry out a thorough examination of a prospective corporation in terms of its core business and subsidiaries: (a late discovery that an associated company is involved in exploitive or dubious activities could be a public

relations disaster);
- an internal review process to critically vet possible corporate supporters;
- something tangible to offer which is attractive for support because it enhances corporate image or market position;
- reference points for the way in which corporate assistance is 'advertised' at the site of its application – in a village, on a vehicle;
- a system enabling field operations to advise on, and if necessary veto, proposed corporate collaboration;
- resources to enable a fairly long process of development, including exposure to the NGDO's work;
- certainty that collaboration will not unacceptably compromise or limit who is assisted, and how.

Corporate contributions can be warm, but of medium to low quality because of the close tie to image and other interests. This type of income is very small within the total funds disbursed by NGDOs, probably contributing less than 1 per cent of the US$9 billion total. Nevertheless, the ongoing Northern political debate about the social function and responsibilities of corporations is creating a re-enforcing environment which NGDOs can capitalise on. But this will be in heavy competition with domestically oriented non-profits who benefit from close proximity in their impact.

NGDO financing in the South and East

At first sight NGDOs in the South and East appear to be in a better position than their Northern counterparts when it comes to sources of finance – five against three. For reasons of history, socio-economic development and culture, reality does not, however, match this picture. Again, we take a tour around each source (arrows 4 to 8 in Figure 6.1); in the next section we analyse critical dynamics between each one which impact on the shape of NGDO communities as well as steer their social and political relationships.

Northern NGDO funding

Historically, channel 4 (Figure 6.1), has been the dominant source of finance for NGDOs in the South and East. Reliable statistics are not available, but informed guesses suggest that up until the late 1980s funds raised by Northern NGDOs from the three channels described previously probably constituted some 90 per cent of income for Southern NGDOs; Eastern NGDOs were yet to be 'discovered'. Though uneven, the trend today is away from an unparalleled dominance of Northern NGDOs as funders because of growth in direct funding from official aid and greater efforts at local fund-raising detailed below.

Some South American countries and South East Asian Tiger economies, such as Thailand and Indonesia, are being placed on the 'fast track' of withdrawal by Northern NGDOs. There are at least three reasons for this shift. First, economic indicators provide less justification for support, fuelling the argument that local NGDOs should access growing local resources. Second, new opportunities in Indochina and Eastern Europe are attracting attention and diverting funds. Third, a more strategic approach to financing is highlighting irrationality in the existing spread of NGDO assistance.

A mix of domestic sources leads to varying temperatures and qualities of Northern NGDOs and their funds. And Northern NGDOs will differentiate themselves more sharply in the future because of their varying capacities to access cold money without cooling off. Some Northern NGDOs will be co-opted, becoming an official aid channel in all but name. Southern NGDOs already see this happening as their previous 'partners' start to call a new tune of neo-realism with market rules. The implications for Southern and Eastern NGDOs are two-fold. First, authentic partnerships with high-quality Northern NGDO partnerships will become more valuable but more difficult to attain. Second, there may not be much difference in dealing with cold NGDOs and other cold sources. In other words, it may be preferable to deal with official donors directly. And this is possible because of direct funding (channel 5 in

Figure 6.1).

Direct funding from official aid

Direct funding by official aid agencies to Southern and Eastern NGDOs (arrow 5), bypassing the North, is a change on the aid scene which began in the 1980s and is gathering momentum. Justifications for direct funding are grouped around issues of greater efficiency in aid delivery; better governance in terms of supporting and building local NGDOs as stronger civic actors; supporting donor sectoral priorities and donor learning about local conditions; and maintaining legitimacy for aid by better demonstrating impact. In addition, Northern NGDOs have found it very difficult to come up with firm evidence that they do add something to development to justify their costs. This inability makes their reservations sound weak and self-pleading.

While seen by some as a mixed blessing or threat, direct funding is generally welcomed by recipients who are disillusioned with the practice of NGDO partnerships with the North; are increasingly capable of negotiating in their own right; and have overtaken Northern NGDOs in their development thinking and strategies towards their own countries.[43] There is, in fact, less difference in dealing with Northern NGDOs channelling aid on essentially official terms and dealing directly with official donors who are slowly interacting with Southern and Eastern NGDOs in more appropriate ways. Harshly put, Northern NGDOs who want to stay in the aid game had better make sure that they have, and can demonstrate, their comparative advantages .

The capacities Southern and Eastern NGDOs require to directly access official aid are the same as for their Northern counterparts, which poses difficulties for weaker organisations. However, Southern and Eastern NGDOs face an additional demand. They must cross a threshold to direct funding by being classed as 'wheat amongst the chaff'.[44] Why? Because NGDOs with no voluntary ethic, understanding or vision are being created by politicians, ex-civil servants and entrepreneurs solely for the purpose of tapping aid flows or building a political base. For them NGDO registration is a strategic convenience. Confined to their offices, official donor staff are too seldom able to verify what they are told. They can be taken in by unsupported but well-formulated proposals, be oversensitive to political name dropping, and may not invest in trusted third-sector links which could provide a third-party opinion – the cocktail party circuit acts as a substitute. Donors often compensate for these weaknesses by recruiting NGDO liaison personnel from the sector. However, local recruitment may import the personal biases and politics of the NGDO community; this cannot be adequately countered because of the high turnover of international supervisory staff, who are generalists anyway. In sum, a distinct requirement for local NGDOs wishing to access direct funding is to establish legitimacy and credibility. A reciprocal requirement for official aid agencies is to gain knowledgeable and independent advice.

Despite different donor positions on the merits and pitfalls of direct funding, there is little doubt that in money volume terms this trend is set to continue. If there is not much to separate cold donors and cooled-off Northern NGDOs in terms of aid quality, the expanded choice of funding sources made available by direct funding could strengthen the negotiating position of competent Southern and Eastern NGDOs. Such possibilities should, however, be approached strategically rather than opportunistically because of potential negative effects on local NGDOs' relationships.

Funding from Southern and Eastern governments

Corresponding to arrow 2 in the North (Figure 6.1), local NGDOs can try and access funds from their governments, both nationally and locally (arrow 6). The funds governments have to give can originate from local taxes or from international aid obtained as grants or loans. In countries with substantial economies, where aid is a small proportion of GDP and NGDO-government relations are positive, there is a potential for NGDOs to access indigenous tax-based funds – South Africa and India provide examples. Even if they had the will, governments in low-income, aid-dependent, resource-poor countries expect NGDOs to bring additional resources into the country, not knock on the door asking for financial support. This is the scenario in most of sub-Saharan Africa where in extreme cases such as Chad, NGDO finance for health services exceeds that of the government department doing similar work.

Where funds are available from (especially poorer) Southern governments, it is increasingly because the official aid system is pushing for NGDOs to be included in the activities they finance governments to do. For example, the new generation of social development funds in Latin America have, on donor insistence, a strong NGDO element.[45] Similarly, bilateral donors try to include NGDOs when their finance needs heating up. What happens when official aid is diverted to NGDOs, or ties them to governments, is discussed below.

NGDOs in Latin America and South East Asia who are being fast-tracked out of Northern NGDOs because of their countries' economic performance are actively looking at ways of obtaining resources from their governments as a matter of right, not privilege.[46] The argument is that they are contributing to socio-economic development and well-being and, like businesses which benefit from investment incentives, local NGDOs are also entitled to supportive state policies and finance. It is too early to tell how successful this reorientation will be, but the switch from higher- to lower- quality funds, which the move from Northern NGDOs to Southern government money implies, introduces a danger zone of co-optation and decreased ability to adopt a critical stance on issues of social justice and rights.[47] Here, lessons can probably be learned from domestically oriented Northern third-sector organisations because many are financed by government.

In Latin America, Mariano Valderrama describes two types of initiatives, in addition to local NGDOs making demands on government.[48] One is self-finance through the promotion of loan and cooperative funding, such as micro-enterprise credit in Peru and FINCA (Campasino Financing Fund) in Costa Rica. Another is Northern to Southern NGDO finance shifting from a grant to an investment logic by, for example, providing credit guarantees for development loans. Research and Applications for Alternative Development (RAFAD) is an early example of a guarantee approach initially applied in West Africa.

For NGDOs in ex-Soviet block countries the dynamic differs. These newly independent states are adjusting to imposed political sovereignty, bringing with it both a loss of financial stability and the benefits of integration associated with the rouble zone and incorporation in the Soviet economy. The tenuous financial situation of Eastern states is not a good starting point for NGDO claims on government resources. In addition, NGDOs are a newly emerged quantity, often existing under inappropriate legislation or in a constitutional limbo. Moreover, they face suspicion from ex-Soviet schooled regimes of being little more than fronts for political interests, or groups out to show up government inadequacies. In the words of a Kazak NGDO leader, dealing with the government calls for 'gritted teeth, keeping your nerve and a lot of patience.'[49] Eastern NGDOs who owe their existence to external aid face a long uphill battle in fund-raising from the state.

The potential for government funding of local NGDOs therefore varies across countries of the South and East, but is generally on the increase, bringing opportunities and dangers. A common drawback with funds from the domestic tax base, or donor funding to governments with an NGDO component, is that both can be used to re-enforce patronage or corruption. The prime capacity required of Southern and Eastern NGDOs, therefore, is to cope with becoming enmeshed in the politics of public finance, followed by competencies to deal with bureaucracies which are perhaps not independent of the regime in power and suffer poor working conditions. Colder aid from Northern NGDOs may reflect self-interest, but corruption is less likely.

The market

The fourth source of funds is from the market

(arrow 7). As for the North, this source can be divided into NGDO direct economic activity and corporate support. Direct economic activity can mean commercial operations or income-generating investments. Concern for self-sustainability is leading more and more Southern NGDOs to embark on direct economic activity, usually with finance from the North. With noted exceptions, results have been disappointing because either the concept was not viable to start with, or the organisation could not cope with the dual management demands of for-profit and non-profit activity under one roof. Sarvadoya's investment in a printing press is an example of the latter. Set against this is the success in commercial income generation of IBASE in Brazil, which raises 44 per cent of its turnover from commercial activity, including the management of an e-mail node.[50]

BRAC in Bangladesh is well known for its local entrepreneuralism, running a cold store, a printing press, a chain of handicrafts stores and garment factories. In 1994, 31 per cent of its income came from business operations.[51] Introducing for-profit activity with a development dimension came naturally to BRAC's founder, Fazle Abed, who was originally in business working with Phillips. He established BRAC at the time of the war of independence against Pakistan in 1971. However, becoming commercial was less natural to staff who objected that potato cold stores would benefit richer farmers.

Deciding to be commercial and non-profit at the same time has major implications.[52] Factors to be considered include the following:

- It is important to overcome entrenched beliefs that business exploitation and profit-seeking is the cause of poverty and injustice and that NGDOs are simply going to add to this. Distrustful of money and business, NGDOs have not developed commercial expertise – in fact, there is a fear that doing so will make them lose their 'non-profit virginity'.
- The organisation as a whole must be convinced that income-generation is vital. In other words, instead of complaining about donor conditions and autocratic attitudes, people from bottom to top must realise that repackaging projects and putting even more effort into finding unexplored donor territory is not a viable way ahead.
- Be aware that adding a commercial operation might mean a loss of cohesion and resulting confusion for existing staff and stakeholders. For example, the Grameen Bank's perceived callousness in getting loans repaid is seen by some as a loss of their commitment to the poor rather than a means of instilling a sense of discipline.
- The concern about exploitation, because this is what NGDOs see around them, has to be overcome by recognising that not all for-profits rip-off workers and damage the environment. A further fear to be tackled is the perception of exploiting 'poverty' and packaging the poor as an aid to generating business.
- NGDOs which have been living in the comfort zone of grants need to rebuild the entrepreneurship existing at their inception. But, with backgrounds in politics, activism and the social sciences, most NGDO leaders do not have the experience necessary to manage commercial ventures themselves. Who should they turn to?
- A change in structure is needed to enable two cultures – each with their own objectives, activities and rewards – to operate alongside each other without interference, but with sufficient interaction to ensure that they both push in the same direction.
- A change in mentality is called for, moving from expenditure budgets, projects and reports to a concern for revenue budgets, profit-and-loss accounts and reinvestment strategies.
- Public suspicion needs to be dealt with, because adding commercial activities can feed a perception that NGDOs are businesses in disguise. In addition, politicians may be less comfortable with an NGDO who enjoys greater financial autonomy than one dependent on external aid which governments can better control.
- Be aware that the legal and tax situation

may not cope with for-profits owned for non-profit purposes. NGDOs must be sure that taxes will not render the whole enterprise a waste of time.

● Be aware that governments may be suspicious about loss of tax revenue and unfair market competition because NGDOs have access to grant funds.

NGDOs pay insufficient attention to establishing necessary preconditions when embarking on profit-making enterprise. Too frequently this new step is simply treated as an add-on to the existing organisation, instead of a decision with far-reaching consequences in terms of organisational development.

Gaining income from investments carries with it the concerns listed above, but the organisational implications may be less severe. For example, investing in a building which provides both NGDO offices and space to rent out need not involve the organisation in day-to-day management; this can be contracted to an agent. PRRM in the Philippines has raised US$12 million by selling land donated to them in the 1970s. Some of the funds will be used to obtain new office premises, including rental space for third parties. The remainder will initially be divided between investment brokers to compare their performance before a final allocation is made.

Endowment funds are another form of investment for a recurrent resource, but substantial amounts are needed to generate a reasonable income. For example, an NGDO with a budget of $300,000 a year and 15 per cent overheads would require an endowment of $450,000 generating 10 per cent interest to cover administrative costs. Where inflation runs into double figures, either the returns need to be far above the inflation rate and with substantial reinvestment, or the endowment sum must be much higher.

Investments generating an untied return are most attractive because they produce high-quality funds. They have also been the most difficult for donors to support for reasons ranging from legitimate worries about governance and probity, to a concern to keep hold of the purse strings. Nevertheless, with

strategic efforts of foundations such as Synergos and Ford in the USA, and the odd one-off grants by donors, such as USAID in Pakistan, slow progress is being made on the establishment of foundation-like organisations (FLOs) in the South and East, such as the West African Rural Foundation (WARF) and the Mozambique Community Development Foundation (MCDF).[53] However, while a high-quality resource, FLOs are not set to produce significant income compared with current levels of external flows to NGDOs. This is unfortunate, because it is access to this quality of money which will shape the NGDO community in the next millennium.

Southern and Eastern NGDOs can also reach the market through local corporate support. The issues raised and competencies needed are not yet that similar to those of Northern NGDOs. The economic situation of many Southern countries offers opportunities not readily available to the North in terms of international corporations which cannot repatriate funds and possibilities for debt-equity swap arrangements. For example, ORAP in Zimbabwe used its access to foreign aid to help a battery company buy out its multinational owner. In return, ORAP gained 10 per cent of the share holding, a seat on the board and technical expertise. On the other hand, where political and economic power are closely tied, or markets are thin and weak with monopoly players, or state ownership dominates enterprise, there may not be much corporate interest or need to promote a positive public image. For this reason, corporate sponsoring of projects is less likely than other options.

Where markets are strong and free, moral and political motives can encourage business to take the initiative in establishing funds for financing social development directly and through NGDOs. Fundaçion Sociale (FS) in Colombia was established 30 years ago by a Jesuit priest in the service of social development and was designed to be self-financing at the outset by running a commercial enterprise. The foundation currently owns 13 companies with a value of US$ 1 billion. Profits are used to run its own development programmes.[54]

In India, corporate philanthropy for social

development has a long history. In 1893 J N Tata established an endowment scheme to educate Indians abroad. Other wealthy industrial families followed suit and today there are almost none without a family philanthropic trust. This initiative was complemented by Ghandi's concept of trusteeship, inspiring the wealthy to start and support schools and hospitals and endow temples. Post-independence government take-over of these facilities and social functions led to a decline in private giving, and family trusts now tend to run their own social development work for populations around the areas where their factories operate. Financing development work as undertaken by foreign-funded NGDOs seldom interests them.[55]

Philippines Business for Social Progress (PBSP), established in 1970 during the Marcos era, was intended to act as a counterweight to ultra-nationalist agitation against what was seen as multinational exploitation. The then chairman of Shell copied a Venezuelan model to set up PBSP and pledged with others an amount of finance, currently set at 1 per cent of net income for social development. Some 0.2 per cent goes to PBSP to utilise as its sees fit, while 0.8 per cent is allocated to social development under the companies' own management. Obviously this is one way that the 180 corporations who are members of PBSP can buy off their social responsibility. Over the years, PBSP established a buffer fund to protect the continuity of its support and now operates with an annual budget of about US\$ 6 million. A proven record in development funding has attracted official aid agencies who provide some \$4 million of this total.[56]

On balance, accessing the market through corporations in the South and East requires financial insight and acumen, together with an ability to recognise and quickly exploit opportunities while barriers to financial flows are removed and markets expand. Fund-raising from market actors is a dynamic country-specific process which is growing in potential as an NGDO financial source.

The gift economy

The gift economy (arrow 8 in Figure 6.1) and its

potential as a source of NGDO finance in the South and East depends on two primary factors. First is the availability of personal economic surplus. Second is a social morality and social relations which induce a sense of personal obligation towards others and the public good. A prerequisite for contributing to the gift economy is an ability to do so, determined by the level and distribution of affluence and disposable surplus. Simply put, if you do not have the money, you cannot give it away. So the level of wealth in society and the extent to which it is concentrated sets conditions for who is able to give and to what extent. In the South substantial proportions of the population live below the poverty line, with wealth concentrated amongst a few families – so the base for giving is narrow. The East is in such a state of flux and recent impoverishment due to devaluation, inflation and external limits set on government expenditures that its gift economy is, at best, embryonic.

However, an ability to give does not mean that people will do so. Social morals, derived from custom, religion and/or ideology, influence whether or not people believe they have an obligation to assist others or personally contribute to the public good. If they do feel this way, it is the nature of social relations which determines if they provide support directly to the individuals or institutions who deserve it, or give indirectly through an intermediary.

In the North, charitable or philanthropic giving has its roots in Christian teaching, while highly individualised social relations have given rise to non-profit intermediary organisations who receive and distribute gifts according to contributors' wishes. In Islamic countries *zakat* is a teaching which has also led to the founding of intermediary organisations. More generally, in the South people are much more likely to give directly to the person or the institution of their choice. Intermediaries are not a common way of expressing social obligation. As Pushpar Sandar says of the Indian situation:

> *'Whereas in the West, individual contributions constitute the bulk of funds available to organised charity, in India this does not appear to be so. This*

is not to say that individuals are any less charitable in India, but only that individual charity is informal and flows spontaneously to individuals needing help on a one-to-one basis and does not go to organised bodies. The significant non-governmental indigenous funds for welfare and developmental work, then, are those from religious bodies and the business sector ...'.[57]

The traditional preference to give directly builds bonds of mutual obligation and assistance which form a safety-net in times of hardship. In the South, reciprocity is part of a survival strategy as well as a way of establishing and maintaining social cohesion where inheriting and fulfilling obligations is an expression of status and power.[58] An additional feature of Southern giving is its orientation towards religious and charitable purposes, not towards long-term sustainable development. This is the government's job. Discussions with NGDOs across the world lead to a consistent assessment that, certainly in the short term, it will be difficult to redirect existing patterns of local charitable, welfare and religious giving towards the type of development work funded by the aid system.

The important conclusion for NGDO strategies is that the necessary preconditions for growth in local giving to intermediaries are not necessarily built into the values or practices of societies in the South and East as in the North. While a gift economy exists, it does not fund third-party organisations since direct one-to-one giving is preferred. In other words, there is unlikely to be much local, good-quality, hot money for NGDOs to access for development as opposed to welfare. In the few cases where an affluent middle class grows rapidly and familial ties loosen, as in the Tiger economies of South East Asia, gifts to intermediaries may be on the increase – the Community Chest in Singapore is one example. Other signs of this happening are moves by transnational child sponsorship and other Northern NGDOs to fund-raise and spend on development work within countries such as Hong Kong, Singapore and Malaysia, instead of remitting funds.

Overall, for most countries the gift economy is unlikely to be a substantial source of local NGDO financing, mainly because it will take a long time for socio-economic conditions to create a widely shared surplus, and for social morality of giving to redirect itself towards funding intermediaries.

Issues and challenges in today's resource trends

The trends identified so far bring two important effects that must also be kept in mind by donors when formulating funding policies and by NGDOs when selecting funding strategies. The first is the response of Southern and Eastern governments towards NGDOs. Second are relationships between NGDOs as civic actors.

Government attitudes

Aid trends are introducing tensions between Southern and Northern NGDOs as they sort out their new divisions of labour. In addition, shifts in funding are influencing relations between NGDOs and governments. Diverting shrinking levels of official aid to NGDOs means less for local politicians and bureaucrats to control, which is not popular. Insisting that NGDOs are involved in bi- and multilateral-funded programmes may not go down well either. Both policies encroach on sovereignty in terms of deciding how resources are divided and by whom – causing antagonism between Southern and Eastern governments and the NGDO community. Setting up commissions to investigate what NGDOs are up to – in India and Sri Lanka – is one sign of regime discomfort. New NGDO legislation and administrative procedures – adopted in Uganda, Kenya, Zambia and Zimbabwe – are another indication that some Southern governments are not prepared to lose influence over funds which used to come to them.

In the extreme, careless diversion of aid from governments to NGDOs can undermine the functions which state and civil society are supposed to fulfill. Supremacy of national governance is compromised as donor conditions change the roles of local institutions; competent civil servants are enticed away because government cannot match NGDO conditions of service. On the ground, NGDOs deliver more than ministries do, which erodes regime legitimacy; aid-driven NGDO expansion may also provide cover to subversive elements, or corrupt organisations, provoking crackdowns which close space for all civic initiatives. In other words, more official aid to NGDOs can work against good governance and the strengthening of civil society: objectives used to justify increased Northern tax money to NGDOs in the first place. Donor practices can undermine their own goals while making life more difficult for legitimate NGDOs.[59]

For NGDOs, changing partners means different dances

NGDOs who decide to follow aid money without paying attention to what this means for identity and long-term relationships between North, South and East risk weakening their contribution to civic development locally and globally. Changing partners means learning new dances, (the contractor waltz), at the cost of forgetting the old ones – such as the solidarity two-step. If NGDOs get seriously out of step in the North, South and East, an influential part of the citizens' sector will be less likely to oversee whatever system of international governance evolves. In turn, weak civic control on governments limits the public's ability to control how transnational markets operate and who wins and loses from how they work.

In deciding strategy, Southern and Eastern NGDOs must look carefully at the costs and benefits of cutting Northern NGDOs out of the aid chain. Instead of switching partners, Northern NGDOs should be pushed harder to deliver on their comparative advantages as intermediaries, which are to:[60]

- help Southern NGDOs retain their autonomy as civic institutions;
- reduce the perception that Southern NGDOs are competing with their governments for aid;
- incorporate appropriate technical assistance that is based on mutual values;

- ensure that aid can be more flexibly applied;
- work against simple substitution of Southern NGDOs for the state in service provision;
- broaden support of Northern constituencies;
- maintain plurality in the aid system;
- strengthen South-North collaboration in policy impacts at the international level by bringing 'testimony' from the lives of poor people and their struggles.

The lower circle in Figure 6.1 is not a realistic representation of the complex NGDO community with sector and interest groups, factions, overlaps and constructed barriers. The different ability of NGDOs to access sources in the South and East may drive more wedges between them. Two splits are reasonably obvious. The first is between NGDOs with the capacity to deal with the official aid system and those that cannot. The second group may be squeezed out and resent it. The second is between transnationals with a built-in capability to take learning from one place and apply it in another, both North and South, placing local NGDOs at a disadvantage, leading to nationalist feelings and resentment again. The capability of NGDO co-ordinating structures to mediate and bridge fund-related divides will be critical in years to come.

Managing deflection and displacement

The picture looks pretty clear: the future of NGDO funding lies in the hands of the official aid system, with the self-financing development banks playing an increasingly dominant role as bilateral funds shrink over the longer term. These trends present managers with the challenges of deflection and displacement. Deflection is a redirection of management focus and energy from the founding purpose and civic constituency. Two types of deflection are likely to occur. The first is satisfying the demands of governmental agendas at the cost of attention to civic roots and constituency. Second, when focusing on development banks, NGDOs can lose sight of the fact that it is the borrower rather than the giver who should be at the centre of attention. Improving the quality of a bank's lending conditions may only re-enforce the problem of lack of borrower ownership and responsibility. Again, it is not a question of either/or. Improving the quality of what IFIs do should be part of the NGDO agenda, but not at the cost of engaging with the borrowing governments. As a strategic first step, it is the dialogue and interaction between development banks and borrowing governments with which NGDOs need to engage; this is now occurring, for example, in the Philippines in preparation for donor consortium meetings.

Displacement arises when new tasks of engaging with the official aid system are taken on without extra capacity. Inevitably the human capacity in time and effort is withdrawn from elsewhere. Making up for displaced capacity is not easy because the interaction is not a 'project' and therefore calls for high-quality money which is in short supply. Serious attention needs to be paid to making good displaced management capacity if an NGDO's effectiveness is not to suffer. Dealing with displacement will put a particular burden and responsibility on a small group of Northern donor NGDOs.

Managing while Moving Away from Aid: NGDO Strategies and Practices

NGDO leaders/managers need to simultaneously manage a mix of funding and multiple donors while pursuing strategies which wean the organisation off aid through building up greater financial self-reliance. The information generated so far can help make choices which reduce dependency on, and increase autonomy within, the international aid system. This section provides ideas on dealing with multiple donors and offers strategic conclusions about a desirable resource mix, with practical advice about how to fund-raise.

Managing multiple donors

Generally, multiple donors are a management burden and an asset at the same time. The burden is essentially one of dealing with low-quality money and individualised demands on time. The blessing is less dependency on any one source, which reduces vulnerability and increases negotiating power. The challenge is to find an optimal number and balance of sources when managing more than one.[61] Conversation with leaders suggests that between five and eight donors is optimum – a few unadventurous and reliable, complemented by others willing to experiment and then perhaps move on. A common way of reducing the disadvantages of multiple donors is to form roundtables or consortia.

Rountables and consortia are structured relationships between an NGDO (often southern) and its donors, where a common set of ground rules are agreed and adhered to by all parties. This structure is used by BRAC and PROSHIKA in Bangladesh and various councils of churches. The format usually involves the following:

- The NGDO preparcs a multiycar programme of activity to be funded, which may be made up of distinct related projects, but is treated as a logical, integrated whole.
- Support is pledged and provided as a proportion of the whole with agreements on performance criteria, overhead levels and admission of other funders.
- A system of periodic monitoring, evaluation and reporting used by all parties, perhaps with joint evaluation teams or other technical support.

Experience suggests that this set-up can work effectively if five conditions are satisfied. These are:

- The NGDO must be strong enough to formulate a comprehensive, detailed statement of what it wants to do, where and why, including frank assessments of its strengths and weaknesses.
- The NGDO must have the capacity to deliver what it has planned, including the capability to monitor, assess and report on what it has or has not achieved.

- Donors must relinquish their 'project possession' way of thinking, supporting instead a coherent programme (even if for domestic consumption they stress activities which correspond to their priorities).
- Donors need to reassess what they consider to be overhead or indirect costs to ensure that process features and the institutional capacity development of the NGDO are properly valued.
- Donors must be able to accept and work with consolidated reporting, both financial and narrative. Translation to individual formats become the donor's responsibility.

While usually to be recommended if the conditions are met, the drawback for NGDOs, as Sarvadoya and ORAP in Zimbabwe found, is that donors can co-ordinate their support and priorities in such a way that it is equivalent to 'ganging up', severely limiting the NGDO's room for manoeuvre. The chance of this happening is greatly reduced if the NGDO can demonstrate real impact. More often than not, multiple donors do not form consortia or roundtables and so it is left to the leader/manager to do just that: provide leadership and management of diverse donors. Box 6.3 summarises the reflections on donor management by a Kenyan NGDO leader who was, at one stage, managing 23 donors.

Donor management is seldom found in the curricula of NGDO management training programmes, but is a crucial demand that must be done well. This gap needs to be filled.

Box 6.3
Managing multiple donors

The trade-off
Establishing a broad donor base involves a trade-off between costs in time, reporting, administration and management, set against reduced vulnerability and greater operating independence. Experience suggests that an NGDO's creative potential is reduced if it is at the mercy of one or two dominant donors, who almost invariably dictate operational requirements. Multiple donors are a demanding, but preferred, financing strategy.

Building relationships with donors
Making the initial contacts and establishing the basic framework of a relationship is crucial for what eventually follows.

- *Initial contact:* Follow up an initial contact as soon as possible to understand the donor's interests, priorities principles and concerns - if any - about working with NGDOs. What is their 'risk threshold' – for instance, their openness to innovation and new ideas? What are the basic requirements for information and how does the approval process work? If you are dealing with a local office, how much authority or influence does it have? Is the donor interested in a long-term relationship and can this be maintained via one person? If no long-term prospects exists, but a 'one-night stand' can provide funds, the decision has to be made to engage or cut losses and get out.
- *Finding project/programme congruence:* To establish where congruence may exist, the NGDO should present its ideas clearly and seek a reaction; if the reaction is not enthusiastic, determine what modifications could elicit greater support.

- *Negotiating areas of flexibility:* Negotiation is required to ensure that a proposal is not simply a write-up of what the donor will fund. A balance needs to be struck, and it is important to agree on implementation expectations – such as pace of activities – as well as monitoring and evaluation requirements; there must also be flexibility along the way.
- *Monitoring the relationship and reporting on activities:* Exploit every opportunity for face-to-face contact. Treat such contacts and visits as supplements, not substitutes, for formal reporting. While generic reporting is preferable, a tailored addenda or covering letter providing more detail about a particular aspect of interest to a donor should be considered.
- *Establishing positive familiarity:* Donors tend to make similar statements which need to be clarified because they can hide significant differences. For example, the assertion that the aim is to fund ideas and innovation may, in an ongoing relationship, be a sign of 'fatigue' and code for withdrawal. The NGDO must be in a position to ease out of the donor, rather than the other way round. One way of testing for fatigue is to withhold a funding request at the end of the cycle but maintain contact, keeping the donor informed of what you are doing. Let any long-term interest in continuation come from them first.

Rules of thumb
- Ensure that the constituency you want to work with is at the centre of your plans and activities.
- Focus on building a relationship of mutual trust and shared ideas, rather than concentrating on money, which should be treated as an instrument – not the object of the interaction.
- Every grant has a cost. From time to time, assess the total 'cost' of each donor relationship. Where familiarity is weakening, this may be a sign to either 'rest' the donor or take the chance: request more funds; however spread the application to others as well.
- Make sure you keep promises, especially with respect to accountability and timely reporting. Never agree on deadlines you cannot deliver.
- Learn to appreciate and incorporate donor ideas, but say 'no' when necessary.
- Remember that donors need NGDOs as much as NGDOs need donors.
- Use common sense and make ethical management principles your guide.

Source: adapted from a contribution by Ezra Mbogori

Strategic choices in funding sources

Based on the previous analysis, and looking ahead, what conclusions can be made about preferred strategies for NGDO financing? The following six conclusions stand out.

- NGDOs everywhere are well advised to spread their income sources, ranking them according to existing potential and trends in quantity and quality. Each NGDO needs to decide on a strategic mix and develop the necessary capacities.
- Southern and Eastern NGDOs are vulnerable to political aid decision-making

in the North, over which they have minimal control or influence. To be viable, autonomous and truly indigenous, resource strategies must be directed at 'rooting' them in their own economies.[62]
- Aid available to NGDOs is getting colder; official funds will start to dominate, allocated on a 'contracting' basis. Avoiding a contractor's role calls for access to (small amounts of) hot funds to protect organisational autonomy.
- High-quality funds generated directly from the market do not carry the complications of public expectations, together with the risk of not living up to them. In other words,

market operation is the preffered source; everything else brings costs and constraints.

- Combining non-profit and for-profit activities must be structured so as to avoid too much of an overlap, but without breaking the relationship between them. Distinct legal entities under separate management, but single ownership, is preferable where the law and the tax situation makes this possible.
- For the South and East, the choice between Northern NGDOs and official aid agencies will be less important because their sources, conditions and obligations are beginning to merge. Only those Northern NGDOs with substantial autonomy from the influence of official aid will remain distinctive, offering the highest potential for authentic partnership.

The future of NGDO viability and third-sector identity, therefore, lies in balancing opportunity with fund-raising strategy.

Translating strategy into practice

Assuming that NGDOs have surveyed the potentials and limitations of different sources, how can they translate their choices into practice? In today's language, how can they mobilise financial alternatives to the aid system? Readings provides useful publications on practical steps. Box 6.4 summarises Richard Holloway's insights.

Box 6.4
Alternative fund-raising

What are alternatives to continued reliance on aid?
There are three components to NGDO finance: self-financing (generating funds from income-generating activities); local fund-raising (tapping economic surpluses generated in-country); and external financing directed specifically at organisational sustainability.

Self-financing
This is generated through:
- sale of products and services which used to be free, including sale of expertise;
- fees and subscriptions;
- interest from investments.

Local fund-raising
This occurs through:
- the general public: mailing, appeals, special events, campaigns, games/lotteries;
- corporate support, including deductions from pay rolls, corporate philanthropy, acting as a supplier of parts or expertise, social investment, sponsored projects;
- national governments as grant aid, project financing, tax exemptions, capital goods, expertise;
- local governments – similar to national governments, but are public resources locally controlled;
- local charities and foundations, including helping new, local funders come into existence and persuading welfare-oriented bodies to support long-term development.

External finance for sustainability

Types of suitable external finance are:

● revolving loan and credit funds which produce a surplus as income;
● (repayable) venture capital to help an NGDO engage in a viable commercial activity, purchase a subsidiary, or build on land as an investment;
● capital required for an endowment fund.

Getting started

Without a benefactor, NGDOs will need to build their own capital fund by a combination of:[63]

● local fund-raising from subscriptions, contracts;
● reducing funding levels though cost recovery;
● creative use of external funds, capitalising on exchange-rate fluctuations, investing reserve on short-term deposits;
● support from grants by educating donors to make lump-sum payments for recurrent costs, such as rent, salaries and consumable items; this can be invested and the income allocated to a capital fund.

How much self-reliance and autonomy?

NGDOs serious about generating funds outside of the aid system are generally disappointed with the modest amount of income they are likely to get from the time and effort involved. In this case, it is important to focus on strategies which finance the core. If this is covered, an NGDO's position towards donors can change for the better.

● *Reduce costs.* NGDOs, especially those in the South and East, have become accustomed to styles of operation which are not cost effective, do not match locally supported non-profits, and place them way beyond the means of the local economy. A first step in embarking on alternative fund-raising for self-reliance is to operate more simply, using public transport instead of four-wheel drives, standardising equipment and sharing facilities.
● *Concentrate on covering administrative and overhead costs.* The most vulnerable NGDOs must aim to finance their core costs without 'skimming' the projects they implement.
● *Recruit people with skills.* NGDOs build up expertise in grant-hunting at the cost of an enterprise mentality and basic for-profit skills. Expanding horizons and contacts to include business-minded people on boards is one way of gaining the insights needed, as is recruitment of commercially trained staff who understand and subscribe to non-profit goals.

Source: adapted from contribution by Richard Holloway

The way to access resources owned by other people depends on the type of resource. What you can do depends on what you want. Table 6.1 offers ideas for accessing key resources NGDOs need.[64]

Table 6.1 How to access other people's resources

Resource	Method
People	hire, borrow, poach, meet, join, visit, learn from
Money	impress, persuade, borrow and pay back, request investment, demand as a right
Equipment	share, pool, buy, borrow
Experience	learn, visit, work with, befriend, offer something in return
Information	borrow, work with, buy, share
Competence	learn from

According to Santar Datta, launching a fund-raising programme involves ten sequential steps, which draw on any of these methods.
The steps include the following:

- *Define the purpose.* Sort out why you want to fund-raise (the ends) from the activity the money will be used for (the means). For example, the goal of improving education is not the same as teaching children.
- *Analyse funding requirements.* Goals and activities may require different types of money, such as one-off investments, ongoing cover for recurrent costs and expertise.
- *Map the potential sources.* Look at the environment to see who has the type of resource you need.
- *Assess potential contributors.* Analyse a contributor's worth against the costs of persuading them to give and collect donations. For example, a monthly collection of $10 from 1000 people might cost more than a single gift but offers long-term continuity.
- *Define a strategy and plan.* For each contributor, detail how you will approach them, the preparations needed and the steps

required.
- *Establish a collection system.* How will the contributor be approached, by whom and how will they be held accountable?
- *Conduct the collection drive.* Put strategies and plans into action.
- *Allocate the resources.* Use the funds raised as promised.
- *Monitor utilisation.* Collect information on what is being done and how it is achieved.
- *Communicate back to contributors.* Build towards a longer-term relationship by informing contributors how their help has made a difference.

Fund-raising is a profession distinct from writing project proposals. Because they have evolved within the framework of aid, Southern or Eastern NGDOs seldom have this type of competence. In the North, some NGDOs have built up significant expertise in mobilising funds from the public and the market. It is time this capacity was prioritised and experiences shared, which is now beginning to happen. The odd case needs to become a standard component in NGDO relationships between North, South and East. Moreover, given the difference in environments, South-South exchanges would be particularly useful.

Irrespective of the fund-raising strategies or methods employed outside of investments, any contributor naturally wants as much of their support as possible to go towards the goal they have been 'sold'. Making this (appear to be) the case – the art of minimising overheads – is both a skill and a trap for NGDOs. This, then, is the final element in resource mobilisation which NGDOs must do properly.

NGDO finance and the dangerous myth: sustainable development is quick, cheap and easy

NGDOs want and need their supporters to believe that they are effective at minimum cost. To this end, the ratio of administrative costs to total income is used as a proxy for efficiency, irrespective of the product.[66] NGDOs have been so successful that, irrespective of the type of development work they do, low overheads are apparently always possible. The American financial magazine *Money* produces a yearly value-for-money ranking of US charitable organisations using one criteria only – administrative costs. 1994 saw the International Rescue Committee at 7.7 per cent, followed by the Mennonites and Save the Children Fund at 11.8 and 17.9 per cent respectively.[67] The magazine has no idea what they actually achieve, which is a vital criteria. Similarly, *Henderson Top 2000 Charities*, a UK publication, 'guarantees you the answer!' about non-profits, again apart from what they achieve.

NGDOs, especially in the North, are in a bind when it comes to the false image they have created – that development itself is easy and can be done on the cheap. So how do they square the circle? The answer is that they fudge by using creative public financial reporting.[68] There are no standardised or legally binding formats or ratios, such as the generally accepted accounting principles (GAAP) used by businesses and their auditors. Only when media disaster strikes is the curtain lifted, shedding light on the way NGDOs allocate expenditures to show themselves in the best possible way. Typical fudges which are used to reduce NGDO overhead percentages are shown in Box 6.5.

Whichever techniques are adopted, they are all counterproductive in one way or another. First, they leave the NGDO vulnerable to detailed enquiry and negative publicity. Second, by obscuring the real costs of doing development work, management is rendered less effective because an important foundation for informed decision-making is missing. Third, by ignoring the fact that different types of activity carry different cost structures, donors can get away with misusing their position. Some donors, such as USAID, do establish realistic overheads through a Negotiated Indirect Cost Rate Agreement for an agreed programme. This is an exception, with UN agencies, such as UNHCR, being apparently the worst at accepting the full costs of the work they fund NGDOs to do.[69]

Box 6.5
Maintaining a perception of minimum overheads

Typical Ways NGDOs Appear to Reduce Overhead Percentages

1. Allocate as many administrative costs as possible to 'programmes'.

2. Charge institutional donors as much as the traffic will bear. Associated techniques are:
    *   claiming overheads on a cost-plus basis;
    *   claiming the same costs from two or more donors;
    *   shifting headquarter expenses around in institutional and project-funding arrangements – different donor 'windows' have different cofinancing conditions which can be exploited for cross-subsidy;
    *   cross financing from very large projects, such as food aid, where relatively small overheads generate sufficient income to subsidise other activities.

3. Finance overseas expenses as 'projects' which can be classed as development expenditures. This method is prevalent amongst Northern donor NGDOs which operate on an unrealistically low fixed-percentage basis agreed with government, as in Scandinavia and the Benelux: 5 per cent in Norway and Sweden, 7.5 per cent in Holland and 14 per cent in Switzerland for 'complex' projects implemented on the government's behalf.

4. Send as many funds as possible overseas, claiming them to be development expenditures. Then repatriate the money needed to finance fund-raising and other local costs as if they have come from a third party. Transnational NGDOs with an international centre are in the easiest position to do this.

Source: adapted from a contribution by Ian Smillie

None of these tricks solve the essential problem which is the calculation and allocation of true costs associated with different types of development work, combined with public honesty. The most critical cause of today's difficulties is that the process costs of development are denied, ignored or just not considered 'real' development. And sadly, this perspective can still be found in professional donors who should know better. Ignorance is no longer an excuse for understanding what sustainable development means in all its dimensions and costs. It really is incumbent on NGDOs, say through their co-ordinating bodies, to confront this issue collectively.

With respect to Northern NGDOs, adherence to the myth indicates that leaders/ managers make an internal calculation that the risks of discovery and negative publicity do not outweigh the benefit of keeping things as they are. This calculation may be faulty; the few NGDOs who are transparent about their costs do not necessarily suffer from it. For example, World Vision Australia has published overheads of 33.7 per cent and has still managed to be the largest public fund-raiser in the country.[70]

In Europe, no individual NGDO or grouping is taking the lead in developing standards for overhead calculations which others could adopt on a voluntary basis. The probable reason is fear of being undercut promotionally by those who keep to their old 'untransparent' practices. Change, if it comes, is more likely to result from external rather than internal pressures. The UK has a Charity Commission which is drafting proposals for accounting

standards which it can enforce.[71] Other countries do not have such a body. Another type of initiative is to establish a *Guide to Good Giving* – a sort of consumer's guide to NGDO effectiveness and costs.[72] This move is likely to be actively contested and declared technically impossible by insecure NGDOs who have the most to hide.

Are there basic principles which could justify categories of expenditure which NGDOs could agree to apply, allowing the public to make a fair comparison of overheads and enabling managers to do their jobs more effectively? At the risk of gross over-simplification in a very complicated area, the following principles are suggested. They flow from the understanding that NGDO work in sustainable development contains the micro-macro, North-South, product-process dimensions explained in previous chapters.

- NGDO expenditures should be categorised according to their interaction with the primary stakeholder. Table 6.2 indicates what this looks like in practice.
- Because of their intermediary position between giver and beneficiary, NGDO fund-raising should be treated as a direct cost. Without the poor, NGDOs cannot exist; without donors they cannot serve the poor. The costs involved at both extremes mirror each other in terms of primary interaction, but not in terms of their proportions, which should be low at the income and high at the expenditure end.

Table 6.2 Categories for reporting expenditure

Expenditure category	Characteristic	Typical examples
Direct operations (micro-development and macro-policy initiatives)	Expenditures incurred in direct transaction with the primary stakeholders, partners or institutions	● pre-investment funds to including participatory planning, studies, stakeholder negotiations; ● all material, financial and process inputs to primary stakeholders: materials, training, exchanges, meetings; ● change agent's personal transport, accommodation and other costs, including skill upgrading; ● costs of first-level managers who interact or negotiate with communities, partners or policy makers; ● costs of information collection and first-level processing for micro- or macro-development; ● cost of lobbying and advocacy, including staff, media, meetings, communications.
Direct fund-raising	Expenditures required to educate, communicate with and collect funds from donors or private contributors	● costs of personnel directly running public education/communication, writing proposals and collecting incomes; ● expenditures to third parties: the media, communication/collection services; ● costs of public information and education.
Administration	Expenditures required to satisfy statutory constitutional, accounting and audit requirements	● costs associated with accountants, financial controllers, purchasing officers, statutory external audits; ● costs associated with management of assets; ● costs associated with trustees or boards complying with legal and constitutional obligations, such as annual and other meetings.
Support	Expenditures on services provided centrally which can be clearly identified; necessary for direct operations or fund-raising.	● costs associated with second and higher management and direction of operations and administration – where necessary, apportioned according to responsibility; ● cost of specialist professional staff; ● costs of monitoring, learning, evaluating and managing information.

It may be unrealistic to expect Northern (and in the future Southern and Eastern) NGDOs to struggle with the re-education needed for the general public to understand why professional development work is not simply a case of shipping money overseas. Altering the public's perception of what development is about – from quick, cheap and easy to slow, costly and complex – has to happen sooner or later. The trouble is, who will take the lead at the risk of losing market share?

But, let's be optimistic and say that re-education does occur and NGDOs provide fair, comparable accounts of their expenditure. Even with new understanding and better figures, the public, and NGDOs themselves, still lack a vital piece of information – what has actually been achieved? Without this measure, high or low overhead percentages are meaningless. The next chapter therefore turns to the problems and possibilities of assessing NGDO development impact and organisational performance.

7

Assessing Development Impact and Organisational Performance

The Importance of Knowing about Change as Well as Action

The previous pages contain many references to this chapter, because knowing what you are achieving crops up in many areas of effective organisation and management. However, when it comes to knowing the results of their efforts, NGDOs rate poorly. It is difficult to find a system that provides reliable evidence of achievement in relation to development goals, and things are not much better with programmes or projects. Past efforts to identify results have been technically inadequate, of low priority and underresourced. Things are, however, changing for the better.

The lack of NGDOs' ability to manage by achievement stems from several factors. First is the complexity of what must be assessed. Second is a major inconsistency between the assumptions of the aid system and how

sustainable development actually occurs. Third is the limitations of the instruments NGDOs use to monitor, evaluate, and review. Fourth is inadequacies in the system which focus on projects rather than on the organisation as a whole. Fifth is a culture which values action more than reflection. Sixth is a lack of benchmarks to compare performance with, compounded by a lack of clarity about objectives and position. Finally come financial considerations; assessment costs cannot always be allocated to project budgets and are therefore treated as overheads which must be kept low. Together these factors prevent NGDOs from assessing themselves and the results of their actions. Combined, these weaknesses make it difficult for NGDOs to prove their legitimacy and to be held accountable.

Recognising Achievements: the Foundation for Effective NGDO Management

The core task of management is to lead an organisation to its purpose. If achievements are not recognised, or can only be guessed at, or must be assumed by logical inference, the basis of management and decision-making is weakened. This insight is nothing new; the question is how does lack of knowledge about results affect NGDOs?

Development results

When NGDO leaders/managers do not recognise the results of their works the following consequences – as outlined in previous chapters – may occur:

- Leaders and managers lack solid grounds to judge consistency between activities, goals and missions; make sound choices between conflicting ways of doing things; ensure that a transfer of 'ownership' to primary stakeholders occurs at the right time and in the right way (described in Chapter 5); and judge how far all relevant stakeholders have been satisfied – in other words assess the adequacy of organisational capacity.
- Cost-benefit appraisal may not be possible, and economic effectiveness therefore cannot be assessed.
- Personnel may only be judged on the basis of effort, not merit, in terms of their

contribution to achieving development goals.

- Authority cannot be delegated with confidence, as there is no external standard against which staff efforts and quality of decisions are judged.

- Legitimacy and accountability remain open to question which: results in a perpetual state of internal anxiety and vulnerability to external appraisal; weakens an NDGO's position as a trusted civic actor; and reduces confidence.

- It is difficult if not impossible to demonstrate the merits of NGDO work, which means: loss of opportunity to persuade others to adopt NGDO practices; loss of potential to scale up by mobilising

more funds; and loss of influence.

- Future sustainability cannot be predicted.

- Lack of demonstrated achievements weakens grounds on which to resist or negotiate alternatives to state-centred policies and practices.

Evidence of these negative outcomes can be found in a spate of NGDO evaluation and impact studies. NGDO effectiveness is suffering badly because leaders, managers and staff do not know or learn about the consequences of their work, although they do learn about implementing activities. Why does the situation persist? What makes it so difficult to find out what is being achieved?

Difficulties in Demonstrating Development Impact

There are three reasons why NGDOs find it so hard to recognise their achievements: problems with assumptions, methodological difficulties and organisational demands. The first two are looked at in this section, organisation in the next.[1]

Promoting human development

Inconsistencies arise between the assumptions shaping the aid system and the way change occurs in real life. What happens is explained with the help of Figure 7.1, which places performance assessment in the context of the aid chain. On the left side are external forces, while on the right are shown the various links in the chain where assessment can be made.

Project-based aid relies on the assumption that a straight line of causes and effects can be defined and put in place. These relationships will guide resources through all organisations in the chain and allocate them in the right way. If you follow the line of a project you can predict future outcomes. Such a system might work if each organisation could shield the flow of resources and organisational behaviour from negative internal and external influences – which they never can. Logical frameworks deal

with such potentially disruptive factors by relegating them to the assumptions column. If everything went according to plan, reaching the desired (hypothetical) impact would be assured in a controlled process where measurement and accountability for performance would be straight forward. But there are two major flaws in this approach related to an NGDO's ability to control the context and the demands of sustainability

False assumption of control

Significant changes occur as the development process moves along the chain and out of aid organisations into society. First, NGDO influence diminishes as other factors come into play. The most important factor in people-centred development is altering human behaviour, which in turn depends on many external historical and local factors, such as power relations, motivation and cultural values. Second, the timescales needed to assess impact are usually much longer than to assess output or outcome. Sustained benefit from tree planting may not be obvious for many years. In other words, some impacts can only be seen long after an activity or project has ended. Third, impacts

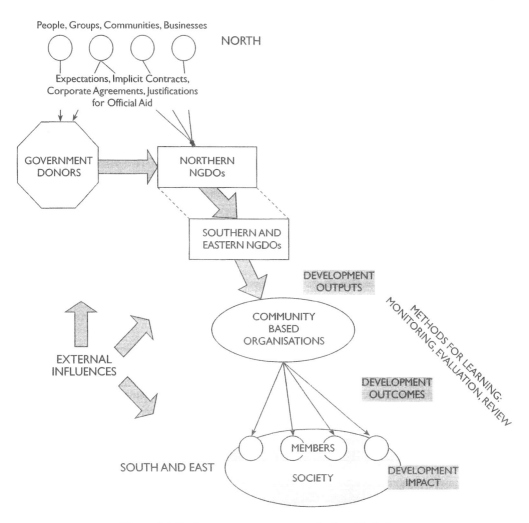

People, Groups, Communities, Businesses

NORTH

Expectations, Implicit Contracts,
Corporate Agreements, Justifications
for Official Aid

GOVERNMENT
DONORS

NORTHERN
NGDOs

SOUTHERN AND
EASTERN NGDOs

DEVELOPMENT
OUTPUTS

COMMUNITY
BASED
ORGANISATIONS

EXTERNAL
INFLUENCES

DEVELOPMENT
OUTCOMES

METHODS FOR LEARNING:
MONITORING, EVALUATION, REVIEW

SOUTH AND EAST

MEMBERS

SOCIETY

DEVELOPMENT
IMPACT

Figure 7.1 Performance measurement in the aid chain

on poverty do not occur only through NGDOs. However, to convince donors and contributors of their worth, an NGDO must show the difference it has made – which is difficult. Fourth it is imposible to predict the future. Furthermore as the number of parties increases along the chain, so does the influence of their own interests and instabilities. For example, frequent turnover of international staff may bring fresh ideas, but it disrupts continuity and commitment to other people's projects while the politics of aid, in particular, create continual disturbances. Relying on predictions of cause and effect is not realistic when it comes to assessing achievements.

Sustainability: merging NGDO efforts with other processes

By the time resources leave the relative shelter of NGDOs and enter the world of communities, families and local culture, uncertainties and external influences increase many fold. This is the point where the demands of sustainability contradict the requirements for an unambiguous demonstration of NGDO achievements. To be sustainable, benefits of external inputs must be generated from changes in economic, social, political, environmental and other processes – which continue once external assistance withdraws. To achieve this, the outcomes of an

NGDO's activities must merge into ongoing processes rather than clearly stand apart from them, a necessary condition if effects are to be clearly attributed to aid resources. If they do their work properly, NGDO effects cannot be kept separate in order to be measured.

In sum, assumptions shaping how the aid system works, and can be measured, are inconsistent with how supported human development occurs and is sustained. NGDOs must therefore create an assessment system which copes with this inconsistency. But before describing how this can be done, methodological issues require attention.

Assessing development initiatives

Assessing an NGDOs development performance is complicated because it involves achievement on at least three levels: operational activities, strategic choices, and organisational standing in society. Ideally, each level must be consistent with those above or below and each calls for different measures and indicators. Figure 7.2 illustrates how development initiatives are meant to work.

Performance assessment

Development initiatives typically start by identifying a problem – for example, a rural population is suffering from malnutrition. Of the many causes identified, one is a significant loss of grain held in traditional family stores. The development initiative therefore introduces a new communal type of low-loss grain store and trains each household and the community in its proper use. The output of the initiative is the number of stores constructed and the number of people trained. This is a measure of the effort expended. However, these numbers do not say anything about the percentage reduction in grain loss – which is the outcome we need to know in order to judge if the initiative has been effective. Furthermore, the outcome is not the same as the solution to the original problem, which is low nutrition. The impact of the initiative will therefore be reductions in malnutrition, in other words the change achieved in relation to the original problem.

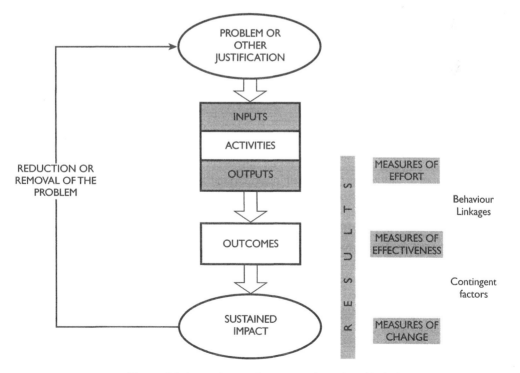

Figure 7.2 Assessing performance along the aid chain

The step from output to outcome is usually determined by people's behaviour and the links made to surrounding processes. For example, are the grain stores used as they should be and if not, why? If men decide that chickens have become a profitable undertaking, perhaps the stores might be used for breeding them instead. What if the rains fail? Nutrition may worsen, even if less stored grain is lost. In other words, the step from outcome to impact depends on many additional factors which the NGO often cannot influence, let alone control. Development initiatives, therefore, call for three points of measurement – outputs, outcomes and impacts, both wanted and unwanted – which can all be classed as results. What is assessed at each point is summarised in Table 7.1. Table 7.2 applies these points of measurement to common types of NGDO initiative.

Often impacts can only be assessed (long) after the original outputs have been achieved when the NGDO has moved on to other

Table 7.1 Assessing development achievements

Point of measurement	What is measured	Indicators
Outputs	Effort	Implementation of activities
Outcomes	Effectiveness	Use of outputs and sustained production of benefits
Impact	Change	Difference from the original situation

Table 7.2 Measures for different types of intervention

	Water supply	Credit for women	Environment	Civil society
Problem	Ill health	Women's vulnerability	Fall in agricultural production	State abuses its authority
Activity	Providing community-managed potable water supplies	Implementing a credit programme for women	Introducing agro-forestry species and technologies	Educating people on their human and civic rights
Output	Number of wells installed	Number of loans given and repaid as agreed	Number of species planted correctly and surviving	Number of participants who attend training courses
Outcome	Sustained availability of clean water with proper domestic use	Increase in disposable female income	Soil fertility stabilised and new agricultural practices applied	More active censure of politicians and public servants
Impact	Reduction in mortality and morbidity	Improved control, choice and status with respect to men	Retention or increase in agricultural productivity	More transparent and accountable state behaviour

activities or places. Consequently, NGDOs tend to report on their efforts and not the outcomes or impacts of their work (this is an abiding legacy of the welfare origins of NGDO activity originally intended to fill gaps and make good social ills). Even worse, objectives are typically framed in terms of activities – which is wrong. In the words of one adviser, 'If you find an NGDO using verbs as an objective, beware!'[2]

Assessing development initiatives in relation to organisation

At some stage, the results of development initiatives need to be related to the organisation as a whole, which brings additional demands for assessment. For example, a vision of a world where children enjoy their rights is translated by an NGDO into a mission of reducing infant mortality. Analysis by the NGDO shows that in the geographic area of concern – say urban slums – girls' lack of knowledge and access to prenatal services are key causes for high infant mortality. Male attitudes towards daughters' education, and government resource limitations, are seen to explain these two direct causes. Two development strategies are therefore selected. One with a long-term perspective is to enhance girls' access to education. A second short-term strategy is to increase the availability of good-quality prenatal services in urban slums.

The long-term strategy leads to two types of development intervention. One is to increase the motivation of men to educate their daughters, the other supports community action to provide additional primary school classrooms. Initiatives to change attitudes would aim at awareness raising and might involve newspaper, radio and television programmes, including educational seminars for industrial workers. Each would have specific measures of

Table 7.3 Organisational goals and measures

Organisational level	Reference points		
Vision	Children enjoy their rights		
Mission	Promote infant survival		

	Strategy 1 (Long term)		Strategy 2 (Short term)	
Problem	Low access to education for girls		High drop rates due to pregnancy	
Objective	Increase level of enrolment		Reduce unwanted pregnancies in school-aged girls	
Activity	Change male attitudes through education	Build more educational facilities	Training to improve the competencies of TBAs	Community mobilisation to operate clinics
Output	Number of men educated	Increase in number of school places relative to school-aged children	Number of TBAs completing training	Increase in number of reliable clinics
Outcome	More men supporting daughters' education	Higher proportion of girls of school age in school	Better quality of advice and preventive services	Greater proportion of girls using reproductive services
Impact	Greater proportion of school-aged girls attend and stay longer in school			

success. The short-term prenatal strategy consists of two interventions: one to improve the skills of traditional birth attendants (TBAs), the second to build up community capacity to finance their work. Again, each requires different measures of achievement. Table 7.3 summarises each level and the measures involved.

This example shows the variety of measures an NGDO needs to assess its organisational achievements. Although knowing what to measure is tough, it is not the most difficult problem to deal with.[3] Table 7.3 also illustrates that an NGDO's vision cannot be an operational measure of its impact because vision is too broad in scope. This raises the question: can NGDOs really demonstrate their impact and, if not, what can they be held accountable for? In practical terms, it is seldom possible for NGDOs to measure their organisational impact, especially for international NGDOs with a global vision and mission. From a performance point of view, for large and international NGDOs, vision and mission function primarily as the reference point for judging coherence between impacts and strategic choices and policy decisions. To be effective, nothing that an NGDO achieves should be in conflict with its guiding vision and purpose.

The process component to performance assessment

In addition to the multiple layers of achievement, complications arise when assessing the way goals are reached. For instance, how can you judge the processes as well as the products of change? In one example, increasing people's access to potable water can be done by installing wells that NGDOs run forever. An alternative is to negotiate community installation, ownership and management of a local water supply. Both improve access to clean water, but the way of doing so is very different. People-centred principles, and eventual NGDO withdrawal, make the second approach more appropriate, but assessing how far people own and manage a water supply is not easy.

Judging the process dimensions of

intervention is particularly important when improving the self-reliance of local organisations. The capacities for an effective local organisation listed below illustrate the process outcomes an NGDO should be facilitating, each of which needs specific measures.[4] The capacities of an effective community-based organisation – which an NGDO should facilitate – are to:

- mobilise and regulate local resources on an ongoing basis;
- manage and account for resources;
- ensure that leadership can be censured and held accountable;
- ensure and enable the ongoing participation of relevant stakeholders;
- cost-effectively translate external support into sustained impacts;
- critically assess public policies and translate them in locally appropriate ways;
- mediate, resolve and manage internal conflicts;
- effectively control an equitable distribution of benefits;
- resist appropriation of benefits by those who should be excluded;
- make legitimate claims on resources and defend local interests towards the government;
- understand and promote civic rights;
- hold NGDOs and other intervening agencies accountable for their behaviour;
- monitor, evaluate and learn from experience.

The processes needed to achieve these requirements are not simple to define or apply.[5] This is one reason why the participant-based measures described earlier are a way forward. People can best measure their own progress. Assessing achievement therefore means mastering the complicated business of measuring products and processes in development initiatives at interrelated levels of external change and in relation to the NGDO's own purpose.

Measures and indicators

Today's focus on demonstrating performance has lead to a flurry of efforts to identify indicators and measures of outputs, outcomes and impacts. The search is tough because of the complexities described in this chapter, and because of a healthy competition between two approaches to measurement: scientific and interpretative.[6] The readings at the end of this book provide a summary of measures and indicators currently applied to different types of development initiative – such as water, environment, shelter, credit, health and AIDS. Relatively less effort is applied to measures and indicators of NGDO organisational performance. The sections below, and the next chapter, look at what is occuring in this area.

Criteria for monitoring and evaluation

The previous sections highlight factors which should play a role when NGDOs assess the results of their work. It is possible, now, to summarise these as criteria an NGDO system should satisfy.

● Operate at different organisational levels, consistent with a framework set by vision and mission.

● Provide information on both tangible and intangible products and processes of development.

● Have reference points or standards against which judgements can be made.

● Offer predictions in terms of sustainability.

● Incorporate a time scale covering future changes.

● Be able to identify the extent of NGDO effects against other factors.

● Be reliable and produce valid information.

● Generate information which is appropriate for different users and timely in relation to decision-making and accountability requirements.

● Be cost effective in relation to the level of resources applied.

These criteria are so difficult to satisfy that most NGDOs simply measure their activities, expenditures and outputs. Moreover, it is rare to find any assessment of the organisation as a whole. The next two sections look at ways of introducing performance assessment in both these areas.

Assessing Performance in Development Initiatives

NGDOs do pay attention to performance but are poor at creating systems which demonstrate actual outcomes. The inadequacy of existing performance measurement is tied to the methods and instruments that systems typically employ. This section therefore looks at ways of altering and increasing capacity in terms of instruments, systems and culture.

NGDO assessment methods: monitoring, evaluation and organisational review

To assess their work and their role NGDOs employ three instruments: monitoring, evaluation and review. Initially, until the late 1980s, these tools were shaped by scientific ways of thinking which assumed that facts

could be established by a neutral, external third-party separate from the people involved. This approach has been increasingly rejected as unfeasible, incompatible with authentic participation and contrary to true people-centred development. Consequently, an alternative, interpretative method is increasingly employed. At the same time the official aid system is putting much effort into improving scientific measures.[7] Where are these developments leading to?

Defining traditional assessment methods

Assessing and managing NGDO work traditionally relies on project-oriented systems of monitoring and evaluation, recently complemented by organisational review. These methods can be defined as follows. Monitoring is an ongoing process of surveillance on the implementation and outcomes of development initiatives and related organisational functions. Monitoring informs operational decision-making. Information gained through monitoring is usually judged against what has been planned or agreed. A principal focus is on internal management factors, such as the costs and timing of inputs and outputs, level of effort and supervision of staff performance. Evaluation is a (semi-)independent assessment of the outcomes, impact and relevance of a development initiative and its associated organisational functions. Evaluations inform decision-making and learning at the strategic or programme level. Information gained through evaluations should attribute change to the NGDO's efforts, identify unintended effects and provide learning for improvement. Review is a periodic (semi-)independent appraisal of an organisation's role and capacity. Reviews primarily inform learning and decision-making at the organisational level. The principal focus is on translating vision into position, public recognition, social legitimacy and future viability in civil society. In other words, it is an holistic appraisal of an NGDO's role. Organisational reviews are not frequently undertaken, although there is some improvement because of an awakening interest in capacity building (the subject of the next chapter).

One important factor to bear in mind is that monitoring, evaluation and review are means to an end, not ends in themselves. They all contribute to present and future effectiveness and impact. The above definitions furthermore include organisational factors.[8] This dimension is added because, for reasons of project-based development history, there is a difference between assessing development and assessing the organisations 'doing' development. This allows, for example, donors to avoid critical scrutiny because monitoring and evaluation are applied to projects 'out there' in the field – as if all organisations in the aid chain are not part and parcel of what happens. In other words, evaluations seldom say anything about the organisational conditions or characteristics which might have contributed to the results.

> What is more, *'although funders may sometimes acknowledge the extent of their influence, they rarely accept responsibility for its consequences. By and large, donors take the stance of an employer or service contractor. Like employers or contractors, donors control many of the conditions affecting performance. However, in a manner similar to employers-contractors, donors typically assign responsibility for results to those whom they finance. They hold grantees accountable for the successful delivery of outcomes and outputs specified in negotiated agreements without considering the determinative nature or impact of their own policies, objectives, requirements, timetables and capabilities on grantees' orientation, scope, capacity and operations.'* [9]

This quotation highlights a major limitation in assessing if NGDOs perform well. By keeping themselves out of the picture, funders deny the existence of an important set of factors which determine NGDOs' achievements. There are few areas of development work carried out by NGDOs which are not, to some degree or another, influenced by the quality of donor assistance. As a matter of principle, good practice and fairness, the donor dimension must be included in any investigation and explanation of NGDO performance. Unless this occurs, learning about NGDOs and their development initiatives will always be inadequate.

Limitations of monitoring and evaluation

Monitoring and evaluation should be straightforward. In projects, monitoring compares what is going on with what was anticipated. Evaluation essentially answers three questions: what has changed; what caused the change; and is the change what was originally intended? In terms of the criteria set above, however, both monitoring and evaluation are difficult for NGDOs in practice, partly because intended outcomes are infrequently identified in advance.

For a start, evaluating change requires a defined baseline for comparisons. The problem is knowing from the outset every factor which is relevant and how all factors affect each other. These relationships are usually complex and can be disputed, especially when the parties involved have different views or theories of cause and change. Furthermore, it is necessary to choose appropriate indicators and decide upon their significance. Finally, it is necessary to know when to stop – to know how much data is too much. The importance of this point is to draw boundaries around what the NGDO intends to negotiate and take on. Because the causes of problems nest in one another from international to local level, the agency must set practical limits and admit to donors and contributors what it cannot tackle.

Indicators can be used for monitoring change. By and large, however, because of the difficulties described above, what is actually monitored are activities and outputs, not organisational functions, outcomes or impacts. Because activities and outputs tend to be biased towards quantitative measures at the cost of qualitative change, the task becomes one of 'making up the numbers'. Monitoring merely highlights targets rather than demonstrating the effects activities have on people's lives. Target-fixation has a number of undesirable effects. First, unintended outcomes or impacts are not recognised or may be ignored. Unless it noticeably disrupts activities, change not in the project's scope does not feature in monitoring set-ups. In addition, unless specifically catered for, achievement of contracted activities takes precedence over sustainability. In other words, activity targets make performance systems focus on the here and now rather than on long-term change. One solution is to include indicators of non-sustainability in monitoring (and evaluation), but this seldom occurs.[10]

The organisational challenge in monitoring is to gather, store and utilise information which serves different levels of assessment. Monitoring must be multifunctional so that information generated at one level is useful at the next. A rule of thumb is that the quality of data collected is negatively related to whether or not the collector requires it. In other words, if I do not need the information for my work, I will spend less effort in obtaining it and ensuring that it is valid. As far as possible, therefore, information should be collected, generated and interpreted by each user. For example, bench-marking of organisational performance needs to be done by leaders/managers because the necessary comparisons call for the type of insight which can only be gained by working at this level.

Once activities are completed, it is time for evaluation. With a good baseline as a reference point, the key is to link effects to causes so that the NGDO's can assess their contribution to change. However, identifying NGDO-induced change from other factors is very difficult. The scientific way of doing this is to employ control groups which are the same in all respects to the groups the NGDO's work with. Nevertheless controls are imperfect as groups and are never identical. Therefore, as well as being costly and time consuming, approaches which try and objectify development measures are at best only fair approximations and at worst numerical misinformation. They may also be unethical, or else involve unpalatable actions, such as denying aid to retain a control sample for comparison.

External evaluations throw up other problems too. They can falsify reality for organisational ends, may not instigate learning, and are seldom placed in a forum with those 'investigated' so that findings can be challenged or rejected. But a more important limitation is that this approach not only separates development from poor people, it places the interpretation of facts in the hands of outsiders. In other words, it disempowers those who should be in the driving seat. The first 20 years of development tried its best to be objective and scientific in monitoring and evaluation. However, growing dissatisfaction with the way scientific approaches treat people as objects has led to the development of alternatives which place people's perceptions at the starting point.[11]

The move to interpretation in monitoring, evaluation and review

An 'interpretative approach' is the label used for monitoring and evaluating social development and organisational performance, highlighting different stakeholders' views and appraisals of situations and events.[12] In this approach, monitoring and evaluation are ongoing situation-specific processes which may be stopped for practical reasons, – for example, money has run out – but will carry on in the minds and lives of those concerned. People evaluate their circumstances continually; life, even in poverty, is much more than a series of aid projects.

Interpretative assessment contains features which bring it closer to satisfying the criteria for effective NGDO monitoring and evaluation. First, it works on the basis of building up the 'truth' from the perspectives of different interested parties. In this sense it is multilevel, as various parties provide inputs. To the extent that individuals bring different levels of experience, a wide spectrum of views can be incorporated. For example, an individual can be a client of a micro-enterprise NGDO and a member of a governing body of a national association of small businesses. The person brings all these perspectives to bear at once. Given that development problems nest in each other, no artificial separation of perspectives must be created for the method to work.[13] Second, because people's lives are affected by diverse factors an interpretative method can disentangle an NGDO's effects from individual factors. In other words, people themselves must identify the complex influences they experience. Third, reference points for predicting sustainability are in-built because they rest with the people concerned. It is the values, aspirations, interests and changes people will act on which are important for assessing outcomes and gauging long-term impact. Fourth, people know about unintended effects and can report them. Unexpected effects are not 'discordant' information which tends to be ignored, especially if it creates difficulties. Finally, if built into the intervention approach, monitoring and evaluating information is generated at little extra cost, being part and parcel of the intervention process. In fact, the interpretative approach to evaluation can itself stimulate and encourage action, as well as re-enforce people's confidence in their abilities and commitment to change.

However interpretation is not all benefit and no costs. Sometimes people merely repeat what the NGDOs wants to hear out of respect or due to a cultural aversion to displease. Furthermore, where dependency has been created, or where an NGDO fulfils a patronage function, or is used by the elite, or has replaced government services which have withered away, people have reason to be dishonest. This drawback may be amplified when third parties are involved, because they can create a perception that negative findings are going to be used against NGDO continuation. In fact, in any evaluation method, needs and interests can lead stakeholders to distort or bias information.

One answer is to employ participatory techniques which stress the learning function of monitoring and evaluation processes, while not ignoring their role in satisfying demands for accountability. MYRADA in South India, for example, has established participatory learning methods (PALM), which form the basis for initial planning, ongoing monitoring and eventual evaluation. PALM takes about five days and sets the criteria for future assessment of the NGDO's interaction with villagers at the first stage of intervention.[14] PROSHIKA, GSS, BRAC and Njera Kori in Bangladesh rely more and more on participant-defined social and economic indicators of positive change, as do ACTIONAID internationally, CIED in Colombia, DESCO and CIED in Peru, PRRM, SCF/UK and HASIK in the Philippines. While not yet mainstream, there is a move to implement negotiated performance indicators as the basis for monitoring and evaluation.

Negotiated indicators, therefore, combine participant measures of change with input from outsiders. Participants provide the initial information, outsiders translate these into measures and feedback in order to interpret results.

Interpretation as a basis for defining, finding and judging achievement calls for participatory competencies founded on a principle of mutual learning. To re-enforce this principle NGDOs could place learning as a budget line item where monitoring and evaluation used to be. Similarly, evaluation units or departments could be renamed Learning Support Centres to bring out the actual purpose of their work and investment.

Not a case of either/or

Are scientific and interpretative approaches to monitoring and evaluation incompatible? The answer is yes and no. The conceptual foundations of the two are mutually exclusive, you either can objectify facts and truth or you cannot. In reality both have their uses, though NGDOs have a bias towards people-centred interpretation. The challenge for NGDOs is to find practical ways of combining the two approaches. One method used is to construct a logical framework and then get different stakeholders to negotiate the performance measures and indicators.[15] In other words, a logically framed agreement brings together relevant stakeholders to discuss what problems are to be solved, why they are there, what can (jointly) be done and how they can be assessed. This approach towards logical framework analysis has certain prerequisites (see Tips). It is too early to know if this hybrid approach will become widespread, but it does offer one practical way ahead.

This section has concentrated on how NGDOs can go about identifying and demonstrating achievements in terms of development initiatives. This must now be placed in the context of the wider organisation: the NGDO's role. The next section looks at the relatively new area of assessing performance for the organisation as a whole.

Assessing Organisational Performance

Knowing about development interventions is a vital condition for effective NGDO management. But leaders/managers and owners also need to know how the organisation is working overall. This calls for motivation to create a self-critical learning culture. Once the motivational bridge is crossed an NGDO must create a fundamental measure of overall

TIPS

➤ Donors and government officials must be prepared to be treated as equals with poor people, not above them.
➤ The capacity of primary stakeholders must be sufficient to enable them to interact on a par with other, stronger stakeholders.
➤ Significant initial effort to engage people in performance dialogues may be required for what is not yet a funded project (initial access to non-project resources can therefore be a limiting issue).
➤ Conflict and its resolution must be a recognised part of the process. This does not mean that differences must be solved on the spot, but that a process is put in place which deals with these conflicts.
➤ It must be accepted that the time required to reach agreed measures can be long, sometimes more than a year.
➤ A system of periodic consultation must be put in place which enables progress indicators to be renegotiated throughout the cycle as events evolve.
➤ The mandates of primary stakeholder representatives should be renewed periodically.
➤ Intervention management is designed to depend on stakeholder dialogue.

performance. This section describes what a measure of organisational performance looks like and how it can be constructed.

Learning from performance

Distressed at their pathetic performance, John Argenti (1993) has taken a large swipe at non-profits. He argues that they either define their purpose by what they do – which makes any level of performance acceptable as long as the money comes in – or retain wide-ranging goals as a defence against external criticism and the discipline of accountable management.[16] This used to be the situation for most NGDOs, and still is for many – which signifies a leadership unwilling to learn or simply intent on surviving where levels of support, rather than impact, are the yardstick for performance. Keeping overheads down is a common scapegoat for low prioritisation and meagre investment in learning, but there is more to it than that. Learning has much to do with the attitudes of leaders/managers, their degree of personal security and an understanding of how they can be most effective.

Equating learning with overheads is wrong. Earlier I argued that the future development role of NGDOs is to learn and demonstrate from experience in order to influence the larger forces which perpetuate poverty. Consequently, assessing results and translating them into organisational learning is central to an NGDO's future development function. Getting this message across to donors and the public is already yesterday's challenge, but is yet to be undertaken by most NGDOs. What learning entails in practice is not solely a question of systems and resources. These are necessary but insufficient on their own. Rather, development should be seen as a continuous process of investigation though implementation.[17] This is a leadership stance which makes a significant difference to whether the NGDO learns or not. The stance needs to encourage questioning; treat error and failure as positive information; value self-criticism, systematic reflection and external challenge; and push boundaries. Learning should also answer the 'why' questions an organisation faces. Paraphrasing the words of

Marie-Thérèse Feuerstein, 'knowing why an organisation is succeeding or failing is even more important than knowing it does.'[18] Examples have been given of NGDOs who have adopted an 'action-learning' way of working. They are 'aware' organisations, which is not the same as being busy or energetic.[19] A common feature of NGDOs following this path is that they are led by reflective-practitioners and their style spreads around. A culture of learning, therefore, not only improves development initiatives but is needed for the effective running of the organisation as a whole. The issue is: what organisational standards of performance should be a leader's/manager's reference point?

Stakeholders draw the NGDO bottom line

Establishing performance criteria for non-profits and then using them for comparative purposes is a conceptual and practical headache.[20] Whichever way the problem is tackled, an NGDO bottom line does not simply appear – it has to be constructed. It must also be interpreted in relation to each individual organisation. Though old, the findings reached in a study by Rosbeth Moss Kanter in 1979 are still appropriate. When evaluating non-profit performance, she concluded that:

- the measurement of effectiveness must be related to a particular context and life stage of the organisation;
- rather than seek universal measures, the need is to identify appropriate questions reflecting multiple criteria;
- the concept of assessing organisational goals should be replaced with the notion of organisational uses, in other words the recognition that 'different constituencies use organisations for different purposes'.[21]

More recently, Peter Drucker reached essentially the same conclusions, namely that:

- performance must be contextually determined and interpreted;
- questions should form the basis of the assessment approach;
- standards must derive from the various

constituencies that the organisation serves;

● the process of organisational assessment should be participatory.[22]

What these summaries show is that NGDOs must be judged from the perspectives of those who affect or are affected by the organisation's behaviour. No universal judgement can be applied. This leads to a definition of an NGDO bottom line – the basic measure of organisational performance – as: *the effective satisfaction of the rights and interests of legitimate stakeholders in keeping with its mission.* This definition is very similar to that for organisational capacity. A high-performing NGDO has the capacity to satisfy or influence its stakeholders in furtherance of its mission. A low-performing NGDO lacks this capacity. But a definition does not imply the existence of a bottom line; this has to be constructed.

Measuring organisational performance

An NGDO bottom line is constructed from the standards set by multiple stakeholders. Previously, stakeholders have been described as individuals or bodies who legitimise an NGDO's existence. However when it comes to

Table 7.4 Typical NGDO stakeholders

Category	Stakeholder	Examples
Formal or legal obligation	Legitimising population (primary stakeholders)	People who are poor, women, children, the disabled, political prisoners, refugees
	Governing body (secondary stakeholder)	Board, constituency/members' council,
	Staff (secondary stakeholders)	Employees' council, volunteer committees
	Funders (secondary stakeholders)	Private contributors Donor agencies Supporting corporations
	Other NGDOs (secondary stakeholders)	Members in co-ordinating bodies and funded consortia
	Governments (secondary stakeholders)	Registrar of NGDOs Collaborating ministries
Effectiveness	Other NGDOs (tertiary stakeholders)	Collaborators in networks or alliances
	Private service providers (tertiary stakeholders)	Marketing/advertising companies Technical consultancy firms
	Public institutions (tertiary stakeholders)	Study and research centres National fora or task forces on policy issues
Imperative interest	Media (tertiary stakeholders)	Investigative journalists News reporters
	Hostile activists (tertiary stakeholders)	Anti-aid interest groups Threatened elites Racist, anti-immigrant groups Political opponents to aid Ex-NGDO employees with a grudge

establishing a bottom line, this definition is not so straightforward.

Stakeholders

The term stakeholder was introduced in the late 1970s. As a tool for strategic planning, the concept helped business managers identify and understand links and interactions with the external environment.[23] A typical definition of stakeholders is as follows:

> *'Stakeholders are all those interested groups, parties, actors, claimants and institutions – both internal and external to the corporation – who exert a hold on it. That is, stakeholders are all those parties who either affect or are affected by a corporation's behaviour, actions and policies.'*[24]

Recognising stakeholders as integral to policy-making better enables organisations to tackle the 'messy' problems of selecting strategies within complex systems and unstable environments. Stakeholder analysis helps discriminate between potentially promising solutions and the 'best' solution. The stakeholder approach accepts that there will be conflicting interests and disagreements which must be taken into account whether the organisation likes it or not. These conditions almost define the setting of most NGDO development and humanitarian work.

There are three common types of stakeholders. First, there are those whom the organisation has a legal or formal obligation towards. This category starts with the population which legitimises the NGDO's existence, its primary stakeholders. This also includes, secondary stakeholders: other parties whom the NGDO is obliged to satisfy, such as the governing body, donors, and government agencies. Another category are those who will help an NGDO to be more effective, such as research and study centres. Third are people, groups and organisations who have an 'imperative interest'; for whatever personal or ideological reason, they wish to influence the NGDO. In this category can be found opponents of aid: the elite who may be threatened by empowerment, groups who have an

opposite set of values, and so. The NGDO may prefer that these groups do not exist, but they do and must be taken into account. Table 7.4 summarises these stakeholder categories.

Sorting out and prioritising legitimate stakeholders is a key pre-condition for starting to construct an organisational bottom line.

Constructing an NGDO bottom line

An NGDO bottom line is a set of performance standards obtained through negotiation with legitimate stakeholders. It defines the minimum organisational capacities an NGDO needs to be effective. The task of reaching a set of organisational performance standards and indicators requires dealing with multiple perspectives, opinions, rights and interests. Sources of tension will accompany any effort to construct a bottom-line. They must be recognised and taken into account. Common examples include:

- differences in relative power of and between the stakeholders (typically, government officials will have more power than peasants and men more than women or children);
- differences in relative influence on the NGDO (donors usually have more influence than recipients);
- differences in formal rights and interests between stakeholders (primary stakeholders seldom gain formal rights with respect to the NGDO; donors do through contracts – the media has no rights, but it certainly has interests which cannot be ignored);
- differences between insiders and outsiders (leader/managers and staff are also stakeholders, as are the governing body).

To successfully define performance standards, NGDOs must be clear about which stakeholder counts most and why. This is difficult but inevitable. It happens anyway in untransparent ways inside the NGDO. It is unlikely that any one stakeholder can be totally satisfied; the issue is to strike an optimum balance between the two, but one that favours the poor. How can this be done? Usually, NGDOs negotiate with stakeholders individually. Field staff do participatory surveys; proposals are written and submitted to donors; boards and executive committees meet to hear of progress, problems and ratify decisions already made; accounts and annual reports are sent to the responsible government department each year, and so it goes on. In each of these transactions, NGDOs take account of the expectations of each stakeholder and juggle with their often contradictory demands.

Today NGDOs are beginning to experiment with systems that reduce the danger of donor and contributor dominance and the internal stress of continual juggling. Two methods make the trade-offs and balancing act more transparent. One approach, the Assembly, tested by Oxfam UK/I, gets various stakeholders together and encourages them to listen to their different expectations.[25] In 1994, some 250 people, drawn from volunteers, Southern NGDO partners, managers, staff representatives, trustees, associates, advisers and donors, were brought together to deliberate on a policy issue: namely, should Oxfam work on poverty in the UK? This question had been unresolved in Oxfam for many years. There are, indeed, many reasons for and many against. Therefore, while retaining authority for the policy decision, the trustees invited others to argue the case. While not binding, the assembly's advice could not realistically be ignored. The result was a recommendation to work domestically, as well as overseas, but with additional funds raised for the purpose.

This is not quite an example of constructing a baseline for performance because the question asked was whether or not Oxfam UK/I should adopt a particular policy. But if performance had been the question, the assembly approach can be a way of providing an answer.

An alternative approach to constructing an NGDO bottom line is a process known as a social audit. It corresponds to a social accounting process which establishes the criteria against which an NGDO's overall achievements are judged by stakeholders, and then later determines the degree to which these criteria have been satisfied.[26] In other words, a social

audit is a periodic assessment of the NGDO's performance against negotiated standards: its bottom line. Social audits are similar to an assembly in that they gather the opinions, expectations and standards set by key stakeholders. In effect, this is an institutionalised way of listening to and being judged by those who have a right to be heard. For this reason, social audits have been defined as: 'an assessment of the social impact and ethical behaviour of an organisation in relation to its aims, and those of its stakeholders'.[27]

Traidcraft, a UK NGDO established to foster fair trade and better returns for producers in the South, has published two social audit reports. The stakeholders considered were: producers in the South, consumers, staff, voluntary product representatives, shareholders and the general public. The audit report for 1992/1993, for example, voiced producers' concerns about pricing structure by the time their products reached the market, and re-emphasised the importance of product development as a form of support which is critical for raising sales, securing markets and increasing value. The staff audit included: verification of compliance with the ratio of highest and lowest income differences, which had been set at a ratio of 3:1; the role and positions occupied by women, which were found to be skewed towards lower-paid and part-time work; investment in staff development, indicated by the number of training days; and the adequacy of the staff association, measured in terms of negotiating skills to redress staff grievances. Economic performance in terms of turnover, profitability, payment to producers and dividends was also reported.[28] The following year's social audit introduced more specific performance indicators and investigated changes in issues raised previously. For example, income paid to producers in the South was seen to increase by 28 per cent, environmental concerns were reviewed and more substantial involvement in lobbying was described.[29]

Applying social audit to NGDO performance is in its infant stage. Nevertheless, as an approach consistent with the ethos of NGDO work, it adds a human element,

TIPS

Undertaking a social audit entails the following steps.[30]

➤ Identify an independent, competent social auditor.
➤ Identify major stakeholders.[31]
➤ Identify the NGDOs' and stakeholders', values, aims and standards for judgement.
➤ Identify the indicators and targets (the bottom line) for assessing an NGDO's performance in relation to its values, and aims.
➤ Design appropriate methods for assessing performance against indicators and targets.
➤ Carry out the assessment
➤ Prepare 'social accounts' (which complement financial accounts).
➤ Obtain verification by an 'audit group'.[32]
➤ Distribute social audits to stakeholders and solicit feedback.
➤ Submit social audits to governing bodies for review and approval.

complementing the auditor's annual accounts.

The two methods described point to ways in which an NGDO can assess its overall achievements, which is more than simply adding up all its development initiatives. However, there is a similarity between the principles of an organisation-wide social audit and the assessment of development which has been negotiated using a logical framework. Both must include significant parties in the definition and measurement of performance. And both help to solve the problems of NGDO accountability and legitimacy.

Before examining the link between accountability and performance, it is important to look at the requirements for performance-based management.

Establishing effective systems for assessing performance

As mentioned earlier, inadequate internal systems frequently prevent NGDOs from recognising their achievements. Typically, management is project-focused. Indicators such as compliance with legislation, achieving bench-marks, optimising returns on financial transfers or staffing levels, gaining the most appropriate ratios of central to operational costs, and so on, seldom feature in small NGDOs and are not always to be found in big NGDOs either. Furthermore, there is little room or finance allocated for the capacity to translate project results into management information. Management information, as opposed to project reporting, is conspicuously absent in NGDOs. These observations are not new. What, therefore, can be done?

Establishing an achievement-oriented monitoring and evaluation system [32]

An effective information system uses monitoring, evaluation and organisational review, as well as social audits, to produce valid information at the right time. Figure 7.3 shows, in a simplified way, the different levels and types of information appropriate to different users in a big, complex operational NGDO. While the items in the figure contribute to effectiveness, the degree to which an NGDO must accomplish some or all will vary significantly. Small NGDOs working in limited areas with few communities may find that the first two levels provide more than enough for their needs. The primary data for policy-oriented NGDOs will often be found at the second level, with primary sources located in alliances. Transnational NGDOs will probably need the capacity for everything.

Examples of achievement-based management information systems are difficult to find in NGDOs, although more energy is being put into creating them. Box 7.1 is an example of NGDO performance in South Africa.

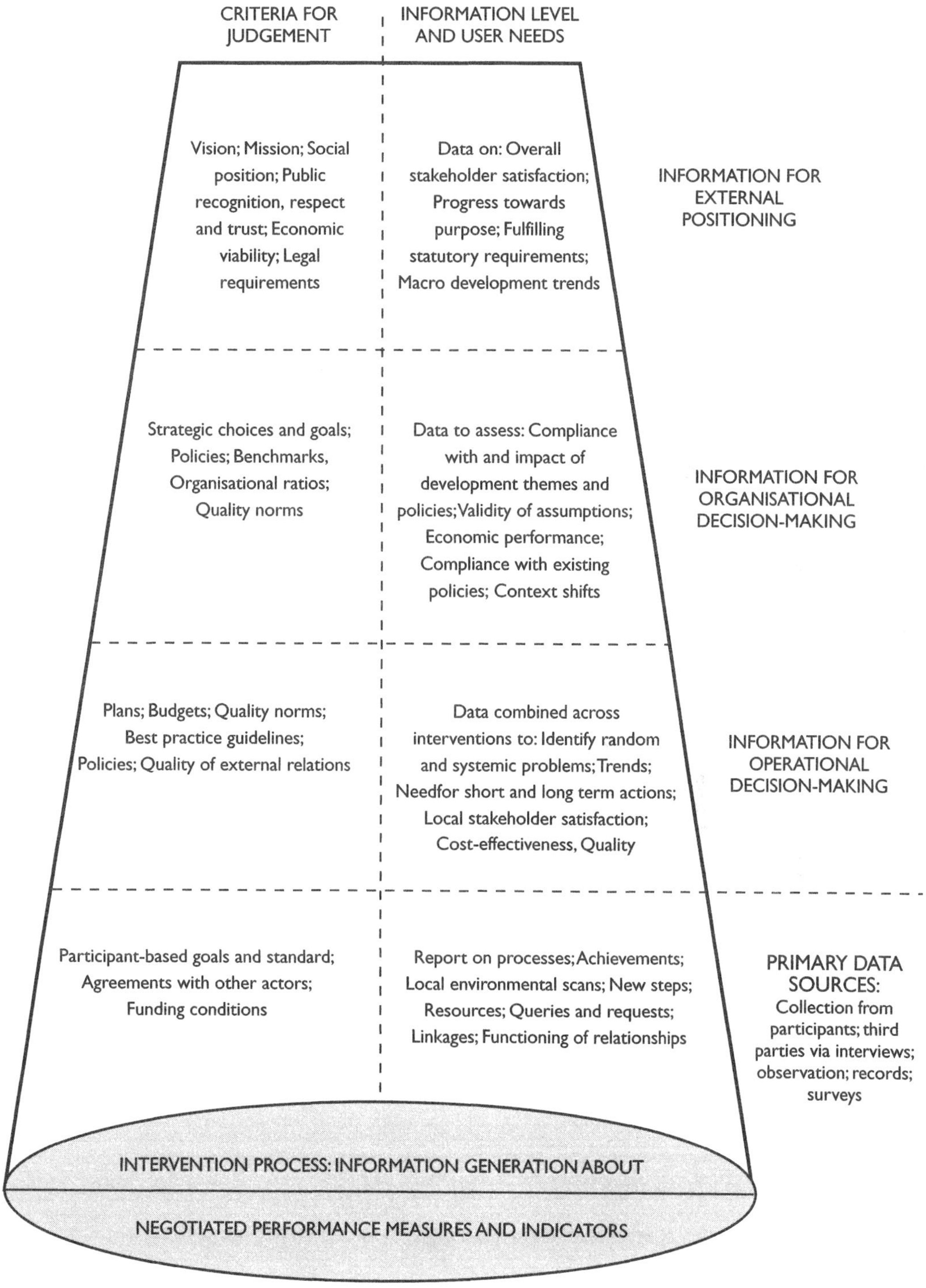

CRITERIA FOR JUDGEMENT	INFORMATION LEVEL AND USER NEEDS	
Vision; Mission; Social position; Public recognition, respect and trust; Economic viability; Legal requirements	Data on: Overall stakeholder satisfaction; Progress towards purpose; Fulfilling statutory requirements; Macro development trends	INFORMATION FOR EXTERNAL POSITIONING
Strategic choices and goals; Policies; Benchmarks, Organisational ratios; Quality norms	Data to assess: Compliance with and impact of development themes and policies; Validity of assumptions; Economic performance; Compliance with existing policies; Context shifts	INFORMATION FOR ORGANISATIONAL DECISION-MAKING
Plans; Budgets; Quality norms; Best practice guidelines; Policies; Quality of external relations	Data combined across interventions to: Identify random and systemic problems; Trends; Need for short and long term actions; Local stakeholder satisfaction; Cost-effectiveness, Quality	INFORMATION FOR OPERATIONAL DECISION-MAKING
Participant-based goals and standard; Agreements with other actors; Funding conditions	Report on processes; Achievements; Local environmental scans; New steps; Resources; Queries and requests; Linkages; Functioning of relationships	PRIMARY DATA SOURCES: Collection from participants; third parties via interviews; observation; records; surveys

INTERVENTION PROCESS: INFORMATION GENERATION ABOUT

NEGOTIATED PERFORMANCE MEASURES AND INDICATORS

Figure 7.3 NGDO information levels

TIPS *Setting up such a management information system calls for a number of preconditions in order to assess development achievement and organisational performance. These include:*

➤ a real commitment to organisational learning;[34]
➤ commitment translated into approved budgets and time scheduling;
➤ an organisational culture of enquiry and investigation rather then response and production.

The steps needed to put such a system in place comprise the following:

➤ For each staff level define the purpose for generating management or decision-making information.
➤ Select information indicators based on use and user.
➤ Determine information sources and the frequency of their availability.
➤ In consultation with users, design appropriate formats and train staff to use them.
➤ Agree on the system to collect and analyse data, allocating responsibility and costs.
➤ Specify where, when and how information will be interpreted, communicated and disseminated, including availability for periodic meetings as inputs to routine processes.

The problem NGDOs face in advocacy work is that their primary stakeholders, the institutions to be influenced, are unlikely to negotiate performance standards or indicators of success. They would probably prefer the NGDO to disappear. In advocacy, direct impact will show up in the degree and direction of policy or behavioural change which occurs due to NDGO argument and pressure. Where regimes are hostile, simply keeping an issue alive may be a sign of achievement. Whatever the context, the

---

Box 7.1
NGDO performance

Training for Efficiency (TOE) was a South African NGDO established to improve the efficiency of other organisations through knowledge and skill-based training courses. In a short time, it established a reputation for bringing substantial improvements, and took pride in the fact that it always completed its yearly plan of activities. In addition, more and more costs were being covered through the fees charged. Board, clients and donors were all positive about TOE's work and viewed it as an example of an efficient, productive organisation. There was general self-satisfaction about the way things were going.

Not surprisingly, therefore, a stunned silence arose when the head of training asked: 'Why do we train organisations to be more efficient? What differences does it make if the filing system works better or if the secretary types with less mistakes?' One staff member put the question another way by asking: 'What difference do we want to make? What are we trying to achieve?' It became clear that TOE's goal was to build an efficient non-profit, non-governmental sector – but was this really what they were doing? A discussion of the ultimate purpose of their work was summed up by the director who said: 'It sounds to me as if we all agree that we want to build a strong civil society by making organisations more effective in

---

achieving goals which increase the depth of democratic participation in South Africa. We want to contribute to people taking more control over their lives.' In other words, the issue was impact, not the efficiency of NGDO activities. And the measure of TOE's performance would be the ability of client organisations to strengthen democratic participation through social, political and economic initiatives. Instead of setting targets for the number of courses to run and participants trained, TOE would need to interact more deeply with NGDOs. But how, then, could TOE's performance be seen through the work of its clients? Changes were sought: in the way beneficiaries make decisions about projects; the information they use to reach decisions; in laws which give people greater control over their lives; and in the number and types of initiatives people take on themselves without support. Assessing beneficiary influence over decisions could be done by looking at their involvement in meetings, what action is taken by whom as a result, and analysis of the organisation's structure, management and accountability.

Further reflection made it clear that increasing the effectiveness of other NGDOs would call for a very different way of working – for example, by targeting NGDOs with similar visions and goals instead of anyone who applied. On this basis, TOE chose very different objectives:

- At least 90 per cent of organisations would have empowering people as their long-term goal.
- By the end of TOE's intervention, at least 50 per cent of organisations would have long-, medium- and short-term goals with indicators for measuring achievement.
- After six months of work with any organisation, TOE would need to identify three areas which became more efficient and demonstrate how this led to greater effectiveness.

The new objectives obviously had many consequences. A team approach was adopted, monitoring and evaluation were carried out differently, services focused on forming long-term relationships complemented by scheduled courses, in-house training became common, and a tighter selection of organisations reduced the numbers but made impacts easier to trace. To back up the change, TOE was renamed Training for Effectiveness. Human resource development was a key tool in bringing about the change in skills.

From this experience, TOE developed a set of questions to use when entering into a dialogue with clients.

- What difference do you want to make? What impact do you want to have?
- Are your activities ends in themselves or do they contribute to the desired impact ?
- Are you targeting the right audience?
- Which of the activities you do well could contribute more towards the changes you desire?
- How could these activities be developed so that they are more effective?
- How will you measure progress? What indicators will you set and what information must be collected to measure the indicators?

The changes proposed made sense to the board and donors, even though it meant working with fewer organisations. Staff motivation increased because it was easier for members to see the effects of their inputs. The original commitment to productivity was not lost, but was placed within the context of what social changes TOE was trying to bring about in.

Source: adapted from a contribution by Marian Nell and Janet Shapiro, Johannesburg

drawback is that the definition of achievement lies within the NDGO itself, because achievement cannot be negotiated.

A way through this is to identify performance measures with those who should benefit from the policy change advocated: the poor, women, the disabled. This is where a strong link between micro- and macro- levels comes into play again. In as far as policy change should benefit those at the economic or political margins, assessment of impact lies with them, as does participation in defining what type of policy reform the NGDO should be advocating.[35]

For all NGDOs, recognising achievements – whether negotiated with stakeholders or not – will contribute to greater effectiveness. It will also help to fulfil external requirements for accountability and legitimacy, which is the final dimension we look at.

Linking Participant-Based Performance to Accountability and Legitimacy

This chapter began by listing negative outcomes if an NGDO could not demonstrate what it had achieved. One such outcome was a reduction in an NGDO's accountability and demonstration of worth. This section looks at the role of showing achievements in maintaining an NGDO's credibility.

Public accountability normally involves a formal notification of activities and expenditures to government. However, where government is itself not legitimate, formal accountability may either not count for much or be counterproductive to the NGDO's principles of working for social justice. In fact, the

Table 7.5 Accountability demands

Stakeholder	Basis of Claim or NGDO Obligation	Ability to Exert the Claim
People who are poor and marginalised	Implicit and moral right because they justify an NGDO's existence	Low due to dependent and disempowered position and lack of capacity to engage and sanction NGDO behaviour.
Governing body	Legal responsibility	Self-perpetuating boards are generally weak because of reliance on information provided by staff. (Staff-based governing bodies suffer from lack of objectivity.)
Staff	Moral and legal obligation	Strong because of control over information, internal processes and interpretation.
Funders	Fiduciary responsibility	Strong because of abiding responsibility or concern for proper use of resources,which can be withdrawn.
Other NGDOs	Mutual protection and promotion	Medium, depending on strength of co-ordinating bodies and structure of NGDO community.
Government	Public and political interest	Medium, depending on the regime in power, its information sources and monitoring capacity.
Media	Public interest	Potentially strong but uneven – government and public perceptions can be influenced for or against NGDOs.

officials to whom NGDOs report are often the very people they are struggling against.[36] In other words, there are many situations where the political economy requires NGDOs to deny or only nominally accept accountability to the state. With this in mind, Table 7.5 gives a picture of the audiences who an NGDO could be accountable to and whose opinions count if the organisation is to stay credible.[37]

Holding NGDOs accountable

In their introduction *to NGO Performance and Accountability* (1995), Mike Edwards and David Hulme make a distinction between two types of accountability: functional and strategic. The first is accountability for the use of resources and their immediate impact. The second is accountability for how the NGDO influences other organisations and the wider environment in the medium to long term. For Edwards and Hulme, a critical issue is the ability of different stakeholders to exert accountability in terms of information, reporting, appraisal and sanctions. For both types of accountability, in their assessment, primary stakeholders score low or nil. For the hypothetical Southern NGDO they take as an example it is the Northern NGDO which scores the highest in exacting accountability.

Accountability to the general public, outside of the legal requirements, is seldom demanded unless the media kicks up a fuss, or those calling for it are contributors to NGDOs in one way or another. Those expecting accountability tend to be the middle class, both in the North and South; their concern is with the allocation of money and the proportion reaching the 'beneficiaries'. Internally, for reasons explained in Chapter 2, staff rather than governing bodies tend to exert the most influence on accountability while, externally, donors usually play the strongest role in holding NGDOs to their word. By and large, accountability rests in the hands of professionals within the aid system. On its own, internal accountability can be effective if staff are – for ideological, political, theological, cultural or other reasons – truly committed to redressing the injustices and deprivations faced by the poor.

This condition often holds for local NGDOs in many parts of South and South East Asia and Latin America – both in and out of the aid system. Any type of formal external accountability is unlikely to ever be as effective as the selfless, self-motivated commitment of this type. However, this level of commitment cannot be assumed to exist for all NGDOs; what is more, personal integrity must be complemented by other ways of ensuring accountability.

One precondition and two steps are needed to enable people who are poor and marginalised to gain accountability from NGDOs, particularly the ability to sanction their behaviour. The precondition is that NGDOs must accept the influence these groups have over them. In other words, there must be a genuine desire to make reverse participation real. The first step is to build up the ability of communities to oversee NGDO's interventions affecting them. This ability has been found to increase at higher levels of CBO federation, such as apex bodies created by the People's Rural Education Movement in Orissa. Another example is development officers employed by AWARE in India. The staff are located in a decentralised management structure where they are accountable to a second-level membership body comprising 10 to 20 village associations.[38] The second step is to negotiate performance criteria on which the NGDO and its staff will be judged and sanctioned.

Broadly speaking, the capacities that communities need to hold NGDOs accountable are no different from the ability to act in an empowered way in society. However, NGDOs too seldom apply participatory, empowering principles and methods to increase their accountability to communities. One organisation who has tried participation in this way is the Aga Khan Rural Support Programme (AKRSP) in Western India.[39] AKRSP asked villagers in the programme area to identify the performance criteria to be applied. This activity produced 15 criteria, grouped around:

- processes of decision-making;
- AKRSP's management style;
- reporting, sharing and acting on information;

TIPS ***Subsequently, applying these criteria to the way the organisation worked produced the following suggestions.***

➤ Brainstorming to generate performance criteria and indicators.
➤ Community ranking of AKRSP against each criteria.
➤ Evaluation workshops should be set up every six months to identify reasons for low rankings, assessment of changes and agreement on further remedial action.
➤ Assessment of AKRSP against other development agencies to illustrate comparative strengths and weaknesses.
➤ Agreement should be made on community involvement in other performance assessments, such as strategic planning prior to external evaluations.

Additional features which evolved once the basic system of NGDO accountability was in place were:

➤ development of a local management information system to further develop local accountability to other institutions and improve feedback capacity;
➤ community involvement in recruitment, performance appraisal and training of NGDO staff.

The major obstacles to introducing this type of accountability were :

➤ anxiety amongst staff in adapting to changes in power relationships;
➤ altering the management style from hierarchical to responsive and flexible;
➤ dealing with the fear of making mistakes;
➤ changing the structure, decision-making, resource allocation and other features of the organisation.

For those wishing to implement a system of accountability to primary stakeholders, the AKRSP experience gives the following pointers:

➤ Pilot the approach before embarking on any large-scale introduction.
➤ Spend time ensuring that senior management remain on board.
➤ Uncouple the process from any decisions about resources, so that the initial evaluation process is not dampened by potential loss of support.
➤ Involve communities from the outset; their motivation depends on involvement now, not later.
➤ Do not use participatory methods for bottom-up accountability if you are not prepared to change your own decision-making processes and accountability structures, particularly towards other stakeholders who are used to having top-down accountability.

● the nature/quality of the programme support provided;
● assistance in gaining access to external institutions and decision-making fora.

Incorporating participant-based accountability should not be idealised or seen as a substitute for other equally valid methods. Communities can be controlled by local elites, and an NGDO's actions can create new socio-economic divisions with a class of haves and have-nots, where the poorest lose out again. However, something can be done to bring primary stakeholders into the accountability equation; NGDO credibility will increasingly depend on it.

Overall, if the political economy – in which

governments are a central player – is part of the development problem; if local elites, rather than the poor, gain hold on NGDO behaviour; if the general public are indifferent; if contributors are satisfied with 'feel good' stories; if the media are concerned mainly with scandal; and if insiders – staff and professional funders – are effectively in control – what can NGDOs do to enhance their external accountability?

One method already described is to self-regulate the NGDO community on the basis of codes of conduct. This type of peer control, common to other professions and business groupings, would be a good start; complemented by an ombudsman as an independent watchdog on how self-regulation was applied. Within an NGDO, in addition to participant oversight, improvements can be sought in strengthening governing boards with people who have integrity, time, commitment and insight into development work, as well as stature and useful social links.

So far the discussion of incorporating accountability has concentrated on operational NGDOs. A similar process can occur between Northern NGDOs and those in the South and East. Again, the purpose is to reduce imbalances in capacity and create a multiple-stakeholder bottom line for donor NGDOs which prioritises recipient standards.[40]

Incorporating bottom-up, community-based accountability, however, is a very difficult reversal for NGDOs and the aid system. Why? Because it is not just a question of applying new techniques and procedures, but of reversing many aspects of organisational culture which lie at the heart of assumptions and behaviour.

Difficult as it may be, nevertheless, the reward at the end is vital for NGDOs' survival and enhanced legitimacy.

NGDO legitimacy and the link to accountability

Legitimacy and credibility are not often used in relation to NGDOs, but these are vital characteristics NGDOs must attain. A working definition of legitimacy is: a valid public perception that an NGDO is a genuine agent of development. In other words, the organisation does what it says it will do and can prove it. Two key words in this definition are 'valid' and 'genuine'. The first requires that public perception is founded on fact. The second implies conformity with generally accepted standards of development behaviour and performance.

Demonstrating achievement is the first step on the ladder to social legitimacy. Without this foundation, legitimacy will always be vulnerable to critical scrutiny. In the end, it is positive changes that an NGDO brings about which justify its existence. Given the conceptual and technical difficulties of demonstrating achievement, however, participant-based measures and indicators may be the most effective means of ensuring NGDO legitimacy. This will tie accountability much more closely to NGDO norms and standards.

This assertion takes us to the question of how NGDOs can assess and improve their legitimacy and credibility. In short, how can they build the capacities needed to be effective? The answer is the subject of the next chapter.

Part 3

Improving and Moving On

8

Improving Performance: Process and Method in Developing NGDO Capacity

Making Capacity Growth a Way of Life

Part II details five areas of organisational capacity that an individual NGDO and the NGDO community require to be effective. This chapter describes how existing levels of capacity can be reoriented and improved through a process called organisational development (OD). In addition, NGDOs are expected to help build the capacity of civil society, which is a wider goal calling for processes of institutional development (ID). This chapter explores how to do both so that capacity growth becomes a new way of life.

Unfortunately, the explanation is not straightforward. First, like other development buzz words, capacity building is used in different ways by different parts of the aid community – there are no shared under-standings. So, we have to begin by bringing some order into the variety of meanings. Second, capacity building is applied at different levels of development action, but the differences involved are seldom clear, leading to confusion and ineffectual strategies. Third, the tools and funding approaches needed for effective civic development have not been put in place and important preconditions for success have been ignored, leading to mediocre activity that primarily serves political ends. In sum, it is all a bit of a mess, so be prepared for difficulty in using capacity growth as a way of increasing the effectiveness of NGDOs and civil society.

What is Capacity Growth all About?

Improving capacity is a common aid objective. Like other development concepts, there is little agreement on the characteristics of organisational capacity or how to increase it. Unfortunately, aid agencies are not guided in capacity building initiatives by a well thought through and conceptually coherent story of what it is all about. By default, and for want of a coherent theory, the common mode of thinking is in terms of supplying packages of knowledge and skills. But without a theory – even with a very small 't' – discussions and initiatives go round in circles, means are confused with ends, processes are undervalued because their merits cannot be understood or assessed, and different levels of action get all mixed up.[1] Under the label of capacity building, a lot of money is spent and wasted. What can be done to redress this situation is set out below using the working definitions found in Chapter 3.

Sorting out the concepts

Increasing capacity for better development impact can be directed at specific organisations and at institutional relations operating at different levels in society. In both cases the task is to initiate changes which serve or better influence sets of stakeholders. Organisational capacity 'emerges' when NGDO staff and volunteers with the necessary competencies interact together in the right way. In short, it is a product of group dynamics properly tailored and focused on mission-derived tasks.[2]

More often than not, realising an NGDO's mission means strengthening the capacities of others. This activity could be directed at the NGDO community or a part of it – for example, coalitions or networks in health, credit, agriculture – as well as grassroots organisations, social movements, associations and trade unions. It can also mean changing the way organisations relate to each other in civil society and towards government and the market. In other words, the NGDO is engaged in processes of institutional development. In any healthy organisation, capacity growth is the result of gaining experience and adapting to the outside world. However, this type of growth can be accelerated through tailored processes of organisational development – capacity seldom improves in sustainable ways when solely based on predefined packages imported into an NGDO or into society at large.[3] From this perspective, it is more appropriate to see change in organisational capacity as a process of inducing growth in human and organisational relationships, rather than a mechanical process of building with known blocks.[4]

Capacity development in different arenas of NGDO action

Mechanically inspired *ad hocism* is probably the best way of describing how the aid system presently understands and deals with the concept of capacity building. One reason is that insufficient distinction is made between capacity building as a means, ends or process and whether it is intended to improve things within the organisation itself, within society at large, or both. Table 8.1 summarises these differences.[5]

The three rows represent internal and external elements of capacity building.[6] Confusion arises from the fact that internal capacity growth is often initiated in order to improve an NGDO's performance in institutional, that is external (civic), capacity building. Put another way, an NGDO's organisational development (OD) is used as a means to achieve sectoral development (SD) or institutional development (ID).[7]

Table 8.1 Concepts of capacity growth

	Means	**Process**	**Ends**
Capacity growth of an NGDO: organisational development (OD)	Strengthens the NGDO's ability to perform specific *functions*, such as capacity building of CBO's.	Brings coherence at all levels of internal action with possibility of continual *learning* and necessary *adaptation*.	Improves NGDO viability, sustainability and direct impact consistent with the chosen *mission*.
Capacity growth of the NGDO community or a subsector of it (eg, health, credit): sectoral development (SD)	Strengthens the ability of the sector (or subsector) to improve overall *civic impact*.	Brings *mutually supporting relations* and understanding amongst subsectors.	Achieves confident and powerful *interaction* with other sectors and social actors based on *shared strategies and learning*.
Capacity growth of civil society: institutional development (ID)	Improves the ability of primary stakeholders to identify and carry out *activities* to solve problems.	Enables and stimulates *stronger civic interactions* and communication, conflict mediation and resolution in society, thereby enhancing social capital.	Increases ability of primary stakeholders to engage with and *influence* the political arena and socio-economic system in accordance with their *interests*.

These types of capacity growth are not mutually exclusive. In fact, to be effective the opposite should occur. A competent NGDO must be able to address any number at once. For example, an NGDO can contribute to the capacity building of informal sector entrepreneurs; facilitate links and relationships between them to form associations which, in their turn, strengthen civil society; and contribute to social capital and affect governance by influencing public policy. Here the NGDO works on institutional means, processes and ends indirectly. Alternatively, an NGDO providing development services, such as credit or health care, learns how to tie its work to parallel initiatives coming from the official aid system – which increases its impact – while collaborating in national networks to lobby and change public policy on informal sector activities. Here NGDO institutional impact is more direct.

There are three important points to bear in mind when looking at the types of capacity growth. First, when moving from top left to bottom right, the scope of required organisational capacities widens and deepens. Second, the degree of control an NGDO has on external change lessens. Third, changing social institutions may mean altering an NGDO's prevailing norms, values or attitudes. For example, the institutionalised low status of women is not located in one place or organisation, it permeates all aspects of life. Yet for NGDOs, institutional change is mainly achieved by changing the roles, policies and relationships of other organisations. In other words, the path to changing social relations is usually indirect.

A more direct approach to institutional change is to stimulate civic action. Because of legal restrictions, financing constraints and innate conservatism in the majority of NGDOs, this strategy tends to be the exception rather than the rule. A vocal minority of NGDOs dedicated to working and building social movements is not the norm. As we saw in the chapter on performance, in order to be realistic about what measures and indicators of achievement are appropriate, it is important to be clear about what dimensions of capacity building an NGDO has in mind. Without this clarity, different expectations about impact can easily arise, especially between Northern NGDOs and their counterparts in the South and East.

Capacity for institutional change

Engaging in the capacity building of social institutions means getting involved in the right way in a complex set of interactions which occur outside of the NGDO. The challenge is to alter dynamic processes and roles between formal institutions of state, market and civil society and the informal forces which often determine how things really work. Figure 8.1 illustrates the dynamics involved.[8]

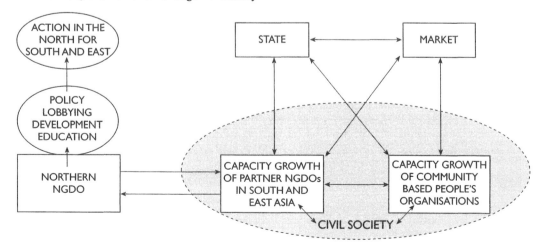

Figure 8.1 Capacity growth for institutional development

Increasing capacity within NGDOs in order to effect changes within social institutions is distinct from capacity that improves the performance of local organisations. For instance, the primary focus is on relationships, roles and power distribution between civic actors and interactions with other sectors of society; it usually calls for multiple levels of intervention locally, nationally and internationally; and it is more difficult to assess in terms of achievement. Consequently, methods, measures and timescales are not the same for developing social institutions and organisations. NGDOs wishing to finance or operate in the institutional arena need to recognise the complexity involved, the reduced control they have and the greater risks they take.

Pitfalls and how to avoid them

Problems arise when concepts of capacity development are not clear because the methods chosen are inappropriate. For example, since the late 1980s, some Northern NGDOs have taken capacity building for institutional development seriously as a funding priority. An evaluation of a Northern NGDO's support to institutional development in Kenya and Zimbabwe indicated misunderstandings with local partners about what was really intended, leading to eventual confusion and disagreement about what should have been achieved and how performance would be assessed. The study also identified a mismatch between the Northern NGDO's roles and instruments. While institutional development was the stated policy goal, the tools applied were still related to project support and project-related ways of thinking.[9] This inconsistency is common.

For effective capacity development of institutions, there are a few rules of thumb.

➤ All parties need to understand and agree on what concepts of capacity are being applied at which level(s) of development. Is greater internal capacity meant to improve direct impact on civic or wider social institutions, such as government and market?

➤ The initial process leading to capacity growth must assess the depth of change needed so that all parties can estimate the probable implications of starting down this particular path.

➤ In order to provide realistic goal-setting and performance indicators, it is necessary to sort out what can be controlled, influenced or only appreciated by NGDOs. Generally, moving from top left to bottom right in Table 8.1 means reduced NGDO control and greater influence of contextual factors shaped by the state and market. This has implications for what can be expected in terms of performance in institutional change.

➤ It is necessary to assess instruments and timescales against each type of capacity to ensure that they will do the job intended. Methods and approaches needed will be specific to OD or ID. It is not always possible to rely on combinations of the old tool kit used for project-based development. What this means is discussed below.

In summary:

● Organisational development and civic institutional development are related, but they are not the same in terms of process and measures.

● The capacities needed for better organisational and institutional effectiveness are related but are not the same.

● For non-operational Northern NGDOs, the route to institutional capacity building and structural change is indirect – through growth in the capacity of Southern and Eastern civic organisations.

● In the South and East, operational NGDOs can have direct and indirect development effects on society, requiring distinct types of organisational capacity. Direct effects are through a capacity to be civic actors, with recognised identity, position, legitimacy and influence. Indirect effects emerge when doing things for other organisations in ways

which improve their self-sufficiency. Best practice in organisational development ensures the growth of both direct and indirect capacity.

Capacity development processes within NGDOs, the NGDO sector and civic institutions

Stimulating capacity growth in NGDO communities and institutions of civil society can be similar, but there is a different mix of stakeholders and processes. These are illustrated in Figure 8.2, adapted from Richard Holloway's work. The diagram shows: an assessment involving different stakeholders, processes to identify areas and types of capacity growth required; and four types of intervention which can be employed singly or together. Subsequent sections explain each phase, but with an emphasis on organisational development within NGDOs.

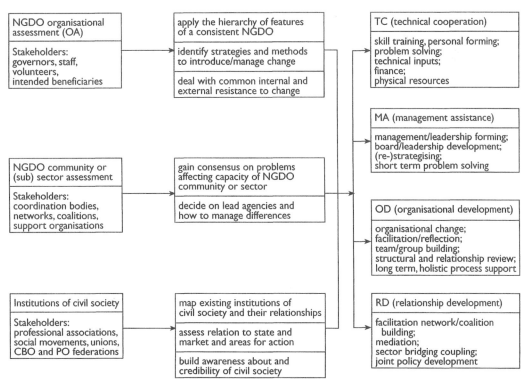

Figure 8.2 Comparing types of capacity development of NGDOs

Organisational Development for Capacity Growth in NGDOs

Improving organisational capacity distinguishes itself from ongoing incremental modifications in NGDOs because it is an explicit set of activities which aim to better organisational performance in relation to mission, context, resources and sustainability. As a type of (self-)development, OD focuses on changing factors which limit capacity but which, unfortunately, can seldom be isolated from others. In organisational analysis everything hangs together. Consequently, organisational development is usually complicated and difficult to restrict to one part of an organisation. Despite the complications, there are a few principles and preconditions which should be followed.

Principles of effective organisational development

While there is no one 'right' way of growing capacity, experience suggests that effective processes of capacity building follow some key rules.

Rule 1: action-learning

Capacity development is best treated as a form of action-learning by staff , volunteers, leaders and governors. Put another way, it should be seen as a type of learning which takes place by going through changes and then reflecting on what has happened. While the capabilities of individuals can be built through skill-oriented, prepackaged training courses, the organisation's overall capacity cannot be improved effectively this way.[10] To be of real use, training must be located within an organisation's development strategy; 'the organisation needs to gain mastery of itself in order to take responsibility for and adequately utilise the individuals it sends for training'.[11] If an OD process goes well it never stops, but becomes a way of life. Instead of a limited, specialised, dedicated set of activities, organisational development becomes part and parcel of the organisation's normal functioning. The process of applying continuous learning is its product.

Rule 2: group facilitation

Organisational development is essentially a process of group-oriented research and reflection. While scale and complexity differ considerably, this basic idea holds true for capacity growth across the spectrum of community-based organisations to transnational NGDOs. Typically, this means bringing facilitators, similar to change agents, into the organisation, instead of taking individuals out for training. Why? Because if there is no third-party involvement, the chances are that 'self-reflection' will be limited: awkward questions that challenge comfortable assumptions are not asked; existing power relations and hierarchy are respected even if they are disfunctional; and lack of input about comparative experience engenders complacency, with insufficient awareness of how things could be done differently and better. Skilled group facilitation is a key component of OD.

Rule 3: stakeholder judgements

Organisational development occurs predominantly amongst NGDO staff. However, the definition of capacity ties performance to what stakeholders experience. Consequently, stakeholder perceptions must be brought into the OD initiative. Eventually, any process of capacity change will have to be assessed through the perspective of those who have a legitimate claim on the organisation.

Rule 4: internal participation

Organisational change should follow the same principles that an NGDO uses to work with communities: honesty, transparency negotiation and participation. This means adopting OD methods which engage everyone and create space in terms of time and resources. Where change is likely to involve reducing staff or substantially altering the mix of competencies, it is obviously unrealistic to expect participatory decision-making to produce consensus on who should go or stay. Eventually, it is the task of leaders to make hard choices, but the point is to ensure that decisions are the result of open consultation.

Rule 5: self-appraisal

Although extreme situations of self-denial or power abuse may exist, the guiding principle for OD is that it is based on self-assessment. This is the only way that responsibility is located within the NGDO – not displaced to outside 'experts'.[12] This is also consistent with the principle of participation outlined above.

Preconditions for effective organisational development

Too often, capacity building measures are adopted in the South and East without putting the necessary preconditions in place. Consequently, results are disappointing, improvements do not occur or are not sustained and relationships with funders become strained. There are at least four types of precondition which need to be considered before starting OD.

Understanding the depth of change needed

Moving left to right in the top row of Table 8.1

explains how OD broadens, from improving specific functions to strengthening an NGDO's overall position in society. Figure 8.3 links this scope of change to time and difficulty. In order to select the right methods, judge the resources needed, and identify likely difficulties, any approach to capacity growth must be gauged in terms of the depth of change required. For example, to improve their effectiveness, over the past few years a fair number of Northern NGDOs have tried to alter organisational behaviour to make it more 'business-like'. The usual way of doing this is to restructure tasks and authority. Too often, however, structural changes have not been complemented by changes in the systems linking people and their activities. Changing organisational behaviour has far-reaching implications and must be tackled in a comprehensive way. Similarly, when Southern or Eastern NGDOs are encouraged, or required, by funders to improve their capacity, the implications are seldom clear. As a result, NGDOs say 'yes' without understanding how far-reaching the process may have to be. Organisational assessment, described below, is one way of identifying all aspects involved, but this step is further down the line. In order to gauge implications and likely levels of resistance, some idea of the depth of change is required.

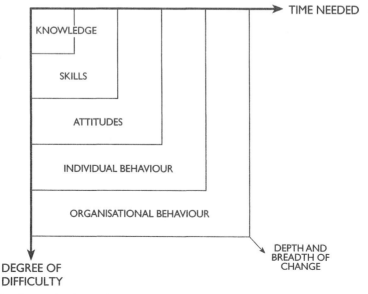

Figure 8.3 Depth of organisational change

Source: adapted from Piers Campbell, 1989

The donor stance

Often the idea that capacity growth is necessary comes out of dialogue between NGDOs and funders. Self-initiated NGDO assessment in relation to performance and major changes in the environment certainly occurs – for example, in post-apartheid South Africa – but is a less frequent source of OD initiatives. Whether or not dialogue is the origin, it is important that donors recognise their own limitations. The tendency, however, is not for donors to say *mea culpa*, but to treat capacity as an internal NGDO affair, independent of financing conditions and expectations. A second precondition, therefore, is to locate OD within the aid system, recognising that the 'overheads game' and the fixation on what NGDOs do rather than what they are create profound constraints which an NGDO cannot change on its own.[13] Without this recognition, starting an OD process can be an exercise in futility, with donors contributing as much to the problem as the solution of capacity growth. When pushed by donors, an NGDO OD process should be treated as a mutual imposition – it takes at least two to do the OD tango in the aid chain.

Initiative, ownership and commitment

Organisational development is less effective if it is imposed from outside rather than self-initiated. Northern NGDOs and donors have a tendency to point out the capacity weaknesses of their partners instead of encouraging and enabling them to critically reflect on their own performance. Consequently, OD becomes a new aid imposition not fully owned by recipient NGDOs. Reflecting on this issue, one Northern NGDO came to the conclusion that its own capacity weaknesses had to be recognised first, as did its historical role in shaping its partners' own incapacity. From here, partners could determine whether or not they wanted to collaborate in an OD process of their own.[14]

Furthermore, ownership must be reflected by commitment from the top, signalled through necessary time and budget allocations. Where chief executives feel threatened or insecure, they may permit OD to go ahead but distance themselves from the process, reserving the right to veto outcomes. This is not an acceptable stance in general, but certainly cannot be tolerated in situations where the depth of change is likely to be far-reaching. Where the leadership of an NGDO, including the governing body, is not prepared to have his or her or their functioning examined in an OD process, the chances are that key elements influencing capacity will not be assessed and that recommendations for change are less likely to be adopted.

Acknowledging the informal

A fourth precondition is that all parties accept that there are informal as well as formal dimensions to organisational capacity. Organisational development should not be treated in isolation from interpersonal relationships and external links which influence how an NGDO operates. For example, relationships with influential families, political leaders, different religious denominations or political factions can all colour how external negotiations take place. In short, OD processes should be designed to take into account both formal and informal factors.

Knowing where to start

It can be argued that growing capacity is only one reason for starting a process of organisational development. For example, OD may be prompted simply because of moving the office to a new building. How, then, is the right process of capacity building initiated? Like so many other development questions, the answer is: it depends. Most importantly, it depends on the stimulus for doing it in the first place. In other words, the eventual OD journey depends on where you are starting from and what needs to change. There are two common situations. First, the need for change is evident. Second, neither forces for change nor consensus about change exist. In the first case, there will be little difficulty in moving straight into an OD process; in the second, an assessment is probably required. We will look at both settings.

Forces for change

There are numerous forces for change. Some are relatively straightforward, such as adopting a new type of technology or scaling up because of demonstrated good work. Others are destabilising and threatening, such as redefining identity and role in society. This happened, for example, in Latin America with the introduction of elected civilian regimes instead of military juntas. Under the military, the NGDO goal was to restore civic rights. Today, the task is to promote sustainable development which benefits the poor. This reorientation may call for a critical stance towards government officials and politicians who were once 'brothers and sisters' in the struggle – as in Chile. Here, a far-reaching process of organisational transformation is called for, where old truths and assumptions must be discarded in order to move on. Where there is internal recognition and agreement on why capacity must be developed or redirected, force(s) for change may already signal what needs to be done and how. Where this is not the case, an initiating step is required, commonly called organisational assessment (OA), but this is not easy to start.

Capacity assessment

Four factors commonly stand in the way of starting and finishing an OD initiative. First, not everyone will agree that there is a significant problem or capacity weakness, partly because this is an admission of inadequacy. It might also suggest a less than competent leadership, which is painful to acknowledge. Second, there is a tendency to keep things as they are rather than embark on the unknown. Third, NGDO monitoring and performance appraisal systems often allow poor practice to go unseen and unchallenged. This also allows effort to be equated with achievement consistent with a culture of 'good works are enough'. Any criticism is seen as unfair because everyone is doing their best. Finally, while the signs of capacity weakness may be clear, the underlying causes may not be apparent or the remedies suggested may give rise to dispute. These, and other issues such as work overload, insecurity and stress, form barriers to recognising internal forces for change.

In my experience, NGDOs are more likely to be prompted into organisational change by external rather than internal factors. External factors can include incentives or threats. Incentives arise from new opportunities to access funds, gain a foothold in policy-making processes, expand existing operations, and improve public profile. Threats appear when funding is likely to be cut or conditions for gaining access are made more difficult; when the media questions the merits of the community as whole; and when governments feel uncomfortable about NGDOs. In Canada, a seminar in 1994 for NGDO leaders on challenges arising from the changing national and international context led to a consensus that change was inevitable and had been so for some time. When asked why necessary change was still not happening, the reply was: 'because things are not hurting enough'.[15] In other words, proactive change did not seem to be possible, unless the leadership was prepared to create an artificial crisis.[16] For this reason, complacency is a major barrier to organisational change.[17]

Too often real pain seems to be the motivation for necessary change in NGDOs. But what if an NGDO decides that it must do something about capacity; where can it start? A sensible answer is to begin by assessing existing organisational capacity.

Assessing Organisational Capacity

There are two major reasons why organisational assessments (OA) are carried out. The first is as a diagnostic tool to identify what organisational development process is needed to increase capacity. Secondly, some donors use forms of OA as an input to financial decision-making. This section looks at both motivations.

Organisational assessment: capacity diagnosis

Organisational assessment can be compared with the entry process used for development interventions described earlier. There are two directions for starting up an OA process which can be called the outside-in and inside-out strategies. Selecting an assessment strategy depends on:

- Purpose: is it, for example, to convince donors of capabilities or to identify reasons for poor performance? In the first case, outside-in may be appropriate, in the second something deeper may be required.
- Organisational complexity: an NGDO's complexity is not simply a function of size in terms of budget and staff numbers, although generally speaking bigger NGDOs tend to be more complex. Breadth of objectives, diversity in resource base and relationship patterns can also lead to very complex features in small NGDOs. In very complex organisations, assessment usually requires tailor-made tools.
- Cost: how much can the organisation afford in terms of direct and opportunity costs? Outside-in tends to be cheaper.
- Level of concern or crisis: where an NGDO faces a severe crisis in terms of viability, or credibility it may be necessary to put effort and resources into OA which are out of proportion to the complexity of the organisation and its level of operation.
- The extent to which it hurts: where self-analysis is likely to be disturbing, it may be appropriate to start with a more superficial type of OA, slowly moving into sensitive areas once confidence has been established.

Wherever possible, these trade-offs should be arrived at following OD rules. If this occurs, an OD process has actually started and the activity becomes more cost-effective because it involves staff participation. Crisis within an NGDO, on the other hand, may preclude full participation and the activity will, of necessity, start without consensus. In such a situation, one function of participatory OA is to provide a forum and process for meeting and mediation. More generally, assessment methods must be able to deal with conflicts as different opinions about strengths and weaknesses are exposed.

The outside-in assessment strategy

Outside-in involves comparison of the organisation to an ideal. Box 8.1 summarises the characteristics of an ideal operational NGDO.[18]

Experience from Bangladesh shows that an important first step is a locally appropriate definition of what an ideal or healthy NGDO looks like, together with measures and indicators.[19] No matter how many organisational generalisations are valid, there will always be cultural, context-specific factors and social problems that a competent NGDO must deal with – for example managing internal ethnic, religious or caste differences. Ideals can be established for different types of organisations – for example, operational, support and advocacy NGDOs – as well as for networks, coalitions and co-ordinating bodies.

Subsequent steps for applying an outside-in assessment strategy include the following:

- Pre-entry: win support and commitment for the exercise from internal and external stakeholders.
- Create one, or a small number of, multiple stakeholder groups. For strongly de-centralised NGDOs, this might mean one in each semi-autonomous entity.
- Define organisationally relevant indicators and measures from the list above and allocate a range of scores, such as high-low, too often-not often enough, 1 to 5, and so on. Measures can come from other NGDOs as a type of bench-marking. Agree on a how to sample and find information on each indicator.
- Gather information on the organisation in relation to each characteristic. For example, an NGDO's statement about position could be: 'nationally we are seen and approached as an extension of rich foreign donors, rather than a small indigenous agency with an empowerment mission'.

Box 8.1
Characteristics of an ideal operational NGDO

An ideal or healthy operational NGDO:

- understands socio-economic and political realities and is able to maintain the POSITION it wants with respect to its values, vision, identity and mission;
- is an AWARE organisation, constantly able to LEARN, review and adapt its position and methods to maintain performance;
- shows DISTINCTIVE COMPETENCE through cost-effective use of resources in achieving its mission;
- is ACCOUNTABLE to its stakeholders and proves its LEGITIMACY through demonstrated IMPACT on poverty and injustice;
- forms STRATEGIC ALLIANCES with others in pursuit of its goals without compromising its position;
- enjoys COMPETENT LEADERSHIP that is visionary, has integrity, is respected internally and externally, can constructively manage inherent organisational tensions, is adept at recognising and resolving conflicts, and is action-oriented;
- has a FINANCIAL BASE that assures AUTONOMY and CONTINUITY, requiring long-term financial strategies and competent management of diverse funding sources;
- has ORGANISATIONAL STRUCTURES and SYSTEMS that: ensure interventions are appropriate to diverse environments and social groups; select and maintain correct priorities and plan for them accordingly; link multiple levels of development action; engage with both organisational and institutional change; achieve sustainable impacts; do not create dependency; empower those served; motivate and develop staff as individuals and teams; are responsive, with high local problem-solving capabilities; and build the capacities of others, particularly CBOs.

- Analyse what each statement says about how reality differs from the ideal. For example, inadequate skill and confidence to take micro-action into the policy arena may suggest individual or organisational weaknesses.
- Decide how to tackle each inadequacy and plan to do so.
- Mobilise any necessary resources, implement the plan and critically reflect on past experience.

A key feature in the success of this strategy is to place the findings within their environmental context, as well as taking into account the organisation's age. Bench-marking should stop the NGDO from blaming everything on outside forces.

The inside-out assessment strategy

The inside-out strategy does not have an ideal type, but takes mission and strategic goals as reference points. The detailed steps to be followed depend on the complexity of the NGDOs concerned and can be found in the referenced publications.[20] Questions to be asked include the following.[21]

- What is our organisation's purpose in society?
- Who do we represent?
- What do the people we represent value or find important in terms of change?
- What results are we achieving?
- What is our strategy and plan for the future?

Answers to these questions should then be checked with written records and other evidence, including inputs from external stakeholders. Staff should then return for a final assessment by comparing two types of information: their own answers and answers produced by other sources. Differences are analysed, causes identified and change planned.[22] Key limitations are the ability and willingness to be self-critical as a group – which may be culturally determined. In addition, it can be difficult to get frank responses from communities, groups or other primary stakeholders, especially when a dependency relationship has been created. In both cases, independent facilitation, input and validation are called for.

Self-assessment in medium-complexity NGDOs

Medium-complexity NGDOs can use a two-stage approach involving a broad reconnaissance, followed by selective, in-depth analysis of areas which are weak or where opinions or perceptions are highly contested.

In stage 1, reconnaissance involves creating a team from different organisational levels which will do the assessment. One way of helping team members reach a common organisational understanding is for them to analyse the NGDO's history. Based on mission, strategic choices and analysis of stakeholder claims and measures, the team identifies key areas for capacity assessment and related information sources. Scales for judgement are agreed upon and the team splits into twos or threes to interview internal and external stakeholders, as well as to review documents. Responses to questions should always be supported by concrete examples from respondents' experience. After data collection, each team constructs a matrix showing assessments for each area of the organisation as seen from the perspective of respondents and other sources. The presentation could be key words, statements or scales. Comparisons between responses are made to see where there is consensus about capacity strengths and weaknesses and to identify contested areas. For example, a problem would be signalled if staff say decision-making is transparent and timely, while primary stakeholders see it as a dark hole. The final matrix, constructed from a critical review of team inputs, is shared with all staff. Feedback becomes part of the second stage.

Stage 2 is an in-depth analysis of critical areas identified in stage 1. One method is to bring diverse stakeholders together for focus-group discussions where an appropriately representative group of individuals is asked to analyse a problem or issue. This approach can have an organisational development effect by strengthening internal-external relationships and by checking if implementation is consistent with goals and operational plans. Inputs to decisions about organisational change, and the necessary OD content and process, come out of the in-depth studies, combined with the overall picture of organisational capacity.

Three drawbacks to the method are, first, respondents' honesty. Second, the quality of individual team members has a significant impact on the quality of the assessment. Finally, this type of process is bound to produce internal tensions. It is therefore vital that OA leads into an OD process where tensions are dealt with constructively. To leave things hanging in the air after an assessment usually makes things worse. In other words, a commitment to following through is essential from the outset. Again, external facilitation can introduce comparative objectivity, compensate for weaknesses in the team and act as a lightening rod for relieving tensions.

Self-assessment in high-complexity NGDOs

In very complex NGDOs, organisational assessment is typically a long process spread over many months. With the likelihood of many discrete departments and layers, it is necessary to determine what are the key functional units which need to be assessed. Functional units (FUs) are not necessarily formal structures, such as cells or departments, but can include management teams, committees and periodically constituted bodies. The key criteria is that the function, however performed, plays a critical role in the NGDO's behaviour, such as management teams.

Assessment in very complex NGDOs requires both facilitation and independent validation. The typical steps in assessment are:

- selection of a core team or task force responsible for the exercise;
- an introductory workshop to clarify both content and process of assessment, followed by identification of functional units to be assessed; each FU is accompanied by indicators, measures and sources of information - this exercise can take one or more weeks;
- splitting of the core team in pairs to carry out an assessment of the FU assigned to them;
- a parallel process of selective validation, carried out by outsiders using the same instruments produced by the initial workshop;
- an assessment workshop, which provides the forum for sharing back the findings of the FU appraisals; identifying contradictions and mismatches; and comparing them with the separate validation to locate biases and explain disparities.

The outputs of the final gathering should be:

- a shared holistic appreciation of organisational capacity;
- an identification of capacity limits in the organisation as a whole and in terms of its constituent parts;
- a prioritised and sequenced proposal for the organisational development activities which need to be undertaken.

Inevitably, there are drawbacks to this approach. First, the core team is very likely to miss some of the specialist expertise needed to assess the functional units. Selective involvement of external specialists can compensate for this, which also builds capacity. Commonly, assessment mixes up what actually exists with what should exist. It is difficult to decide on criteria for judging competencies, especially if the NGDO is implementing a new strategy. External validation can help deal with this, but

awareness of the problem is important to start with.

The costs and benefits of this assessment method are less easy to judge than if outsiders are hired to do it – principally because the opportunity costs of staff time are difficult to estimate. This is one reason why allocation of time and budgets are vital. Similarly, staff availability must be scheduled into their work. Finally, personal biases inevitably find their way into the process. This introduces distortions that are worse the more secretive the organisation is. While independent validation can help reduce personal bias, a culture of openness is the key condition to solving the problem from the start.

Additional observations

Each of the assessment methods described above conforms to the basic principles set out at the beginning of the chapter. If done properly, each produces a baseline profile of organisational capacity which is owned within, has identified the causes rather than the symptoms of capacity limitations, and summarises the principal areas where organisational change should occur, perhaps with an OD plan. If done properly, the OA exercise has already produced organisational development outcomes in terms of greater awareness, has stimulated internal motivation for change, and has improved relationships and generated new insights. In other words, distinctions between this type of organisational assessment and the stage of organisational development become blurred. In most cases, one overlays the other.

Capacity assessment for donors

The capacity assessments described above apply to all NGDOs, but have most relevance for those who are operational. A different type of capacity assessment is applied by donors who want to either decide about funding, or how to tailor their support to the capacity needs of the recipient. How can they do this? Usually, with difficulty, given the often severe constraints on donor staff time. There are, however, tips for donors which create a profile of the NGDO in question. The example below is for an operational NGDO; modifications would be needed for lobby and advocacy organisations, networks or consortia.

Constructing an NGDO profile

The objective of a profile is to create a fair and dynamic picture of the organisation.[23] This calls for an understanding of organisational processes and the selection of information which is realistically obtainable in the time allowed. In this sense, a partner profile is less of a tool than a checklist to guide donor staff who are not organisational specialists and to help them interpret what they find. Within each category, questions about abilities can be asked. For example, is the NGDO able to report on and analyse its experiences? Is the NGDO able to create a budget consistent with its plans? Is the NGDO able to hold its position in society? In general, a question-based format is the most useful; but answers only have meaning in relation to a wider context. Box 8.2 shows categories which can be used.

Although obtaining sound information is a major problem for many donors, both governmental and non-governmental, the best strategy is to gain as many insights from as many sources as possible. Information coming only from the NGDO itself is highly risky and needs validation.

At least two factors must be brought into such interpretation and assessment. First, the age of the NGDO. Younger organisations will be less likely to have consolidated their capacities and ways of working than older ones, and it may just be the energy and drive of a young organisation which is needed – a capacity in itself. Second, the local environment must be considered. Where regimes have actively worked against NGDOs or other autonomous bodies, it may be reasonable to find capacity weaknesses. The question is whether there is potential for capacity growth?

Donors funding NGDOs need competencies to interpret and contextualise, which is seldom a topic in their training or a criteria for selection. Tools only provide data, the real job is forming a fair judgement – which depends on the insights and quality of donor staff. Tools are no short cut to professional competence. In addition, as a matter of principle and best practice donors must be able to answer for their own organisation the questions they ask of others. Doing so will give them a feel for the difficulties involved and provide concrete examples of what they are looking for because the jargon used in OD is vague and confusing.

From Capacity Assessment to Capacity Growth

One way or another, NGDOs reach the conclusion that they need more capacity. Through assessment, or in other ways, NGDOs should have identified areas where growth must be achieved. This section examines how organisational development can be carried out. Four topics need to be covered. First, there is a hierarchy within any OD strategy which must be respected. Second, there are basic ways of introducing and managing change, involving points of entry or themes which act as the leading idea around which OD activities take place. Third, internal resistance must be dealt with. Fourth, appropriate institutional and human resources must be selected to help in the change process.

Respect the OD hierarchy

Processes of organisational change should not create inconsistency between the organisation and its mission. To ensure this does not happen, it is necessary to respect the organisational hierarchy which makes up an effective NGDO. In other words, there is a sequence to be followed, as described by CDRA.

The basic order in which capacity building occurs is: conceptual framework first; appropriate organisational attitudes leading to vision and strategy; followed by structure (organisational form), which

Box 8.2
Donor checklist for NGDO capacity

Nominal data:
- name, legal status, name of officers;
- type of constituency it represents.

Identity and historical trajectory:
- mission statement; does it make sense and is it realistic?
- can the NGDO explain the causes of the problems it is addressing?
- how has the NGDO evolved in terms of scope of operational activity?
- are organisational adaptations a response to crises or the result of strategic thinking?

Governance, management and organisation:
- is the governing body truly non-governmental?
- does the governing body exert proper oversight and does it really carry responsibility?
- is the leadership still the founder or has there been a transition?
- is the management style appropriate to the mission, activities and context?
- is the organisational set-up and culture appropriate for the tasks and their scope?

Programmes, projects and policies:
- are programmes, projects and activities coherent with each other and with the mission?
- do necessary policies exist on gender, environment, and sustainability?
- can the NGDO produce clear, internally consistent proposals and intervention frameworks?
- is the NGDO able to assess costs and benefits of its work?

Implementation:
- does the NGDO have the technical skills required?
- does the NGDO have an effective approach for its work with CBOs; can it target and who does it reach?
- does it apply participatory methods and demonstrate community involvement in decision-making?
- are its physical resources looked after and well maintained?
- is a monitoring system in place, does it disaggregate information by gender and does it extend beyond outputs?

Performance track record:
- can the NGDO show sustainable outcomes or impact at any level; has its work been replicated or used by others?
- are evaluations and other studies carried out regularly?
- is there evidence of learning from evaluation findings?

Administration:
- are financial reports produced on time and properly?
- are audit reports satisfactory?

Financial resources:
- has there been continuity in donor support?
- is a strategy for own financing in place or being planned?

Links:
- does the NGDO network have strong links within the NGDO community and to other social institutions?
- is it a recognised, respected institutional actor?

Financing perspective:
- what is needed for the NGDO to be better?

- is there potential for any type of scaling up?
- what is the longer-term perspective for viability?

Summary assessment:
- does the NGDO have the basic competencies required and can it obtain others it may need?
- does the NGDO potentially meet donor priorities and criteria and vice versa?
- what is the type and duration of assistance required?
- how can viability be assisted and assured?
- what adaptations to funding methods need to made to ensure that finance is effective?

in turn gives content and energy through skilled individuals. The whole is then supported by adequate resourcing. Needs change with respect to all these elements as the organisation develops, but the central point is this: intervention or work on any of these elements will not prove effective unless sufficient work is done on preceding elements in the hierarchy.[24]

Although the degree of complexity will alter as an NGDO becomes established, matures and grows, the basic hierarchy remains the same and must be checked before an OD process begins. The rule of thumb, therefore, is to check and respect the hierarchy, even if the change you intend to make appears to be limited to one aspect of the organisation.

Introducing and managing change

Those responsible for improving effectiveness have to make key decisions about how the change process will be managed.[25] They must decide how staff will be engaged and how the process will be overseen to its conclusion. Some of the major choices available are described below.

The point of entry

Any process that stimulates capacity growth needs a point of entry or focus, or guiding theme. Such a focus is like a washing line on which activities can be hung, linking together what may be a wide variety of changes.

Assuming the hierarchy of change is respected, points of entry include:

- strategic leads – changing mission, goals, tasks and activities;
- cultural leads – changing attitudes, values and group relations;
- structural leads – changing the divisions of competencies and authority;
- system leads – changing procedures, sequences of work, communication/information flows;
- resource leads – changing the mix and level of financial and other resources;
- plan and budget leads - changing the way resources are allocated and accounted for;
- people lead – changing the human resources available in terms of knowledge and skills;
- technology leads – changing the principle assumptions, hardware and software used in the core work;
- relationships lead – changing the pattern and content of external relations;
- performance leads – changing the quality of outcomes.

None of these are mutually exclusive and one is unlikely to be sufficient on its own. The leading idea would normally be defined by specific capacity limitations or by the primary force for change. For example, weak social positioning and influence would call for a strategic lead; inadequate community ownership may call for a (soft) 'technology' lead in terms of participatory methods.

How will change be introduced?

Leaders/managers face a difficult choice in bringing about change. They can decide to adopt the following alternatives.

- Implement change directly, by instruction.
- Trickle-down change by starting with managers and then reaching each level of staff.
- Implement multi-level changes by including appropriate staff: this is sometimes called a vertical-team or coalition approach.
- Comprehensive change, where staff, structures and systems are altered all together in a single, comprehensive step.

Needless to say, what is most appropriate depends on the depth of change called for and the types of capacity to be increased. A common situation amongst Northern NGDOs is to undertake a strategic review and then be stuck with the repercussions. In cases of far-reaching, strategy-lead change, for example, where priorities, structure, ways of working and relationships all have to alter, the risks associated with change can be reduced by establishing a task force to pilot all changes on a small scale. The task force builds up practical experience of how an, essentially, new organisation would function. Once this has been tried, tested and demonstrated to the rest of the organisation, it can be introduced 'overnight' – thereby avoiding a long drawn-out, destabilising and confusing transition where bits of the organisation are working simultaneously in the old and the new set-up. Most cases are best approached incrementally. Given the nature of NGDOs, a multi-level team or coalition approach would be most consistent with preferred practice.

How will the change process be managed?

Various options for change management exist. Again, the best choice depends on organisational circumstances and the depth of change envisaged. In general, the deeper the change, the higher the level of authority needed to see it through. Common options include the following.

- The leader(ship) controls the process directly.
- A change manager/co-ordinator is appointed who reports to the senior management and is empowered to act with their authority.
- A participatory group are given delegated authority to monitor and guide change, with line managers remaining responsible for capacity development within their sphere of control.

Each option has its merits and drawbacks. A leader-controlled process is less likely to be participatory and tends to be used when resistance is high. The second option requires consensus, but may suffer from confusion about who has the last word. Option three works best when there is little resistance, and multiple changes affecting many parts of the organisation must be harmonised. An important way to steer change is through resource allocations. Control over budgets and time in terms of reducing workloads can do a lot to encourage co-operation and keep up momentum. Creating a change budget also signals that management is serious and that change is not simply business as usual.

Resistance to change: sources and remedies

It would be too optimistic to assume that all change for capacity growth will be universally embraced and simply flow into and throughout the organisation. Leaders/managers must be prepared to recognise and deal with passive and active obstacles to altering how things work. Where is resistance likely to come from and what can be done about it?

Resistance to change

There are three typical sources of resistance to organisational change, summarised in Box 8.3. The organisation can be 'stiff', people can actively or passively resist, and external

---

Box 8.3
Typical sources of resistance to change

Organisational sources:
- an overstructured, centralised authority which constrains movement outside of existing parameters;
- lack of, or a contested, development analysis (theory of cause and change) resulting in unclear objectives and operational rationale – this allows any change initiative to be countered on the grounds that it will not make a difference;
- poor internal communication which permits or encourages misinformation;
- an aversion to disrupting existing operations with an inability to make space for change.

Human sources:
- self-interest;
- fear of the unknown;
- lack of perceived benefits;
- lack of trust and misunderstanding;
- different perception of the present and future situation;
- avoiding disruption of existing work;
- denial that forces for change exist or are significant;
- unconscious or wilful ignorance.

Relational sources:
- fear of loss of livelihood;
- comfort, habit and dependency;
- moral outrage that the NGDO is not fulfilling its promises, is deceitful and unreliable, with threats of media exposure;
- partners may have powerful allies in society which can be turned against the NGDO;
- unshared perceptions about the need for change, or that the change intended is right, casting doubts and uncertainty within the NGDO.

---

relations can put up barriers to altering the way things are. For example, aggrieved partners can mobilise the media and politicians to influence decisions in favour of the status quo. In other words, an NGDO is seldom fully autonomous in decision-making; outside relationships may both demand and discourage change at the same time.

Countering resistance

A common way of visualising resistance is as forces of varying intensity lined up against the forces for change. Strategic options that are available to alter the balance of power in favour of change are:

- increase the forces for change;
- decrease or remove sources of resistance;

- turn negative forces against into positive forces for change.

The following actions can be combined to complement any one of these strategies.

- Build coalitions for change with like-minded individuals.
- Change styles of management and leadership to increase trust.
- Modify staff attitudes and values.
- Allocate responsibility for the change process to those who inspire confidence.
- Ensure open management of the change process.
- Promote wide and systematic communication.
- Provide personal counselling.
- Solicit suggestions on ways to go about

Table 8.2 Types of intervention for capacity growth[26]

Type of Intervention	Technical Cooperation (TC)	Management Assistance (MA)	Relational Development (RD)	Organisational Development (OD)
Purpose	To improve operational and technical skills	To improve specific organisational areas	To improve civic and intersector interaction	To improve the organisation overall
Methods	• HRD options (Ch 4) • technical inputs • finance • physical resources • counterparts/ advisers	• HRD options • management/ leadership forming • board + leadership development • strategic development • short-term problem-solving	• coalition building • joint policy development • mediation • civic linking • sector coupling and networking	• HRD options • organisational change consultancies • 'partnering' • strategic development exercises • team/group relationship exercises
Approach	Problem-solving	Problem-solving + counselling	Mobilising and bridging	Facilitating

effecting change.
● Involve principle stakeholders in an advisory capacity and as an educational opportunity.

The process of capacity development

From an understanding of what changes are needed, an appropriate mix of interventions can be selected. Table 8.2 shows four basic intervention types to choose from: technical cooperation (TC), management assistance (MA), organisational development (OD) and relationship development (RD).

Generally speaking, the deeper the behavioural change required, the more likely that an NGDO will require OD-type interventions. Technical cooperation can usually be applied to deal with limited areas of operational change, while management assistance – in the form of counselling, cadre-forming programmes, internal workshops – is more likely to deal with relationship and decision-making issues. Relationship development is designed to bring together, mediate between, focus and link NGDOs, as well as help them interface with other sectors. Organisational development, is the most far-

reaching type of intervention, where no part of the organisation is likely to remain untouched. Our attention concentrates on OD because it covers the most extreme cases and in doing so deals with more extensive capacity development.

The intervention framework applied for interaction with communities (described in Chapter 5) can also be used for NGDO capacity growth; Figure 8.4 is an adapted version of this. Stage 1, entry, calls for the preconditions to be implemented and an assessment to have taken place so that the necessary organisational changes are understood. In addition, management of the change process should already be sorted out in terms of responsibilities and resources. Stage 2 implements the change along the theme(s) selected; group-oriented activities are usually a central part. Team-building exercises, in-house training, human-resource development, and workshops with external stakeholders are all typical activities which support the lead theme. In stage 3, change is well underway and organisational life is associated with an increase in performance that is appreciated by stakeholders.

It is apparent from Figure 8.4 that organisational development cannot be measured

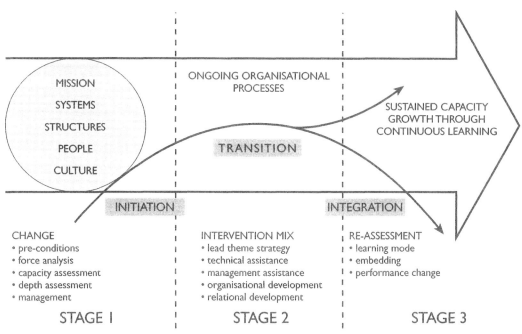

Figure 8.4 Introducing organisational change

in numbers of outputs – such as seminars and workshops attended – or in greater academic qualification of staff, but in the time it takes to achieve behavioural and development change.

The facilitation process: partnering and accompanying

The approaches to organisational assessment described so far called for an independent input to guide the process, provide external validation, and introduce additional skills and comparative experiences. Similar inputs are valuable for making the OD process more effective. When there is a need for fundamental change in an NGDO, the most useful type of input is one which is long term. This type of assistance corresponds to the 'partnering' described when

working with CBOs. The practice of 'partnering' in NGDO organisational development is summarised in Box 8.4.

One limitation to adopting an 'accompanying' processes in OD is the reticence of funders to meet the costs of periodic external inputs which cover the three stages. There is still a naive hope that a project-type magic bullet, such as training, will do the trick. It will not. The best that professional NGDO-OD consultants can do in this situation, therefore, is place the occasional inputs they are asked to provide, such as a project appraisal, an evaluation, or a workshop, in an OD framework.

In addition to OD process guidance, there are other supporting resources that NGDOs can draw on to assist in capacity growth. These resources are described below.

Selecting Resources to Support NGDO Capacity Development

Recent increases in resources allocated to NGDO capacity growth have brought with them a demand for services which can support organisational assessment and change. However, because of unbalanced funding strategies, the

growth in demand is outstripping the supply of services needed. Consequently, there are services on offer which are not professionally sound. Because the situation is changing so rapidly, this section is restricted to a brief

Box 8.4
The art of partnering and accompanying

Accompanying and partnering

Accompanying is a process of moving along side by side in dialogue and experimentation which creates organisational improvement and yields knowledge about change. This description can apply to 'authentic partnering' between Northern and Southern or Eastern NGDOs and between a consultant and an organisational client.

Principles and practices

At its core, partnering requires the right personal competencies and relationships revolving around:

● a commitment to learning as an attitude and ethic;
● a spirit of dialogue which searches for new meaning that cannot be found individually;
● honest recognition of mutual weaknesses and strengths;
● seeing totalities and people at all levels, not just bits and pieces of each other;
● agreeing on expectations — is what we want from each other clear, fair and realistic?
● using rigorous techniques as well as impressions to ensure accuracy and fairness;
● in decision-making, treating others as you wish to be treated yourself.

Pitfalls and how to avoid them

● Partnering can create a level of mutual dependency which blinds individuals to other ideas and ways of doing things. Ensure periodic third-party inputs to create 'space' to question assumptions and choices.
● Local staff employed by foreign agencies may suffer from dual allegiances, leading to confused attitudes and behaviour. Ensure that operations are based on locally inspired vision, mission and strategies within a guiding framework.
● Information exchange is frequently reduced to narrative reports, audits and evaluations. Deeper interaction must be valued and built in through long-term visits.
● Reports or agreements may not always be followed up. Set standards for response time and make sure content is adhered to.
● Routines can thwart creative dialogue. Adopting a team-based relationship can work against this, as can joint workshops to assess progress and give new impulses.
● Emotional attachment is as unhealthy as clinical detachment. Team approaches can help to retain the critical balance.
● Northern and Southern NGDOs can over or underestimate their importance in the aid process. Learning circles, and multi-agency discussion groups can assist in seeing one's own place in the whole.
● Northern agencies should use internal human resource development to positively refocus staff.
● There is no agreement or strategy for dealing with things when they go wrong. Bringing in an evaluator is not the solution. Instead, an arbitrator and arbitration process can be agreed upon before they are needed; this avoids power politics.

Source: adapted from a contribution by Tom Lent, Redd Barna, Guatemala analysis of what appears to be happening; pointers are then offered for NGDO leaders/managers and donors who are looking for competent, cost-effective assistance in capacity development.

Services to support capacity growth

There are eight major types of supplier who assist in the capacity development of NGDOs.[27] Generally, each supplier has a mix of

Table 8.3 Services that support NGDO capacity growth

Capacity for what? Type of supplier	Community development	NGDO self- development	Institutional development
International NGDO support organisations	unsuitable	probably suitable but not cost-effective	suitable and cost-effective
National NGDO support organisations	potentially high	potentially high	potentially high
NGDO training centres	not very useful	very useful for individuals	unlikely to be very appropriate
Donor NGDO support projects	ranging from high to low	probably high for projects	ranging from high to low
Academic training institutions	medium if there are specialists	low potential	potentially high for analysis
Government training institutions	limited potential	unsuitable	low
Dedicated consultancy firms	uncertain, depending on individuals concerned	potentially high depending on individuals	uncertain, depending on individuals concerned
Management accounting firms	unsuitable	useful for selected functions	unsuitable

competencies and comparative advantages in relation to the types of NGDO capacity described at the beginning of this chapter (Table 8.1). The summary in Table 8.3 comments on the ability of each supplier to: support the capacity growth of community-based organisations (CBOs); effectively achieve the NGDO's mission; and strengthen (civic) institutions in society.

Of most interest is a new type of NGDO being established to provide competent OD assistance to NGDOs, – known as NGO support organisations (NGOSOs). Support NGDOs differ from NGDO co-ordinating bodies (which can play similar roles) in that they are not mandated by, and do not represent, an NGDO constituency or membership; are designed to

gain skills and knowledge from action-research with NGDOs and the aid system; and share what they have to offer though publications, training courses, seminars, and in-house consultancy. Institutional and organisational capacity development is their major strength.

The mission of NGOSOs is to strengthen other NGDOs, internationally, regionally or nationally, as well as to participate in policy dialogue within the NGDO community and the official aid system. International examples are IRED in Africa, Asia and Latin America, IDR in the USA, INTRAC in England, El Taller in Tunisia, FOCUS in Thailand, PRIA in India, CDRA in South Africa and EASUN in Tanzania. These bodies co-exist with training-based international NGDOs and programmes, such as Selly Oak Colleges in the UK and World Learning's School of International Training in Vermont.

Increasingly, international support NGDOs are directing their efforts towards assisting a growing number of national NGDO support organisations, for example, the NGO Resource Centre (NGORC) in Pakistan, CORAT in East Africa, Center InterBilim in Kyrghystan, PRIP in Bangladesh, MODE in the Philippines, DESCO in Peru and Sambhav Social Service Organisation in Madhya Pradesh. The relationship between national and international NGDO support organisations appears to result from personal contact and trust, pivoting around a reasonably well-shared view of the NGDO sector in society and a commitment to participatory approaches.

There are also a growing number of national NGDO support organisations emerging from the provision of training or evaluation services which are focussing on capacity development of operational NGDOs. However, few are capable yet of providing a 'partnering' approach of long-term interaction and counselling. Some national NGDO support organisations start life as donor-funded projects implemented by Northern NGDOs in the South and become autonomous national bodies – PACT/PRIP is an example in Bangladesh. A similar project in Namibia is run by World Education, an American NGDO. Whether indigenous or imported, national NGDO support organisations are a new and potentially critical resource which can accelerate capacity growth in NGDOs.

Together, international and national NGDO support organisations should offer the most appropriate type of support for the different types of capacity growth. They are not, however, present in sufficient numbers in the countries which need them. Nor have they gained the degree of practical exposure required to professionally assist operational and/or policy-oriented NGDOs in capacity growth and change processes. Unfortunately, as noted for EASUN, funding arrangements based on one-shot inputs rather than long-term processes do not increase their professional exposure either. In sum, there is a shortage of competent advisers with a track record of assisting NGDOs in OD processes. Initiatives are afoot to change this situation, but the lack of professional skills is opening up opportunities for other types of suppliers.

The individual counts most

Experience suggests that while different types of service institutions can act as a filter when looking for support in capacity growth, it is the individual who counts most. Selecting the right person as consultant, trusted adviser or counsellor determines whether or not they can be used as a practical resource. Unfortunately, a lot of money and energy is wasted because NGDOs and donors – who too often choose the consultant – do not know how to select and use such people effectively. Milan Kubr's book (1993) is therefore a must for anyone called upon to hire or use consultancy expertise.[28]

What should you look for in a consultant? The answer, again, is it depends. Firstly, examine what stage you are in. Exploring capacity growth is different from having a clear idea of what should to be altered and how. Secondly, what is the likely depth of change? The deeper the change, the more open, flexible and unregimented the consultant should be. In the words of one practitioner in the field:

> ... watch out for the OD practitioner who offers you 'ready to wear' models for your organisation to slip into – not wanting to get into the uncharted waters of your own organisation's unique issues and responses. The practitioner who brings a 'patent method' as 'the method for all situations' is a sign that they are more dominated by the method than master of it.... Beware of those who offer to provide you with the expert answers - rather than help you work through tentative, experimental responses of your own.[29]

Third, what is your freedom of choice? There is an unfortunate policy in the official aid system, and a habit with Northern NGDOs, to choose consultants from the country where the funds

A rule of thumb for NGDOs after consultation with the funder, is to insist on producing the final terms of reference for the work and to sign the contract with the consultant; payment should be made by the funder only after the NGDO's instruction.

come from, or local people if they are qualified and cheap. This limits the freedom of Southern and Eastern NGDOs to be in control of the recruitment process. Therefore, within the parameters set, your choice may be limited to those whom donors trust.

There is every reason, when NGDO leaders/managers are unsure of how to deal with problems, to rely on an expert's solution. However, ultimately the 'answer' lies within NGDOs themselves. A consultant who approaches NGDOs without any answers is probably more honest and knowledgeable about how NGDOs work. To be fully effective, a consultant must have an understanding of an NGDO's situation and goals, together with comparative experiences and opinions which, if they make sense, may be worth trying.[30] But this is the point – they are not solutions; rather they are ideas. The issue for NGDOs is to identify the problem themselves then work on it. This calls for process-consultation.[31]

This section concentrates on how to create capacity within NGDOs. One reason for doing so is to improve their ability to impact on the way society works, that is to change the institutions which make up civil society. The next section looks at what we can learn about this area.

$TIPS$

To recap, the type of institution to which he or she belongs is a first guide to the expertise, values, mind-set and approach a resource provider is likely to have. But, eventually it is the individual(s) concerned who must be judged for their suitability. Rules of thumb for selection are:

➤ the person has a demonstrated track record in the area needed;
➤ he or she (for deep change) can adopt an open-ended process approach to the interaction;
➤ he or she can listen and respond without imposing;
➤ he or she is not dependent on the funder for a substantial part of their income;
➤ choose people you can get on with and trust.

Strengthening Civil Society

Strengthening the institutions of civil society is a fairly recent addition to the aid system's goals. It is has become both an objective and condition of donor financing in the 1990s as part of a new policy agenda for aid.[32] Under the label of 'reforms for good governance', political conditions are being applied to aid grants throughout the world, especially in countries where civil society is considered to be deficient, as in the countries newly independent from the Soviet Union. These nations are therefore good places to learn about how the concept of civil society is being applied in the context of aid and the role NGDOs play. This concluding section looks at the strategies and methods NGDOs can adopt to strengthen the capacity of civic institutions.

Chapter 1 explained where the concept of civil society has come from and why it is being promoted as a way of achieving better governance, – a pluralistic, democratic set-up similar to those in the North. Strengthening civil society calls, first, for a clarification of what the aid system has in mind when it uses the concept. Second, it is important to look at how strategies are translated into practice. Are the same old tools being used to achieve new goals? Finally, suggestions are made on how to promote a more organic form of civic growth.

How civil society should not grow

The aid system has adopted a 'mirror' view of civil society. In other words, countries which do not have the types of organisations and institutional configurations found in the democratic, market-based North should be quickly helped to create them.[33] The approach therefore concentrates on establishing a plurality of organisations and enabling legal frameworks with a particular division of roles, responsibilities and power between state, market and civil society. In this way a pattern of institutional roles and relationships is created which works at home. Inevitably, domestic concerns of reducing the size of government, privatising and using the voluntary and private sector to provide social services also feature in aid when it comes to building civil society.

However, within the wide range of organisations and activities which are thought to make up civil society, the aid system is quite selective. By and large, only a small range of civic organisations are supported; these are primary intermediaries with specific agendas such as human rights, environmental concerns, gender, and AIDS. Mass organisations, unions, diverse professional associations, recreational or cultural bodies, and the multitude of special interest groups which are a substantial part of Northern civil society, and which are not in the business of delivery, are commonly ignored. For practical purposes, no meaningful distinction is made between CBOs and NGDOs. Because they do not employ organisational mapping based on a coherent theory, as far as the official aid system is concerned NGDOs are part of a homogenous category which can be equated with civil society as a whole.[34]

The aid system also ignores historical experience. It focuses on creating the formal structures of civil society as if the roots do not matter. But it cannot be assumed, for example, that a Northern NGDO approach will work in the South and East where historical conditions are not the same. By undervaluing local conditions, furthermore, external agencies take an oversimplified view of what must be done. For example, in Cambodia, years of internal strife and genocide under Pol Pot have eroded one of the most fundamental conditions for civic relations: trust. In the words of one survivor, Maes Nee:

> *In the Khmer Rouge time, trust was systematically destroyed. A friend would be asked to spy on a friend, and the next day the second of the partnership would be asked to spy on the first. Even today, people meet and recognise those who betrayed their loved ones.*[35]

Some NGDOs recognise that they must assist in building trust as the most essential foundation of civic life. But the methods they, and the official aid system, adopt are strongly conditioned by today's aid priority – micro-credit – which may not be the most appropriate in the Cambodian context. Maes Nee again:

> *I believe that if you start rebuilding by putting in projects that the village has never seen before, you are not restoring, you are making something different and you could be causing great confusion.*
>
> *Many loan schemes are an example of this. Because village people want money you can easily start a loan scheme. You can persuade people to make groups of five and to guarantee each other. But do not believe that you*

have rebuilt trust... It is not a way of redeveloping the structures of community; the agency becomes like a money lender and borrower becomes the client. If the borrower does not have the money to give back at the time, s/he will borrow from another money lender or will sell an asset. The agency may think that the loan scheme is a success because of a 100 per cent repayment. Full repayment is not difficult to achieve, but to understand the effects of this on the lives of the people and the spirit of the village is very difficult.[36]

Discounting the significance of historical preconditions and a narrow 'mirrored' idea about civil society promotes an imbalanced set of civic organisations without social or cultural foundations. The relative inattention to preconditions – such as trust – and appropriate ways to evolve them is the reason for the unsustainability of many projects. There are ways out, for example by using (formal and informal) organisational mapping, to understand weaknesses, opportunities and gaps in relationship patterns. But these are not systematically employed to see where civil society stands in relation to itself, to the state and the the market.

What causes aid agencies to short-cut best practice in strengthening civil society is a political imperative. In the words of Eva Mysliwiec:

...the work of NGOs in Cambodia has been shaped not only by the Cambodians' perceptions or former experiences of development but by many other factors as well, especially the politicization of aid. That, unfortunately, has been one of the few constants in an ever fluid situation.[37]

In sum, supplying aid to create allies is as important, if not more so, than being effective. How are NGDOs responding to this reality in countries of the East where 'producing' civil society is a top priority?

NGDO strategies for strengthening civil society

An NGDO strategy to strengthen civic institutions can contain any number of the capacity building dimensions explained in this chapter. Two choices, however, present themselves: supporting a civic organisation for what it is or supporting it for what it does. Ideally, a balance will be achieved between the two. Initiatives for helping NGDOs to be themselves should ensure that the organisation and its mission are recognised and valued in society. Specifically, as we saw in resource mobilisation, a priority would be to create local economic and political conditions which support indigenous NGDOs. Strategic and operational competencies should also be developed. Unfortunately, the thrust of external aid appears to be unbalanced; absorption of project-finance appears to be the first priority, while civic value and economic rooting come second, if at all.

'I am tired of classes on proposal writing', says Igor Kokarev, President of the Citizens Foundation [in Russia], which seeks to revitalize and inner-city neighbourhood. 'You should teach our business about giving,' he tells a visiting American.[39]

Observation of Northern NGDOs and the aid system in Kazakstan and Kyrghistan indicates that local NGDOs are being stimulated and supported as carriers of the aid agenda, with projects as the currency. Crudely put, the project is the organisation. In other words, the mainstream approach to capacity development of civic institutions does not respect the OD hierarchy set out above. Social needs and delivery of services are used as the starting point, not civic identity. While pragmatic, this approach has long-term weaknesses. Eventually, the realisation dawns that a civic organisation has different qualities than a contractor and is more than a sequence of projects. And when the money stops, which it will one day, local NGDOs will not have initiated sufficient civic strength in order to be recognised as legitimate institutions rather than extensions of international aid. Why? Because external project-based funding imports all sorts of foreign behaviours and life styles which are copied by local NGDOs, but are not socially appropriate or economically viable.

The role models that foreign NGDOs provide often do not reflect either good practice or the situation of non-profits back home. An article by two NGDO activists in Kazakstan lists the following images created by the way Northern NGDOs operate.[40]

- Expense is no object.
- There is a proliferation and overpayment of staff. Local presence calls for four or five local staff to support one foreigner, with the salaries of janitors being greater than doctors.
- Paperwork and bureaucracy abound. Form overrides content because specific formats must be retained at the cost of a voluntary ethos which motivated activists to establish an NGDO.
- Foreign NGDOs lack co-ordination. Local NGDOs are called for a meeting about the same topic by different Northern agencies who can't or won't co-ordinate what they do.
- There is an inability to tackle common structural issues together.
- Lack of contextualisation. NGDO activists who retain a job in government cause confusion about their commitment rather than a realisation that having more than one occupation is both an ingrained and a sensible strategy given the insecurity of Northern funding.
- Foreign models are too often imported. Without experience in Central Asia, Northern NGDOs rely on what they know about work in the poorer South, where highly qualified human resources, access to the latest thinking and technologies are less common. They proceed to treat Kazak NGDOs as incapacitated from the outset.
- Northern NGDOs only superficially understand local communities. Without time or resources to learn before leaping, staff of Northern NGDOs turn up with a paper thin level of understanding about the country the people or the history and proceed to learn on the job.
- The lucky dip. The short-term nature of Northern NGDO staff leads to a high turnover, and steep learning curves. For a local NGDO, your partner is more the individual you deal with than anything else.
- Personal ambitions and foibles often influence who gets recognised and supported and who does not.

All in all, its looks as if the scramble for the East has brought with it much of the worst rather than the best of what international aid has to offer. NGDOs wishing for change from this mode will find it very difficult to do so if they do not have a well thought-through strategy for strengthening civil society based on their own theory, civic position and comparative advantages. The options for such a strategy are summarised below.

NGDO strategic options: accelerating the growth of civil society

There are five complementary areas in which Northern and local NGDOs can act to strengthen civil society.[44]

- *Primary civic action:* here the founding elements of civil society – informal and formal autonomous associations of people – are built. Specific attention is paid to growing an independent economic base, democratically oriented organisational capabilities, and civic rights.
- *Secondary civic action:* this involves fostering supportive capacities for primary civic actors, such as intermediary NGOs – as well as, information sources, communication channels, public information systems and an independent media.
- *Relationship action:* this facilitates the 'horizontal' linking of primary civic actors, as well as 'vertical' second-level associations and alliances with different types of civic actor in order to realise common agendas.

- *Political action:* this allows others to take on advocacy roles at different levels of political and bureaucratic decision-making; make public decision-making more inclusive; increase awareness of citizenship, civic rights and responsibilities; and highlight acceptable norms and sanctions for politicians and public servants.[42] This is not the same and should not be confused with party-political action, which is another function emerging from civil society.

- *Direct institutional action:* here activities promote or strengthen public acceptance and valuing of citizen initiatives; create a supportive environment of values, legislation and social convention; and create fora or recognised places and systems for dialogue within civil society and between civil society and other sectors

NGDOs who attempt to strengthen civil society need to be aware of the challenges and complications which go with it. This is not an attempt to put NGDOs off the idea. In my view, a lot of what NGDOs have been doing for years can be understood within a civil society framework. However, civic goals must be made more explicit and pursued on the basis of competent strategies chosen by NGDOs themselves, instead of simply adopting or reacting against the official aid system's priorities and practices. Strategies to strengthen civil society are of critical importance for NGDOs. Ultimately, this new force in local, national and international development may, in the long run, supplant NGDOs themselves. What the future holds is therefore the last topic of this book.

Future in the Balance: the NGDO Horizon and Beyond

The Future for NGDOs

I have emphasised in previous chapters that through learning, NGDOs become more effective. However, NGDOs cannot move forward only on the basis of yesterday's experience. In fact the rapid collapse of a complete socio-economic system in the former Soviet Union made past lessons of little use. The end of the Cold War has caused a quantum shift in the global context in which NGDOs operate. Such a transformation makes analysis of trends a questionable approach.[1]

To set out perspectives on future NGDO development we start by looking at the post-Cold War rationale for aid. Sections two and three review NGDOs in their new global circumstances, suggesting two major directions for their efforts – supporting the growth of individual organisations and learning from practice in order to gain leverage on aid, states and markets. Both strategies call for a shift in priorities and tactics.[2] The final question of whether or not NGDOs will continue to be significant actors in social change leads to speculations on the relationship between technology and alternative organisational forms which are emerging in civil society in order to pursue anti-poverty and social justice agendas.

Amidst all the uncertainties there is one fact. If NGDOs want to remain relevant in reducing poverty and injustice later on in the next century, they cannot continue as before; they must make choices – their future lies in their own hands.

Perspectives on Aid, Development and NGDOs: Is the System Past its Sell-By Date?

The aid system is undergoing a fundamental shake-up. Quantity and quality are both changing and this is happening irrespective of the level of public support in the North. In addition, the role of aid in promoting development is set to diminish as commercial capital forms a larger proportion of external investment. This section reviews what appears to be happening with an updated justification for continuing aid. From here, perspectives are drawn on the challenges and opportunities facing NGDOs in the next ten to fifteen years.

States, markets, poverty and the aid system

UNDP's 1996 *Human Development Report* provides additional evidence that removing constraints on capital markets and opening up trading systems, while more efficient than other ways of generating economic growth, do not necessarily lead to greater well-being or equity for society as a whole. Inequality in wealth distribution and economic growth rates has been widening both within and between continents, countries and citizens. Despite international aid, the poor are increasing in absolute and proportional terms. Changes in this state of affairs must be sought in economic policies, which guide and control markets, and in social policies which affect who wins and who loses from growth.

An issue for the coming years, therefore, is the position governments take to either prevent market-related poverty occurring through equity-oriented policy choices, or dealing with its consequences through incentives and expenditures on unemployment benefits, subsidies, social safety nets and other compensatory measures. A complicating factor in extreme cases, to be found in parts of Asia and sub-Saharan Africa, will be the economic, political and individual capability to do anything about material deprivation, political exclusion or failure to respect people's rights – especially when they result from a government's misuse of its power. In short, tackling structural poverty and injustice will be a question of political will, economic capacity and the civic strength to hold leaders to account.

Part of a government's policy to tackle poverty can be to involve both economic and social sectors in joint action. Such an approach is occurring almost everywhere in the world, under labels of corporate social responsibility or corporate philanthropy. There are also appeals to old traditions of charity, self-help and mutual support (carrying a new Northern label of communitarianism).[3] However, the trend towards totally free markets appears to be tempered by the experience of the social malfunctions and instability which unimpeded markets can cause. Be that as it may, the current strategy in the North is a shift from a welfare to a 'share-fare' state, where responsibility for social well-being is allocated according to individual circumstances and spread around all sectors. What does this imply for the aid system? Why spend public money on it?

Despite its changing fashions, for 30 years the international development system has worked on the assumption that concessionary financial transfers, now complemented by capacity building measures, will make the difference to poverty levels and should be assigned according to some measure of poverty-related need. Meanwhile, under the surface, Cold War strategic interests shaped who got what amounts of aid and when. While East-West political rivalry is at an end, national strategic interests remain and will continue to influence the relative allocations of development funding while it lasts. However, the nature of what is considered to be a Northern strategic interest has shifted to emphasise the dangers of deprivation in the South and East. Examples of poverty's unwanted effects on the North are: internal and hence international destabilisation due to 'transitional' impoverishment as former communist countries move to market-based economies; domestic tensions and pressures caused by economic migrants; insecurity caused by conflicts and civil wars due to competition over limited or dwindling resources; and reservoirs of disease which do not respect national borders and also act as sources of drug resistance due to inadequate medical services. In short, poverty in the South and East is seen to be a source of international instability and insecurity which aid can help to neutralise. Today, we are dealing with a case of aid as enlightened Northern preventive self-defence, not a moral obligation of rich to poor.

Quantity of aid and public judgement

Government allocations to the aid system are stagnating. The year 1995 saw official aid as a proportion of Northern national gross domestic product drop to 0.27 per cent, its lowest average for 20 years.[4] Recent study has thrown doubts on the 'public fatigue' explanation of why aid budgets are being reduced. No convincing evidence has been found positively linking levels of public support for aid to the level of GDP actually allocated. In fact, public support for aid has, generally speaking, remained constant while official aid levels have risen and fallen.[5] Studying the poor correlation, Daniel Yankelovich (1996) argues that individual or public awareness is a step towards – but is not the same as – an individual or public judgement about aid on which people will act and politicians will listen. 'What people need more than information is enough time, help and incentive to decide which values to sacrifice when values conflict with one another, as they do in the case of development assistance.'[6] This finding calls into question assumptions NGDOs have used in their development education efforts which concentrate on informing people about the inhumane situation facing millions in the South and, now, the East.[7] The NGDO challenge will be to move beyond knowledge to assist people in making judgements which put pressure on politicians.

Northern citizens face a problem in forcing policy-makers to act in favour of maintaining or increasing aid levels and to take more account of the South or East in domestic policies. Their problem stems from a fundamental ambivalence when faced with the trade-offs involved. Citizens in the North do feel compassion and retain the idea that poor people elsewhere deserve support; many are enlightened enough to see that this can help them too. But social needs and problems at home also demand

attention, and it is a lack of clarity about how development aid works and relates to domestic concerns which reduces public confidence in its merits. This lack of clarity stems from the fact that the vast majority of Northern populations gain their understanding about the South and East from brief reports in the media, with television playing a dominant role. Development, that complex, slow process of self-improvement, is undermined by messages and images of misery, atrocities and disasters. NGDOs are way down the list of information sources about the developing world.[8]

While of little apparent impact in terms of aid levels, the case for public involvement in issues of development is becoming stronger than ever due to the processes of globalisation. Northern NGDOs must therefore focus on engaging a wider audience.[9] The OECD report on public attitudes to international aid makes the following recommendations for increasing Northern domestic support.

➤ Factual information on development issues must be better.
➤ Answers to why development is important for the Northern public must be given.
➤ There should be no 'mixed signals'; this occurs when development policy does not have clear goals or is not a coherent part of foreign policy.
➤ Public disillusionment should be reduced by ensuring that development activities bring about policy goals.
➤ While striving for mass support, NGDOs should start by expanding the existing constituency and develop its sophistication by moving from information and awareness to judgement.
➤ An appeal must be made to the values which people hold, emphasising particular national traditions and concerns.

I am, however, doubtful about the success or appropriateness of a future development strategy which continues to emphasise more aid as the way forward. One possible alternative to more aid is better aid: making serious efforts to increase the impact of what is available. There is a lot of scope for improvement in the quality of aid, but whether this will happen is another matter.

Improving the quality of aid

The quality of aid is changing through opposing forces. On the one hand, there are signs of improvement as bilateral agencies, the UN system and some development banks move closer to good practice in sustainable human development by taking on board the results of their own and NGDO development experience.

Set against this are parliamentary audit requirements and political demands to satisfy national interests with predetermined short-term performance. The more that NGDOs can point out these and other contradictions, as well as demonstrating practical alternatives which are more effective, the greater the probability that quality constraints will be removed.

Aid is also suffering from an overload of expectations. As experience grows, new goals are added without old ones being withdrawn. Today, as a conservative list, international aid is meant to:

- sustainably reduce poverty;
- ensure people's access to basic needs;
- halt and redress environmental degradation;
- pay special attention to gender and the situation of women;
- engage the 'unbankable' poor as economic actors in an expanding market place;
- empower the marginalised to act as citizens in a push for better governance;
- strengthen civil society with a reform of social institutions and;
- ensure human rights are respected.[10]

This list is enough to tax the effectiveness of any institution and leads to unrealistic expectations, which can only engender disappointment. As if this was not enough, Roger Riddell (1996) points out that an insufficiently recognised but ground-shaking shift is taking place, with a reorientation of the purpose of aid towards capacity growth. In other words, the task of aid is to bring peoples and countries of the South and East into a position where they can 'achieve the ends of development for themselves'.[11] This ability will be the primary criteria for success, instead of the percentage reduction in deprivation which aid has brought about. In as far as aid dependency has or is still reducing the ability for local or national self-development, the charge that aid is part of the problem – and not the solution – will continue to be levied against the system as a whole.

In reviewing the future of international co-operation for development, Mike Edwards (1996) identifies three conditions which have significantly reduced aid effectiveness and

impact. So far, the aid system has lacked the 'three Cs' of: '*consistency* (with local goals and realities delinked from the volatile selectivity imposed by foreign policy concerns); *continuity*, (in strategies, personnel, approaches and level of resourcing over the very long term); and *coherence*, between different components of aid and development action.'[12] Redressing these systemic weaknesses is a precondition for improving quality in the instruments applied. Interventions or better-designed projects will, for example, still be undermined if they are contradicted by other aspects of aid, due to a lack of coherence and co-ordination. In particular, I do not see an acceptance of a more open-ended, experimental approach to development work which reflects the way diverse societies 'generate' and reduce poverty over time.[13] Adopting a more inquisitive rather than prescriptive approach would better fit the differences between countries and peoples and the complex, open-ended nature of progress and social change. Put another way, agencies have to move away from the idea and practice that what is learnt in one place can be transported to another. The official aid system still lies hamstrung by a fixation on searching for and applying uniform answers.

The limitations caused by this stance are important for NGDOs. A greater proportion of their finance is set, in the short term, to come from bilateral agencies – whose resources are on the decline – and in the longer term from the self-financing multilateral banks. Participating, without question, within the development framework set by these institutions can threaten NGDO sustainability because their comparative advantages and public credibility as agents of effective change will be jeopardised. But reactive questioning will cut little ice. What is needed is questioning on the basis of conceptually sound and demonstrable alternatives – this requires organisational investment and a reasonably autonomous position. The practical resources, furthermore, which NGDOs need to identify alternatives in turn calls for high-quality money, which is unlikely to come from official aid or development banks and must be sought elsewhere. A key issue in accessing high-quality aid is tied to the evolution of Northern NGDOs and the ability of Southern and Eastern NGDOs to wean themselves off aid for at least their core financial needs.

Overall, it is difficult to find the significant forces which will increase the quality of aid required to make a noticeable impact on poverty levels, especially when arrayed against market and geo-political forces which are gaining in significance. Continual pressure by NGDOs and others, backed up by cogent analysis and other ways of stimulating development, is what is required – there do not appear to be any magic bullets.

The concentration of high-quality funding power

Earlier I signalled the danger of NGDOs being exclusively financed by low-quality, cold money. NGDOs face 'cooling-off'and being lifted away from their civic roots. In this way their roles as lobbyists and advocates may be compromised. Countering this danger depends on accessing high-quality funds which, in relative terms, are going to be in shorter supply. Therefore, whether they want it or not, Northern NGDOs who control shrinking proportions of high-quality money are going to gain more power over the nature and eventual quality of NGDO activity elsewhere. In this category of Northern NGDOs can be found the US foundations, Dutch co-financing and German political foundations, the Oxfam family and NGDOs in Scandinavian countries who enjoy continuity in state funding without significant political interference.

This handful of Northern financing NGDOs will increasingly determine which NGDOs in the South and East enjoy higher levels of autonomy from government and the official aid system. In addition, they will influence the level, direction and agendas of non-project and non-service delivery activity – for example, in policy studies and lobbying, innovation, real capacity growth, research, publications, networking and the existence of higher aggregations of NGDOs such as co-ordinating bodies. Put another way, unless care is taken, truly non-governmental development agendas, initiatives and active

relationships will cluster around the choices of a small Northern grouping, mirrored by a group of NGDOs in the South and East fortunate enough to have access to their funds.

Will this be a problem? The answer is unclear. In as far as mechanisms are created which ensure a true balance between North, South and East, in setting and pursuing agendas, global collaboration will lead to more effectiveness at all levels of NGDO development action and should be welcomed. Conversely, where fads, fashions, personal preferences, entrenched interests, arbitrariness and lack of transparency prevail in who gets financed for what, the evolution of NGDO communities in the South and East will suffer. Existing NGDO collaborative bodies in the North, South and East could take the lead by getting together to help their members think through the issues, strategies and mechanisms needed to ensure that concentration of high-quality funding power is matched by mutual responsibility and strategic coherence.

A related issue is the division of donor labour where the official aid system finances NGDOs' operational work while core organisational costs are met by NGDO sources. There are already signs of this division occurring. This creates both a paradox and an important opportunity. The paradox is that an NGDO fully financed by the official aid system, with no alternative funding input, might be little more than a contracting parastatal. But if core costs are met from NGDO funds, the financiers of operational work are effectively enjoying an unwarranted subsidy. A way out of this paradox – which makes non-official aid go further – is to ensure that an NGDO's core funds are used to control the way official aid money is applied. In other words, the opportunity is to use non-government core-funding to ensure sufficient learning together with the autonomy needed to gain maximum influence on how official aid is used. In this way, Northern contributions to the organisational costs of NGDOs in the South and East can have a significant heating effect. This is one strategic way to gain leverage on cold money. If leverage is not present a significant value-added of high quality Northern funds will be lost. Using high-quality NGDO resources to replicate government delivery programmes, or to reduce the costs of the official aid system, is a grossly ineffective, inappropriate policy. But there is a more fundamental issue which needs NGDO policy attention in the North, South, and East. This is their response to being credible agents in global development.

The sustainable NGDO will be the credible NGDO

Despite stagnation in levels of official aid, NGDOs are currently favoured in terms of the proportion of governmental assistance they are receiving. Bar a major loss in public confidence, this situation is likely to continue in the medium term. But this advantage is countered by a levelling-off in the growth of public giving which may tilt the overall mix of NGDO resources towards tax-based funds. For the foreseeable future, the financial sustainablity of NGDOs will still depend on their ability to raise funds from professional givers and development bankers, while their autonomy will depend on the degree to which they can convince the broader public that they are worthy of their core support. A key feature of accessing both sources will be an NGDO's credibility.

The most important factor for NGDO credibility and legitimacy is demonstrating effective performance. Difficult as it is, especially for non-operational and advocacy NGDOs, identifying their contribution to change will be an essential element in successful fund-raising. In addition, growing demands for independent 'consumer guides' to charitable giving will keep up the pressure for third-party assessments and comparisons of an NGDO's 'value for money'. Credibility, however, is an area where Northern NGDOs face increased vulnerability. First, scandals about abuse of office and excessive

salaries in the USA and financial incompetence (the UK Salvation Army lost millions in investments recommended by dubious advisers) have already reduced public trust in non-profits.[14] And, like SCF/USA, other Northern agencies will face a critical review of the way they apply donor funds to finance overheads. One recent study about Bolivia suggests that only US$15 to $20 out of every $100 applied to social development projects run by NGDOs actually reach the designated beneficiaries, most of the rest being absorbed in administrative costs and professional salaries.[15] Fund-raising mines have been sown, and unless NGDOs start disarming them through public re-education it is only a matter of time before there are other victims.

In contrast, in the South and East a high degree of public scepticism appears to accompany NGDOs, especially regarding their recent supply-led growth. Scandals in the South and East are therefore less likely to lead to a public loss of trust which is expressed in reduced support – seldom large anyway. But credibility and public trust will still be important in societies that are learning what domestic NGDOs are all about, especially in cases where governments are indifferent to poverty or incapable of doing much about it.

Secondly, Northern NGDOs are losing legitimacy because of growing opposition from counterparts in the South and East. The South is challenging the way the North makes decisions, the positions they take on international issues and the generally ineffective role they play in changing their own societies. The East is irritated by Northern NGDOs' assumptions about local incapacity and the patronising attitude inherent within the aid system.[16] Direct funding is one factor shifting North-South/East power relationships away from the North; together with greater efforts at self-financing, this is translating into a growing Southern and Eastern assertiveness.

NGDOs in the Service of People: Building Local Institutions

Looking at the dynamics of the aid system, there are two strategies NGDOs should adopt in a 10- to 15- year time horizon. The first is to not get caught in the role of (international) social welfare

provider – despite the fact that this is a function needed in many countries – by concentrating on building people's capacities to look after and demand for themselves; this is complemented by

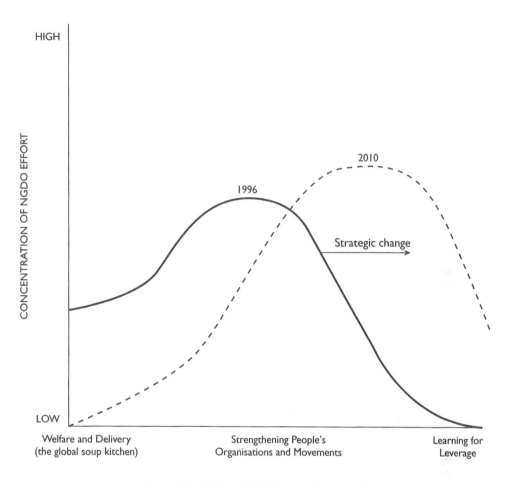

Figure 9.1 Shift in NGDO strategies and roles

a second strategy of gaining leverage on structural changes to governments and markets which benefit the poor. What these choices entail is summarised in Figure 9.1 and forms the subject of the next two sections.

People's organisations: from self-help to self-service and civic engagement

A common intention of NGDOs is that communities and groups are strengthened to the extent that they are able to provide for themselves or access the services they need without the help of an intermediary. While examples of this evolution are unevenly spread across the world, there is an upsurge of community-based, grassroots organisations which are working to change their lives and society.[17] As civic actors CBOs/GROs have two long-term advantages over NGDOs in promoting well-being and justice. First, they can generate their own resource base and are in principle self-sustainable. Second, as people-based organisations they can be directly representative and mandated to speak and act on behalf of members' interests. Obviously, this aspect should not be overidealised because both theory and field study shows that unless conscious effort is made, inherent tendencies to be undemocratic, unaccountable and exploitative of members' interests come to the fore.[18] Nevertheless, people's organisations are in a better position to push for the social, political and economic changes they want than those doing so in their name but not accountable to them.

The trend towards supporting local CBOs has been underway for some time, but for many NGDOs this is still within a framework of communities and groups acting as project carriers. As pointed out by Roger Riddell (1996), building capacity is now the development objective – initiatives to improve well-being are part of the process of doing so. People's organisations can also function as a civic springboard for direct political engagement. For example, they can sponsor trusted individuals onto development committees and strategically vote their candidates into elected posts. Furthermore, the autonomy resulting from self-financing should also encourage collaboration with others in civil society. NGDOs can act as shields for a while. However, there always remains the issue of the organisation's self-interest and the degree to which it is prepared to be vulnerable on behalf of others. An NGDO is unlikely to go to the wall for those it serves, so it is the strength and resilience of the people themselves which count in the long run. In sum, the more competent people's organisations there are to do development work for themselves, the greater the need for NGDOs to act as facilitators, bridges and brokers and less as resource intermediaries.

Social movements: a flexible force for change

There is almost as much discussion and lack of consensus on the nature and form of social movements as there is about civil society. This is not the place to elaborate on the debates, but it is important to say that – for our purpose – a social movement is taken to be a core group of activists with a sufficiently shared ideology and set of activities who wish to bring about change in the existing order of things.[19] The feminist, environmental and peace movements are modern examples, with agrarian, labour, universal suffrage and other movements as their historical predecessors, but not necessarily today's role models.

Social movements do not have one particular organisational form or predefined constituents. At any moment, a movement may be composed of individuals, organisations, networks or whatever else finds common cause with the issue, the values and the basic ideology of those already involved. An ethos of changing the way society works, it is argued, differentiates new movements from those which, historically, agitated for satisfaction of members' needs and civil rights. For example, while activists in the women's or environmental movements may be personally spurred by the issues involved, this does not mean that they only want greater equity and justice or cleaner air for themselves, but for women and people everywhere. 'New' movements seek to change the social order for the good of all, not necessarily for themselves alone, which may bring them into confrontation with organised labour, business and government.

To be a 'citizens' movement' requires attention to obligations, duties and sacrifices as well as assertion of rights. It also requires forms of participation which are not bureaucratised, hierarchical and which avoid corporate tendencies found in well-established interest groups. Membership can be broad and is not restricted to those with a narrow set of social, political or economic characteristics. However, to be effective, the capacity to mobilise and manage action in political and social arenas – through demonstrations, voting and direct action – is crucial. Strategies and tactics adopted by movements use both conventional and unconventional forms of political action. In the peace and anti-nuclear movements, educational campaigns, broadcasts, conferences, and public lectures all had their place next to direct action, such as blocking roads and other forms of civil disobedience. The art is to utilise all resources available, adapted to the issue, context, nature of the opposition and political opportunities which arise.

These characteristics are distinctive from the intermediary functions of NGDOs who, while perhaps sharing the same goals of social reform, are less able to engage with power holders because of their legal status and often narrow or non-existent social base. From an NGDO perspective, social movements are not just natural and important allies in realising their goals but a potentially important source of legitimacy. However, allying with social movements will not be a panacea because movements themselves face some basic predicaments. As Dalton and Kuechler (1990) point out:

> *They face a choice between being pragmatically successful (in broadening their popular bias and reaching more modest policy goals) and being true to their fundamental beliefs. This dilemma is particularly apparent with regard to internal organisation. By their very nature, movements value openness and immediate participation, which at the same time seriously restrict their effectiveness and efficiency in reaching policy-oriented goals. Social movements on the whole are rather amorphous; leadership is established informally, based on charisma, rather than formally defined procedures. The characterisation of movements as 'networks of networks' ...is very much to the point.*[20]

A way of dealing with the problems movements face is hinted at in the last sentence: to treat them as networks, which is the emerging organisational form of civil society. Civic networks may be the long-term key to gaining a balancing hold over states and markets, but this prospect lies with the distant future.

The role of NGDOs as service providers

The strategy discussed above plays down the future role of NGDOs as service providers, and in my view this is right if the task is simply to behave as governments do. The benefit of NGDOs is when they provide services differently and more appropriately for people who are poor, be it in education, health or water supply, particularly when this is part of an approach which aims to grow human capacity, and social relations. The big NGDOs (BINGOs) in Bangladesh – BRAC and Grameen – exemplify this approach, providing social and financial services and on a significant scale. In the process they reorient what government – and on occasion businesses – do by showing that alternatives work.

In Figure 9.1 an NGDO replica of government welfare is the 'global soup kitchen' dimension of aid.[21] The abiding problem with fulfilling a welfare role, however, is sustainability. Where an NGDO's ability to be a soup kitchen comes from government funds, nationally or internationally, social change is unlikely to occur. This is not to argue that where states are weak and poor such services are not necessary, but that this activity does not always qualify as 'development'. Indeed, unless NGDOs are distinctive in the services they provide, their comparative advantages over governments will be difficult to find, beyond being underfinanced and therefore 'cheaper' – which regimes then use as a means of gaining cost-effectiveness through privatisation.[22]

The second strategy for NGDOs therefore, is to gain leverage by learning about and demonstrating alternatives, such as 'services with a difference' and agitating for policy reforms. Unlike capacity growth of people's organisations and movements, a 'learning for leverage strategy' has traditionally been less well explored and therefore is dealt with in more detail.

An NGDO Strategy: Learning for Leverage

At first, NGDO competence was built up from local action – from doing things with and for people who are poor and marginalised. Realising the limitations of this effort, the past ten years or so have seen local action complemented by NGDO attempts to scale up their impact by getting bigger and doing more – through diffusion of experience and by gaining influence on macro-policy.[23] NGDOs need to prioritise this last strategy because – as global poverty and aid trends show – they will never have anywhere near the resources required to address the scale of the problem. They need to get to the heart of causes. Aside from local limitations in physical resources and adverse natural conditions, these causes are due to human choices leading to exploitation at all social and geo-political levels, usually accompanied by a denial of basic rights.

NGDOs need to push forward on leverage so that their primary goal eventually becomes one of influencing the larger forces which cause deprivation, using local development action and service delivery as their tools. In other words, the immediate shift needed in NGDO thinking is to learn in order to apply leverage on others – the shift in Figure 9.1. Today, NGDO activity is concentrated towards the left of the figure. Moreover, as social budgets are cut, funding to fill in the gaps left by governments is creating pressure to move even further left. However, strategically, from the perspectives of enhanced effectiveness, value for money and greater scale of impact, this is the wrong direction in which to go. The NGDO strategic challenge is to use service delivery and other development activities as sources of experimentation, innovation, demonstration and learning for leverage. The comprehensive studies led by John Farrington (1993) show, for example, how this is being done in extending agricultural innovation.[24] As Figure 9.1 suggests, it is

Table 9.1 Learning within NGDOs

Who should be learning?	What should they be learning about?
Field staff	• participation in practice; • effective empowerment; • local level collaboration with government and other NGDOs; • gender dimensions of local development.
Technical specialists	• best practice in their area of expertise; • ways of integrating with other disciplines; • how to improve cost-effectiveness; • how existing internal and external policies affect performance.
Operational managers	• what factors make interventions/projects work well or badly; for example funding conditions; • how to be more cost-effective; • how to co-ordinate internally and externally.
Fund-raisers/development educationalists	• principles and insights to be used in negotiation with professional donors; • new messages to get across to private contributors; • examples of impact and what made things work or fail.
Leaders	• how policy choices and strategies work out in practice; • how to make external relationships more effective; • how best to exert influence; • what environmental factors have had unforeseen effects and which must be taken into account; • the quality and costs of donors.
Governors	• the degree of stakeholder satisfaction; • consistency between mission, strategy and impact; • improving social standing and credibility of the organisation.

unrealistic to expect all NGDOs to work purely on the basis of learning for leverage. Nevertheless, while many NGDOs still concentrate their efforts on direct development action to solve problems, satisfy needs and build capacities – singly or in alliance with others – they must pay more attention to exerting leverage than is currently the case. This section looks at how to introduce such an emphasis in terms of methods and tactics.

Learning for leverage in practice

Moving towards a learning-for-leverage strategy raises a number of questions, such as who should be learning, about what, to apply leverage to whom, in what way?[25] Chapter 7 made the case for learning in the context of assessing performance, and described levels of information which produce lessons for structural leverage. Table 9.1 represents this information in terms of who should be trying to learn about what.

There is no reason why an NGDO should bring in-house all the expertise it needs to learn in these areas. Collaboration with sensitive academics, institutes for applied social studies and other NGDOs with suitable expertise can all be tried. Increasingly, some types of leverage will require a strong mix of NGDO operational learning and grassroots testimony, combined with sound macro-analysis which professional researchers can provide. In forging the necessary productive relationships, cultural differences between practitioners and researchers will be a crucial obstacle to overcome.[26] Irrespective of who does what, the items listed in Table 9.1 can be grouped into eight areas:

- functional, participatory learning about operations in the field – what works for who, what does not and why;
- intervention/project-based learning about why negotiations do or do not happen and how development approaches can be improved;
- organisation-oriented learning about how the whole NGDO functions and how it can be made more effective;

- civic learning about how NGDO activities work their way into, and influence, the ability of civil society to interact with government and market;
- policy-linked learning, which looks for patterns in experience and generic features, which shape the overall development process and the aid system;
- advocacy-linked learning, which searches for examples and 'people's stories'; which can underpin pressure for change;
- scientific learning about the relation between trends, actions and context, which can contribute to renewal of vision, mission and strategies as well as the propagation of new ideas or understandings about development;
- learning about learning by critically reviewing the internal processes being used when compared to their leverage effects.

Leveraging who with what?

Assuming that an NGDO has got its learning act together, the next question is what sort of leverage should be applied to whom? Direct leverage for an NGDO typically involves engaging with more powerful actors to change how they behave. Indirect leverage involves informing and supporting others, such as people's organisations and social movements. Here, we focus on direct leverage.

At its most basic, direct leverage involves finding the sensitive spot in another organisation and applying the right sort of pressure, in other words the most appropriate type of input that will cause change. At this stage only broad generalisations can be made about the probable best fit between the target of leverage and the best instrument to apply. There are at least six instruments NGDOs can apply when trying to influence others: demonstration; public-policy advocacy; political lobbying; monitoring of compliance with public policies and laws; propagating new ideas and findings from studies; and research and public education. Previous chapters have analysed the types of activities associated with each and how success can be measured in terms of: changes in aid

Table 9.2 Probable fit between who to lever with what

Who to lever Instruments for leverage	Other NGDOs	Aid agencies	Government[27]	NGDO supporters	General public	Business
Demonstration of practical development alternatives	high	high	medium	high	medium	medium
Policy advocacy based on field testimony and validated 'stories':						
• alternatives to existing policies	medium	high	high	high	medium	medium
• lessons on better implementation	medium	high	high	low	low	low
Lobbying in political arenas, events and via constituencies	low	high	high	high	medium	medium
Monitoring reports on legal and policy compliance and impact	low	medium	high	low	low	high
Findings of applied research with new insights, ideas, frameworks or policy options	high	high	medium	low	low	medium
Development education	low	medium	low	high	medium	?

policy and practice; legal and public-policy reform; economic, corporate and market reform; greater inclusiveness and accountability in political processes and governance; and the strengthening of civic organisations and institutions. Table 9.2 sets out the probable fit between types of leverage and development actors.

Demonstration is most likely to impact those doing similar activities and supporters who gain greater confidence in the NGDO's competence. However, unless the approach adopted by the NGDO corresponds with the organisational structure of government, for example by focusing on an administrative area as the CONVERGENCE network is doing in the Philippines, it may be more difficult to convince those responsible of the merits of the NGDO alternative. Increasingly, NGDOs will need to exert leverage on local as well as national governments, and will have to tailor their way of working accordingly. If the setting is right, demonstrations can also influence business; for example, energy-saving devices have developed

into commercially viable products and industries.

Both policy advocacy and lobbying can be aimed directly at governments and politicians and can be pursued indirectly through constituencies and mobilisation of the wider public. Only when the issue has strong resonance is the general public likely to act in support of an NGDO. Consequently, greatest leverage is most likely through direct interaction with governments and aid agencies.[28] Policy which affects businesses often results in galvanising the opposition, as is the case of rain forest preservation in Brazil, promotion of generic rather than brand mark drugs, and advancing the merits of small-scale rather than giant dams.

Monitoring and reporting on the extent to which a public body fulfils the intentions of its policy commitments, or applies the law as it should, can – depending on the political context – be very effective in relation to modifying government behaviour, especially when there are opportunities to publicise details in

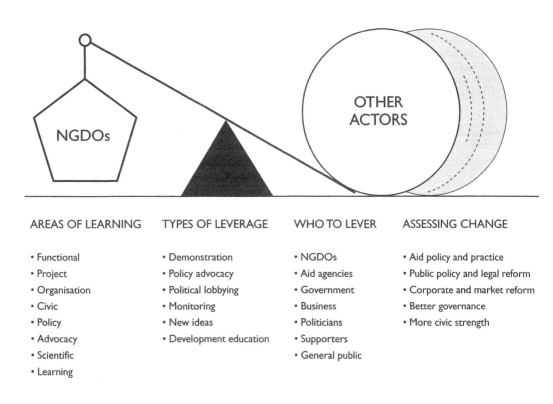

AREAS OF LEARNING	TYPES OF LEVERAGE	WHO TO LEVER	ASSESSING CHANGE
• Functional	• Demonstration	• NGDOs	• Aid policy and practice
• Project	• Policy advocacy	• Aid agencies	• Public policy and legal reform
• Organisation	• Political lobbying	• Government	• Corporate and market reform
• Civic	• Monitoring	• Business	• Better governance
• Policy	• New ideas	• Politicians	• More civic strength
• Advocacy	• Development education	• Supporters	
• Scientific		• General public	
• Learning			

Figure 9.2 Learning for leverage

international fora. This may, however, be a high risk approach where the regime in power is autocratic or worse. Impact on business can also be significant when, for example, adherence to environmental or safety standards is in question.

For the reasons detailed above, development education has not been very successful in gaining leverage through broad public action. New strategies are needed which will lead to less ambivalent, positive public judgement on international co-operation. To sum up, gaining leverage means choosing the right sort of learning to influence the most significant actor(s) with the most effective instruments. This strategy is illustrated in Figure 9.2 and is followed by a look at important tactics.

From barricades to martial arts: complementing a leverage strategy with appropriate tactics

To be effective, new strategies must be supported by appropriate tactics. In the case of learning for leverage, the key tactical change is to move away from the notion of manning the barricades against political imperialism and market exploitation, be it local or international. Instead, what is needed are tactics which draw on the principles of martial arts – such as judo and jujitsu – using the momentum and energy of the opponent to knock them off balance and throw them in the direction wanted. The parallel in international aid is to identify and exploit contradictions and weaknesses in the aid and economic system, its agents, and in the political system with its power holders.

Martial arts is a more subtle approach, demanding greater insight into how systems operate. For example, capital accumulation by poor people can be used as a bargaining chip in policy negotiations, while parallel markets and barter trade can alter how local markets function. The fair trade movement has shown that, when presented with alternative choices, people are prepared to pay more, threatening the market share of commercial competitors. Barter economies are another example and these are springing up in localities within London and internationally. Exploiting market imperatives may call for temporary tactical alliances with strange bedfellows. For example, Greenpeace has found that its campaigns for stricter pollution controls are being actively supported by businesses which aim to clean up the environment. Combining their efforts strengthens pressure and leverage on governments who, whatever other functions they give up, will retain a monopoly role in enforcing public policy.

In politics, one martial arts tactic is to make use of the 'reverse hold' which clients have on patrons who have to deliver in order to hold on to their position. For example, by playing one patron off against another, clients can gain leverage on political decisions and public resource flows, which is how 'pork barrel' constituency-based politics works anyway. The general point is that while there is a time and place for confrontation with power holders, this cannot be the premise. Indeed, a long-term aim for NGDOs and other civic organisations is to reach a position where governments and businesses acknowledge and respect citizen power as the complementary 'third force'.

The tactics and strategies described will probably see NGDOs through the next 15 years or so. The final section contains longer-term speculations that move beyond the aid system as a way to foster social changes in a global world. What is suggested may, indeed, be optimistic, but there are already signs around that NGDOs can move in this direction.

A Long-Term View: Civil Society and NGDOs Beyond the Aid Horizon

When thinking about writing a book like this, I asked a few individuals for critical feedback on an initial outline. One respondent argued that my efforts would be more useful if the last chapter I had in mind became the first chapter of a different book dedicated to helping newly emerging civil organisations find their feet.[29] In his view, aid-dependent NGDOs were already becoming extinct. Some will stay around for emergency and humanitarian work, but his argument was that the era of externally financed development is on its way out, taking NGDOs with it, to be replaced by locally rooted change agents and international exchanges. As you can see, I did not take up his suggestion because, while agreeing with much of his diagnosis, I do not share the inevitability of this perspective.

Part of the problem with predicting the future of NGDOs are the assumptions made about what the emerging world order will look like. Are we in for a (long) period of disruption until the new world framework settles down or is a higher level of instability the new natural order? An answer to this question is important for NGDOs.

Will a turbulent future save NGDOs: the transformation from development to relief?

Speculations on what NGDOs will face in the long term are tied to assumptions about whether or not the world is set for increasing conflict or is on the path to a new, stable, economic and political world order.[30] Various 'futurists' suggest that the relative period of 'equilibrium' in international relations caused by Cold War dominance is now being 'punctuated' by a, perhaps long, period of uncertainty and radical environmental change as new forces vie for dominance.

Some observers argue that the variety of

changes and trends are producing a convergence of forces which will threaten global stability in the future. Examples are: technologies which make communication easier, where imbalances in acquiring information will be increasingly important; the rise of competing trading blocks with unaccountable self-serving transnational corporations; demographic imbalances which create migration pressure; competition for natural resources such as water; the advance of capitalist relations which focus more people's aspirations, demands and attentions on the same finite resources; a dimished role for nation states due to globalisation, which is further threatened by growing demands for self-determination or greater autonomy by subnational groups; and competition and clashes between religions and cultures.[31]

Ironically, NGDOs will do better the less stable the world becomes. Why? Because in a quest to guide 'stability' in favour of those vying for power, finance will become increasingly available to agencies who can deliver 'stabilising' social services. Transnational corporations are unlikely to be favoured as their allegiance will be less certain and more difficult to control than NGDOs. Furthermore, civil conflict, as subnational groups assert their rights to recognition and autonomy, or border conflicts over natural resources, may generate a continual demand for humanitarian assistance which NGDOs can respond to and thrive on. In short, a world in a continual state of domestic and international friction will maintain a role for NGDOs – but with the balance of effort and international aid tilted towards relief and humanitarian assistance rather than development. If this happens, the choice facing many NGDOs is transformation to relief to survive. We will then shift our language to talk of NGROs – non-governmental relief organisations – which already exist in the form of various NGDOs 'without borders'.

This section does not follow the assumptions of increasing global conflict, but looks to a future where sooner or later action against poverty will not be based on aid.

Eliminating aid dependency

NGDOs in the South and East have a very high level of aid dependency which makes them vulnerable. Insiders estimate that 95 per cent of NGDOs will collapse if aid is stopped.[32] However, many of what are today's NGDOs in the South and East will not disappear; instead the 'D' of development will fade away to be replaced by the 'W' of welfare as NGDOs take on the function of contracted non-profit providers of socially affirming public services – rather than agents of social change.

The diminishing of aid versus the economic growth and social policies of recipients will determine the proportion of NGDOs that collapse or make the transition to a new welfare order. In richer Southern and Eastern countries, as in the North, government finance will be available for non-profits to provide social services rather than social change, which is already happening in the newly industrialised economies of South East Asia. In the poorest countries, NGDO presence will be sustained by funds which continue to be disbursed by the self-financing development banks – who are unlikely to make themselves redundant.[33] There will also remain a set of transnational NGDOs with sophisticated skills in public fund-raising that will have a pivotal role to play in learning for leverage if they realise that operational size does not equate with structural impact.

While the omens for NGDOs may not be encouraging, one reason I do not share the idea of their inevitable demise is that they can still choose to transform themselves. Many, however, will not, and for them the ongoing transition and changes within the aid system will be a crisis resolved by take-over, absorption or collapse. Nevertheless, Southern and Eastern NGDOs can make the effort to root themselves in their own economies and societies. Northern NGDOs can reorient themselves away from reliance on official aid and a delivery model of international development if they wish. The previous chapters have suggested ways of doing so. In other words, ignorance of the possibilities available is no longer a valid excuse. Whether they transform themselves or not, NGDOs with social change agendas will be surrounded, and probably overshadowed, by other civic organisations. The ability of civic organisations to organise and act nationally and internationally is already being abetted by the rapidly expanding global information infrastructure and by communications technology.[34] Independent of NGDOs, though sometimes nurtured by them, other civic actors unrelated to the aid chain are (re-)establishing themselves in the pursuit of change; resource transfer is not what they are about.

After a brief review of the forces driving civil society, this final section looks at three longer-term issues for NGDOs based on the prediction that aid will diminish as the way of helping poorer countries develop. The first issue, therefore, is the replacement of the NGDO notion that development comes through aid. Second, is the removal of international cooperation as the monopoly of the few. Third is the establishment of a new dimension to civil society: the emergence of mutlilevel citizens' networks which will oversee states and markets nationally and internationally. Over the horizon, NGDOs will need to make choices about their own position in a new global civic arena; transformation could be the answer they will have to face.

Forces within civil society

Much has already been said about civil society. This section briefly reviews why we can expect current trends in civic development to continue. Civil society is a messy concept employed to describe how nation states evolve and how societies behave.[36] Irrespective of how the concept is defined or misused for economic or political reasons, civil society is increasingly seen as an expression of citizens asserting themselves. The long-term development questions are, first, where will power lie within civil society and, second, how will civil society exert its influence? Only sketchy, uncertain answers are possible by looking at the forces involved.

To work effectively, markets require and generate incentives coupled to labour, capital, technology and information. Combined, these factors instigate greater 'modularity' in the way people think and act – collective traditions weaken and individual interests come to the fore. While one product of modularity is alienation and a reduction in social cohesion, another is greater freedom to associate with others beyond customary roles and obligations. The 'modularising' dimension of market-based economic forces will continue to be a source of civic development, but one which has no built-in mechanism to ensure harmony or coherence in the associations created or the interests they pursue.

Privatisation will place more economic power outside of the state – not just in the hands of business but of citizens as consumers. This shift has political implications: it will increase people's autonomy to chose and act accordingly. Furthermore, market reliance on open information flows, systems and technologies also aids people's access to non-market information. In other words, overall, market-oriented development can be expected to create forces which will enhance civic association and action. While unlikely to disappear, nation states which rely on markets for growth will have a lesser role to play in determining how people gain their livelihoods and in regulating how they learn, think and act. Greater literacy and higher levels of education result in a more critical and insightful population, who are less easy to manipulate for self-serving political ends. What is more, an economically empowered citizenry and larger middle class brings higher expectations about political voice and choice. This is not to ignore civic struggle, such as the recent civic unrest in Indonesia and armed revolt in Mexico. The point is that factors of a structural nature are working in favour of civil society becoming a force to be reckoned with.

What is far from clear, however, is where power will lie in civil society. Will it be concentrated or spread? What dominant values will be aspired to? Will there still be divisions along class, gender, ethnic, educational or other lines, allowing manipulation and exploitation by old or new elites? Will civic attitudes be massaged and directed by the media and directed by politicians to identify new enemies – domestic and international terrorists, for example – in order to justify constraints on civil freedoms and rights? The answers will surely differ between countries and over time. The challenge for NGDOs will be to achieve strong social values of equity and justice, coupled with dialogue and mediation.

Civic institutions will also need to take their place in negotiating policies and practices which ensure that markets are both sustainable and capable of improving social well-being. In other words, though distinct from political parties, civil society is a political actor; it has political interests which vie to be heard. A third voice at the power table will make social choices more complex, but of better quality, as more perspectives are voiced. This means, for example, that the old social contract idea of government, business and labour sitting down to chart a country's future will no longer be adequate. A search for new forums of dialogue, appropriate to a country's history and circumstances, is becoming a matter of urgency. NGDOs have a role to play here too, at home and abroad, as part of a wider set of civic interests. What this might mean is discussed next.

From development through aid to development through civic co-operation

International aid is being down-graded as *the* instrument for poverty reduction in the South and East. In as far as aid funding was ever a significant factor in how poorer countries developed,[36] decreasing levels of assistance and the rapid expansion of foreign investment will supplant the role aid has to play. A positive response to this will not be to lament and lobby for increases in aid – which is too often today's response – but to look more comprehensively at the domestic and international policies and strategies countries adopt: do they bode well for poor and marginalised people in the North, South and East? In other words, the challenge for Northern NGDOs is to take a holistic view of the behaviour of their countries towards others rather than isolating aid allocations and pushing them forward as the major solution to poverty.

Processes of globalisation, which have been going on for years, are integrating economies, eroding aspects of national sovereignty and making domestic policy choices – such as flexibility in labour markets – increasingly dependent on external factors. Correspondingly, national policies such as trade conditions will increasingly have external implications which affect the prosperity of other countries, with the poorest being at the receiving end. With aid diminishing in significance, there are real implications for NGDOs. First, their sights must be set beyond aid to other areas of national policy. For example, quality controls to protect domestic consumers may have negative impacts on poor Southern producers, and this consideration must be brought into decision-making. Secondly, the message that aid to the South and East is an important part of the answer, if not the answer itself, must give way to the message that, like it or not, interdependence between people is increasing; responsibility for understanding and dealing with interdependence, lies with everyone. In some areas, such as the environment, this concept is already underway. In others, such as food security, health, social stability and working conditions, global links are still not readily apparent.

In short, aid supply can no longer be the predominant basis of Northern NGDO relationships with their constituencies. Establishing a sense of international co-operation, and shared global responsibility, needs to be part of the future agenda. Moving towards co-operation calls for different strategies and tactics, as well as relearning old ways of thinking.

Civic co-operation rather than aid

While it can help push in the right direction, learning-for-leverage does not directly address the need to move from aid transfer to civic co-operation. This shift calls for a radically new approach to an old idea. In the 1970s a strong case was made for development to concentrate on building people-to-people relationships between North and South.[37] The intention was to promote mutual understanding and solidarity as a counter to the perception – pushed by elites – that the mass of people in the North and South have no common interests, but are simply in competition for jobs, and economic security. It was this thinking which led to the 'hot money' analysis and approach to development.[38] Such a strategy has been tried spasmodically by NGDOs, usually under the label of 'twinning' between schools, local governments, minority and women's groups, indigenous people, farmers, and unions.

Why, outside of child sponsorship, did this global human-relations strategy for international development never became mainstream? One probable cause is that project-based development is 'neater' than orchestrating thousands of relationships, while projects lend themselves better to aid as the business of professionals. Another possible reason is that a strategy of 'mass linking' was not in the interest of power holders during the Cold War. Therefore, development as a business progressed and along with its increasing professionalism came an aversion to trusting lay people to 'do it right'. It would be too risky, mistakes would be made, misunderstandings would occur because of language and cultural differences, disappointments would arise, prejudices would be re-enforced and so on. Best leave it to the experts as intermediaries, translating both ways and, in the process, creating an enclosed aid imperium with its own hierarchy, rites of passage, jargon, culture and codes.

If there was unequivocal evidence that aid professionals had got it right, the attitude just described might have been justified. But study after study shows that we have not got it right as often as necessary to demonstrate that we are indeed professional in terms of knowing the right thing to do and then doing the right thing well. Professionals in the official aid system have become, by and large, a privileged self-serving class too isolated from the societies in which they work. The picture in the NGDO community has been different but is becoming less so because of pressure to adopt the inappropriate role models of official aid. The strategic challenge for the next century, therefore, is to seriously open up the international aid system.

Opening up has potentially dramatic

implications for NGDOs who have carved out a niche by acting as funding intermediaries. In a more open set-up, the role of NGDOs changes from intermediaries which pass resources along the aid chain to bridges, information brokers and facilitators of relationships between civic groups, organisations and movements in the North, South and East. For Northern NGDOs not already involved with people-to-people development, the major change is to envisage the world as an ever-growing web of *non-exploitive relationships* and to facilitate this process. This does not deny the usefulness of service delivery. But these activities should be placed in a larger framework of civic action with learning-for-leverage serving as one tool, complemented by greater effort at forming relationships between people.

The move proposed is to concentrate on linking people of North, South, East and West and trusting them to learn about each other – mistakes and all. This is not an argument for throwing away all that has been learnt during 30 years of NGDO development effort. It is critical that accumulated experience is included in a process of encouraging civic actors in international development. In other words, the task is to de-professionalise the development industry in a professional way, with NGDOs learning how to be effective brokers and facilitators of societies learning about international co-operation.

One speculation is that the accelerating growth of stronger citizens' organisations and social movements in the South and East, coupled to more rapid, accessible and inexpensive (electronic) communication, may provide part of what was missing in the 1970s. While realities are very different for small-scale fishermen in Nova Scotia and Senegal, the problems they face of diminishing fish stocks are not. Fish have yet to recognise national borders and civic organisations and communication do not need to do so either. Where local organisations and common interests exist, and communication is easy and cheap, new opportunities for joint action can be created – facilitated but not managed by intermediaries. Linking people can become mainstream if NGDOs are prepared to use communication more effectively to orchestrate a transformation.

NGDOs and transformation to civic networks

The position of NGDOs in civil society is the final topic that needs to be discussed; it can hold NGDOs' long-term future in the balance – on the one side renewal and relevance, on the other irrelevance and decline. It is probably no overstatement to say that civic networks are seen as a new force shaping the world. Some observers go so far as to argue that transnational networks will be the means by which civil society restructures the global political order.[39] And if this is not the ultimate result NGDOs are looking for, what is? Networks has already been the subject of Chapter 5, but restricted to relations within the NGDO community. The prospect facing NGDOs is to accept that they are a small but potentially significant part of an expanding web of civic organisations, many – but by no means all – of which share their values and desired direction for social change. The following quotation by Ronfeldt and Thorup (1993) sets the scene for what can emerge.

> *The new, multi-organisational, NGO-based networks are setting in motion new dynamics that promise to shape civil society at local, national, regional and even global levels. Civil society seems to be the home realm for the network form, the realm that will be strengthened more than any other. This form seems to have particular advantages where the members – as often occurs in civil society – are all committed to being autonomous and independent to avoid hierarchical controls, yet have agendas that are interdependent and benefit from consultation and co-ordination.*[40]

Until today, for two reasons networks have been a relatively neglected and powerless form of organisation. First, unlike states and markets, analysts have not treated networks as social systems to be reckoned with. Second, the power

of networks has been limited by their inability to appropriate economic surpluses in order to form higher levels of association which are able to interface on a par with governments and businesses. Nevertheless, things are changing in favour of network power. Technology has begun to provide the means by which citizen networks can aggregate at any level while retaining autonomy and independence. They can do so without having to construct a hierarchical structure for control and appropriation of surpluses. This is possible because communication service providers, strung around the Internet, provide a means to relate and organise without any necessary financial aggregations and transfers between network members. We are entering an era when organisations called networks are virtual and real at the same time.

The most promising long-term future for NGDOs dedicated to change through the power of third-sector leverage is to become nodes, hubs, enablers and supporters of civic networks. Straddling countries, regions, continents and the globe, and electronically linked, people-to-people networks are set to take the place of NGDOs in shaping world development. But what use are virtual networks for the poor and marginalised? Will the technical paraphernalia needed to link into networks be another tool for exclusion? Perhaps not. For the Corfan people living deep in the Amazon rainforest on Ecuador's border with Colombia, a Corfan chief armed with high-tech communications equipment is already able to negotiate with Petroecuador, the national oil company which has plans to penetrate the forest.[41] Twenty or more years from now this may be so common place that it does not merit a book. NGDOs are in an excellent position to be part of this. It is up to them.

The question of choice: finding the will to transform

There is no inevitability about the future of NGDOs. They have the freedom to work for what they believe in, adapted to different global circumstances. Figure 9.3 summarises the previous discussion in terms of the choices

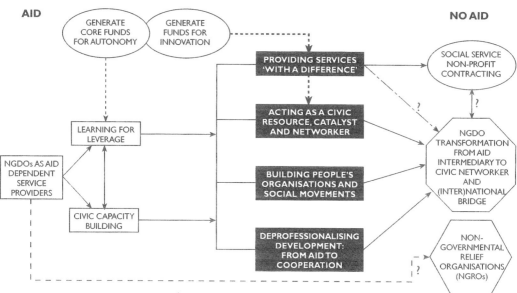

Figure 9.3 Transforming NGDOs

facing NGDOs within and beyond today's aid horizon. A critical factor in making choices will be an NGDO's ability to raise resources which secure both autonomy and capacity for innovation. Without these, contracting in the aid system and then for national and local governments is a likely future. The question-marks signal problem areas. NGDOs may argue they can shift back and forth from service 'delivery with a difference' to civic networking or effectively combine public contracting and networking roles. I am doubtful that this shift will work out in practice – the organisational balancing act needed is too great. It is also difficult to see how both roles can work together; the organisational tensions involved will be a constant source of anxiety and juggling. In other words, choices made in the coming years will probably initiate some options at the expense of others. Making the right choice is the name of the game for NGDOs, and there are signs that a few NGDO leaders are fully aware of this fact. Their problem is how to put this idea across to governing bodies and staff.

Perhaps inevitably, books about NGDOs all have to choose whether or not to end on an upbeat note. Two recent examples deal with this dilemma by having more than one ending, or by presenting a variety of scenarios from which to choose.[42] What is common to both is the fact

that when the environment transforms itself, organisations have to make choices. For all sorts of reasons, NGDO horizons are cloudy and any sunshine will be hard to find unless they create it themselves. This book has therefore been about how NGDOs can improve their role in creating a brighter and sustainable future for people who are economically poor, for those who are physically marginalised or abused, for the many who are politically disempowered, for minorities who are culturally threatened and, if they succeed, for NGDOs themselves. But no amount of writing can substitute for the most fundamental precondition for change: the will to do so. Finding the will to change is the first step in making this book of practical use. But where will the will come from?

It seems to me that this is a moment in NGDO history when leaders have to be precisely that – motivators charting future directions for development and then mobilising followers. Previous chapters have described how this can be done, but have also pointed out that, too often, necessary organisational change in NGDOs does not occur soon enough. Instead, it is time to initiate a dialogue within and between NGDOs on a tranformation in international development that is not premised on resource transfers. The ball is in the court of NGDO leaders and governors to generate a vision of the future they want *beyond aid*.

References

Publications that are asterisked are particularly recommended by the author.

AALAE (1992) (Partners or Foes?: The Great Debate) *The Spider*, vol 6(1), African Association for Literacy and Adult Education, Nairobi

AALAE (1995) *Towards a New Development Paradigm: Findings from Case Study Research of Partnerships in Africa* African Association for Adult Literacy and Education and Synergos Institute, Nairobi and New York

AAPAM (1986) *The Ecology of Public Administration and Management in Africa* African Association for Public Administration and Management, Vikas, New Delhi

Achterhuis, H et al (1993) *Het Orkest van de Titanic: Werken aan Andere Noord-Zuid Verhoudingen*, [The Orchestra of the Titanic: Working on Alternative North-South Relations] StudentAid/VU Press, Brussels

ADAB (1995) *NGO Programs Effectiveness Review* Australian International Development Assistance Bureau, Canberra

Aderinwale, A [ed] (1995) *Corruption, Democracy and Humna Rights in East Africa* Africa Leadership Forum, Ota, Nigeria

*Adriondack, S (1992) *Just About Managing?: Effective Management for Voluntary Organizations and Community Groups* London Voluntary Service Council, London

African Rights (1994) 'Humanitarianism Unbound?: Current Dilemmas Facing Multi-Mandate Relief Operations in Political Emergencies' Discussion Paper No 5, November, Africa Rights London

Alegre, A (ed) (1996) *Trends and Traditions, Challenges and Choices: A Strategic Study of Philippine NGOs* Ateno Center for Social Policy and Public Affairs, Manila

Alianza (1995) *Progression Indicators* Alianza Para Desarrollo Juvenil Comunitario, Guatamala City

Alliband, T (1983) *Catalysts of Development: Voluntary Agencies in India* Kumarian Press, West Hartford, Connecticut

Anderson, M (1996) *Do No Harm: Supporting Local Capacities for Peace Through Aid* Collaborative for Development Action, Cambridge, Mass

*Anderson M and Woodrow, P (1989) *Rising from the Ashes: Development Strategies in Times of Disaster* Westview, Boulder

ANGOC (1988) *NGO Strategic Management in Asia: Focus on Bangladesh, Indonesia and the Philippines* Asian NGO Coalition, Manilla

Anheier, H (1989) 'Private Voluntary Organizations and Development in West Africa: Comparative Perspectives , in James, E [ed] *The Nonprofit Sector in International Perspective* Oxford University Press, New York

Anheier, H (1994) 'Non-Governmental Organizations and Institutional Development in Africa: A Comparative Analysis' , in Sandberg, E [ed] *The Changing Politics of Non-Governmental Organizations and African States* Praeger, Westport

Anheier, H (1995) 'Theories of the Nonprofit Sector: Three Issues' *Nonprofit and Voluntary Sector Quarterly* vol 24 (1), pp 15–23

Anheier, H, Rudney, G and Salamon, L (1992) 'The nonprofit sector in the United Nations system of national accounts: definition, treatment and practice' Working papers of the Johns Hopkins Comparative Nonprofit Sector Project, No 4, The Johns Hopkins Institute for Policy Studies, Baltimore

Anheier, H and Seibel, W (1990) *The Third Sector: Comparative Studies of Nonprofit Organizations* de Gruyter, Amsterdam

Archer, R (1994) *Markets and Good Government: The Way Forward for Economic and Social Development* Non-Governmental Liaison Service, Geneva

Archer, D and Cottingham, S (1996) *Action Research Report on 'REFLECT': Regenerated Frierian Literacy Through Empowering Community Techniques* Overseas Development Administration, London

Arellano-Lopez, S and Petras, J (1994) 'Non-government Organizations and Poverty Alleviation in Bolivia' *Development and Change* vol 25 (3), pp 555–568

Argenti, J (1993) *Your Organization: What is it for?* McGraw-Hill, London

Arthur, L and Preston, R (1996) *Quality in overseas consultancy: understanding the issues* The British Council, London

Austin, G (1993) *The Process of Change: A*

Synthesis Study of Institutional Capacity Development Projects and Experience Overseas Development Administration, London

Austin, V (1984) *Rural Development Management* Batsford, London

Avina, J, Lessik A, Gomez, A, Butler J and Humphreys, D (1990) *Evaluating the Impact of Grassroots Development Funding: An Experimental Methodology Applied to Eight IAF projects* The InterAmerican Foundation, Rosslyn, Virginia

Bak, P and Chen, K (1991) 'Self-Organised Criticality' *Scientific American*, January pp 46–53

Baldwin, G (1990) 'Non-Government Organizations and African Development: An Inquiry', [Background papers: long-term perspectives study for sub-Saharan Africa, institutional and sociopolitical issues] The World Bank, Washington, DC

Baldwin, G (1992) 'Targets and indicators in World Bank population projects' Policy research working paper no. 1048, Population and Human Resources Department, World Bank, Washington, DC

*Ball, C and Dunn, L (1995) *Non-Governmental Organisations: Guidelines for Good Policy and Practice* The Commonwealth Foundation, London

Bamberger, M (1988) 'The Role of Community Participation in Development Planning and Project management' [Policy development report series] Economic Development Institute, The World Bank, Washington, DC

Barbedette, L *et al* (1995) *Charter For Evaluations Made During Development Work* Fondation de France, Paris

Barclay, A *et al* (1993) *Development through PVOs and NGOs: Assessment Design* United States Agency for International Development, Washington, DC

Barrett, L (1993) 'The Relief Game' *West Africa*, May

Barrig, M and Wehkamp, S (eds) (1994) *Engendering Development: Experiences in Gender and Development Planning* NOVIB/Mujeres

Batchelder, D (1988) 'Experiential Learning in a North-South Context' *NGO Management*

vol 11, pp 19–21, International Council of Voluntary Agencies, Geneva

*Batsleer, J, Cornford, C and Paton, R (1991) *Issues in Voluntary Non-Profit Management* Addison Wesley and The Open University, Wokingham and Milton Keynes

Bebbington, T and Mitlin, D (1996) 'NGO Capacity and Effectiveness: A review of themes in NGO-related research recently funded by ESCOR' (mimeo) International Institute for Environment and Development, London

Bello, W (1994) *Dark Victory: The United States, Structural Adjustment and Global Poverty* Third World Network, Penang

Bendahmane, D (1991) 'Performance Review for NGOs' *Grassroots Development* vol 15 (2), pp 31–37, InterAmerican Foundation, Rosslyn, Virginia

Bennett, J (1994) *NGO Coordination at Field Level: A Handbook* International Council of Voluntary Agencies, Geneva

*Bennett, J (1995) *Meetings Needs: NGO Coordination in Practice* Earthscan, London

Berg, E (1994) *Improving Technical Cooperation: Some Key Issues* OECD, Paris

Berg, R (1987) 'Non-Governmental Organizations: New Force in Third World Development and Politics', Distinguished speaker series, No 2, Center for Advanced Study of International Development, Michigan State University, East Lansing

*Bhatnagar, B and Williams, A (eds) (1992) 'Participatory Development and the World Bank: Potential Directions for Change', Discussion paper, No 183, The World Bank, Washington, DC

Billis, D (1989) 'A Theory of the Voluntary Sector: Implications for Policy and Practice', Working paper, No 5, Centre for Voluntary Organisation, London School of Economics

Billis, D (1989) 'Towards a Distinctive NGO Management Training' *NGO Management* vol 15, pp 20–21, International Council of Voluntary Agencies, Geneva

Billis, D (1990) 'The Roots of Voluntary Agencies: A Question of Choice' *Non-profit and Voluntary Quarterly*

Billis, D and MacKeith, J (1993) *Organising NGOs: Challenges and Trends in the Management of Overseas Aid* Centre for

Voluntary Organisation, London

Bjur, WE and Zomorrodian, A, (1986) 'Towards Indigenous Theories of Administration: an international perspective' *International Review of Administrative Sciences* vol 52 (4), pp 397–420

Black, M (1992) *A Cause for Our Times: Oxfam the First 50 Years* Oxfam, Oxford

Blair, H *et al* (1994) 'Civil Society and Democratic Development: A CDIE Evaluation Design Paper', United States Agency for International Development, Programs and Operations Assessments Division, Washington, DC

Blaney, D and Pasha, M (1993) 'Civil Society and Democracy in the Third World: Ambiguities and Historical Possibilities' *Studies in Comparative International Development* vol 28(1), pp 3–24

Blankenberg, F (1993) 'The Institutional Support Model: A reflection on the experiment in three Latin American Countries, 1989–1992' Policy Support Unit, NOVIB, The Hague

Body Shop (1996) *The Body Shop Approach to Ethical Accounting* Body Shop, London

Bolling, L and Smith, C (1982) *Private Foreign Aid: U.S. Philanthropy for Relief and Development* Westview Press, Boulder

Booy, D (1989) *Institutional Development: A Guide for Development Practitioners* University of Guelph, Guelph, Ontario

Boschuyt, J (1995) 'Capacity Development: How Can Donors do it Better' Policy management brief, No 5, European Centre for Development Policy Management, Maastricht

Bourguignon, E (1979 *Psychological Anthropology: An Introduction to Human Nature and Cultural Differences* Holt, Rinehart and Winston, New York

Bowden, P (1986) 'Problems of implementation' *Public Administration and Development* vol 6 (1), pp 61–71

Bowman, C (1990) *The Essence of Strategic Management* Prentice Hall, London

Bratton, M (1990) 'Non-Governmental Organizations in Africa: Can They Influence Public Policy?' Development and Change, vol 21 (3), pp 87–119

Brautigan, D (1991) *Governance: A Review* Policy and Review Department, The World Bank, Washington, DC

*Brett, E (1993) 'Voluntary Agencies as Development Organizations: Theorizing the Problem of Efficiency and Accountability' *Development and Change* vol 24(2), pp 269–304

Bridges, W (1991) *Managing Transitions: Making the Most of Change* Addison-Wesley, Wokingham

Brinkerhoff, D (1979, 'Inside Public Bureaucracy: Empowering Managers to Empower Clients' *Participation Review* vol 1 (1), Cornell University, Ithaka

Brinkerhoff, D (1992) 'Looking out, looking in, looking ahead; guidelines for managing development programs', *International Review of Administrative Sciences* vol 58, pp 483–503

Brinkerhoff, D (1994) 'Institutional Development in World Bank Projects: analytical approaches and intervention designs' *Public Administration and Development* vol 14, pp 135–151

Brinkerhoff, D and Goldsmith, A (1992) 'Promoting the Sustainability of Development Institutions: A Framework for Strategy' *World Development* vol 20 (3), pp 369–383

Brinkerhoff, D and Ingle, M (1989) 'Integrating Blueprint and Process: a structured flexibility approach to development management' *Public Administration and Development* vol 9, pp 487–503

Brinkerhoff, D and Klauss, R (1985), 'Managerial Roles for Social Development Management' *Public Administration and Development* vol 5 (2), pp 145–156

Brodhead, T and Herbert–Copley, B (1988) *Bridges of Hope: Canadian Voluntary Agencies and the Third World* The North–South Institute, Ottawa

Brown, D (1988a) 'Organizational Barriers to NGO Strategic Action', reprint from *NGO Strategic Management in Asia: Focus on Bangladesh, Indonesia and the Phillipines* ANGOC, Manila

Brown, D (1988b) 'Private Voluntary Organisations and Development Partnerships', reprint from Khandwalla, P [ed] *Social Development: A New Role for the Organisational Sciences* pp 71–88 Sage, Newbury Park

Brown, D (1990) 'Bridging Organizations and Sustainable Development', Working paper, No 8, Institute of Development Research, Boston

Brown, D (1991) 'Methodological Considerations in the Evaluation of Social Development Programmes: An Alternative Approach' *Community Development Journal* Oxford University Press, Oxford

Brown, D and Covey, J (1987) 'Development Organizations and Organization Development: Towards an Expanded Paradigm for Organization Development' *Research in Organizational Change and Development* vol 1, pp 59–87, JAI Press, Boston

Brown, D (1994) 'Creating Social Capital: Nongovernmental Development Organizations and Intersectoral Problem Solving', *IDR Reports* vol 11 (3), Institute of Development Research, Boston

Brown, D and Covey, J (1987) 'Organizing and Managing Private Development Agencies: A Comparative Analysis', Working paper No 2129, Institute for Social and Policy Studies, Yale University, Boston

Brown, D and Korten, D (1989) 'Voluntary Organizations: Guidelines for Donors', Working paper 258, Country Economics Department, The World Bank, Washington, DC

Brown, D and Tandon R (1990) *Strengthening the Grass-Roots: Nature and Role of Support Organisations* Society for Participatory Research in Asia, New Delhi

Brown, D and Tandon, R (1992) 'Multi–Party Cooperation for Development in Asia', *IDR Reports* vol 10 (1), Institute of Development Research, Boston

Bruckmeier, K and Glaeser, B (1992) *Institutional Development and Environment: Analysis and Recommendations* Deutsche Gesellschaft für Technische Zusammenarbeit, Berlin

Brudney, J (1990) 'Volunteering in the Public Sector: Emerging Issues', in *The Nonprofit Sector [NGO's] in the United States and Abroad: Cross–Cultural Perspectives* Independent Sector and United Way, Washington, DC

Bryant, C and White, L (1984) *Managing Rural Development with Small Farmer Participation* Kumarian Press, West Hartford

Bryson, J (1988) *Strategic Planning for Public and NonProfit Organisations: A Guide to Strengthening and Sustaining Organizational Achievement* Jossey–Bass, London

*Burke, W (1992) *Organization Development: A Process of Learning and Change* Addison–Wesley

*Burkey, S (1993) *People First: A Guide to Self–Reliant, Particatory Development* Zed Press, London

Burnell, P (1991) *Charity, Politics and the Third World* Harvester–Wheatsheaf, Hemel Hempstead

Burnell, P (1993) 'Debate: Third World Charities in Britain to 2000' *Community Development Journal* vol 28 (1), pp 66–81, Oxford University Press, Oxford

Butler, P and Wilson, D (1990) *Managing Voluntary and Non–Profit Organisations: Strategy and Structure* Routledge, London

Callahan, W (1995), 'Non–Governmental Organizations, Non–Violent Action, and Post–Modern Politics in Thailand', *Sojourn* Vol 10 (1), pp 90–115

Campbell, P (1989) *Relations Between Southern and Northern NGOs: Effective Partnerships for Sustainable Development* International Council of Voluntary Agencies, Geneva

Campbell, P (1990) 'Strengthening Organisations' *NGO Management*, vol 18, pp 21–24, International Council of Voluntary Agencies, Geneva

*Carlsson, J, Kohlin, G and Ekbom, A (1994) *The Political Economy of Evaluation: International Aid Agencies and the Effectiveness of Aid* St Martin's Press, London

Carnall, C (1992) *Managing Change* Routledge, London

*Carroll, T (1992) *Intermediary NGOs: The Supporting Link in Grassroots Development* Kumarian Press, West Hartford

Carroll, T, Schmidt, M and Bebbington, T (1996) *Participation Through Intermediary NGOs* environment department papers, participation series, no. 031, The World Bank, Washington, DC

Carty, E (1990) *Development Education and Non–Governmental Organisations: Mediums, Methods and Messages* MPhil Thesis, Institute of Development Studies, University of Sussex, Brighton

Carvalho, S and White, H (1993) *Performance Indicators to Monitor Poverty Reduction* The World Bank, Washington, DC

Case, R (1987) *How Are We Doing? A Framework for Evaluating Development Education Programs* Interaction, New York

Casley, D and Lury D (1982), *Monitoring and Evaluation of Agricultural and Rural Development Projects* Johns Hopkins, Baltimore

Cassen, R (1986) *Does Aid Work?* Oxford University Press, Oxford

CCIC (1988) *Mind if I Cut In?* Canadian Council For International Cooperation, Ottawa

CCIC (1996) *From Donors to Global Citizens* Canadian Council for International Co-operation, Ottawa

CDRA (1994) *Annual Report (1993/94)* Community Development Resource Associations, Cape Town

CDRA (1995) *Annual Report (1994/95)* Community Development Resource Associations, Cape Town

CDRA (1996) *Annual Report (1995/96)* Community Development Resource Associations, Cape Town

Cernea, M (1988) 'Nongovernmental Organizations and Local Development' discussion paper no 40, The World Bank, Washington, DC

Cernea, M (1993) 'Culture and Organization: The Social Sustainability of Development', *Sustainable Development* vol 1 (2), pp 18–29

Chamberlain, H (1993) 'On the Search for Civil Society in China' *Modern China* vol 19 (2), pp 199–215l

Chambers, R (1983) *Rural Development: Putting the Last First* Longman, Harlow

Chambers, R (1987) 'Normal Professionalism and the Early Project Process: Problems and Solutions' Paper presented at a conference on project identification in developing countries, Institute for Development Policy and Management, University of Manchester

Chambers, R (1994) 'Paradigm Shifts and the Practice of Participatory Research and Development' working paper No 2, Insitute of Development Studies, University of Sussex

Chambers, R, (1997), *Whose Reality Counts? Putting the First Last* IT Publications, London

Chambers, R, Longhurst, R and Pacey, A (eds), (1981), *Seasonal Dimensions to Rural Poverty* Frances Pinter, London

Chang, C and Tuckman, H (1994) 'Revenue diversification among non–profits' *Voluntas* vol 5 (3), pp 273–290

Chazan, N, Harbeson, J and Rothchild, D (eds) (1993) *Civil Society and the State in Africa* Lynne Rienner, Boulder

Chepkwony, A (1987) *The Role of Non–Governmental Organizations in Development: A Study of the National Christian Council of Kenya (NCCK 1963–1978)* Studia Missionalia Uppsaliensia, Uppsala

Cherrett, I *et al* (1995) 'Redefining the roles of environmental NGOs in Africa' *Development in Practice* vol 5 (1), pp 26–35

Cheung–Judge, M–Y, and Henley, A (1994) *Equality in Action: Introducing Equal Opportunities in Voluntary Agencies* National Council of Voluntary Agencies, London

Chomsky, N (1994) *World Orders Old and New* Pluto Press, London

Chossudovsky, M (1996) 'The World Bank derogates women's rights: outcomes from Beijing' *Development in Practice* vol 6 (1), pp 65–66, Oxfam, Oxford

Choudhary, A and Tandon R (1989) *Participatory Evaluation: Issues and Concerns* Society for Participatory Research in Asia, New Delhi

Clark, J (1991) *Democratizing Development: The Role of Voluntary Organizations* Earthscan, London

Clark, J (1993) *The State and the Voluntary Sector* HRO working paper no 12, World Bank, Washington, DC

Clayton, A, [ed] (1994) *Governance, Democracy and Conditionality: What Role for NGOs?* INTRAC, Oxford

Cohen, J (1991) 'Expatriate Advisors in the Government of Kenya: Why they are there and what can be done about it' development discussion paper, No 376, Harvard Institute of International Development, Cambridge

Coleman, G (1991) 'Investigating Organisations: A Feminist Approach', occasional paper 37, School for Advanced

Urban Studies, University of Bath, Bath

Commonwealth Secretariat (1986) *Decentralization for Development* A Selected Annotated Bibliography, April, Commonwealth Secretariat, London

Commonwealth Secretariat (1987) *Women in Management: An annotated bibliography with emphasis on Commonwealth sources* Human Resource Development Group, Commonwealth Secretariat, London

Constantino–David, K (1995) 'Community Organizing in the Philippines: The Experience of Development NGOs', in Craig, G and Mayo, M (eds) *Community Empowerment: A Reader in Participation and Development* Sage, London

Conyers, D (1984) 'Decentralization and development: a review of the literature', *Public Administration and Development* vol 4, pp 187–197

Cooke, B (1996a) *Participation, (Process) and Management: Lessons for Development in the History of Organisation Development* Working Paper 7, Human Resources Development Group, Institute for Development Policy and Management, Manchester University, Manchester

Cooke, B (1966) *From Process Consultation to a Clinical Model of Development Practice*, discussion paper no 48, Institute for Development Policy and Management, Manchester University, Manchester

Cooperrider, D, Ludema, J, Srivstva, S and Wishart, C (1995) *Appreciative Inquiry: A Constructive Approach to Organizational Capacity Building, Weatherhead School of Management* Case Western Reserve University, Cleveland

Corkery, J, Land, A and Bosuyt, J (1995) 'The Process of Policy Formulation: Insitutional Path or Institutional Maze?' Policy Management Report 3, European Centre for Development Policy Management, Maastricht

Costello, S (1994) *Managing Change in the Workplace* Mirror Press, New York

Coudere, H (1994) *Van project tot belied: Evaluatiemethodes voor niet–gouvernementele ontwikkelingssamenwerking* [From project to policy: Evaluation methods for non–governmental development cooperation] NCOS, Brussels

Covey, J (1992) 'A Note on NGOs and Policy Influence' *IDR Reports*, (9)2, Institute of Development Research, Boston

Covey, J (1994) 'Accountability and Effectiveness of NGO Policy Alliances' *IDR Reports* vol 7 (2), Institute of Development Research, Boston

Covey, J and Brown D (1994) 'Forming a Multi–National Development Coalition: Diversity and Oppression in Organisational Relations' *IDR Reports* vol 11 (8), Institute of Development Research, Boston

Cracknell, B (1983 *The Evaluation of Aid Projects and Programmes* Overseas Development Administration, London

*Craig, G and Mayo, M (eds) (1995) *Community Empowerment: A Reader in Participation and Development* Zed Press, London

Crewe, E (1994) *Expatriates Working for Sustainability* School of African and Asian Studies, University of Sussex

Crosby, B (1991) 'Planning and Strategic Management: What are they and how are they different?' technical notes, No 1, implementing policy change project, United States Agency for International Development, Washington, DC

Crosby, B (1992a) 'Management and the Environment for Implementation of Policy Change: Part One Political Mapping' technical notes, No 4, implementing policy change project, United States Agency for International Development, Washington, DC

Crosby, B (1992b) 'Management and the Environment for Implementation of Policy Change: Part Two Policy Environment Mapping Techniques' technical notes, No 5, implementing policy change project, United States Agency for International Development, Washington, DC

Crosby, B (1992c) 'Stakeholder Analysis: A Vital Tool for Strategic Managers' technical notes, No 2, implementing policy change project, United States Agency for International Development, Washington, DC

Cumming, L and Singleton, B (1995) 'Organizational Sustainability – An End of the Century Challenge for Canadian Voluntary International Development Organizations' Paper presented at the eleventh annual conference for the study of international development, Montreal

Daimond, L, Linz, J and Lipset, S (eds) (1988) *Democracy in Developing Countries* Lynne Reiner, Boulder

*Dalton, R and Kuechler, M (eds) (1990) *Challenging the Political Order: New Social and Political Movements in Western Democracies* Polity Press, Cambridge

DANIDA (1994) *Evaluation Report: The Local Grant Authority of Danish Embassies* vol 1, Ministry of Foreign Affairs, Danish International Development Agency, Copenhagen

Dartington, T (1989a) 'Management Learning and Voluntary Organisations' discussion document, No 1, The Management Unit, National Council for Voluntary Organisations, London

Dartington, T (1989b) 'Management Competencies and Voluntary Organisations' discussion document, No 2, The Management Unit, National Council for Voluntary Organisations, London

Dartington, T (1994) *Leadership and Voluntary Organisations*, The Management Unit, National Council for Voluntary Organisations, London

Datta, S (1996) *Fund Raising for Development Action* Society for Participtory Research in Asia, New Delhi

Dawson, E (1995a) 'Women, Gender and Impact Assessment: A Discussion Paper' Oxfam, Oxford

Dawson, E (1995b) 'Novib and Oxfam UK/I Impact Assessment Research Programme Phase III – West Africa' Oxfam, Oxford

de Bunt, P (1993) *Management van Verandering en de Rol van de Organisatie–Adviseur* [The Management of Change and the Role of the Organisational Adviser] Samson, Alphen aan de Rijn

Deacon, D, Fenton, N and Walker, B (1995) 'Communicating Philanthropy: the media and the voluntary sector in Britain' *Voluntas*, vol 6 (2), pp 119–139

Devine, J (1996) 'NGOs: Changing Fashion or Fashioning Change?' *Occasional Paper* 02/96, Centre for Development Studies, University of Bath

Dichter, T (1987a) 'The Contexts and Culture in which PVOs/NGOs Manage', Technical paper for the meeting of the advisory committee on voluntary foreign aid, Technoserve, Boston

Dichter, T (1987b) 'Development Management: Plain or Fancy? Sorting Out Some Muddles' *Findings* Technoserve, Connecticut

Dichter, T (1989) 'Development management: plain or fancy? Sorting out some muddles' *Public Administration and Development* vol 9, pp 381–393

Donnelly–Roark, P (1991) 'Grassroots Participation: Defining New Realities and Operationalizing New Strategies' discussion paper, UNDP, New York

Dorr, D (1991) *The Social Justice Agenda: Justice, Ecology, Power and the Church,* Gill and Macmillan, London

Doub, M (1996) *Supporting the support organizations: A case study of collaborative regional suport organizations [NCRSO] in India* Institute of Development Research, Boston

Douxchamps, F (1995) *Relationships between NGOs and Official Aid Agencies: Partners or Contractors* COTA, Brussels

Drabek, A [ed] (1987) 'Development Alternatives: The Challenge for NGOs' *World Development* vol 15, Oxford

Dreesman, B (1987) 'Northern NGOs: tradition, change and challenge' *The Courier* Commission of the European Community

Drucker, P (1989a) 'What Business Can Learn From Nonprofits' *Harvard Business Review*, July–August, pp88–93

Drucker, P (1990a) 'Lessons for Succesful Nonprofit Governance' *NonProfit Management and Leadership* vol 1 (1), pp 7–14

Drucker, P (1990b) *Managing The NonProfit Organization: Principles and Practices* HarperCollins, New York

Drucker, P (1993) *The Five Most Important Questions You Will Ever Ask About Your NonProfit Organization: Participant's Workbook* Drucker Foundation/Jossey–Bass, San Francisco

DSA (1994) 'The Academic–Practitioner Interface' report of a workshop held in Manchester on June 30th Development Studies Association, London

Duel, C and Dutcher, L (1987) *Working*

Together: NGO Cooperation in Seven African Countries InterAction, New York

Duffield, M (1993) 'NGOs, Disaster Relief and Asset Transfer in the Horn: Political Survival in a Permanent Emergency' *Development and Change* vol 24, pp 131–157, London

EASUN (1996) *Participatory Intervention Approaches* Final Report of a Mini–Consultation, East African NGO Support Unit, Arusha

Eaves, A (1992) 'EXTIE's NGO Monitoring System' mimeo External Relations Division, The World Bank, Washington, DC

ECA (1990) *African Charter for Popular Participation in Development and Transformation* Economic Commission for Africa, Addis Ababa

*Eckman, K (1993) 'Use of Indicators of Unsustainability in Development Programs' *Impact Assessment* Fall, vol 11

ECPDM (1995) 'Civil Service Reform: Improving the Capacity of Governments to Formulate and Implement Development Policy' *Bulletin* vol III (1), European Centre for Development Policy Management, Maastricht

*Edwards, E and Hulme, D (eds) (1995) *Non–Governmental Organisations Performance and Accountability: Beyond the Magic Bullet* Earthscan, London

Edwards, M (1993) 'Does the doormat influence the boot?: critical thought on UK NGOs and international advocacy' *Development In Practice* vol 3 (3), pp 163–175, Oxfam, Oxford

Edwards, M (1996b) 'Becoming a Learning Organisation, or the Search for the Holy Grail?' Paper presented at the Aga Khan Foundation Round Table on Systematic Learning: Promoting Support for Canadian Development Co–operation, Ottawa

Edwards, M (1995) *Approaches to Work in South Asia: A Report to Save the Childrens Fund–UK* December, Save the Children Fund, London

Edwards, M (1996a) 'International Development NGOs: Legitimacy, Accountability, Regulation and Roles' Discussion paper for the Commission on the Future of the Voluntary Sector and the British Overseas Aid Group, Save the Children Fund, London

Edwards, M (1996b) *The Future of International Co–operation* Save the Children Fund, London

*Edwards, M and Hulme, D (eds) (1992) *Making a Difference: NGOs and development in a changing world* Earthscan, London

Edwards, M and Hulme, D (1996a) 'NGOs and Development: Performance and Accountability in the Post Cold–War World', *World Development* forthcoming

*Edwards, M and Hulme, D (eds) (1996b) *Too Close for Comfort? NGOs, States and Donors* Earthscan, London

Egland, J and Kerbs, T (eds) (1987) *Third World Organizational Development: A comparison of NGO Strategies* Henry Dunant Institute, Geneva

*Ekins, P (1992) *A New World Order: Grassroots Movements for Global Change* Routledge, London.

El Taller (1991) *The Fruit Ripens: A Latin American Perspective on Networking* El Taller Foundation, Tunis

Elliott, C (1989) *Comfortable Compassion: Poverty, Power and the Church* Hodder and Stoughton, London

Esman, M and Uphoff, N (1984) *Local Organisations: Intermediaries in Rural Development* Cornell University Press, Ithaca, N.Y.

Etzioni, A (1971) *A Comparative Analysis of Complex Organizations: On Power, Involvement and Their Correlates* The Free Press, New York

Farer, T (1993) *The Western Hemisphere's Prospect,* Essays on Human Rights and Democratic Development, no. 1, International Centre for Human Rights and Democratic Development, Ottawa

Farrington, J and Bebbington, A (1993) *Reluctant Partners?: Non–Governmental Organizations, the State and Agricultural Development* Routledge, London

Fernandes, R (1995) *Backwards and Forwards to Civil Society* World Council of Churches, Geneva

Fernandes, R and Carneiro, L (1991) *NGOs in the Nineties: A Survey of their Brazilian Leaders* ISER, Rio de Janeiro

Fernando, S (1986) *How Networks Function: Some Structural and Interactional Aspects of the IRED Network in Asia: Colombo* Development Innovations and Networks, Sri Lanka

Fernando, S (1991) 'NGOs in Liberal Democratic Society: The Case of Sri Lanka', occasional paper series, Development Innovations and Networks, Sri Lanka

Ferris, E (1992) 'Non–Governmental Organisations in the International Refugee System: Churches and NGOs', in Ferris, E (ed) *Beyond Borders* World Council of Churches, Geneva

Feuerstein, M T (1988) *Partners in Evaluation: Evaluating Development and Community Programmes With Participants* Macmillan, London

Fierlbeck, K (1997) 'Civil Society' , in Rai, S and Grant, W (eds) *Globalizing Democracy: Power, Legitimacy, and the Interpretation of Democratic Ideas* Manchester University Press

*Fisher, J (1990) 'Local Governments and the Independent Sector in the Third World', Paper prepared for the spring research forum on The NonProfit Sector In the United States and Abroad: Cross Cultural Perspectives, Boston, Massachusetts

Fisher, J (1993) *The Road to Rio: Sustainable Development and the Nongovermmental Movement in the Third World* Praeger, New York

Fisher, J (1994) 'Is the Iron Law of Oligarchy Rusting Away in the Third World?', *World Development* vol 22 (2), pp 129–143

*Flood, P, Gannon, M and Paauwe, J (1996) *Managing Without Traditional Methods: International Innovations in Human Resource Management* Addison–Wesley, Wokingham

Fowler, A (1982) 'Temperatures in Development Funding, The Hot Money Model' *Development: Seeds of Change,* vol 2, pp 81–82, Society of International Development, Rome

Fowler, A (1984) 'Management at Grass Roots Level for Integrated Rural Development in Africa with Special Reference to Churches', working paper 419, Institute of Development Studies, University of Nairobi, Nairobi

*Fowler, A (1988) 'Non–Governmental Organizations in Africa: Achieving Comparative Advantage in Micro– development', discussion paper, 249, Institute of Development Studies, University of Sussex

Fowler, A (1989a) 'Why is Managing Social Development Different' *NGO Management Newsletter* No 12, International Council of Voluntary Agencies

Fowler, A (1989b) *Guidelines and Field Checklist for Assessment of Community Organisations* The Ford Foundation/CARE, Nairobi

Fowler, A (1990a) 'Doing it Better? Where and how do NGOs have a 'comparative advantage' in facilitating development', *Bulletin* vol 28, pp 11–20, Agricultural and Rural Development Extension Department, University of Reading

Fowler, A (1990b) 'Some Thoughts on Human Resource Development Strategy For Leaders and Senior Cadres of Non–Governmental Development Organisations in Africa', in Fowler, A, Campbell P and Pratt B *Institutional Development and NGOs in Africa* International NGO Training and Research Centre, Oxford

Fowler, A (1991a) 'Building Partnerships between Northern and Southern NGOs: issues for the 1990s, *Development in Practice* vol 1 (1), pp 5–18, Oxfam, Oxford

Fowler, A (1991b) 'The Role of NGOs in Changing State–Society Relations: Perspectives from Eastern and Southern Africa', *Development Policy Review* vol 9 (1), pp 53–83, Overseas Development Institute, London

Fowler, A (1992a) 'Participation for Citizenship: The New Challenge in Africa's Development' *People First* vol 1 (1), pp 5, Economic Commission for Africa, Addis Ababa

Fowler, A (1992b) 'Non–Governmental Organisations as Agents of Democratization: An African Perspective' *Journal of International Development* vol 5 (3), pp 325–339

Fowler, A (1992c) 'Decentralization for International NGOs' *Development in Practice* vol 2 (2), pp 121–124, Oxfam, Oxford

Fowler, A (1992d) 'Distant Obligations: Speculations on NGO Funding and the Global Market' *Review of African Political Economy,* November, vol 55, pp 9–29, Sheffield

Fowler, A (1992e) 'Prioritizing Institutional Development: A New Role for NGO Centres for Study and Development' *The Gate Keeper Series* no 35, International Institute for Environment and Development, London

Fowler, A, Campbell, P and Pratt, B (1992) *Institutional Development and NGOs in Africa: Policy Perspectives for European Development Agencies*, October, International NGO Training and Research Centre and NOVIB, Oxford/The Hague

*Fowler, A (1993) 'Development, Democratisation and NGOs: Lessons from Experience' *Development and Democracy* vol 7, pp 9–18, Urban Foundation, Johannesburg

Fowler, A (1994) 'Capacity Building and NGOs: A Case of Strengthening Ladles for the Global Soup Kitchen?' *Institutional Development* vol 1 (1), pp 18–24, Society for Participatory Research in Asia, New Delhi

Fowler, A and James, R (1994) 'The Role of Southern NGOs in Development Cooperation: A Review', occasional paper, 2, International NGO Training and Research Centre, Oxford

Fowler, A, Goold, L and James, R (1995) 'Practical Guidelines for Self–Assessment of NGO Capacity', occasional paper, 10, International NGO Training and Research Centre, Oxford

Fowler, A (1995) 'Assessing NGO Performance: Difficulties, Dilemmas and a Way Ahead', in Edwards and Hulme (eds) *Beyond the Magic Bullet: NGO Performance and Accountability in the New World Order* Earthscan, London, pp 143–157

Fowler, A and Biekart, K (1996) 'Do Private Aid Agencies Really Make a Difference', in Sogge, D (ed) *Compassion and Calculation* Pluto Press, London

Fowler, A (1996) 'Strengthening the Role of Voluntary Development Organizations: Nine Policy Issues Facing Official Aid Agencies' in *Strengthening Civil Society' s Contribution to Development: The Role of Official Development Assistance* report of the Overseas Development Council/Synergos Institute, Washington DC/New York, pp 21–23

Fox, L (1995) *How New Funding Mechanisms Could be Used to Support Civil Society: A Preliminary Study of Existing Experience* October, Synergos Institute, New York

Fox, L (1996) 'Strengthening Civil Society Finance in Development: The Role of Official Development Assistance', in *Strengthening Civil Society's Contribution to Development: The Role of Official Development Assistance* pp. 12–20, Report of a Conference Organized by the Overseas Development Council and The Synergos Institute, Washington DC/New York

Foy, C and Helmich, H (eds) (1996) *Public Support for International Development*, OECD, Paris

Frankenberger, T (1993) 'Indicators and Data Collection Methods for Assessing Household Food Security' *Household Food Security: Concepts, Indicators Measurements* UNICEF/IFAD, New York/Rome

Freeman, R (1984) *Strategic Management: A Stakeholder Approach* Jossey–Bass, San Fransisco

Friere, P (1973 *Education for Critical Consciousness* Seabury Press, New York

Galloway, R (1993) 'Global indicators of nutritional risk [II]',working paper 6, Human Resources Development and Operations Policy, World Bank, Washington, DC

Galtung, J (1975) 'The Centre–Periphery Model in Development', *Development* Society for International Development, Rome

Garcia–Zamor, J–C [ed] (1985) *Public Participation in Development Planning and Management: Cases from Africa and Asia* Westview Press, Boulder

Gariba, S, Kassam, Y and Thibault, L (1995) *Report of the Study of Partnership and Institutional Strengthening* Partnership Africa Canada, Ottowa

Gellner, H (1994) *Civil Society and its Rivals* Methuen, London

Geneva Group (1992) *How to Run a Small Development Project* IT Publications, London

Gerson, P (1993) 'Popular Participation in Economic Theory and Practice',working paper 18, World Bank, Washington, DC

Gianotten, V (1986) *Methodological Notes for Evaluation* Food and Agriculture Organisation, Rome

Gibson, K (1995) 'Becoming Self–Sufficient: The Experience of US NGOs in Achieving Sustainability', *MULBERRY Series,* vol 5, Olive

Information Services, Durban

Goetz, A–M (1992) 'Gender and Administration' *Bulletin* vol 23 (4), Institute of Development Studies, University of Sussex, Brighton

Goldsmith, A (1991) 'Institutional Development for Agricultural Research: Concepts, Models and Methods', *ISNAR Staff Notes* pp 91–115, International Service for National Agricultural Research, The Hague

GOM (1991) *Significance of the Co–financing Programme: An Exploration* Gemeenschappelijke Overleg Medefinanceiering, Oegstgeest

Goold, E (1994) 'Sierra Leone: DELTA dilemmas hierachy and tradition, participation and change', *Rural Extension Bulletin* vol 6, University of Reading, Reading.

Gorman, R [ed] (1984) *Private Voluntary Agencies as Agents of Development* Westview Press, Boulder, Colorado

Graham, P (1991) *Integrative Management: Creating Unity From Diversity* Blackwell, London

Greeley, M, Kabeer, N, Davis S and Hussein, K (1992) *Measuring the Poverty Reduction Impact of Development Interventions* Institute of Development Studies, University of Sussex

Griffiths, G (1987) 'Missing the poorest: Participant identification by a rural development agency in Gujarat', discussion paper 230, Institute of Development Studies, University of Sussex, Brighton

Grindle, M and Thomas, J (1991) *Public Choices and Policy Change: The Political Economy of Reform in Developing Countries* Johns Hopkins, Baltimore

Grønbjerg, K (1993) *Understanding Nonprofit Funding*, Jossey–Bass, San Francisco

GTZ (1988) *ZOPP [Objectives–oriented project planning] in brief* Deutsche Gesellschaft für Technische Zusammenarbeit, Frankfurt–am–Main,

*Guba, E and Lincoln, Y (1989) *Fourth Generation Evaluation* Sage, London

Hage, J and Finsterbusch, K (1987) *Organizational Change as Development Strategy: Models and Tactics for Improving Third World Organizations* Lynne Reiner, Boulder

Hailey, J (1995) 'International Organisation Assessment: Lessons from Development Agencies and International NGOs', Paper presented at the British Academy of Management Annual Conference, Manchester

Hall, B (1992) *Learning Lessons: Global Networking and International Non–Governmental Organizations* INGO Division, Canadian International Development Agency

Hall, P (1995) 'Theories and Institutions' *Nonprofit and Voluntary Sector Quarterly* vol 24 (1), pp 5–13

Hall, R (1991) *Organizations: Structures, Processes and Outcomes* Prentice Hall, Englewood Cliffs

Hallowes, D (1995) 'Of Partners and Patrons: NGO Perceptions of Funders' *AVOCADO Series* No 5, Olive Information Services, Durban

Hammond, A, Adriaanse, A, Rodenburg, E, Bryant, D and Woodward, R (1995) *Environmental Indicators: a systematic approach to measuring and reporting on environmental policy performance in the context of sustainable development* World Resources Institute, Washington, DC

Hancock, G (1989) *The Lords of Poverty* The Atlantic Monthly Press, New York

Handy, C (1985) *Understanding Organisations* Penguin, Harmondsworth

*Handy, C (1988) *Understanding Voluntary Organisations* Penguin, Harmondsworth

Handy, C (1989) *The Age of Unreason* Pan Books, London

Handy, C (1995) *The Empty Raincoat* Arrow, London

Harder, M (1992) *Voluntary Service: Current Status Report Volunteer Management Cycle* Henry Dunant Institute, Geneva

Harding, D (1995a) 'Mistrusting Broken Images: Facing our Inadequacies in Organisational Thinking' *OD Debate* vol 2 (3), Olive Information Services, Durban

Harding, D (1995b) 'Why Care About OD?' *OD Debate* vol 2 (4), Olive Information Services, Durban

Harding, P (1991) 'Qualitative indicators and the project framework' *Community Development Journal* vol 26 (4), pp 294–305; Oxford University Press, Oxford

Harris, T (1970 *I'm OK–You're OK* Pan, London

Harriss, J, [ed] (1982) *Rural Development: Theories of peasant economy and agrarian change* Hutchinson, London

Hashemi, S (1991) 'The NGO Participatory Development Paradigm', *World Development* vol 3 (4), pp 421–425

Heimovics, R, Herman, D and Jurkiewicz–Coughlin, C (1993) 'Executive Leadership and Resource Dependence in Nonprofit Organizations: A Frame Analysis', *Public Administration Review* September/October, vol 5 (5)

Herman and Associates (1994) *The Jossey–Bass Handbook of Non–Profit Management and Leadership* Jossey–Bass, San Francisco

Herman, R and Heimovics, R (1994) 'A cross–national study of a method for researching non–profit organisational effectiveness' *Voluntas* vol 5 (1), pp 86–100, Manchester University Press

Herzlinger, R (1996) 'Can Public Trust in Nonprofits and Government be Restored?' *Harvard Business Review*, pp 97–107 March–April

Hewison, K (1993) 'Nongovernmental organizations and the cultural development perspective in Thailand: a comment on Rigg', *World Development* vol 21 (10), pp 1699–1708

*Hind, A (1995) *The Governance and Management of Charities* Voluntary Sector Press, London

Hirschman, A (196)7 *Development Projects Observed,* Brookings Institute, Washington, DC

Hofstede, G (1983) *Culture and Management Development* Management Training Branch, International Labour Organization, Geneva

Hofstede, G (1984) *Culture's Consequences: Culture and Work Related Values* vol 5, Cross–Cultural Research and Methodology Series, Sage, Beverly Hills

Hofstede, G (1991) *Cultures and Organisations: Software of the Mind* McGraw Hill, Maidenhead

Hoggett, P (1992) 'A New Management in the Public Sector' *Policy and Politics* vol 19 (4), pp 243–256

Holland, J and Henriot, P (1983) *Social analysis, linking faith and justice* Center of Concern, Washington DC

Holloway, R (1994) *Alternatives to External Donor Funds for South Asian NGOs – What do we know and what do we need to know* Aga Kan Foundation, Ottawa

Holloway, R (1995) 'The Non–Profit Sector: Trying to Categorise in Bangaldesh' *Institutional Development* vol 2 (1), pp 40–48, Society for Participatory Research in Asia, New Delhi

Holmberg, J, Bass, S and Timberlake, L (1991) *Defending the Future: a Guide to Sustainable Development* International Institute for Enviroment and Development, London

Honadle, G (1982) 'Rapid Reconnaissance for Development Administration: Mapping and Moulding Organisational Landscapes' *World Development* vol 10 (8), pp 633–649

Honadle, G (1986) 'Development Management in Africa: Context and Strategy – A Synthesis of Lessons from Six Agricultural Development Projects', special evaluation study 43, United States Agency for International Development, Washington, DC

Honadle, G, and van Sant, J (1975) *Implementation for Sustainability: Lessons from Integrated Rural Development* Kumarian Press, West Hartford, Connecticut

*Hope, A and Timmel, S (1984) *Training for Transformation* vol 1–3, Mambo Press, Gweru

Horch, H–D (1995) 'On the socio–economics of voluntary organisations' *Voluntas* vol 5 (2), pp 219–230

Hordijk, A *et al*, (1995) *Programme Evaluation Institutional Development: Experience of NOVIB Patners in Kenya and Zimbabwe* September, NOVIB, The Hague

Horton–Smith, D (1995) 'Some Challenges in Nonprofit and Voluntary Action Research', *Nonprofit and Voluntary Sector Quarterly*, 24(2), pp 99–101

Howell, J (1993) 'The Poverty of Civil Society: Insights from China', discussion paper 240, School of Development Studies, Univeristy of East Anglia, Norwich

Howes, M (1992) 'Linking Paradigms and Practice: Key Issues in the Appraisal, Monitoring and Evaluation of British NGO Projects' *Journal of International Development* vol 4 (4), pp 375–396

Howes, M (1996) 'NGOs and the Institutional Development of Membership Organisations' *Journal of International Development* forthcoming

Hoyer, H (1994) 'Reflection on Partnership and Accompaniament' *Institutional Development* vol 1 (1), pp 46–51, Society for Participatory Research in Asia, New Delhi

*Hudock, A (1995) 'Sustaining Southern NGOs in Resource–Dependent Environments' *Journal of International Development* vol 7 (4), pp 653–668

Hudock, A., (1996) 'Institutional Interdependence: Capacity Building Assistance for Intermediary NGOs in Sierra Leone and the Gambia', Paper presented at Development Studies Association Annual Conference, September, Reading

Hudson, M (1995) *Managing Without Profit* Penguin, London

Hulme, D (1989) 'Learning and not learning from experience in rural project planning' *Public Administration and Development* vol 9, pp 1–16

Hulme, D and Turner, M (1990) *Sociology and Development Theories, Policies and Practices* Harvester Wheatsheaf, Hertfordshire

Hulst, W and van de Veen, H (1992) 'Wat doen ze met ons geld?' [What do they do with our money?] *Onze World* July–August, Amsterdam

Human, P and Zaaiman, A (1995) *Managing Towards Self–Reliance* Phoenix, Cape Town

Huntington, S (1993) 'The Clash of Cultures' *Foreign Affairs* vol 72 (3)

Hyden, G (1983) *No Short Cuts to Progress: African Development Management in Perspective* University of California Press, Berkeley

ICSW (1988) *Justice in the Aid Relationship?: A Dialogue on Partnership* International Council on Social Welfare, Vienna

ICVA (1985 *Suggested guidelines on the acceptance of government funds for NGO programmes* International Council of Voluntary Agencies, Geneva

ICVA (1986–1990) *NGO Management: Newsletter of the NGO Management Network* vol 1–18, International Council of Voluntary Agencies, Geneva

ICVA (1988) 'Relations Between Southern and Northern NGOs in the Context of Sustainability, Participation and Partnership in Development', discussion paper, International Council of Voluntary Agencies, Geneva

ICVA (1990) *Relations Between Southern and Northern NGOs: Policy Guidelines* International Council of Voluntary Agencies revised, Geneva

ICVA/ANGOC (1989) *Institutional Development of NGOs: An Annotated Bibliography* International Council of Voluntary Agencies and the Asian NGO Coalition for Agrarian Reform and Rural Development, Geneva and Manila

IDR (1990) *Formulating Strategy: A Planning Guide* Institute of Development Research, Boston

IDS (1986) 'Aid Effectiveness' *Bulletin* vol 17 (2), 2, Institute of Development Studies, University of Sussex, Brighton

IFRG (1993) *Local Fund Raising for East African NGOs* International Fund–Raising Group, Kenya NGO Council, London/Nairobi

IFRG (1995) *Fund Raising for a Better World* International Fund Raising Group, London

IIED (1994a) Special issue on 'Participatory Tools and Methods in Urban Areas', *RRA Notes* vol 21, International Institute for Environment and Development, London

IIED (1994b) Special Issue on Training, *RRA Notes* no 19, International Institute for Environment and Development, London

IIED (1995a) 'Critical Reflections From Practice' *PLA Notes* no 24, International Institute for Environment and Development, London

IIED (1995b) 'Participatory Learning and Action' *PLA Notes* no 22, International Institute for Environment and Development, London

Independent Sector (1990) *The Nonprofit Sector [NGO's] in the United States and Abroad: Cross–Cultural Perspectives* [spring research forum working papers], Independent Sector and United Way, Washington, DC

INTRAC/South Research (1994) *A Tool for Project Management and People Driven Development* International NGO Training and Research Centre/South Research, Oxford and

Brussels

IRDC (1993) 'Institution Building' *IRDC Currents* International Rural Development Centre, Swedish University of Agricultural Science, Uppsala

James, E (1989) *The Nonprofit Sector in International Perspective: Studies in Comparative Culture and Politics* Oxford University Press, Oxford

James, R (1994) 'Strengthening the Capacity of Southern NGO Partners' *Occasional Papers Series* no 5 vol 1 (5), International NGO Training and Research Centre, Oxford

James, W and Caliguire, D (1996) 'Renewing Civil Society', *Journal of Democracy* vol 7 (1), pp 56–66

Jelinek, M, Smiricich, L and Hirsch, P (1983) 'Organizational Culture–Introduction: A Code of Many Colors' *Administrative Science Quarterly* vol 28 (3), pp 331–338

Jena, N (1995) 'People's Participation in Development: A Comparative Analysis of some Development Projects in India' *Participation and Governance* vol 2 (5), pp 13–20, Society for Participatory Research in Asia, New Delhi

JICA (1995) *Participatory Development and Good Governance: Report of the Aid Study Committee* Japan International Co–operation Agency, Tokyo, March

Jones, M and Mann, P (eds) (1992) *HRD: International Perspectives on Development and Learning* Kumarian, Boulder, Colorado

Kanter, R (1979) 'The Measurement of Organizational Effectiveness, Productivity, Performance and Success: Issues and Dilemmas in Service and Non–Profit Organizations' *PONPO Working Paper,* vol 8, Institution for Social and Policy Studies, Yale University, Boston

Kanfer, F and Goldstein, A (eds) (1980) *Helping People Change* Pergamon, New York

Kanter, R (1989) 'The New Managerial Work' *Harvard Business Review* vol 6, pp 85–92, Boston

Kanter, R (1993) *Men and Women of the Corporation* Basic Books

Kanter, R and Summers, D (1987) 'Doing Well While Doing Good: Dilemmas of Performance Measurement in Nonprofit Organizations and the Need for a Multi–Constituency Approach', in Powell, W [ed] *The Nonprofit Sector: A Research Handbook* Yale University, Boston, pp 154–166

Kaplan, A (1994) 'NGOs, Civil Society and Capacity Building; Towards a Development Strategy' *AVOCADO Series* vol 5, Olive Information Services, Durban

*Kaplan, A (1996) *The Development Practitioner's Handbook* Pluto Press, London

Karas, J and Coates, B (1994) *Indicators for Sustainable Development* New Economics Foundation, London

Kardam, N (1993) 'Development Approaches and the Role of Policy Advocacy: The Case of the World Bank' *World Development* vol 21 (11), pp 1773–1786

Kawohl, W (1990) 'South–North NGO Relationships: Towards true partnerships? A Case Study of Dutch CFAs and Southern NGDOs' (mimeo) Master's thesis, Institute of Social Studies, The Hague

Keehn, M and Kniep W (1987) *So You Want to Evaluate? Building evaluation into program planning for development education* InterAction, New York

Kelleher, D and McLaren, K (1996) *Grabbing the Tiger by the Tail: NGOs Learning for Organisational Change* Canadian Council for International Co–operation, Ottawa

Kennedy, P (1993) *Preparing for the Twenty–First Century* Harper Collins, New York

Khan, A (1996) *Some Recent experiences of NGOs in Influencing Public Policy in India* Society for Participatory Research in Asia, New Delhi

Khan, S (1994) 'Ranking Social Development Indicators: A Discussion Paper', November, ActionAid, London

Kievelitz, U and Reinke, R (1992) 'Rapid Appraisal of Organisational Cultures: A Challenge for Field Work' *RRA Notes* no 12, International Institute for Environment and Development, London

Kiggundu, M (1994) *Managing Organisations in Developing Countries,* Kumarian Press, West Hartford

Kinyanjui, K (1982) 'The Church and Development' *AACC Bulletin* vol X11 (1), pp 25–31, All Africa Conference of Churches, Nairobi

Klittgard, R (1993) *Tropical Gangsters* Simon and Schuster

Korten, D (1980) 'Community Organisation and Rural Development: a Learning Process Approach' *Public Administration Review*, pp 480–511

Korten, D (1990) *Getting to the 21st Century: Voluntary Action and the Global Agenda* Kumarian Press, West Hartford

Korten, D (1991) 'International Assistance: A Problem Posing as a Solution' *Development Seeds of Change*, No 2/3, Society of International Development, Rome

Korten, D (1995) *When Corporations Rule the World* Earthscan, London

Korten, D and Klauss, R (1984) *People Centred Development: Contributions to Theory and Planning Frameworks* Kumarian Press, West Hartford

Korten, F and Siy, R (eds) (1988) *Transforming a Bureaucracy: The Experience of the Philippine National Irrigation Administration* Kumarian Press, West Hartford

Kotter, J (1996) *Leading Change* Harvard Business School Press, Boston

Krystall, A, Young, S and Waithaka, D (1995) 'NGOs in Kenya: A Review', Report of a Study for Swedish International Development Agency, Matrix Development Consultants, Nairobi

Kubr, M (1993) *How to Select and Use Consultants: A Client's Guide* ILO, Geneva

Kuratov, S and Solyanik, S (1995) 'The Glimmer and Glare of Cooperation', *Ecostan News* August, Almaty

Lal, D (1994) 'Participation, markets and democracy', working paper 12, The World Bank, Washington DC

Lawrie, A (1993) *Quality of Service: Measuring Performance for Voluntary Organisations* National Council of Voluntary Organisations/Director of Social Change, London

Leach, M (1989) *Governance and Control in Value–Based Organizations* December, Institute of Development Research, Boston

Leach, M (1995) 'Models of Inter–Organisational Collaboration in Development' *Institutional Development* vol 2 (1), pp 27–49, Society for Participatory Research in Asia, New Delhi

Leat, D (1993) *Managing Across Sectors: Similarities and Differences Between For–Profit and Voluntary Non–Profit Organisations* VOLPROF, City University Business School, London

LeCompte, B (1986) *Project Aid: Limitations and Alternatives* Development Centre, OECD, Paris

Lee, R (1994) 'From Projects to Advocacy' *Development and Democracy* vol 7, pp 34–43, Urban Foundation, Johannesburg

Lent, T (1988) '5000 Years of Experience: Training and Organizational Development' *NGO Management* vol 9, pp 17–18, International Council of Voluntary Agencies, Geneva

Leonard, D and Marshall, D (1982) *Institutions of Rural Development for the Poor: Decentralization and Organizational Linkages* Institute of International Studies, Berkeley

Lessem, R (1989) *Global Management Principles* Prentice Hall, London

Leurs, R (1993) 'Resource Manual for Trainers and Practitioners of Participatory Rural Appraisal', *Papers in the Adminstration of Development* vol 49, Development Aminstration Group, Birmingham University

*Lewis, R (1996) *When Cultures Clash: Manging Successfully Across Cultures* Nicholas Bealey, London

Lewis, D, Sobhan, B and Jonsson, G (1994) *Routes of Funding, Roots of Trust?: Swedish Assistance to Non–Governmental Organisations in Bangladesh* Swedish International Development Agency, Stockholm

*Lewis, J, et al (1988) *Strengthening the Poor: What Have We Learned?* Overseas Development Council, US–Third World Policy Perspectives, no 10, Washington, DC

Lindenburg, M and Crosby, B (1989) *Managing Development: The Political Dimension* Kumarian Press, West Hartford

Lipshutz, R (1992) 'Reconstructing World Politics: The Emergence of Global Civil Society' *Millenium*, vol 21, pp 389–420

Lissner, J (1977) *The Politics of Altruism: A Study of the Political Behaviour of Voluntary Agencies* Lutheran World Federation, Geneva

Little and van de Geer (1994) *Goal Oriented Project Planning: Manual for Individual*

Procedures Little and van de Geer, Arnhem

Longwe, S (1995) 'A Development Agency as a Patriachal Cooking Pot: The Evaporation of Policies for Women's Advanacement', paper presented at seminar on Women's Rights and Development, One World Action, London

Lovell, C (1992) *Breaking the Cycle of Poverty: The BRAC Strategy* Kumarian Press, West Hartford

Lukes, S (1974) *Power, A Radical View* Macmillan Press, London

MacDonald, M (1994a) *Gender Planning in Development Agencies* Oxfam, Oxford

MacDonald, M (1994b) 'Gender in Partnership: Eurostep Gender Workshop 2', Eurostep, Brussels

MacKeith, J (1993) *NGO Management: A Guide Through the Literature* Centre for Voluntary Organisation, London School of Economics, London

Madrinan, C (1995) 'Influencing Policy – The NGO Lobby on Multilateral Development Banks' *Institutional Development* vol 2 (1), pp 69–74, Society for Participatory Research in Asia, New Delhi

Malena, C (1992) 'Relations between Northern and Southern Non–Governmental Development Organisations' M Phil Dissertation, Institute of Development Studies, Brighton

Malena, C (1995a) 'Relations Between Northern and Southern Non–Governmental Development Organizations' *Canadian Journal of Development Studies* vol 16 (1), pp 7–30

Malena, C (1995b) *Working with NGOs: A Practical Guide to Operational Collaboration between The World Bank and Non–Governmental Organizations* Operations Policy Department, World Bank, Washington, DC

Mamdani, M and Otim, P (1994) *Report of a Survey on Training Needs Assessment of Non–Governmental Organisations [NGOs] in East Africa* Centre for Basic Research/Danish Association for International Cooperation, Kampala and Copenhagen

Maren, M (1994) 'A Different Kind of Child Abuse' *Penthouse*, December, pp 46–74

Marsden, D and Oakley, P (eds) (1990) *Evaluating Social Development Projects*

Oxfam, Oxford

Marsden, D, Oakely, P and Pratt, B (eds) (1994) *Measuring the Process: Guidelines for Evaluating Social Development* International NGO Training and Research Centre, Oxford

Mascarenhas, J (1992) 'Participatory Rural Appraisal and Participatory Learning Methods: Recent Experience from MYRADA in South India' *Forest, Trees and People Newsletter* vol 10–17

Mason, R and Mitroff, I (1981) *Challenging Strategic Planning Assumptions* Wiley, London

McCarthy, K (1989) 'The Voluntary Sector Overseas: Notes From the Field' working papers, Center for the Study of Philanthropy, City University of New York

McKenna, E, and Beech, N (1995) *The Essence of Human Resource Management* Prentice Hall, London

Mendoza, G (1976) 'The Transferability of Western Management Concepts and Programs, an Asian Perspective', in Stifel *et al* (eds) *Education and Training for Public Sector Management in Developing Countries* Rockefeller Foundation, New York, pp 61–72

Miller, E (1979) 'A "Negotiating Model" in Integrated Rural Development Projects', in Gordon Lawrence, W (ed) *Exploring Individual and Organizational Boundaries* John Wiley and Sons, Chichester

Miller, V (1994a) 'Policy Influence by Development NGOs: A Vehicle for Strengthening Civil Society' *IDR Reports* vol 11 (1), Institute of Development Research, Boston

Miller, V (1994b) 'NGOs and Grassroots Policy Influence: What is Success?' *IDR Reports* vol 11 (5), Institute of Development Research, Boston

Mills, D (1988) 'Direct Funding: Implications for Caribbean NGOs' *Development* vol 4, pp 19–25, Society for International Development, Rome

Mink, O, Shultz, J and Mink, M (1991) *Developing and Managing Open Organizations: A Model and Methods for Maximizing Organiational Potential* Somerset, Austin,

*Mintzberg, H (1994) *The Rise and Fall of Strategic Planning* Prentice Hall, New York

Mintzburg, H (1979) *The Structuring of Organisations* Prentice Hall, Englewood Cliffs,

New Jersey

Mitroff, I (1983) *Stakeholders of the Organisational Mind* Jossey–Bass, San Fransisco

*Mooney, T [ed] (1995) *The Challenge of Development in Conflict Zones* Organisation for Economic Co–operation and Development, Paris

*Moore, M (1995) *Institution Building as a Development Assistance Method: A Review of Literature and Ideas* Swedish International Development Authority, Stockholm

Morato, E (1993) *Strategic Intervention for Development Managers* vols I and II, Asian Institute of Management, Manila

Morehouse, W (1991) 'Grass Roots Power: Limiting the Damage from Development Assistance' *Echoes* pp 5–20, International Group on Grass Roots Initiatives, Utrecht

*Moris, J (1981) *Managing Induced Rural Development* International Development Institute, Bloomington

Moris, J (1976) 'The Transferability of the Western Management Tradition to the Non–Western Public Service Sector', in Stifel et al (eds) *Education and Training for Public Sector Management in Developing Countries* Rockefeller Foundation, New York, pp 73–83

Morss, E and Gow, D (1985) *Implementing Rural Development Projects: Lessons from AID and World Bank Experiences* Westview Press, Boulder

Morss, E (1984) 'Institutional Destruction Resulting from Donor and Project Proliferation in Sub–Saharan African Countries', *World Development*, 12(4)

Moser, C (1993) *Gender Planning and Development: Theory, Practice and Training* Routledge, London

Mosley, P and Hudson, J (1995) *Aid Effectiveness: A study of the effectiveness of overseas aid in the main countries receiving ODA assistance* Overseas Development Administration, London

Muchunguzi, D and Milne, S (1995) *Perspectives from the South: A Study on Partnership* CIDA, NGO Division, Ottowa

Murray, V and Tassie, B (1994) 'Evaluating the Effectiveness of Nonprofit Organizations', in Herman, R (ed) *The Jossey–Bass Handbook of Nonprofit Leadership and Management* Jossey–Bass, San Fransisco

Murrell, K and Duffield, R (1985) *Management Infrastructure for the Developing World: a Bibliographic Source Book* Kumarian Press, West Hartford

Mutahaba, G (1989) *Reforming Public Administration for Development: Experiences from Eastern Africa* African Association for Public Administration and Management, Kumarian Press, West Hartford

Myers, R, Ufford, P and Magill, M–S (1989) *On–Site Analysis: A practical approach to organisational change* Oscar Publishers, Etobicoke, Ontario

Mysliwiec, E (1993) 'Cambodia: NGOs in Transition', in Utting, P (ed), *Between Hope and Insecurity: The Social Consequences of the Cambodian Peace Process* United Nations Research Institute for Social Development, Geneva, pp 97–141

Nadler, D and Tushman, M (1988) *Strategic Organization Design: Concepts Tools and Processes* Scott, Foresman, Glenview, Illinois

Nair, B, Mehta, M and Sawhney, M (1995) 'Gender Sensitivity and HRD Policies', Discussion note, HRD Academy, Indian Institute of Management, Ahmedabad

Narayan, D (1993) *Participatory Evaluation: Tools for Managing Change in Water and Sanitation* World Bank, Washington, D.C.

Narayan, D (1995) *Designing Community Based Development*, Participation Series 007, Environment Department, World Bank, Washington, D.C.

Narkwiboonwong, W and Tips, W (1989), 'Project identification, formulation and start-up by voluntary organizations (NGOs) in Thailand's Rural Development', *Public Administration and Development*, vol 9, pp 201–214

Ndegwa, S (1996) *The Two Faces of Civil Society: NGOs and Politics in Africa* Kumarian Press, West Hartford

New Economics Foundation (1995) *Social Audit Resource Kit* New Economics Foundation, London

Ng'ethe, N and Kanyinga, K (1992) 'The Politics of Development Space: The State and NGOs in the Delivery of Basic Services in

Kenya', Working paper 486, Institute of Development Studies, University of Nairobi

Ngugi, A (1994), *Portraits in Participation: Case Studies in Participation from Eastern Africa* CARE International, Nairobi.

NGLS (1992) *Culture and Development, Voices from Africa* Non–Governmental Liaison Service, Geneva

NORAD (1991) *Support to Non–Governmental Organisations' Activities in Developing Countries* Norwegian Agency for International Development, Oslo

NOVIB (1991) 'Strengthening organisations for self–supporting development project policy of NOVIB/ Guest–at–your–Table in the Nineties', NOVIB, The Hague

NSR (1991) *Strengthening the United Nations for the 1990s* North–South Roundtable, Society for International Development, Rome

O' Brien, P (1989) 'Programme advisory note on the appropriate use of volunteers in development: An overview' United Nations Volunteers Programme, Geneva

*O' Leary, M and Simmons, M (1995) *Reflections: A Record of Training from the Evolution of Krom Akphiwat Phum* Overseas Development Bureau of Australia, Canberra and Krom Akphiwat Phum, Battambang

Oakland, J (ed) (1989) *Total Quality Management*, Cotswold Press, Oxford

Oakley, P (1987) 'Participation: State or process, means or end?', *Bulletin*, vol 11, pp 3–9, University of Reading

Oakley, P (1991) *Projects With People: The practice of participation in rural development* International Labour Office, Geneva

Oakley, P and Marsden, D (1982) *Approaches to Participation in Rural Development*, International Labour Office, Geneva

ODA (1992) *Report of Working Group on ODA/NGO Collaboration* Overseas Development Adminstration, London

ODA (1994) 'Stakeholder participation in aid activities', Draft technical note, Overseas Development Administration, UK

ODA (1995a) *A Guide to Social Analysis for Projects in Developing Countries* HMSO, London

ODA (1995b) 'Guidance on How to do Stakeholder Analysis of Aid Projects and Programmes', July, Social Development Department, Overseas Development Administration, London

ODA (1995c) *Institutional Development* Technical note 14, Government and Institutions Department, Overseas Development Administration, London

ODI (1988) 'Development Efforts of NGOs' *Development* vol 4 pp 41–46, Society for International Development, Rome

ODI (1996) 'The Impact of NGO Development Projects', Briefing paper 2, Overseas Development Institute, London

ODI/ECPDM (1995a) *European Union Aid Agencies Comparative Management and Effectiveness Volume II: Six Donor Studies* Overseas Development Insititute/European Centre for Development Policy Management, London/Maastricht.

ODI/ECPDM (1995b) *European Union Aid Agencies Comparative Management and Effectiveness Volume I: Comparative Overview of EU Aid Agencies* Overseas Development Insititute/European Centre for Development Policy Management, London/Maastricht

OECD (1988) *Voluntary Aid for Development: The Role of Non–Governmental Organisations* Organisation for Economic Co–operation and Development, Paris

OECD (1992) 'The Evaluation of Non–Governmental Organisations' Activities, Organisation, Methodology and Results' Organisation for Economic Cooperation and Development, Paris

OECD (1995) 'Statistics of Official Funding to NGOs', (mimeo), Organisation for Economic Cooperation and Development, Paris

Oestergaard, L (ed) (1993) *Gender and Development: A Practical Guide* Routledge, London

Okada, T (1994) *The Global Information Infrastructure and the Work of Private Voluntary Organisations* Food for the Hungry, Washington, DC

Oliveira, A, and Tandon, R (eds) (1994) *Citizens: Strengthening Global Civil Society* CIVICUS, Washington, DC

Osborne, D (1993a) 'Good Governance Initiatives in the Global Context' *Hong Kong Public Administration*, vol 2 (2), pp 107–116,

Hong Kong

Osborne, D (1993b) 'Action for Better Government: A Role for Donors', Bulletin, vol 24 (1) Institute of Development Studies, University of Sussex

Ostrom, E (1990) *Governing the Commons: The Evolution of Institutions for Collective Action*, Cambridge University Press, Cambridge

Otero, M and Rhyne, E (eds) (1994) *The New World of Micro–Enterprise Finance: Building Healthy Financial Institutions for the Poor* Kumarian Press, West Hartford

Oxfam (1985) *The Field Directors' Handbook: An Oxfam Manual for Development Workers* Oxford University Press, Oxford

Oxfam (1994) 'Oxfam Assembly 1994: talking, listening and sharing' Assembly Office, Oxfam, Oxford

Oxfam (1995a) *Guidelines for Strategic Planning, Action Planning and Reporting* Overseas Division, Oxfam, Oxford

Oxfam (1995b) 'Women and Culture' *Gender and Development*, vol 3 (1) Oxfam, Oxford

*Oxfam (1996) *Handbook of Development and Relief* Oxfam, Oxford

PAC (1990) *Partnership: Matching Rhetoric to Reality* Partnership Africa, Canada, Ottawa

PACT (1989) *Trends in PVO Partnership* Private Agencies Collaborating Together, Washington, DC

PACT (1993) *Options for Sustainability: Reader and Report on Endowments as a Modality for Funding Development Work* PACT/PRIP, Bangladesh

Paez, C and Noel Elano, J (1993) 'Financial Sustainability: The Philippine NGO Experience' *Transnational Associations*, vol 5, pp 298–291, New York

Patel, R and Jorgensen, L (1997) *Direct Funding from a Southern Perspective – Strengthening Civil Society?* International NGDO Training and Research Centre, Oxford, forthcoming

Paul, S (1983) *The Strategic Management of Development Programmes: Guidelines for Action* International Labour Organisation, Geneva

Paul, S (1987) 'Community Participation in Development Projects: The World Bank Experience', Discussion paper 6, The World Bank, Washington, DC

Paul, S (1993) 'Making "Voice" Work: A Citizens' Report Card on Public Agencies' October (mimeo), report to PRDPF, The World Bank, Washington, DC

Perera, J (1995) 'In Unequal Dialogue with Donors: The Experience of the Sarvodaya Shramadana Movement' *Journal of International Development*, November – December, vol 7 (6)

Phelps, E (ed) (1975) *Altruism, Morality and Economic Theory* Sage, New York

Picciotto, R (1994) *Institutional Learning and Bank Operations: The New Project Cycle* Operations Evaluation Department, World Bank, Washington, DC

Porter, D, Allen, B and Thompson, G (1991) *Development in Practice: Paved with Good Intentions* Routledge, London

Porter, D and Kilby, P (1996) 'Strengthening the Role of Civil Society? A Precariously Balanced Answer' *Australia's Aid Program*, pp 81–94, Monash Asia Institute

Powell, M (1995) 'Culture: Intervention or Solidarity?' *Development In Practice*, vol 5 (3), pp 196–206, Oxfam, Oxford

Powell, W (ed) (1987) *The Non–Profit Sector: A Research Handbook* Yale University Press, New Haven

Pratt, B and Stone, A (1994) *Multilateral Agencies and Southern NGOs: A Position Paper* International NGO Training and Research Centre, Oxford

PRIA (1982) 'Participatory research: an introduction', Participatory research network series No 3, Society for Participatory Research in Asia, New Delhi

PRIA (1990) *Strengthening the Grassroots: Nature and Role of Support Organisations* October, Society for Participatory Research in Asia, New Delhi

PRIA (1992) *Training of Trainers: A Manual for Participatory Training Methodology in Development* Society for Participatory Research in Asia, New Delhi

PRIA (1993) *Process Documentation in Social Development Programme* Society for Participtory Research in Asia, New Delhi

PRIA (1994) *Participation and Governance*

vol 1 (1–2), Society for Participatory Research in Asia, New Delhi

PRIA (1995) *A Manual for Participatory Training Methodology in Development* Society for Participatory Research in Asia, New Delhi

*Putnam, R (1993a) 'The Prosperous Community: Social Capital and Public Life' *The American Prospect*, Spring pp 35–42

Putnam, R (1993b) *Making Democracy Work* Princeton University Press, Princeton

Rahema, M (1981) *Some Dimensions of People's Participation in the Booma Sena Movement* United Nations Research Institute for Social Development, Geneva

Rahema, M (1985) 'NGO work of organising the poor' *Dossier,* vol 50, International Fund for Africultural Development, Rome

Randel, J and German, T (eds) (1994) *The Reality of Aid* Earthscan, London

Randel, J and German, T (eds) (1995) *The Reality of Aid* International Council of Voluntary Agencies/ActionAid, Geneva and London

Randell, J and German, T (eds) (1996) *The Reality of Aid* Earthscan, London

Randon, A and Perri (1994) 'Constraining campaigning: the legal treatment of non–profit policy advocacy in 24 countries', *Voluntas*, vol 5 (1), pp 27–58

Rao, T (1994) 'Human Development – 1994: HRD Strategies for India and Other Developing Countries', Occasional paper 3, Academy of Human Resource Development, Ahmedabad

Rau, Z (1992) *The Re–emergence of Civil Society in Eastern Europe and the Soviet Union* Westview Press, Boulder, Colorado

Ravallion, M (1992) 'Poverty Comparisons: A Guide to Concepts and Methods', Living Standards Measurement Study working paper 88, The World Bank, Washington, DC

Renshaw, L (1994) 'Strengthening Civil Society: The Role of NGOs', *Development*, vol 4, pp 46–48, Society for International Development, Rome

Richie–Vance, M (1991) 'The Art of Association: NGOs and Civil Society in Colombia', Country focus series 2, InterAmerican Foundation, Rosslyn

Riddell, R (1990) 'Judging Success: Evaluating NGO Approaches to Alleviating Poverty in Developing Countries', April, Working paper 37, Overseas Development Institute, London

Riddell, R (1996) 'Trends in International Co–operation', Paper presented at the Aga Khan Foundation Round Table on Systematic Learning: Promoting Support for Canadian Development Co–operation, Ottawa

Riddel, R, Bebbington, A and Peck, L (1994) *Promoting Development by Proxy: An Evaluation of the Development Impact of Government Support to Swedish NGOs* Swedish International Development Agency, Stockholm

Riddell, R, Bebbington, A and Davis, D (1995) *Developing Country NGOs and Donor Governments* Overseas Development Institute, London

Riddell, R and Robinson, M (1992) 'The Impact of NGO Poverty Alleviation Projects: Results of the Case Study Evaluations', Working paper, 38, Overseas Development Institute, London

*Riddell, R and Robinson, M (1995) *Non–Governmental Organizations and Rural Poverty Alleviation* Clarendon Press, Oxford

Rief, C (1992) 'The Benefits and Risks of Going to Scale', Discussion paper presented to an international seminar on 'Going to scale: BRAC's Experience (1972–1992) and Beyond', Bangladesh Rural Action Committee, Dhaka

Robinson, M (1991) 'Development NGOs in Europe and North America: A Statistical Profile' *Charity Trends*, pp 154–165, Charities Aid Foundation, Tonbridge

Robinson, M (1991a) 'Evaluating the Impact of NGOs in Rural Poverty Alleviation: India Country Study', Working paper 49, Overseas Development Institute, London

Robinson, M (1991b) 'Participatory Impact Evaluation: Reflections from the Field', Paper presented at the Development Studies Association Meeting, 11–13 September, Swansea

Robinson, M (1993c) 'Governance, Democracy and Conditionality: NGOs and the New Policy Agenda', in Clayton, A (ed) *Governance, Democracy and Conditionality: NGOs and the New Policy Agenda* International NGO Training and Research Centre, Oxford

Robinson, M (1995) 'Strengthening Civil

Society in Africa: The Role of Foreign Political Aid', *Bulletin*, vol 26 (2), pp 70– 80, Institute of Development Studies, Brighton

*Robinson, M and Thin, N (1994) *Project Evaluation: A Guide for NGOs* Overseas Development Administration, London

Roche, C (1994) 'Operationality in turbulence: the need to change', *Development in Practice*, vol 4 (3), pp 160–172, Oxfam, Oxford

Roche, C (1995) 'Institutional Learning in Oxfam: Some Thoughts', (mimeo) Policy Department, Oxfam

Roling, N and de Zeeuw, H (1983) 'Improving The Quality of Rural Poverty Alleviation', *Final Report of the Working Party on The Small Farmer and Development Co–operation* International Agricultural Center, Wageningen

Rondinelli, D (1983) *Development Projects as Policy Experiments: An Adaptive Approach to Development Administration* Methuen, London

Rondinelli, D (1986) 'Improving development management: lessons from the evaluation of USAID projects in Africa', *International Review of Administrative Sciences*, vol 52 (4)

Rondinelli, D (1989) 'Decentralizing Public Administrations in Developing Countries: Issues and Opportunities', *Journal of Social, Political and Economic Studies*, vol 14 (1)

Ronfeldt, D and Thorup, C (1993) *North America in the Era of Citizen Networks: State, Society and Security* Rand Corporation, Santa Monica

Rooley, R and White, J (1989) *Management Needs of Voluntary Organisations*, Cranfield School of Management, Cranfield

Rosenau, J (1990) *Turbulence in World Politics: The Theory of Change and Continuity* Harvester-Wheatsheaf, New York

Ross, J, Maxwell, S and Buchanan-Smith, M (1994) 'Linking Relief and Development', Discussion paper 334, Institute of Development Studies, University of Sussex, Brighton

Rossiter, J and Palmer, R (1991) 'Northern NGOs: Some Heretical Thoughts', *Refugee Participation Network*, vol 10, pp 11–15, Queen Elizabeth House, Oxford

*Rossum, C (1993) *How to Assess Your Organization with Peter Drucker's Five Most Important Questions: User Guide* Drucker Foundation/Jossey–Bass, San Francisco

Rowlands, J (1995) 'Empowerment Examined', *Development in Practice*, vol 5 (2), pp 101–107, Oxfam, Oxford

*Rubin, F (1995) *A Basic Guide to Evaluation for Development Workers* Oxfam, UK

Rugh, J (1986) *Self–Evaluation: Ideas for Participatory Evaluation of Rural Community Development Projects* World Neighbours, Oklahoma

*Sahley, C (1995) *Strengthening the Capacity of NGOs: Cases of Small Enterprise Development Agencies in Africa*, NGO Management and Policy Series No 4, International NGO Training and Research Centre, Oxford

Salamon, L (1994) 'The Rise of the Nonprofit Sector', *Foreign Affairs*, vol 73 (2), pp 109–122

Salamon, L M and Anhheier, H (1992) 'Toward an understanding of the international nonprofit sector', Working papers of the John Hopkins Comparative Nonprofit Sector Project 1, John Hopkins Institute for Policy Studies, Baltimore

Salamon, L and Anheier, H (1994) *The Emerging Sector: An Overview* Institute for Policy Studies, The John Hopkins University, Baltimore

Salamon, L (1993) 'The Nonprofit Sector and Democracy: Prerequisite, Impediment or Irrelevance?' Paper presented at a symposium on democracy and the non-profit sector, Alpen Institute, mimeo

Salano, A (1994) *Las ONGs y los cambios en les conceptos y les modalidades de la cooperación internacional* FASE–ALOP, Brazil

*Salmen, L (1992) 'Beneficiary Assessment: An Approach Described', Working paper 1, Poverty and Social Policy Division, The World Bank, Washington, DC

Salmen, L (1993) *Reducing Poverty: An Institutional Perspective* The World Bank, Washington, DC

Sandar, P (1990) 'A History of Philanthropy in India', Report to the Ford Foundation, New Delhi

Sandberg, E (ed) (1994) *The Changing Politics of Non–Governmental Organizations and African States* Praeger, Westport

*SCF (1995) *Toolkits: A Practical Guide to Assessment, Monitoring, Review and*

Evaluation, Development Manual 5, Save the Children Fund, London

SCF (UK) (1994) *Country Strategy Paper Support Pack* Overseas Department, Save the Children Fund, London

Schearer, S B (1994) *The Citizen's Global Trust Fund for Communities* Synergos Institute, New York

Schearer, S and Tomlinson, J (1995) 'Case Studies of Partnership Efforts to Address Poverty and Development Problems in Africa' Policy Discussion Paper, May, Synergos Institute

Schein, E (1987) *Process Consultation: Volume II Lessons for Managers and Consultants*, Addison-Wesley, Wokingham

Schein, E (1988) *Process Consultation Volume I: Its Role in Organization Development* Addison-Wesley, Wokingham

Schlanger, J (1992) 'Les agencias de cooperacion al desarrollo en les años 90', in *Construyendo juntos el futuro*, Insitute of Social Studies/DESCO, Lima, pp 148–150

Schmidt, M and Marc, A (1994) 'Participation in Social Funds', Environment department papers 004, The World Bank, Washington, DC

Schneider, B (1988) *The Barefoot Revolution: A Report to the Club of Rome* Intermediate Technology Publications, London

Schutte, L (1995) *Case Study Project on the Process and Techniques of Foundation-Building in the South: The Kagiso Trust South Africa* Witswatersrand University, Johannesburg

*Scott, W (1987) *Organizations: Rational, Natural and Open Systems* Prentice Hall, Englewood Cliffs, New Jersey

Scott, W and Meyer, J (1994) *Institutional Environments and Organizations: Structural Complexity and Individualism* Sage, London

*Semboja, J and Therkildsen, O (eds) (1995) *Service Provision Under Stress: States and Voluntary Organisations in Kenya, Tanzania and Uganda* James Currey, London

Sen, A (1982) *Poverty and Famines: An Essay on Entitlements and Deprivation* Clarendon Press, Oxford

Senge, P (1990a) 'The Leader's New Work: Building Learning Organisations', *Sloan Management Review Reprint Series*, vol 32 (1),

Massachusetts Institute of Technology, Boston

*Senge, P (1990b) *The Fifth Discipline: The Art and Practice of the Learning Organisation* Doubleday, New York

Serageldin, I and Tabaroff, I (1992) *Culture and Development in Africa*, vols 1 and 2, Proceedings of an International Conference, 2–3 April, The World Bank, Washington, DC

Serrano, I (1994) *Civil Society in the Asia–Pacific Region* CIVICUS, Washington, DC

Shah, P and Shah, M (1995) 'Participatory Methods for Increasing NGO Accountability: A Case Study from India', in Edwards, M and Hulme, D *Non–Governmental Organisations Performance and Accountability: Beyond the Magic Bullet* Earthscan, London, pp 183–191

Shaw, J, Kirkbride, P and Rowland, K (1993) *Research in Personnel and Human Management* JAI Press, Greenwich and London

Shearer, B (1995) *The Emerging Role of Civil Society in International Development: Challenges to Foreign Aid Programs*, Synergos Institute, New York

Schearer, S and Tomlinson, J (1995) *Case Studies of Partnership Efforts to Address Poverty and Development Problems in Africa: Policy Discussion Paper* May, Synergos Institute

*Shetty, S (1994) *Development Projects in Assessing Empowerment* Society for Participatory Research in Asia, New Delhi

Sibanda, H (1994) 'NGO Influence on NGO Policy Making in Zimbabwe' *IDR Reports*, vol 11 (2), Boston

SID (1992) 'Culture, Identity and Global Change' *Development Seeds of Change*, vol 4, Society for International Development, Rome

Sidzoo E, [ed] (1993) *Ontwikkeling ssamen werking Voorbij: naar een cultuurbewuste benedaring* [Beyond Development Cooperation: towards a culture conscious approach] Netherlands Vereniging voor Cultuur en Ontwikkeling/Reseau Sud Nord Cultures et Developpement, Amsterdam and Brussels

Siegel, D and Yancey, J (1992) *The Rebirth of Civil Society: The Development of the Nonprofit Sector in Central Europe and the Role of Western Assistance* Rockefeller Brothers Fund, New York

Singh, N and Titi, V (1994) *Sustainable Livelihoods in Africa: Policy and Community Transition Through Listening and Learning* International Institute for Sustainable Development, Winnipeg

Sklias, P (1993) *The International Political Economy of Non-Governmental Development Organizations (NGDOs): The case of the European Community* Hellenic Institute of Cooperation and Solidarity, Athens

*Small, C (1997) *NGO Management in Conflict Situations* International NGO Training and Research Centre, Oxford, forthcoming

Smillie, I (1987) 'Northern "Donors" and Southern "Partners": Arguments for an NGO Consortium Approach', Paper presented at a workshop on Strategic Issues in Development Management, organized by the Commonwealth Secretariat, the University of Warwick, Warwick

Smillie, I (1994) *Mixed Messages: Public Opinion and Development Assistance in the Nineties* Organisation for Economic Co-operation and Development, Paris

*Smillie, I (1995a) *The Alms Bazaar: Altruism Under Fire – Non-Profit Organizations and International Development* IT Publications, London

Smillie, I (1995b) NGOs: *Learning, Evaluation and the Real Life of Seals* Organisation for Economic Co-operation and Development, Paris

Smillie, I (1995c) *The Cherry Orchard: UNHCR, CARE Canada, and the Low Cost of Assisting Refugees* United Nations High Commission for Refugees, Geneva

Smillie, I, Douxchamps, F, Sholes, R and Covey, J (1996) *Partners or Contractors? Official Donor Agencies and Direct Funding Mechanisms: Three Northern Case Studies – CIDA, EU and USAID* International NGO Training and Research Centre, Oxford

*Smillie, I and Helmich, H (eds) (1993) *Non–Governmental Organisations and Governments: Stakeholders for Development,* Organisation for Economic Co-operation and Development, Paris

Smiricich, L (1983) 'Concepts of Culture and Organizational Analysis' *Administrative Science Quarterly*, vol 28 (3), pp 339–358

Smith, B (1985) 'Non–Profit Organizations and Socioeconomic Development in Columbia', Working paper 2093, Institute for Social and Policy Studies, Yale University

Smith, B (1989) 'NonProfit Organizations and Socioeconomic Development in Latin America', Working papers, Centre for the Study of Philanthropy, City University, New York

*Smith, B (1990) *More Than Altruism: The Politics of Private Foreign Aid* Princeton University Press, Princeton

Smith, C (1994) 'The New Corporate Philanthropy' *Harvard Business Review*, May–June pp 105–116

Smith, J, Pagnucco, R and Romeril, W (1994) 'Transnational social movement organisations in the global political arena' *Voluntas*, vol 5 (2), pp 121–154

*Smith, S and Lipsky, M (1993) *NonProfits for Hire: The Welfare State in the Age of Contracting* Harvard University Press, Cambridge, Massachusetts

Smith-Sreen, P (1995) *Accountability in Development Organizations: Experience in Women's Organizations in India* Sage, New Delhi

Smolar, A (1996) 'Civil Society After Communism: From Opposition to Atomization' *Journal of Democracy*, vol 7 (1), pp 24–38

*Sogge, D (ed) (1996) *Compassion and Calculation* Pluto Press, London

Somerset Group (1993a) *Consulting Roles* Somerset Consulting Group, Austin, Texas

Somerset Group (1993b) *Consulting Journal*, Somerset Consulting Group, Austin, Texas

Spitzberg, I (1987) *Exchange of Expertise: The Counterpart System in the New International Order,* Westview, Boulder, Colorado

Sumariwalla, R (1993) *Helping to Build Civil Societies Worldwide* The United Way, Alexandria

Stacey, R (1996) *Complexity and Creativity in Organizations* Berrett–Koehler, New York

Staudt, K (1990) *Women, International Development and Politics: The Bureaucratic Mire* Temple University Press

Stewart, F (1995) 'Groups for Good or Ill', Paper presented at the 40th Anniversary Conference, Queen Elizabeth House, Oxford

Stewart, I and Joines, V (1987) *TA Today: A New Introduction to Transactional Analysis,*

Lifespace Books, Nottingham

Stiefel, M and Racelis, M (1990) 'The Role and Responsibilities of Government and Development and Donor Agencies', Paper prepared for the International Conference on Popular Participation in the Recovery and Development Process in Africa, Arusha

Stockhausen, J (1983) *The Financing of Self-Help Organizations in the Developing Countries* Friedrich Ebert Stiftung, Bonn

Streeten, P, Emmerij, L and Fortin, C (1992) *International Governance* Institute of Development Studies, University of Sussex, Brighton

*Swieringa, J and Wierdsma, A (1992) *Becoming a Learning Organization: Beyond the Learning Curve* Addison-Wesley, Wokingham

*Tandon, R (1989) *NGO–Government Relations: A source of life or a kiss of death?*, Society for Participatory Research in Asia, New Delhi

Tandon, R (1991a) 'Civil Society, The State and the Role of NGOs', Occasional paper, Institute of Development Research, Boston

Tandon, R (1991b) 'Holding Together: Collaborations and Partnerships in the Real World' *IDR Reports*, vol 8 (2), Institute of Development Research, Boston

Tandon, R (1995) *Networks as Mechanisms of Communication and Influence* Society for Participatory Research in Asia, New Delhi

Tandon, R (1996) *Organisational Development in NGOs: An Overview* Society for Participatory Research in Asia, New Delhi

Tanton, M (ed) (1994) *Women in Management: A developing presence* Routledge, London

Taylor, L and Jenkins P (1989) *Time to Listen: The Human Aspects in Development*, Intermediate Technology Publications, London

Tendler, J (1982) 'Turning Private Voluntary Organisations into Development Agencies: Questions for Evaluation', Program evaluation discussion series 12, United States Agency for International Development, Washington, DC

Tennyson, R (1994) *Tools for Partnership Building* The Prince of Wales Business Leaders Forum, London

Tennyson, R with Marriage, M and Simpson, S (1994) *What is Partnership?: A collection of essays on the theme of cross-sector partnerships for sustainable development* The Prince of Wales Business Leaders Forum, London

Theunis, S (ed) (1992) *Non-Governmental Development Organisations of Developing Countries* Martinus Nijhoff, Dordrecht

Thomas, A (1994) 'Does Democracy Matter? – A comparison of NGOs' influence on environmental policies in Zimbabwe and Botswana', draft *GECOU Working Paper*, ESCOR Project, Setting Environmental Agendas: NGOs, Democracy and Global Politics, at the Open University, Milton Keynes

Thomas, A (1995) 'NGO advocacy, democracy and policy development: some examples relating to environmental policies in Zimbabwe and Botswana', Global Environmental Change – Open University Workshop, Open University, Milton Keynes

Thomas, L (1994) 'HRD Needs of Non-Governmental Organisations' Occasional paper 2, Academy of Human Resource Development, Ahmedabad

Thomas, S (ed) (1993) *Understanding Advocacy: Report of the First ACTIONAID Advocacy Workshop* ACTIONAID, New Delhi

Thurow, L (1996) *The Future of Capitalism* William Morrow, New York

Tilakaratna, S (1987) *The Animator in Participatory Rural Development (Concept and Practice)* International Labour Office, Geneva

Tongswate, M and Tips, W (1988) 'Coordination between Government and Voluntary Organizations [NGOs] in Thailand's Rural Development' *Public Administration and Development* vol 8, pp 401–420

Traidcraft (1993) *Social Audit 1992/1993* Traidcraft, Gateshead

Traidcraft (1994) *Social Audit 1993/1994* Traidcraft, Gateshead

Trompenaars, F (1993) *Riding the Waves of Culture: Understanding Cultural Difference in Business* Nicholas Brealey, London

Tvedt, T (1995) *Non–Governmental Organisations as Channel for Development Assistance: The Norwegian System* Ministry of Foreign Affairs, Oslo

UNCHS/World Bank (1995) 'Urban Indicators Review: The Survey Instrument', Indicators Programme: Monitoring the City, volume 2, United Nations Centre for Human Settlements/ World Bank, Nairobi/Washington, DC

UNDP (1990) *Human Development Report* United Nations Development Programme, Oxford University Press, Oxford

UNDP (1991a) *Human Development Report* United Nations Development Programme, Oxford University Press, Oxford

UNDP (1991b) *Holding Together: Collaborations and Partnerships in the Real World* Bureau for Asia and the Pacific, UNDP, New York

UNDP (1993) *Building Development Projects in Partnership with Communities and NGOs: An Action Agenda for Policy Makers* Bureau for Asia and the Pacific, UNDP, New York

UNDP (1994) *Human Development Report* United Nations Development Programme, Oxford University Press, Oxford

UNDP (1996) *Human Development Report* United Nations Development Programme, Oxford University Press, Oxford

UNICEF (1990) *How to Organize and Run Training Workshops* UNICEF, New York

UNICEF (1993) *Visualization in Participatory Programmes: A manual for facilitators and trainers involved in group events* UNICEF, Dhakar, Bangladesh

UNIFEM/UN–NGLS (1995) *Putting Gender on the Agenda: A Guide to Participating in UN World Conferences* UNIFEM/UN–NGLS, New York and Geneva

Uphoff, N (1986) *Local Institutional Development: An Analytical Sourcebook with Cases* Kumarian Press, West Hartford

Uphoff, N (1987) 'Relations Between Governmental and Non-Governmental Organisations and the Promotion of Autonomous Development', Paper presented at the Experts' Consultation on the Promotion of Autonomous Development, 27–30 October, Noordwijk

Uphoff, N (1988) 'Para-Projects as Alternative Models of International Assistance for Self-Sustainable Development in the 1990s', Supplementary Paper for Colloquium on the Changing Nature of Poverty in the 1990s: A Policy Perspective, Michigan State University, Michigan

Uphoff, N (1991) 'A Field Methodology for Participatory Self-Evaluation' *Community Development Journal*, vol 26 (4), pp 271–286

*Uphoff N (1992a) *Learning from Gal Oya: possibilities for participatory development and post-Newtonian social science* Cornell University Press, Ithaca, NY

*Uphoff, N (1992b) *Local Institutions and Participation for Sustainable Development* Gatekeeper Series 34, June, International Institute for Environment and Development, London

Uphoff, N (1995) 'Why NGOs are not a Third Sector: a Sectoral Analysis with Some Thoughts on Accountability, Sustainability and Evaluation', in Edwards, M and Hulme, D (eds) *Non-Governmental Organisations Performance and Accountability: Beyond the Magic Bullet*, Earthscan, London, pp 17–30

Urquhart, B and Childers, E (1990) *A World in Need of Leadership: Tomorrow's United Nations* Development Dialogue, vol 1–2, Dag Hammarskjöld Foundation, Uppsala

USAID (1982) *Effective Institution Building: A Guide for Project Designers and Project Managers Based on Lessons Learned from the AID Portfolio* AID Program Evaluation Discussion Series Report 11, Washington, DC

USAID (1989a) *AID Evaluation Handbook* AID Program Design and Evaluation Methodology Report 7, Agency for International Development, Washington, DC

USAID (1989b) *Methodologies for Assessing the Impact of Agricultural and Rural Development Projects: A Dialogue* AID Program Design and Evaluation Methodology Report 11, Agency for International Development, Washington, DC

USAID (1989c) *Indicators for Measuring Changes in Income, Food Availability and Consumption, and the Natural Resource Base* AID Program Design and Evaluation Methodology Report 12, Agency for International Development, Washington, DC

USAID (1989d) *Accelerating Institutional Development* PVO Institutional Development Evaluation Series, US Agency for International Development, Bureau for Food, Peace and Voluntary Assistance, Washington, DC

USAID (1990) *Responding to Change:*

Private Voluntarism and International Development Advisory Committee on Voluntary Foreign Aid, United States Agency for International Development, Washington, DC

USAID (1994) 'Civil Society and Democratic Development: A CDIE Evaluation Design Paper', Working paper 211, Centre for Development Information and Evaluation, Washington, DC

USAID (1995) *Core Report of the New Partnerships Initiative* July, United States Agency for International Development, Washington, DC (draft)

Vaill, P (1990) *Managing as a Performing Art* Jossey-Bass, San Francisco

Valderrama, M (1995) *Peru and Latin America in the New Outlook for International Cooperation* Peruvian Social Studies Centre, Lima

van Dijk, M-P (1987) 'Collaboration between government and non-government organizations,' *Development: Seeds of Change*, vol 4, pp 117–121, Society of International Development, Rome

van Dijk, M-P (ed) (1989) *Huidige en Toekomstige Rol van Particuliere Ontwikkelingsorganisaties* [Present and Future Role of Non-Governmental Development Organsiations] Society for International Development and Growth Dynamics Institute, Erasmus University, Rotterdam

van Dijk, M-P (1994) 'The Effectiveness of NGOs: Insights from Danish, British and Dutch Impact Studies' *Schriften des Deutschen Ubersee–Instituts Hamburg*, vol 28, pp 27–42

van Rooy, A (1996a) 'The Growing Influence of NGOs in World Conferences: Canadian and British Lobbying at the 1974 World Food Conference and the 1992 Earth Summit' *World Development*, Washington, DC (forthcoming)

van Rooy, A (1996b) 'Civil Society: The Development Solution', Background paper for the Civil Society Research Project, July, North–South Institute, Ottawa

van Sant, J (1987) *Benefit Sustainability* September, Development Alternatives Inc, Chapel Hill

*van Til, J (1989) *Mapping the Third Sector: Voluntarism in a Changing Social Economy* The Foundation Centre, New York

VeneKlasen, L (1994) 'Building Civil Society: The Role of Development NGOs', Concept paper 1, InterAction, Washington, DC

Verhagen, K (1987) *Self-Help Promotion: a Challenge for the NGO Community* CEBEMO/Royal Tropical Institute, Oegstgeest

*Vincent, F (1989) *Manual of Practical Management: Third World Rural Development Associations* Vols I and II, Development Innovations and Networks, Geneva

Vincent, F (1992) 'For Another Kind of Partnership: New Relationship Between NGOs and Governments', Documents of the Colombo Colloquy, No 05, Development Innovations and Networks, Sri Lanka

*Vincent, F (1994) *Alternative Financing of Third World Development Organizations* Development Innovations and Networks, Geneva

*Vincent, F and Campbell, P (1989) *Towards Greater Financial Autonomy, A Manual on Financing Strategies and Techniques for Development NGOs and Community Organizations* Development Innovations and Networks, Geneva

Vivian, J and Maseko, G (1994) 'NGOs, Participation and Rural Development: Testing the Assumptions with Evidence form Zimbabwe', Discussion paper 49, United Nations Research Institute for Social Development, Geneva

van Tiln, J and Hegyesin, G (1996) 'Education and Training in Non-Profit Management'; paper presented at the International Society for Third Sector Research; Mexico City, July

von Glinow, M (1993) 'Diagnosing "Best Practice" In Human Resource Management Practices' in Shaw, J, Kirkbride, P and Rowland, K *Research in Personnel and Human Management* JAI Press, Greenwich and London, pp 95–112

von Nostrand, C (1993) *Gender Responsible Leadership: Detecting Bias, Implementing Interventions* Sage, London

Voorhies, S (1993) 'Working with Government Using World Bank Funds', Staff working paper 16, World Vision International, Monrovia

Wapenhans, W (1992) *Effective*

Implementation: key to development impact Portfolio Management Task Force, World Bank, Washington, DC

Weil, S and McGill, I (eds) (1990) *Making Sense of Experiential Learning: diversity in theory and practice* Society for Research into Higher Education and the Open University Press, Buckingham

Weisbrod, B (1975) 'Towards a Theory of the Voluntary Non-Profit Sector in a Three Sector Economy' Phelps, E (ed) (1975) *Altruism, Morality and Economic Theory* Russell Sage, New York, pp 171–196

*Weisbord, M (1991) *Productive Workplaces: Organising and Managing for Dignity, Meaning and Community* Jossey-Bass, Oxford

Wheatley, M (1994) *Leadership and the New Science* Berrett Koehler, San Francisco

Whitaker, B (1974) *The Foundations: An Anatomy of Philanthropy and Society* Eyre Methuen, London

White, G (1994) 'Civil Society, Democratization and Development [1]: clearing the analytical ground' *Democratization*, vol 1 (3), pp 375–390

White, S (1996) 'Depoliticising development; the uses and abuses of participation' *Development in Practice*, vol 6 (1), pp 6–15, Oxfam, Oxford

Whiting, S (1989) *The Non-Governmental Sector in China: A Preliminary Report* July, (mimeo) The Ford Foundation, Beijing

Wield, D (1995) 'Beyond the Fragments: Integrating Donor Reporting Systems to Support African Universities: Final Report to SAREC', January, Centre for Technology Strategy, Open University, Milton Keynes

Wiggins, S (1985) 'The Management of Rural Development Projects in Developing Countries', Farm Management Unit Study 5, University of Reading

Williams, S with Seed, J and Mwau, A (1994) *The Oxfam Gender Training Manual* Oxfam, Oxford

Wils, F (1995) *NGOs in Latin America: Past Strategies, Current Dilemmas, Future Challenges* International NGO Training and Research Centre, Oxford

Wim, P (1989) *Development at the Grassroots: A Social Approach* World Bank, International Economic Relations Division, Washington, DC

Winter, A (1995) *Is Anyone Listening?:*

Communicating Development in Donor Countries UN Non-Governmental Liaison Service, Geneva

*Wolfe, A (1989) *Whose Keeper?: Social Science and Moral Obligation* University of California Press, Berkeley

Woods, A (1995) 'An Analysis of the Overseas Development Administration's Proposal to Directly Fund Southern NGOs', MSc dissertation, University of London, London

World Bank (1992) *Governance and Development* April, The World Bank, Washington, DC

World Bank (1994a) *The World Bank and Participation* Operations Policy Department, World Bank, Washington, DC

*World Bank (1994b) *World Bank Sourcebook on Participation* Environment Department, the World Bank, Washington, DC

World Bank (1996) *The World Bank and NGOs* Poverty and Social Policy Department, World Bank, Washington, DC

World Vision (1996) *NGOs and the World Bank – Critical Engagement* World Vision UK, Milton Keynes

*Wuyts, M, Mackintosh, M and Hewitt, T, (eds) (1992) *Development Policy and Public Action* Open University/Oxford University Press, Milton Keynes and Oxford

Yankelovich, D (1996) 'Public Judgement on Development Aid', in Foy and Helmich (eds), *Public Support for International Development* Organisation for Economic Co-operation and Development, Paris, pp 55–66

Young, G, Samarasinghe, V and Kusterer, K (1993) *Women at the Centre: Development Issues and Practices for the 1990s* Kumarian Press, Connecticut

Zadek, S (1996) 'Looking Back from 2010', in Sogge, D [ed] *Compassion and Calculation* Pluto Press, London, pp 24–35

*Zadek, S and Evans, R (1993) *Auditing the Market: A Practical Approach to Social Auditing* New Economics Foundation/ Traidcraft, London and Gateshead

Zadek, S and Raynard, P (1949) *Accounting for Change: The Practice of Social Auditing* New Economics Foundation, London

Zadek, S and Szabo, S (1994) *Valuing Organisation: The Case of Sarvodaya* New Economics Foundation, London

Notes

Introduction

[1] In reviewing current research on non-profits, Hall argues that the current task is not to appropriate or apply theory from elsewhere, but to build theory (Hall, 1995; Horton-Smith, 1995). This book may make a modest contribution by describing the behaviour of NGDOs which includes cross-cultural and cross-national dimensions.

[2] The business management guru Peter Drucker first voiced the heretical idea that non-profits had something to teach business (1989a); he later he went on to establish a Foundation for the study and improvement of non-profit management.

[3] Handy, 1985, p. 10.

Chapter 1

[1] The topic of this book allows for a simple distinction between countries which provide and countries which utilise development assistance. The terms used to describe this difference are the North, comprising the 21 OECD countries, and the South, comprising traditional recipients of aid. Countries previously in the Soviet Union, currently in transition to market-based economies, which also receive aid will be referred to as the East.

[2] Between 1985 and 1995, the proportion of poor people in the world grew by 17 per cent to 1.6 billion, with income distribution worsening within and between countries (UNDP, 1996). Today, the top 20 per cent of the world population receives 82.7 per cent of world income, the bottom 20 only 1.4 per cent. These disparities are skewed against women.

[3] As it stands, international aid relies on a deficit view of the South and East; that these countries lack money, expertise and, now, appropriate capacity and institutions for generating growth. An alternative view is that power relations aided by differential control on and access to markets, keep people poor and marginalised. Thus, mobilisation and empowerment are called for; trying to make good deficits that will be appropriated by the better placed is not the answer to poverty alleviation. Another view, put forcefully forward by Graham Hancock (1989), is that the aid system in fact worsens poverty because it is exploitive, self-serving and dependency-creating, delivering more to the North than to the South (Korten, 1991).

[4] A distinction is usually made between absolute and relative poverty. Absolute poverty is typically set at the level of expenditure required for a minimum adult food intake of about 2250 calories per day, plus the consumption of a few non-food necessities. Relative poverty is calculated as the proportion of the population with consumption expenditure below a cut-off point chosen as a percentage of the average expenditure of the poor.

[5] The writings of Amartya Sen have shifted thinking about the nature of poverty. His position, with its notion of 'entitlements' is premised on the right to life and livelihood which many NGDOs would ascribe to (Sen, 1982).

[6] Poverty lines are commonly constructed to assess and compare the proportion of people who can be classed as poor. This measure is normally calculated on the basis of per capita income or consumption which are assumed to reasonably equate with well-being, which is not necessarily the case. The Human Development Index developed by UNDP (1991a), recognises other dimensions of poverty that cannot be expressed by consumption.

[7] Not only do most NGDOs not have a clear theory of the causes of poverty, even less have a theory – even with a small 't' – of social change to underpin their strategies and operational methods.

[8] Governance is a post Cold War dimension to development, introduced by the official aid community to further the conditions they believe to be necessary for the effective functioning of market economies. The mode of governance being put forward imposes a Western model which commonly ignores the historical and cultural realities of many countries in the South and East.

9   Fowler, 1992a.

10 Chambers, 1983, pp. 108-114.

11 Lewis, et al, 1988.

12 The formulation 'broad-based growth' is adopted to differentiate from the discredited 'growth with trickle down' approach propagated in the 1960s.

13 Fierlbeck, 1997, is a good critique and Oliveira and Tandon (eds.), 1994, a good comparative overview.

14 Julie Fisher identifies the creation of networks between grassroots organisations (GROs) as a key step in forming social movements which are often a major force for change in the existing political and economic order, (Fisher, 1993, p. 207). See also Chapter 9.

15 Reviews of NGDO performance indicate that financial appraisals, such as cost-benefit analysis, are a major area of NGDO weakness.

16 I am grateful to Tom Lent for this formulation and many other comments on drafts of this chapter.

17 Rowlands, 1995.

18 Friere, 1973; Shetty, 1994, pp. 5-10.

19 There is still no real resolution on whether empowerment implies a zero or positive sum game. In other words, does power gained by one group mean a corresponding loss for another, or does power alter bargaining relations at a new level of total power? See Hulme and Turner, 1990.

20 This framework could be shifted upwards so that micro becomes the national level with macro corresponding to the international order. Shifting the framework downwards permits analysis of what goes on within households, for example, differences in well-being between men, women and children, and in relation to power in communities and local institutions.

21 Chapter 2 explains the difference between institution and organisation.

22 Some political scientists will have a problem with the notion of a 'growing' civil society as it implies that it does not yet exist. In my view, civil formations are always present but may not be in a form that is recognised or valued as such by Western eyes.

23 This is supposed to be an effect of structural adjustment reforms.

24 The separation between political and economic power is an important precondition for the evolution of a 'modern' type of civil society (Gellner, 1994).

25 Public choice theory suggests that it is not possible for government agents to represent the interests of other parties in decision-making (Gerson, 1994).

26 This is actually a naive statement because in many countries the major economic policy choices are determined by bond markets and IMF and World Bank conditions, irrespective of what people's chosen representatives might prefer to decide.

27 van Rooy, 1996a.

28 A summary of best practice in credit for the unbankable is Otero and Rhyne, 1994.

29 For an analysis of NGDO experience in policy advocacy see Edwards, 1993. For comparison of influencing the World Bank, UNDP and The Ford Foundation in the area of gender see Kardam, 1993.

30 There seem to be two distinctive uses for the term 'development education'. In the South it has been applied to empowerment. It is used instead of 'conscientisation' because it is less likely to attract unwanted government attention. In the North this term often corresponds to public education about development.

31 Social Watch is a recent example of an NGDO initiative to systematically gather and publish information on governments' compliance with commitments they made at the Social Summit (Insititute de Tercer Mundo, 1996).

32 This shift in stance is a feature of new social movements discussed in Chapter 9.

33 For some economists, the cost-benefit case for participation has still not been sufficiently demonstrated resting on an assumption that 'participation' is only significant in micro-development work done by soft social scientists. This is a gross misreading of the principle which is equally relevant for negotiating loans. Lack of 'ownership' of loans by governments due to

inadequate involvement, for instance, participation of recipients, was identified as one reason for the decreasing performance of the Bank's lending portfolio (Wapenhans, 1992). The principle of participation, as a stance in all lending interactions, makes business sense.

34 The term 'authentic participation' comes from Oakley, 1991.

35 Fowler and Biekart, 1996.

36 OECD, 1995. This report also confirms the 8.2 per cent reduction in total ODA between 1992 and 1993. 1995 recorded a further fall of 9.3 per cent to US$59 billion.

37 UNDP estimates that, at best, NGDO initiatives may assist only 20 per cent of the world's poor, but less is more probable (UNDP, 1994).

Chapter 2

1 An example is to be found in Sjef Theunis, 1992.

2 There are major arguments against this shorthand. The first is political and is a reaction against a state-centric view of society. People have always been doing things for others; this has never been the sole terrain of governments. In addition, in non-Western societies, much of economic life is informal and closely tied to household survival and social reproduction (Tandon, 1991a). The second argument stems from today's thinking in management science which sees organisations as complex systems with characteristics which can be found in state, market and voluntary organisations and which are showing signs of converging, making the sector view outdated and unhelpful in understanding the way they work. Finally, the three-sector view does not readily display power relations between the sectors, which tends to work against the interests of the poor. Despite these arguments, the three-sector model is still one of the least difficult ways to sort out the organisational world, there is no really practical alternative on offer, yet!

3 Co-operatives are a special mix of the two in that they are expected to make money for members while selling goods and services to third parties.

4 Salamon and Anheier, 1994.

5 Compliance is the technical term used for gaining required behaviour (Etzioni, 1971).

6 Empowering staff is now a fashion with the business sector – an area where they can potentially learn from non-profits.

7 A distinguishing feature of business and non-profit service providers is thought to lie in attitudinal differences which result from the principle of re- or non-distribution of profits. Businesses re-distribute profits to owners and sometimes to employees leading to acquisitive self-interested stances and extractive interactions with clients which is not the case with value-driven employees leading to better client-centred performance. This is one reason, for example, that people expect better treatment – in the widest sense – from a hospital run under the auspices of a charity or religious order than one run as a profit-making venture. Different operating principles give rise to different qualities of inter-personal behaviour.

8 Forming cartels and lobbying legislators are two common ways in which business try to shape the environment in their favour.

9 I am grateful to David Brown of IDR for this observation and other suggestions on a draft of this chapter.

10 Exceptions can be found in Northern hospitals or educational establishments, usually religious in nature, which recover the full cost of services from patients.

11 It could be argued that there is little real difference because shareholders are in a similar position to donors. While perhaps in a similar position theoretically, this is not the case in practice. Shareholder behaviour differs markedly because (a) real-time market information on share values allows continuous comparative decision-making, which is not the case for the voluntary sector; (b) the bulk of commercial investments are made by professional institutional shareholders, rather than individuals, and (c) the moral return expected by donors to voluntary

organisations is intrinsically different from economic returns, which calls for management to use other measures.

12 Summaries and critiques of NGDO comparative advantages are in Tendler, 1982; Fowler, 1988, 1990a.

13 The technical term for this is 'fiduciuary trust', in other words the confidence that funds will be applied for the purposes and in the ways agreed irrespective of a formal contract.

14 Chapter 6 contains the relevant figures.

15 Horch argues that four effects in the aid system reduce the level of member-solidarity within non-profits. His effects correspond to the overlapping and shifting resource base of NGDOs. His hypotheses are: a) the greater the degree of monetarisation of a voluntary association, the less the degree of member solidarity; b) the greater the formalisation the less the solidarity; c) the greater the financial commercialisation, the less the solidarity; and d) the greater the externalisation of financing the less the solidarity (Horch, 1995). All these features alter the culture of the organisation and the firmness of position in the third sector.

16 An observation of Dr. Rajesh Tandon, Executive Director of PRIA, New Delhi.

17 Sogge (ed.), 1996.

18 Economists apply the notion of transaction costs to explain this difference. The more transactions and time involved in reaching a decision the more its costs. There is, however, increasing evidence that performance in implementing decisions decreases if those who have to do so are not consulted, hence the economic attraction of quality circles in production processes. The current fashion in business for facilitative and consultative management, instead of the more traditional direct approaches, suggests that, again, for-profits may have something to learn from NGDOs on striking a balance between the two.

19 Uphoff, 1995.

20 My thanks go to people too numerous to name who have contributed to this list.

21 The beliefs which a person holds are the most fundamental basis for their behaviour and underpin their values.

22 Fowler, 1991a.

23 Presentation by Dr. Hussein Adam at the Conference of the African Studies Association, 2–9 November 1990, Baltimore.

24 A chief executive can be instrumental in shaping board composition. In such a situation the oversight role of the board can be severely weakened and public accountability lost all together.

Chapter 3

1 There are cases where an NGDO's existence is itself a desired result. This can occur where political regimes are authoritarian.

2 See Lessem, 1989, pp. 556-574.

3 The reorientation of DESCO cost 30 staff positions.

4 There is obviously a danger of Western ethnocentric values being pushed and this type of exercise is a minefield of absolutism versus relativism. But to ignore these difficulties does not make them go away, as any international NGDO will tell you – be it in dealing with salary differences between local and expatriate staff or 'imposing' gender as an issue. In fact, one sign of a professional NGDO is that they have worked through such areas of contention and found their own, often uneasy, solutions which become part and parcel of organisational culture.

5 The planning exercise can and should be used to clarify, share, reaffirm and internalise identity.

6 I advise NGDO managers to read Mintzberg (1994).

7 Bouwman, 1990.

8 Further readings contain examples of the recently published NGDO strategic planning guides.

9 An extreme case I came across was where only three out of 11 existing Southern partners would qualify within the strategy chosen by a Northern NGDO.

10 Confusingly, the term 'programme' is also

used by official aid agencies as the label for pre-agreed allocations of funds to NGDOs. In other words not project by project funding.

11 I am grateful to Simon White, formerly Oxfam Systems Manager for this information.

12 Having spent some time as a donor, I know only too well of conversations about funding criteria, priorities and preferences which appear in proposals. The 'echo' effect.

13 Mintzburg (1979 pp. 479-480), in his seminal book on organisational structure speculated on the existence of a type specifically attuned to non-profit activity – he termed this the missionary structure. He could not make up his mind whether it was just a hybrid of the five other types he had defined or was indeed a sixth, co-ordinated through standardisation of norms, or ideology.

14 If a book is a place for voicing personal laments, one of mine is the damage being done to NGDOs by consultants who have insufficient understanding of the missions, contexts and the on-the-ground nature of sustainable development activity. Such advisers are hired, in part, because of commercialising pressures which places a false premium on for-profit experience. Consequently, interpretations and explanations are generic, partial and make inappropriate comparisons, which leads to less than adequate advice.

15 The concept of integrated development, for which there are still contending interpretations, has been around since the 1970s. The basic obstacle to truly people-centred development is the paradox that organisations need missions which tend to isolate out and prioritise only certain parts of the human condition.

16 The background and perspectives of the chef executive are vital in setting the overall balance between the 'doing' and administration of development.

17 The term 'structured flexibility' was used by Brinkerhoff and Ingle (1989) in relation to development management. From an organisational perspective, structured flexibility is a relationship between people, structure and systems which produces processes that integrate organisational consistency, such as common planning, human resource management and paperwork, with a capacity to continually reconsider, learn and adapt.

18 For a discussion on trade-offs in decentralisation see Fowler, 1992c.

19 The separation of responsibility and accountability is an all too common feature on NGDO management which often stems from personal insecurity within the leadership.

20 Mark Leach identifies franchising as one of six partner-type relationships derived from a study of PLAN International in India (Leach, 1995).

21 Blankenburg, 1993

22 Leach, op cit.

23 Evaluation has not been mentioned, because this is a means for learning – not a function in and of itself.

24 Edwards, 1995, p. 3; Carroll, 1992.

25 A more far-reaching approach is to allocate an agreed amount to the change agent set against negotiated, monitored performance criteria, empowering him or her to manage expenditures with stakeholders.

26 Another reason for this is that core organisational costs are 'skimmed' off of implemented projects.

27 A term borrowed from Ian Smillie.

28 A good example of the internal critical reflection process is to be seen in the CDRA 1995/1996 Annual Report.

29 This listing draws, amongst others, on an unpublished draft paper by Chris Roach of Oxfam UK/I.

30 Many big US NGDOs also have such offices with their headquarters in cheaper locations.

31 A more technical decision is whether advocacy and lobbying is treated as an operational area or as a staff function. In other words, does it rank equally with micro development in directly 'producing' the organisation's purpose or is it treated as a supportive task? When treated as an

operational function, collaboration needs to be structured along the lines of a matrix where staff in different departments form teams around an agreed action and campaign. When regarded as a supportive function, advocacy and lobbying skills are more easily seconded.

32 Cross-cutting issues, such as debt and gender equity, have no natural geographic 'home'. Consequently, there is no straightforward criteria for allocating them to an operational region. Be that as it may, NGDOs must continually draw on evidence from real life experience. So, even if advocacy staff are located in a central unit, financing from all regional budgets would help tie cross-cutting issues to reality in the South and East.

33 I am grateful to Tom Carroll for these observations.

Chapter 4

1 See publications of the South-North Network Cultures and Development as well as NGLS, 1992; Sidzoo (ed.), 1993; Cernea, 1993.

2 *Cultures and Development*, No 24, 1996, p. 14.

3 Hofstede, 1983, 1984; 1991.

4 op cit, 1991, p. 54.

5 op cit,1991, p. 99.

6 A common outcome of these preferences is a less strict dividing line between public and private goods, called corruption.

7 Attention to the cultural dimensions of development is relatively recent and not taken with the seriousness it deserves, partly because it throws up awkward issues about the North's cultural traits and their implicit imposition through aid.

8 Hofstede, 1983, p. 40.

9 Class of international air travel is another proxy indicator of life-style orientations.

10 The same measure can be applied to consultants' fees.

11 Theunis (ed.), 1992, p. 278.

12 Perera, 1995.

13 Zadek and Szabo, 1994; Lewis 1996.

14 This statement does not imply that it is

illegitimate to induce cultural change, only that it must not be imposed.

15 The issue of cultural acceptance and relativism becomes emotionally loaded when it concerns topics such as protection of human rights, female genital mutilation, gender equity and so on. While likely to remain unresolved between different cultures, the point of departure for international NGDOs is that if you want to operate in someone else's country, the onus is on you to show respect – not blind acceptance – for your host's cultural mix. It is not just morally right, it is good development practice because sustainability is a more likely outcome.

16 Graham, 1991.

17 Observers of management in the South note that how a leader or manager is appreciated by staff has as much to do with the person's linkages into wider society as is does with their formal role and position.

18 There is a trend towards team-leadership in Northern NGDOs which includes the chief executive and senior managers. Team management is then found at other levels.

19 Fernades and Carneiro, 1991, p. 6.

20 Ninos de les Andes works for the rights of children. Its founder, Jaime Jaramillo, is a strong, high profile spokesperson whose confrontational style has led to friction with the state and local jealousy, resulting in the witholding of licences and personal vendettas.

21 Interview with Farouk Ahmed, Executive Director, PROSHIKA.

22 One such programme is being jointly developed by BRAC in Bangladesh, ORAP in Zimbabwe and World Learning of the USA.

23 A report of this dialogue has been published entitled *Singing the Same Song*.

24 A more detailed proposal on content can be found in Fowler, Campbell and Pratt, 1992, Appendix II.

25 This section draws on input and advice from Nicky May. I am very grateful for her guidance and education on gender in development and in NGDOs.

26 Moser, 1993; Oestergaaard, 1993.

27 See *The Oxfam Handbook of Development and Relief*, 1993, pp. 200-211.

28 Goetz, 1992.

29 My own observations suggest that a comparison between non-profits and commercial companies would show a higher proportion of women further up in the organisation, but I do not know of any study which would confirm or refute this.

30 Golf courses, clubs and male toilets are not unusual locations.

31 MacDonald, 1994b.

32 A new field in HRM for some NGDOs emerges from their work on complex humanitarian emergencies (CHE). Increasingly, NGDOs must deal with trauma and psychological stress experienced by staff working in CHEs where their 'neutrality' rests on a knife edge. Providing an adequate psycho-social support system must now be added to the HRM repertoire.

33 For an introduction to HRM, see McKenna and Beach, 1995.

34 Bureaucratic hygiene is the boring but necessary routine tasks which keep the organisation 'clean' and healthy. Typically, these include filing documents, timely response to correspondence, regular staff appraisals, the discipline of accounting and donor reporting and so on.

35 Organisational psychology applies psychological insights to understand how groups behave. Basic psychological features, such as need for respect, avoidance of fear and anxiety, aggression, dependency and so on, steer people towards or away from particular types of organisations. The three organisational sectors in society described in Chapter 2 offer different sorts of solutions to psychological pre-dispositions and needs. The state sector provides authority and strong leadership which may satisfy a person's need for security and dependency. Business and the market can satisfy needs for aggression towards, or flight from, enemies. The third sector offers association and 'pairing', satisfying the need for an ideal relationship, human solidarity and oneness (Dartington,

1994).

36 The mechanism of buying competent people out of NGDOs into the official aid system is creating an unhealthy upward spiral in NGDO costs because they have to compete to retain or attract people who can do the work donors expect with the necessary quality. In turn, donors must pay more to attract NGDO people and so it goes on.

37 Where economies are collapsing, who can take issue with an individual choosing for the means to educate children and build up reserves.

38 Constantino-David, 1995, p. 156. This article is a good examination of the trade-offs between internal–external community organisers.

39 Burkey, 1993, p. 73-83.

40 Umtali, quoted in Burkey, op cit, p. 76.

41 For a survey of training in participatory development approaches see IIED, 1994b.

42 DELTA is Development Education and Leadership Training for Action, which uses a neo-Freirian approach to community mobilisation. See Hope and Timmel, 1984.

43 Empowerment of staff is a prevailing concern, or fashion, with the Western business world. The trust which this involves is, however, difficult to cultivate when career guarantees turn out to be worthless because of down-sizing. Too much trust can also lead to bankruptcy as it did with Tim Leason and Barings Bank.

44 See Berg, 1994, and further readings. The widely acknowledged failure of technical assistance (TA) has still not led to necessary changes in donor behaviour. Under the headline 'Reliance on overseas experts decried', it was pointed out by the World Bank representative in Nairobi that spending on technical cooperation in some African countries has exceeded wage bills of the entire civil service. It was questioned whether such spending had produced commensurate returns. The conference at which this took place agreed that it had not. Reported in The Daily Nation, 19th January, 1996. TC is probably one of the most lamentable shortcomings and wastes

in international aid.

45 Crewe, 1994, p. 1.

46 Organisational induction to NGDOs is usually a sorry, hurried affair. Culture, ritual and language are all to be learnt by exposure to the job, hopefully before the project ends or the contract is over.

47 This section draws on a study commissioned by ActionAid UK.

Chapter 5

1 A key factor influencing the choice of a local organisation is whether or not the intervention will provide a private benefit (such as higher individual income) or a public good (such as a communal water point or road). Complex cases occur when collective control is required to obtain individual benefit, as in small-scale irrigation schemes or individual credit which rely on mutual social control (Uphoff, 1992).

2 This not an overidealised view of tradition, which often provides an oppressive form of security, the Indian caste system being one example. The point is not to assume that new is better but to start from the principle of respecting what exists.

3 A useful article on comparative experience of NGDOs building local institutions is Howes, 1996.

4 Promoted by reflective-practitioners, like Anisur Rahman, an intervention approach to development has been around since the 1970s but has not become mainstream.

5 Ten Week Development Management Course of the Society for Participatory Research in Asia, New Delhi.

6 For a model of negotiation which reconciles top-down and bottom-up approaches, see Miller 1979.

7 Jena, 1995.

8 'Appreciative Inquiry' is a recent future-focused addition to the participatory development tool kit which could be applied in an entry process. The method emphasises that people build on positive experiences towards a desired future instead of starting with their needs and structural

constraints as problems to be solved (Cooperrider et al, 1995). My own view is that entry should focus on dialogue towards joint action using a mix of methods which bring together past learning, present difficulties and potentials, and a future vision founded on local values and aspirations.

9 A crucial difference is between project and programme funding, explained in Chapter 6.

10 Petty and Chambers, 1993.

11 Robert Chambers has drawn attention to the disparity between outsiders' measures of poverty and those of poor people themselves. Whose measure counts most? From a people-centred development perspective, it is far more likely that people's motivation will stem from their own experience and reality of poverty (Chambers, 1997).

12 The difference between outputs, outcomes and impacts in development is explored in Chapter 7.

13 The advantage of a mobilisation-only approach contradicts the conclusion reached in Chapter 1 and only works if there are other resources around to be mobilised and accessed by the poorest. If not, mobilisation-only can simply lead to frustration.

14 For example, the IFI process of design using external consultants keeps control out of the hands of the borrower until the loan is approved. The struggle then is to ensure ownership is transferred. Often this does not occur, contributing to a significant reduction in performance of a lending portfolio.

15 Expatriate-dominated, project-management units set up by donors, with government-seconded staff paid additional allowances to reduce internal friction, are notorious obstacles for the responsible ministries being able to feel and exercise real ownership.

16 Project thinking and funding has worked against many NGDOs adopting an intervention approach in their work and relationship with CBOs.

[17] Howes, 1996.

[18] Stewart and Joines, 1987.

[19] On a ranking of over-loaded and abused concepts in the development lexicon, 'partnership' probably ranks second to 'participation', with 'empowerment' a close third. These terms are appropriated by agencies and turned into institution-specific instruments, often totally distorting their original meaning, undermining their value and usefulness. It is vitally necessary for healthy relationships to clarify what a development organisation understands by the terms it uses.

[20] Both quotes from Valderrama, 1995.

[21] Putnam, 1993a, 1993b.

[22] Brett, 1993.

[23] Emerging evidence supports the argument that shared organisational culture, decentralisation and staff participation are good for business performance (Stewart, 1995). This position calls for the empowerment of employees in for-profit enterprise.

[24] Churches, trade unions, women's organisations can most easily identify with a constituency elsewhere, referred to as their 'natural' partners (Fowler, 1991a).

[25] CDRA, 1996, p. 19.

[26] Interview with Farouk Ahmed, Executive Director of PROSHIKA.

[27] Leach (1995) identifies six types of collaboration between international and national NGDOs.

[28] The benefits are not mutually exclusive; in fact they tend to nest in each other up the scale, each higher level incorporates those below. For example, information exchange is found in all other levels, consortia contain alliances, and so on.

[29] Bennett, 1994, 1995.

[30] For those with an academic interest in networks, telecommunications theory offers a good starting point.

[31] A common process in network evolution is for a small group of NGDOs working on the same issue to decide to launch a network with one member acting as the administrative home. Obtaining donor funding shifts the network into a more formal status.

[32] Network financing is fashion driven, with UN Conferences – Environment, Social Development, Women, AIDS, Sustainable Cities – being natural sources of temporary money for national, continental and global NGDO networks. Donor appreciation of the continuing value of informal networks does not appear to be high (Fisher, 1993, p. 158).

[33] Membership of many networks is also used to increase the chance of accessing resources, by increasing the likelihood of being invited to international conferences.

[34] Information from Allan Kaplan, CDRA, Cape Town.

[35] Personal communication.

[36] The initiative had a turbulent start as a reaction against the Philippine government's intention to claim Global Environment Funds with the help of the World Wildlife Fund.

[37] Implicitly, of course, these policies do become binding to the extent that they condition the banks' behaviour in negotiating with NGDOs in relation to grants, loans or economic and sector work.

[38] While NGDOs might argue that the best regulation is no regulation, this is not socially responsible. However, in principle, NGDOs should not have to face more stringent regulation than other legally constituted bodies, as for example, charities do in Britain (Edwards, 1996a).

[39] Competition for representation is not unknown; some might say it is too common.

[40] Official donors have had a hand in starting new or converting old NGDO co-ordinating bodies with very mixed results, particularly negative when these bodies are used as funding channels to their members. Inappropriate funding by official aid has been identified as the greatest threat to consortium (read co-ordinating body) viability (O'Brien, 1991).

[41] A number of unsuccessful candidates in Cambodia's UNTAC-managed elections have created NGDOs as shadow parties in waiting.

[42] Personal communication from Jon Bennett.

[43] UNDP advocated a policy of including an

amount equivalent to 0.5 per cent of project funds to enable NGDOs to support and engage with their co-ordinating bodies. This valuable suggestion of enabling supply instead of funding demand was not taken up. Enabling demand is an innovation long overdue in the aid system.

44 A co-ordinating body's ability to act as a mediator and bridge within the sector and to others is greatly increased when its staff have backgrounds in different institutions.

45 Interview with Quazi Faruque Ahmed, ADAB Chairman.

46 A list by Ball and Dunn, 1995 p. 65, offers some pointers.

47 The fashionable term is an 'enabling environment'.

48 Tandon; 1989

49 The change of regime in South Africa has caused turmoil for local NGDOs who no longer have the anti-apartheid struggle as primary rationale and source of identity. What is their role? How should they relate to ANC brothers and sisters in arms who are now ministers and senior civil servants?

50 There are instances, examined in Chapter 2, where by default or design NGDOs are not legally recognised.

51 Farrington and Bebbington, 1993.

52 Smith, 1990, p. 259-261.

Chapter 6

1 Smillie and Helmich (eds), 1993.

2 Interview with Martha Arengo and Glen Nimnicht, founders of CINDE.

3 The level of official funds invested in development education is dismally low (Randell and German, 1994).

4 Smillie and Helmich, op cit.

5 NOVIB, 1991.

6 Blankenburg, 1993.

7 The Ford Foundation is a positive example. Wield (1995) illustrates how conflicting donor administrative demands mess up African institutions.

8 Dreesman, 1987.

9 In mid 1996, two-thirds of the way through their electoral term, Britain's Conservative government decided to reduce aid

allocations by 20 per cent and concentrate on the world's 20 poorest countries.

10 This fortunate situation stems from the history and domestic role of NGDOs and the nature of a political system based on proportional representation and coalition government. Essentially two-party systems are less reliable when it comes to funding NGDOs over the long term as Canada, Britain and USA demonstrate.

11 Commercial banks are uncomfortable extending overdrafts to NGDOs, especially in the South and East, firstly because they seldom have assets as collateral. Additionally, in event of default, banks do not want to be seen harassing an NGDO through the courts for re-payment; it is bad for their public image.

12 The reason usually put forward for delay is lack of necessary reporting information from the recipient. While often true, the carrot and stick of timely reporting giving timely payment is often too crude for the real-life situation of development in resource-poor environments – which calls for other principles and mechanisms, such as operating floats covering at least two reporting cycles.

13 Fowler, 1982.

14 It is the anonymity of multilateral money that makes the personal values and anti-poverty commitment of IFI and bilateral staff so vital if any heating is to take place within their system.

15 Scandals have recently erupted in the USA involving chief executives of very large non-profits: United Way of America and the National Association for the Advancement of Coloured People. Being financed by an individual is obviously no guarantee against corruption or misuse of power. (Herzlinger, 1996).

16 Fowler, 1992d.

17 The hidden cost for many is stress and burn-out.

18 ODA, 1995b.

19 Riddell, Bebbington and Davis, 1995.

20 Adapted from Fowler, 1992d.

21 *Onze Wereld*, The Hague, 1992, pp. 9-11.

22 Wolfe, 1989.

23 Figures are, however, not available for the growth in a gift economy in the South.

24 Robinson, 1991 and unpublished information provided by the OECD statistical office.

25 Chapter 9 examines the post-Cold War justification for international aid.

26 Robinson, 1991a, contains comparative figures of NGDO dependency on official funds in the North – highest in Canada and Scandinavia, lowest in Britain and Ireland.

27 A more recent study is Fox, 1995.

28 For Canada, the EEC and USA, see Smillie, Douchamps and Sholes/Covey, 1996.

29 A classic example is South Africa. The EEC had a special fund for South African NGDOs channelled through a group of Northern agencies, sustaining some of them. As soon as sanctions were lifted, the EEC opened its own liaison office in Johannesburg and started to deal directly with the South African NGDOs who had been the indirect recipients of EEC support, cutting out the Northern intermediaries.

30 World Bank, 1996b.

31 Pratt and Stone, 1994.

32 Burnell (1991, p. 221) suggests that raising money from official aid may be cheaper than collecting from the public. I am not so sure this is the case, as opportunity costs for NGDOs are seldom calculated.

33 Governments can rightly ask about the mandate that entitles NGDOs to engage in deliberations between multilaterals and governments. Even though the mandate of many Southern and Eastern governments is suspect or disputed, NGDOs need a good answer.

34 Compiled and published by The International Rivers Network, 1847, Berkeley Way, Berkeley, CA 94703, USA.

35 Malena, 1995.

36 One of the largest stumbling blocks to NGDO collaboration with the World Bank are its procurement procedures (Voorhies, 1993). This is a publication worth reading for NGDOs thinking of working with the Bank.

37 USAID, 1995; JICA, 1995.

38 Maren, 1995b.

39 *The Guardian*, 14 December 1994.

40 Investments are a common area of ethical concern which gained prominence in the disinvestment and boycott of European companies with large holdings in South Africa during apartheid.

41 Smith, 1994.

42 Tennyson, 1994.

43 Patel and Jorgensen, 1997.

44 This does not imply that there are no illegitimate Northern NGDOs, only that they lack political cover, and are more easily spotted and reported on by other NGDOs and the media.

45 Schmidt and Marc, 1994.

46 Interviews with NGDOs in Thailand and the Philippines.

47 NGDO self-censorship and compliant attitudes due to dependency on official aid can already be found in Europe. SCF-UK, tempered its criticism of the UN for this reason (Edwards, 1993).

48 Valderrama, 1995.

49 Translated comment made by the director of Green Salvation, Kazakstan.

50 Interview with IBASE staff.

51 Bangladesh Rural Advancement Committee, *Annual Report*, 1994.

52 This section draws, with my thanks, on the comments and unpublished work of Richard Holloway.

53 Shearer, 1994; Fox, 1996.

54 Interview with Enrique Anrade of Fundacion Sociale.

55 Sandar, 1990.

56 Interview with director of PBSP.

57 Sandar, op cit.

58 African countries work on the basis of affinity and kinship: an 'economy of affection' overlaid by modern institutional forms inherited from colonial powers (Hyden, 1983).

59 Fowler, 1996, is a detailed examination of potential pitfalls in donor pro-NGDO policies and what can be done about them.

60 Fowler and James, 1996.

61 Hudock, 1995, provides good readings on optimising resources.

62 Some countries – Chad, Central African Republic, Bhutan – are themselves not

economically viable as modern states. They exist at an unsustainable level by the grace of aid. Here, the potential for NGDOs to become economically rooted in the foreseeable future is very slim. Their autonomy will remain in doubt.

63 Vincent and Campbell, 1989, is one of the most useful books around for leaders or managers who wish to embark on self-financing strategies.

64 Adapted from visual aids prepared by Richard Holloway.

65 Datta, 1996.

66 Andrew Hind provides a good analysis of the ratio game for UK NGDOs (Hind, 1995, pp. 174-188).

67 This section draws on contributions from Ian Smillie.

68 Books published by IRED, written by Fernand Vincent, offer practical advice on how to do this.

69 UNHCR is effectively trying to misuse the partnership label to insist that, as they are not contractors, NGDOs must cover all overhead costs of UNHCR-funded activity from other resources (Smillie, 1995c).

70 *World Vision News*, special edition, Melbourne, 1991.

71 The standards are known as the Statement of Recommended Practice on Accounting by Charities (SORP), explained in Hind, 1995, p. 183.

72 A 1994 proposal for such an initiative in Canada met a lot of resistance from NGDOs as well as CIDA.

Chapter 7

1 I am grateful to Abigail Krystall for advice and collaboration in the writing of this section and other comments on the chapter.

2 Comment made by Abigail Krystall to participants of a workshop for staff of Norwegian Church Aid.

3 The basic challenge is to identify the right indicators of change; examples are in the readings.

4 Shetty, 1994.

5 For a useful approaches see: Fowler, 1989b, Uphoff, 1991.

6 The competition is healthy because it sharpens the search, which increases the quality of what is being done. But it is also false because the world of social development measurement is not either/or, but and/and.

7 For example, Carvalho and White, 1993.

8 See further readings on performance assessment in development and on development organisations.

9 Krystall, Young and Waithaka, 1994.

10 This sensible suggestion, can be found in Eckman, 1993.

11 For a description of this evolution see Guba and Lincoln, 1989.

12 Marsden, Oakley and Pratt, (eds), 1994; and readings.

13 The macro-micro linking of development influences and impacts is a common weakness in monitoring and evaluation, in part because projects tend either to work only at one level at a time or do not integrate very well when attempts are made to couple many levels at once.

14 Mascerenhas, 1992.

15 For details and practical examples see: INTRAC/South Research, 1994.

16 Argenti, 1993. A common justification for this behaviour is that 'professional' management was not consistent with the culture and voluntary ethos of non-profits. There are few NGDO leaders/managers today who would hide behind this façade. It is not a question of professional management – the poor have an absolute right to professionalism – but of using appropriate performance measures.

17 Peter Senge's book, 1990b, is probably one of the best-known introductions and explanations of what it takes to be a learning organisation.

18 Feuerestein, 1983, p. 7.

19 I borrow the term 'aware organisations' from Allan Kaplan of CDRA, Cape Town.

20 See further readings for Chapter 2, this chapter and Kanter, 1979; Kanter and Summers, 1987.

21 Kanter, 1979, p. 36.

22 Drucker, 1990b; 1993.

23 See Freeman, 1984 and further readings.

[24] Mitroff, 1983, p. 2.

[25] Oxfam, 1994.

[26] For the principles of social audit, see Zadek and Evans, 1993.

[27] Conference presentation by the director of Traidcraft UK, Manchester, July, 1994.

[28] Traidcraft, 1993.

[29] Traidcraft, 1994.

[30] Obtained from an analysis of a social audit resource kit (New Economics Foundation, 1995).

[31] Traidcraft's social audit comprised four stakeholder perspectives: producers, staff, consumers and shareholders.

[32] The audit group comprises stakeholder representatives who check the audit report for anomalies as well as providing advisory support throughout the audit process.

[33] This section draws on training materials developed by Salil Shetty.

[34] Typical obstacles to learning in NGDOs have been summarised by Chris Roche of Oxfam UK/I (1995b). These include: weak systems, staff insecurity and turnover, work overload leading to defensive behaviour, territorialism, ambivalent commitment. Nobody is openly going to come out against learning, resistance is passive and/or blamed on lack of time, energy, resources.

[35] For advocacy performance indicators see Miller, 1994b.

[36] I am grateful to Salil Shetty for critical comments on this and other sections of this chapter.

[37] While understandable, not including opponents in stakeholder analysis introduces a serious limitation which shows up when they start to act against a development initiative.

[38] Information from Tom Carroll from a 1988 study carried out by NOVIB.

[39] Shah and Shah, 1995.

[40] A parallel trend with government is the creation of citizen's scorecards, for assessing the quality of public agencies (Paul, 1993).

Chapter 8

[1] Rick James's survey of Northern NGDO capacity building documents the mess quite well (James, 1994).

[2] E. Miller, 1989.

[3] Exceptions do arise in capacity improvements which are tightly bounded – for example, when computerising an accounting system.

[4] Burke, 1992.

[5] Adapted from Bebbington and Mitlin, 1996, p. 11.

[6] I am grateful to Richard Holloway for focusing my attention on the inter-NGDO dimension of capacity growth and other comments on this chapter.

[7] This relationship should be clear, because NGDOs are social change organisations whose effects are external.

[8] Adapted from Hordijk *et al*, p. 70.

[9] Hordijk, *et al*, pp. 64-75.

[10] Honadle and Hannah, 1982; Reilly, 1987; Fowler, Campbell and Pratt, 1992.

[11] *ibid*, p. 10.

[12] Schein, 1988.

[13] Technically, this means applying a resource dependency framework as part of the OD approach. In fact, reducing the degree to which resources limit capacity is a priority for NGDO OD today. See readings for Chapter 6.

[14] Deliberations of staff in the Norwegian Church Aid's Region for Eastern Africa.

[15] Leadership in Turbulent Times', Ganonoque, Ontario, May 1994.

[16] With foresight, this strategy was adopted by the management of Digital Equipment Corporation (DEC) as a way of positioning the company prior to the slump in the computer market in the early 1990s. Convincing staff to change when things are going well is almost a contradiction in terms, so a sense of crisis had to be artificially created. DEC had strategically 'right-sized' before market forces made this a necessity for others.

[17] Kotter, 1996, is a useful guide to introducing change.

[18] Ideal types have long been out of favour in sociology, but many NGDOs have told me how useful it is to have a reference point for judging themselves, so here is one.

[19] D. Brown, 1993.

[20] Fowler, Goold and James, 1995.

[21] Adapted from Drucker, 1993. More detailed questions are in Fowler, Goold and James, 1995.

[22] Rossum, 1993, provides a method and workbook for engaging staff in this exercise

[23] Drawing on unpublished work of INTRAC, Carol Sahley provides a very useful summary of capacities which can be used in a profile. Sahley, 1995, pp. 58-59.

[24] CDRA, 1995, p. 9.

[25] Useful guides to this section containing more detail specifically for NGDOs are: Human and Zaaiman, 1995, Chapter 8; Sahley, 1995; Kelleher and McLaren, 1996.

[26] Adapted from training materials prepared by Richard Holloway and Liz Goold.

[27] This section draws on Fowler, Campbell and Pratt, 1992.

[28] Kubr, 1993. He lists eight selection criteria: professional integrity; professional competence; rapport with the individual; assignment design; capability to deliver; ability to mobilise further resources; the cost of consulting services; the reputation or image of the consultant.

[29] Harding, 1995.

[30] Cooke, 1996a.

[31] See Schein, 1988, for models of consultation.

[32] Robinson, 1993.

[33] There are all sorts of conceptual problems about cause and effect relationships between state, civil society, markets and political systems. NGDOs seldom have the intellectual power to work their own way through this maze and go along with answers underpinning financial flows.

[34] There is movement in this situation with, for example, USAID applying the notion of civic advocacy organisations as a focal point for its democratisation strategy (Hansen, 1996).

[35] Nee, 1995, p. 21.

[36] *ibid*, pp. 49-50.

[37] An example of civil society mapping is Holloway, 1995.

[38] Mysliwiec, 1994, p. 102.

[39] 'Charities Find Western Ways Don't Always Work in Russia', *The Chronicle of Philanthropy*, May 2, 1996.

[40] Kuratov and Solyanik, 1995.

[41] For elaboration on some of these areas see, VeneKlassen, 1994.

[42] For the relation between development participation and citizenship, see Fowler, 1992a.

Chapter 9

[1] It is a time when all writers must offer some speculations about the NGDO future. See Fisher, 1993; Smillie, 1995a, Chapter XIII; Sogge, 1996, Chapter 7; Edwards and Hulme, 1995, Part III; Edwards and Hulme, 1996.

[2] Speculations on a new world order are in the readings for Chapter 1.

[3] In the North this carries the new label of communitarianism: Etzioni, 1993.

[4] ActionAid, 1996.

[5] Foy and Helmich (eds), 1996, p. 11.

[6] Yankelovich, 1996, p. 64.

[7] For a study on NGDO development education, see Carty, 1990.

[8] Rice, 1996, p. 12.

[9] *ibid*, p. 12-13.

[10] Riddell, 1996.

[11] *ibid*, p. 7.

[12] Edwards, 1996c, p. 11.

[13] The World Bank is showing interest in a new – more experimentally oriented – project cycle along lines proposed by Denis Rondinelli (Rondinelli, 1983; Picciotto, 1994). It is far from clear if this will be adopted.

[14] Herlinger, 1995. CARE Canada has also been the subject of hostile press and television reports about its work and use of funds.

[15] Charlton and May, 1995. This takes us back to the issue in Chapter 6 of defining what constitutes an overhead.

[16] Interview with Katalin Ertsey, NGO consultant in Hungary.

[17] See readings for Chapter 2.

[18] For theories of why communal organisations have inherent difficulties with accountability, see Ostrom, 1990; Brett,

1994. For field studies confirming the theory see Carroll, 1992; Smith-Shreen, 1995.

[19] Dalton and Kuechler, 1990.

[20] *ibid*, pp. 288-289.

[21] Fowler, 1994b.

[22] This is the situation in the USA (Smith and Lipsky, 1993) and is showing up in Europe and the aid system.

[23] Edwards and Hulme, 1992, pp. 15.

[24] Farrington, *et al*, 1993.

[25] This section draws on work done by Mike Edwards, 1996b.

[26] In June 1994, the Development Studies Association of UK and Ireland held a workshop to look at improving the interface between development practitioners and academics (DSA, 1994).

[27] This column assumes that the regime in power has some popular legitimacy, is interested in development and not just staying in control by any means.

[28] Philippine NGDOs, for example, came together to agree on issues in the field of land and housing, leading to a concentration of effort on reforming the government's housing programme and specific laws regulating access and title to land (PHILSSA, 1995).

[29] The commentator was Tim Brodhead, who has my sincere thanks for provoking a serious re-think about what I originally intended.

[30] I am grateful to John Hailey for discussions contributing to this section.

[31] See, for example, Kennedy, 1993; Huntington, 1993; Korten, 1995; Thurow, 1996.

[32] During trips in Latin America and Asia, I asked NGDO leaders to estimate the proportion of organisations which would survive a withdrawal of aid from the North. A common response everywhere was 95 per cent.

[33] This comment alludes to the Fifty Years are Enough Campaign pursued by NGDOs during 1994 and 1995.

[34] Okada, 1994.

[35] Katherine Fierlbeck (1997) points to the benefit of ambiguity for donors pushing a liberal agenda.

[36] The 1995 study by Mosley and Hudson indicates that aid to many countries has no significant impact, in part because of the wide range of responses to aid adopted by the public and private sector.

[37] Galtung, 1975; Lehmann, 1986.

[38] Fowler, 1982.

[39] Lipschutz, 1992.

[40] Ronfeldt and Thorup, 1993, p. 11.

[41] *Amazon Stranger*, by Mike Tidwell, published by Lyons and Burford, 1996.

[42] Ian Smillie, 1995, provides the first; David Sogge, *et al*, 1996, the second.

Readings

Chapter 1: Understanding International Development

The purpose of development co-operation

Going through World Bank annual *World Development* reports and the *Human Development* Reports from UNDP is as good a way as any of looking at issues and contending positions on aid. While few would oppose the goals of a more equitable, just society and sustainable economy, many critics contend that the development model being applied is actually making things worse for the poor and for a healthy global physical environment; see, for example, Bellow, 1994. Other observers of the aid scene focus not on the goals and models but on the inadequacies, waste and self-serving nature of the methods and instruments being applied; see Hancock,1989; for NGDOs, see Sogge, 1996.

Civil society

Civil society is a complicated area made more so by the rapidly growing amount of contradictory writing. For academic theory, see Chazan, Harbeson and Rothchild (eds), 1993; White, 1994; Blaney and Pasha, 1993. Gellner, 1994 offers a challenging view and Fierlbeck, 1997, unpacks the concept and shows how it is being (mis)used by the aid system. A good critical look at assumptions about civil society and democracy is Salamon, 1993.

The volume published by CIVICUS, 1994, provides a very useful, but uneven, continent-by-continent review. For practical applications, see: Asia-Pacific region, Serrano, 1994; for Bangaldesh, Holloway, 1995; for Colombia, Richie-Vance, 1991. Siegel and Yancey, 1992, and Rau, 1992, review the emergence of civil society in eastern Europe and the Soviet Union. China is assessed by Chamberlain, 1993, and Howell, 1994. Tandon, 1991a, Sumariwalla, 1993; USAID, 1994; VeneKlasen, 1994; Renshaw, 1994; Robinson, 1995; Porter and Kilby, 1996, all look at how civil society can be strengthened by NGDOs.

Democratisation, good governance and NGDOs

For the theory of democratisation with a Western bias, see Diamond, Linz and Lipset, 1988, 1993.

There are different perspectives on governance, one division being between the economic view of actors like the World Bank and political interpretations. For a sampling of perspectives on markets and good governance, see Brautigan, 1991; Lal, 1992; World Bank 1992; Archer, 1994. On governance in relation to official aid there is Osbourne, 1993a, 1993b. On participation related to governance, see PRIA, 1994. On culture and governance, see Landell-Mills, 1992; Lawyers Committee for Human Rights, 1993.

When it comes to changing governance at the global level, see North-South Roundtable, 1989, 1991; Urquhart and Childers,1990; Streeten, Emmerij and Fortin, 1992. A special issue of *Third World Quarterly*, Vol. 16, 1995, is devoted to NGOs and global governance.

Relationships between NGOs, democratisation and and governance can be found in Clark 1991; Fowler, 1991b, 1993; Salamon, 1993: Clayton (ed.), 1994; Ndegwa, 1996. The governance agenda is bringing together NGOs who were previously separated between those involved in development and human rights: so it is worth looking at Farer, 1993.

Micro development

The extensive literature on rural development seldom addresses the causes of poverty, concentrating on strategies and actions. In addition to the endnotes, useful and not too academic works are: Chambers, *et al*, 1981; Harris (ed); 1982; Chambers, 1983, 1997; Lewis, *et al*, 1988; Porter, Allen and Thompson, 1991. When it comes to the practice of micro-level development the following are worth looking at: Honadle and van Sant, 1975;

Durning, 1989; Taylor and Jenkins, 1989; Wim, 1989; Burkey, 1993; OXFAM, 1995; O'Leary and Simmons, 1995. The reader edited by Craig and Mayo, 1995, provides a good summary of where things stand. A not widely known but excellent treatment of rural development theory and practice can be found in Röling and de Zeeuw, 1983.

Gender, women and development

For texts on gender in the planning, financing and implementation of development work, see: Commonwealth Secretariat, 1987; Oestergaard, 1992; Moser, 1993; Young, *et al*, 1993; MacDonald, 1994; Williams, *et al*, 1994; Barrig and Whekamp, 1994; Chossudovsky, 1996. Getting gender on the UN development agenda is described in UNIFEM/UN-NGLS, 1995.

Development projects and participation

Hirschmans's 1967 insights into the fundamental shortcomings of projects as the instruments for development are, unfortunately, still valid. Typical problems arising from the project mode of development and possible solutions can be found in Morss 1984; Lecomte, 1987; Uphoff, 1988.

For descriptions on how to identify, start up and run development projects, see: Honadle, 1986; Geneva Group, 1992; Morss and Gow, 1985; Narkwiboonwong and Tips, 1989. In addition, much recent project management literature is linked to the widespread introduction of logical framework analysis and its associated implementation requirements; for example, GTZ, 1988; Little and van de Geer, 1994.

Further to items included in the endnotes, for critical discussions on the concept and nature of participation – particularly in relation to international aid – see: Economic Commission for Africa (ECA), 1990; for UNDP, Donnelly-Roark, 1991; ODA, 1994; White, 1996. Bhatnagar and Williams, (ed), 1992, is a particularly good compendium.

For participation within the context of projects and their management, see: Bryant and White, 1984; Korten and Klauss, 1984; Garcia-Zamor (ed), 1985; Oakley, 1987; Bamberger, 1988. Experiences of people's participation in World Bank Projects are analysed in Paul, 1987. When it comes to NGDO practice in participation, including targeting, processes of relationship change and so on, see: Griffiths, 1987; for environment, Ngugi, 1994. Vivian and Maseko, 1994, take a critical look at NGDO participatory practice in Zimbabwe. Two publications on participation directed at World Bank staff, but with far wider application, are World Bank 1994a, and for best practice by type of development activity, World Bank 1994b.

Local institutions and their development

Esman and Uphoff, 1985, and Uphoff 1986, 1992, are still probably the most useful publications on local institutions in development. One asset is their separate treatment of common development sectors such as health, water supply and agriculture. They have probably only been overtaken by publications in the area of credit and micro-enterprise institutions. Cernea, 1996, provides a cogent statement of the significance of social organisations, in development. For research on capacity building of local institutions see Bebbington and Mitlin, 1996; Howes, 1996.

Conscientisation and empowerment in development

For a critical analysis of the principles underlying power, see Lukes, 1974. The notion of conscientisation is strongly associated with Paulo Friere, 1974. For a comprehensive look at empowerment in theory and practice, see Hulme and Turner, 1990; Shetty, 1994; Rowlands, 1995. For practical methods of development education in the process of conscientisation, see Holland and Henriot, 1983; Hope and Timmel, 1984 (revised 1996). For research on what is cited to be a major revision in the application of the Frierian principles to adult literacy, see Archer and Cottingham, 1996.

Reforming bureaucracy

Looking at constraints, opportunities and methods for bureaucratic reform see: Brinkerhoff, 1979; Korten and Siy, 1988; Corkery, Land and Boschuyt, 1995. For restructuring state institutions and decentralising bureaucracy see: Conyers, 1984; Commonwealth Secretariat, 1986; Kruit, 1989; Mutahaba, 1989; Rondinelli, 1989; Salmen, 1993. Hoggett, 1992, and Lindenburg and Crosby, 1989, analyse new public sector management and its political dimensions respectively. For an example of a consumer perspective on public sector reform see Paul, 1993.

Advocacy and public policy reform

For a country (Northern) comparisons on legal constraints to policy campaigning, see Randon and Perri, 1994. For advocacy work, see: Bratton, 1990; Wuyts, *et al*, 1992; Grindle and Thomas, 1991; Clark, 1991; Crosby, 1992a, 1992b; Smillie, 1994; Thomas (ed), 1993; Lee, 1994; and Miller, 1994a, 1994b. NGO experience in advocacy at multilateral conferences is illustrated by van Rooy, 1996a. The workings of the American foreign aid system are described in Morrison and Purcell, 1988. For those wanting to influence multilateral financial institutions, such as the World Bank, see Kardam, 1993; Madrinan, 1995.

Chapter 2 Understanding NGDOs

Organisational theory

For good summary works, which unfortunately do not spend that much time on non-profits, see: Scott, 1987; Hall, 1991. The writings of Charles Handy and Gareth Morgan are usually stimulating and useful: Handy, 1978, 1985, 1988, 1989; Morgan, 1986, 1989. For an open systems approach see Mink *et al*, 1991.

Institutions and organisations

This confusing area is captured reasonably well in Scott and Meyer, 1994; while Goldsmith, 1991, provides a good review in the context of development action. An old but useful book linking institutions to development work is Leonard and Marshall, 1982.

The organisation and features of non-profits

For a comprehensive, but slightly dated reader on non-profit organisations, see Powell, (ed), 1987. The thrust is essentially American, which can to some extent be balanced by more recent studies: Independent Sector, 1990; McCarthy, 1989; Anheier and Seibel, 1990.

For historical and theoretical treatments of the third sector, including the search for definitions and analysis of their size and scope, see: Whitaker, 1974; Weisbrod, 1975; Billis, 1989a, 1990; James, 1989; Anheier, Rudney and Salamon, 1992; Salamon and Anheier, 1992, 1994. The book by van Til, 1989, shows how to map the third sector from a Northern perspective. Comparisons of similarities and differences in the organisation and management of business and non-profits can be found in Leat, 1993. NGDO governance is analysed by Leach, 1989.

Chapter 3 Organising Non-profits for Development

Designing organisations

An easy-to-read introduction to organisational design is Nadler and Tuschman, 1989. For structure analysis and choices, Mintzburg, 1979, is still a good starting point.

NGDOs in development work

Useful general publications on the role and issues related to NGDOs in development are: Gorman (ed), 1984; OECD, 1988; Cernea, 1988; Overseas Development Institute (ODI), 1988; Berg, 1987; Korten, 1990; Burnell, 1991; Clark, 1991; Fowler, 1993; Fowler and James, 1994; Riddell and Robinson, 1995. Butler and Wilson's book, 1990, draws conclusions by comparing NG(D)Os with such different missions that it is not as useful as the title suggests. Comprehensive overviews covering all the major aspects of NGDOs are: Drabeck (ed), *World Development*, Supplement Vol 15, 1987; and Edwards and Hulme (eds), 1993, 1995, 1996b; Smillie, 1995a; Carroll, 1992. These four provide a comprehensive entry into the world of NGDOs.

Though collected at random and variable in their purpose, age and quality, for regional and country studies, see: Latin America, Smith, 1990; Bolivia, Arellano-Lopez and Petras, 1994; Africa, Baldwin; 1990, Anheier, 1994; West Africa, Anheier, 1989; Asia, Bowden 1989; India, Alliband, 1983; Thailand, Hewison, 1993; Canada, Brodhead and Herbert-Copley, 1988; Europe, Sklias, 1993; China, Whiting, 1989; Philippines, Alegre, 1996.

NGOs in relief, humanitarian assistance and conflict

For NGOs in complex humanitarian emergencies; see: Anderson and Woodrow, 1989; Bolling and Smith, 1982; Ferris, 1992; Barrett, 1993; Duffield; 1993, African Rights, 1994; Mooney, 1995. The link between relief and development is explored in Ross, Maxwell and Buchanan-Smith, 1994. Of the few organisational analyses of NGOs in conflict situations see Burns and Bradbury, 1995; Small, 1996. Ways of minimising negative effects of aid in emergency situations are detailed in Anderson, 1996.

From social vision to development action

As both a broad and selectively deep review, the old *Oxfam Field Director's Handbook* and the new *Oxfam Handbook of Development and Relief* stand on their own (Oxfam, 1985, 1996). However, the latest volume is very uneven in its treatment of topics and does not constitute a handbook in the area of NGDO management and organisation.

A useful general work on organisational strategy, including non-profits, is Bryson, 1988. For strategic planning and strategic management in the context of development see, Paul 1983; Rondinelli, 1983; Crosby, 1991; Bowman, 1990. Old and new critiques of the strategic planning fashion are Mason and Mitroff, 1981; Mintzburg, 1994.

For NGDO-specific strategic planning methods, see: IDR, 1990; Oxfam, 1995a; Save the Children Fund (SCF/UK), 1994. For NGDO strategic management, see ANGOC, 1988; Morató, Jr., 1993. Problems with NGDO strategic management can be found in Brown, 1988a.

The organisation of NGDOs

There are many publications describing NGDOs in terms of what they do; there are only a few which attempt to look at their internal functioning. One detailed study of Oxfam UK/I is Black, 1992. MacKeith, 1993, provides a rough guide through the management literature on NGDOs, and Billis and MacKeith, 1993, using British examples, provide a simple review of some of their internal challenges. For NGOs in Latin America, see Carroll, 1992. Analysis of organisational issues in non-profits can be found in: Dichter, 1988, 1989; Fisher, 1994; Human and Zaaiman, 1995; and for the consequences of the changing nature of aid in Brazil, see Salano, 1994. Management of a big NGDO can be found in Lovell, 1992.

The role of the Church in development

Although dated, for a good review of the history and issues related to the church in development, see, Lissner, 1977. For a seminal study of the developmental role of Protestant churches in Kenya, see Chepkwony, 1987; for a critical reflection on the church's development role, AACC, 1982, Kinyanjui, 1982; Elliott, 1989; Dorr, 1991, Goold, 1994.

For a review of the church's internal organisational problems related to integrated rural development in Africa, see Fowler, 1984. For organisational dimensions of the global development set-up for Protestant churches, see Egland and Kerbs (eds), 1987.

Chapter 4 Enabling and Empowering NGDO People

Culture in and of organisations

An acknowledged leader in this field is Geert Hofstede, 1984, 1991. For an application of his work to development, see Hofstede, 1983. A different approach is Fons Trompenaar, 1993, who uses three cultural orientations as the basis for problem-solving. For academic treatments: Ouchi, 1980; Jelenek *et al*, 1983; Smiricich, 1983. For discussion on whether or not Western management is transferable to developing countries, see Mendoza, 1976; Moris, 1976; Bjur and Zomorrodian, 1986. Lewis, 1996, is a recent practical treatment of managing across cultures.

Relations between culture and development

Publications by the Brussels-based, South-North Network Cultures and Development are a critical source in this area. For an introduction to an analysis of the interrelationship between culture and human psychology, see Bourguignon, 1979. Cernea, 1993, explores the link between culture and sustainability. For more general writing on this relationship, see Klittgard, 1989; NGLS, 1992; Seregeldin and Tabaroff, 1992; contributions in SID, 1992; Hewison, 1993; Zadek and Szabo, 1994. The Oxfam Journal *Development in Practice*, 1990-1995, contains over a dozen articles on culture in the context of development; see also Powell, 1995.

General works on managing people

Ronnie Lessem (1989) provides one of the most comprehensive publications on management, drawing on psychological as well as cross-cultural perspectives. Peter Vaill (1990),

describes management in ways that correspond to the captain on board an NGDO — not steering a super tanker, but white-water rafting. For a good guide to enabling people to work effectively in (Western) organisations, see Weisbord, 1991. For those interested in total quality management there is Oakland, 1989.

Pauline Graham (1991) argues strongly against the division between managers and leaders. For an attempt to relate complexity to management, see Wheatley, 1994; Stacey, 1996. Publications which illustrate when the tasks of for-profit management begins to look like NGDO management are Kanter, 1989; Senge, 1990a.

While NGDOs seem to be beating a retreat from valuing innovation in human resource management, the 1996 book by Flood, Gannon and Pauwe on non-traditional methods and Lessem's writings (1989) will hopefully give pause for thought.

Non-profit leadership and management

Of the growing number of publications in this area, see: Handy, 1988; Hudson, 1994. One of the most practical and accessible books on non-profit management is Sandy Adironack, 1992. On non-profit management competencies, see Dartington, 1989a, 1989b, and other publications from the National Council of Voluntary Organisation's management unit. The Academic Journal *Nonprofit Management and Leadership*, is a useful reference for those interested in non-profit research, as is *Voluntas*. Peter Drucker's contribution to this field is Drucker, 1990. An article tying together non-profit leadership and resource dependency is Heimovics *et al*, 1993. A recent comprehensive reader, although with a Northern bias, is

Herman and Associates, 1994. Batsleer, Cornford and Paton, 1991, address common NGO management issues.

Managing development

A substantial amount of material can be found in this area, but almost exclusively from a public sector perspective. General publications, some with an African bias, are: Austin, 1984; Bryant and White, 1983; Hyden, 1983; Murrell and Duffield, 1985; Wiggins, 1985; AAPAM, 1986; Bowden, 1986; Honadle, 1986; Rondinelli, 1986; Dichter, 1989; Brinkerhoff, 1992; Fisher, 1994; Kiggundu, 1994. Though old, the book on development management by John Moris, 1981, remains one of the best. For distinctive management features of development work, see: Brinkerhoff and Klauss 1987; Brown and Covey, 1987; Fowler, 1989.

NGO management applied to development

The series *NGO Management Newsletter* produced by the International Council of Voluntary Agencies (IVCA) from 1985–1990 yields a wealth of practical information and insights. For a critical view see Dichter, 1987a, 1987b, who argues that NGDOs are too interested in the nuances of development management while they still have to get the basics right. For issues of managing volunteers, see Brudney, 1990; Harder, 1992.

Gender, women and organisation

While there are overlaps with texts on the organisational position of women, in the area of gender in organisational culture, see: Staudt, 1990; Goetz, 1992; Tanton (ed), 1992; Oxfam, 1995, Longwe, 1995. For women in organisations, see: Coleman, 1991; Kanter, 1993; von Nostrand 1993; Tanton, 1994; Chueng-Judge and Henly, 1994; Nair, Mehta and Sawney, 1995.

Human resource management and development

For short, useful articles on training for NGDOs, see Batchelder, 1988; Lent, 1988; Billis, 1989b; Campbell, 1989. For examples of analysis of NGDO training needs, see Rooley and White, 1989; Thomas, 1994; Mamdani and Otim, 1994. A more substantial treatment of learning from experience is Weil and McGill (eds), 1990. For HRD in a wider perspective, see Rao, 1994; Jones and Mann (eds), 1992. Ideas about identifying best practice in HRM is described by von Glinow, in Shaw *et al*, 1993. An excellent source of ideas and examples for trainers and facilitators has been produced by UNICEF 1990 and 1993 (Bangladesh).

A useful survey of management training for non-profits is van Til and Heygesi, 1996. For transactional analysis methods, see Harris, 1970, and Stewart and Joines, 1987. For practical training of change agents, the volumes by Hope and Timmel, 1984, are still amongst the best. More recent is PRIA, 1992, 1995; Burkey, 1993. Case studies for use in training can be found in Taylor and Jenkins, 1989. Advice on resources for case study methods is given by Zwick and Brown, 1994. An excellent, practical, comprehensive guide to the forming of NGO staff is O'Leary and Simmons, 1995. Leurs, 1993, provides a PRA training manual as does Mascarenhas *et al* 1991; and in a special training issue *RRA Notes*, IIED Notes, 19,1994. Strategies for forming senior cadres of NGDOs are given in Fowler, 1990 (reprinted as an Appendix in Fowler, 1992b).

Expatriates and technical assistance

An old but still relevant critical review of technical co-operation is Spitzburg, 1987. What should have been the nail in the coffin of TC in the official aid system was Elliot Berg's submission to the DAC. But, as he points out, old habits die hard (Berg, 1994). The search for alternatives can be seen in Boschuyt *et al*, 1991. A useful analysis of expatriates, again from a governmental perspective, is Cohen, 1991. An excellent treatment of expatriate issues for NGDOs is Crewe, 1994.

Chapter 5 NGDO Relationships

Engaging primary stakeholders

For organisational features of an intervention approach to development work, see Fowler, 1988; EASUN, 1996. For a treatment of rural development interventions as a form of action research, see PRIA, 1982. A comprehensive review of the participatory design of projects is Narayan, 1995. Negotiation in rural development work is addressed in Miller, 1979.

In addition to Stan Burkey's book, 1993, one of the best appraisals of the role of change agents is by Tilakaratna, 1992. See also, Rahema, 1981, 1985. The literature on participatory rural appraisal is growing rapidly. The best resources are the PLA Notes (formerly RRA Notes) published by the International Institute of Environment and Development (IIED). For tools and methods applied in urban areas, see, *RRA Notes* No. 21, 1994; for critical reflections, *RRA Notes* No. 24, 1995. See also Kar and Backhaus, 1994.

Relations between NGDOs

For a Northern analysis of partnerships between Northern and Southern NGDO, see: Brown, 1988b; PACT, 1988; ICSW, 1988; PAC, 1990; ICVA, 1988, 1989; Fowler, 1991; Malena, 1992, 1995; Kawohl, 1993; Leach, 1995; Smillie, 1995. Critical Southern perspectives on partnership can be found in: Tandon, 1991b; AALAE, 1992, 1995; Schlanger, 1992; Salano, 1994; Muchunguzi and Milne, 1995. For policy alliances, see Covey, 1992.

In the area of co-ordination, while lacking a framework, Duell and Dutcher, 1987, assess the contextual conditions, dynamics, costs and benefits of co-operation using evidence from seven African countries. The different possibilities and difficulties between NGDO co-ordination in emergency relief and stable development settings stands out. A more recent, multicontinent analysis of NGDO co-ordination experience has been edited by Jon Bennett, 1995; for a practical how-to guide to setting up co-ordinating bodies, see Bennett, 1994. Descriptions of types of NGDO networking, are contained in Fernando, 1986; El Taller, 1991. Fisher, 1994, Chapter 6, is a useful review of NGDO networks, although the term covers almost any form of NGDO interaction or collaboration. See also Hall, 1992; Tandon, 1995.

NGOs relations with governments in the South and East

The following documents look at interactions in the areas of development action and policy reform. A useful typology of NGDO–state relations in the South and East is provided by Tandon, 1989 and 1991a; while Clark, 1993, offers a thematic analysis. For definitions and applications of the notion of development space for NGDO activity, see Ng'ethe and Kanyinga, 1992. Fisher, 1990, also looks at space in NGDO interactions with local government, an important but neglected area which will gain in significance in the years to come. Earlier articles on this topic are Uphoff, 1987; van Dijk, 1987. Country and region-specific studies are: for Sri Lanka, Fernando, 1991; Thailand, Tongswate and Tips, 1986; for Cambodia, Callahan, 1995, Mysliwiec, 1994; for Africa, Sandberg, 1994; for East Africa, Fowler, 1991; for Latin America, Smith, 1989, 1990; Carroll, 1992; for Colombia, Smith, 1985. Readings on civil society are also relevant.

A summary analysis of detailed research on NGDO operational relations with Southern governments in agricultural innovation is Farrington and Bebbington, 1994. Separate studies are published for Africa, Asia and Latin America. Publications on NGDO–government relations also carry the label partnership – for example, UNDP, 1991b; Vincent, 1992. In addition to Khan, 1996, NGDO advocacy is covered in Chapter 2 readings.

NGDO multisector relations

Analyses of NGDOs as bridging organisations is provided by Brown, 1994; analyses of multisector relationships in development are to be found in Brown and Tandon, 1992; Covey and Brown, 1994; with summaries of practical experiences in Africa, in AALAE, 1995, and globally in Shearer and Tomlinson, 1995. Divisons of labour emerging to fill the space left by an ineffectual state are described in Stiefel and Racelis, 1990; Semboja and Therkildsen, 1995.

Chapter 6 Mobilising Financial Resources

For an overview on NGDO funding and trends see: Fowler, 1982, 1992d. For Southern NGDO resources, see Hudock, 1995, 1996. Detailed analysis including problems and methods for researching non-profit financing is found in Grønbjerg, 1993. Chang and Tuckman, 1994, construct a diversification index to help measure financial stability and viability.

NGOs, public image and fund-raising

For the rationale to altruism and public-giving see: Phelps (ed), 1975; Wolfe, 1993. A critical look at Northern NGDO public fund-raising practices is Hulst and van der Veen, 1992. Carty, 1990, looks at development education; Smillie, 1995 and Foy and Milmich, 1996, appraise the link between public opinion and funding. How journalists view and report the voluntary sector along the lines of a 'hierachy of credibility' is to be found in Deacon, et al, 1995. How to communicate with the general public is in Winter, 1995.

NGDOs and official aid

A substantial amount has been written about NGDO relationships with the official aid system. ICVA, 1985, provides NGO guidelines for accepting government funds which are still valid today. A good, recent review of issues arising from the relationship between NGDOs in 13 OECD countries, and their governments' aid agencies as well as the European Union, is Smillie and Hilmich, 1994. Appraisals of NGO-donor relations are: Douxchamps, 1995; Smillie, Douxchamps and Sholes/Covey, 1996. Randell and German (1996) in the annual publication *The Reality of Aid*, contains good analyses of official funding trends.

An introduction to the direct official funding debate is Mills, 1988. Donor views and analysis of their policies and practices in this area can be found in ODA, 1992; NORAD, 1991; Pratt and Stone, 1994; Woods, 1995; USAID, 1995. Riddell, Bebbington and Davis, 1995, contains a comprehensive review of experience. Fowler, 1996, summarises the policy issues donors face in dealing directly with Southern and Eastern NGDOs. Fox, 1995, provides an analysis of current practices and alternatives. For NGO experiences of dealing with official donors see: Voorhies, 1993; Hallowes, 1995; Perera, 1995; Patel and Jorgensen, 1997. For a very useful donor's view on what makes an effective, participatory NGO, including NGDO organisational indicators see: Carroll, Schmidt and Bebbington, 1996. Malena, 1995, is a practical guide on working relationships between NGDOs and the World Bank, albeit from the perspective of Bank staff. Reviews of experience with NGDO donor consortia are not easy to find. One for BRAC in Bangaldesh is Smillie, 1987.

NGOs and alternative sources: corporations and the market

On corporate financing see: Smith, 1994; Tennyson, 1994; Tennyson, with Marriage and Simpson, 1994. On alternative financing and self-reliance see: Stockhausen, 1983; Vincent and Campbell, 1989; PACT, 1993; Paez and Elano, 1993; Vincent, 1994; Holloway, 1994; Gibson, 1995; IFRG, 1993, 1995; Cumming and Singleton, 1995; Valderamma, 1995. For experience in setting up foundation-like organisations, see Fox 1995b; Shearer, 1995; Schütte, 1995.

Chapter 7 Managing by Achievement

An introduction to the theory, practice and evolution of evaluation as an approach to performance assessment is Guba and Lincoln, 1989. Evaluating social development is found in Marsden and Oakley (eds), 1990; Marsden, Oakley and Pratt (eds), 1994; Brown, 1991. The book by Carlsonn, Kohlin and Ekbom, 1994, is a good starting point for understanding why the aid system is ambivalent towards performance assessment. Tendler, 1982; Riddell, 1990; Howes, 1992; Fowler, 1995; and Fowler and Biekart, 1996, cover the basic problems of assessing development and NGDO performance.

Assessing development performance

Performance appraisals of the official aid system can be found in Cassen, 1986; IDS, 1986; ODI/ECPDM, 1995a, 1995b; Mosley and Hudson, 1995; and ODI, 1996. For issues of selecting qualitative and/or quantitative measures, see: Ravallion, 1992; Greeley *et al*, 1992; Harding, 1994; Khan, 1994. For introductory publications on theory, principles, methods and experiences of traditional approaches, see: Casley and Lury, 1982; Cracknell, 1983; Gianotten, 1986; ECA, 1989; USAID, 1989a; Barclay *et al*, 1993. For alternative and participatory approaches: Feuerstein, 1988; Choudhary and Tandon, 1989; Avina, *et al*, 1990; Robinson, 1991b, 1991c; Uphoff, 1991; Brown, 1991; Coudere, 1994; Eckman, 1993; PRIA, 1993. For ethical principles and best practices in development evaluation, see: Barbedette *et al*, 1995.

Performance indicators and assessment applied to rural and urban poverty, well-being and sector-specific projects are discussed in: USAID, 1989b, 1989c; Baldwin, 1992; Carvalho and White, 1993; Frankenberger, 1993; Galloway, 1993; Hammond, et al, 1995; Narayan, 1993; Khan, 1994; UNHS/World Bank, 1995. For local organisations and institutional development: Fowler, 1989b; Uphoff, 1991; Alianca, 1995. For sustainability, Holmberg, et al, 1991; Karas and Coates, 1994.

Empowerment and civil society: Shetty, 1994; Blair *et al*, 1994. For development education: Case, 1987; Keehn and Kniep, 1987. For assessing policy advocacy, Covey, 1992; Lee, 1994; Miller, 1994b.

Assessing organisational performance

For a critical look at current thinking about organisation performance, especially the inability of non-profits to measure what they do, see Argenti, 1993. For readings on measuring performance in non-profits see: Kanter, 1979; Kanter and Summers, 1987; Lawrie, 1993; Herman and Heimovics, 1994; Leat 1993; Murray and Tassie, 1994. Stakeholder analysis can be found in Mitroff, 1983; Freeman, 1984; Crosby, 1992c; Fowler , 1994; ODA 1995b.

Organisational performance of NGDOs, see: Bendahmane, 1991; OECD, 1992; Carroll, 1992; papers in Edwards and Hulme (eds), 1995; Edwards and Hulme, 1996. For social audit and ethical accounting, see: Zadek and Evans, 1993; Traidcraft, 1993; Zadek and Raynard, 1994; New Economics Foundation, 1995; Body Shop, 1996. Appendix 2 in Carroll, 1992, is a useful list of organisational assessment indicators. Peter Drucker's five question approach (Rossum, 1993; Drucker, 1995) is about as basic as you can get. At the other extreme is the NGDO assessment framework applied by the World Bank, Eaves, 1992.

Studies of NGDO micro-development and policy impact

Reviews of methodological and other issues are Riddell, 1990; Robinson and Thin, 1994. Practical guides are: Oxfam, 1995; Rubin, 1995; SCF, 1995. Donor-related NGDO multi-country studies are: Australia, ADAB, 1995; Sweden, Riddell, Bebbington and Peck, 1994; Denmark, DANIDA, 1994; Norway, Tvedt, 1995; the Netherlands, GOM, 1993; Great Britain, Riddell and Robinson, 1992; Riddell and Robinson, 1995. For critical comparisons and findings of these studies see: van Dijk, 1994; ODI, 1996. For policy influence: Sibanda, 1994; Thomas, 1994, 1995; van Rooy, 1996a; Khan, 1996; *Third World Quarterly*, Vol. 16, No. 3.

Organisational learning and management

The best-known introductions to organisational learning are Senge, 1990a, 1990b; Swieringa and Wierdsma, 1992. For learning in development work: Korten, 1980; Hulme, 1989; Uphoff, 1992; Petty and Chambers, 1993; Singh and Titi, 1994. For learning in NGDOs:

Dartington, 1989; Smillie, 1995b; Roche, 1995; Edwards, 1996b.

NGDO accountability

Verhagen, 1987, was one of the first systematic reviews of dilemmas associated with accountability with member-based NGDOs, confirmed by Smith-Shreen, 1995. The papers in Edwards and Hulme, 1995, provide a comprehensive assessment of the topic, but lack a governmental view.

Chapter 8 Improving Performance: Process and Method in Enhancing NDGO Capacity

General works about organisation development and managing change

There are many books on organisational development and change. Simple introductions are Burke, 1992; Costello, 1994. For managing change see, Bridges, 1991; Carnall, 1992; Kotter, 1996.

Organisational complexity

For complexity theory as applied to organisations see, Wheatley, 1994; Stacey, 1996. Bak and Chen, 1991, look at how complex systems organise themselves.

Consultants

For advice on selecting and using consultants, see Kubr, 1993; Arthur and Preston, 1996. A good introduction to a consultant's role is Weisboid, 1987; Schein, 1987,1988; de Bunt, 1993. Consultant's competencies, skill assessment and practical methods of skill aquisition are described in Somerset Group, 1993a, 1993b.

Capacity and institution building

Capacity building is an end as well as a means in development. Additional readings to Chapters 1 and 2, are USAID, 1982; Hage and Finsterbush,

1987; ICVA/ANGOC, 1989; IRDC, 1993; Kaplan, 1994; Kaplan, 1996, ECPDM, 1995. Blair, *et al*, 1994, have designed a method for assessing civil society, which is not easy.

Assessment of organisational capacity (OA)

There is not much available in this area. For (rapid) assessment in relation to the public sector, see Honadle, 1982. For applications to (US) non-profits, see Rossum, 1993; IDR, 1993; Fowler *et al*, 1995, Hailey; 1995.

Development of NGO organisational capacity (OD)

James 1994 study on Northern NGDO understanding and approaches to OD is a good description of present practice. Further critical reviews can be found in various issues of *OD Debate*, published by OLIVE, South Africa, especially Harding, 1995a, 1995b. See also, Fowler, 1992c, 1994; Fowler *et al*, 1992.

For the theory and practice of OD for NGDOs, see: Brown and Covey, 1987b, 1989; Covey, 1988; Booy, 1989; Campbell, 1989, 1990; Myers *et al*, 1989; CDRA, 1984, 1985; Leach, 1994; Kaplan, 1994; Fowler *et al*, 1995; Gariba *et al*, 1995. Recent, very useful guides to OD are, for micro-enterprise NGDOs, Sahley,

1995; and more generally Kelleher and McLaren, 1996; Tandon, 1996.

Specialist resources for assisting the growth of organisational capacity

There are a growing number of support NGDOs, dedicated to strengthening NGDO and civic capacity: PRIA, 1990; Fowler, 1992e; Doub, 1996.

Civic institutional development (ID)

Moore's 1995 study is a good introduction to ID in the context of international aid. Analysis of past experience of OD/ID are Brown and Tandon, 1990; Brinkerhoff and Goldsmith, 1992; Bruckmeier and Glaeser, 1992; Austin, 1993; Boschuyt, 1995; Brinkerhoff, 1994. Cherrett *et al*, 1995, provide a practical look at redefining institutional roles in relation to environmental sustainability in Africa.

Chapter 9 Future in the Balance

The new world order

For speculations on the new world order and the changing context of NGDO work see: Schneider, 1988; Rosenau, 1900; Ekins, 1992; Kennedy, 1993; Chomsky, 1994; Salamon, 1994; Huntington, 1993; Thurow, 1996; Korten, 1996.

The future of the aid system

On the new policy agenda for aid, see Robinson, 1993. For a summary of trends in international development see: USAID, 1990; Riddell, 1996; and the future of NGDOs, van Dijk (ed), 1989; USAID, 1990; Achterhuis *et al*, 1993; Burnell, 1993; Smillie, 1995a; Sogge (ed) 1996; Zadek, 1996; Edwards and Hulme (eds), 1996; CCIC, 1996; Devine, 1996. Moving beyond aid: Korten, 1990; Sidzoo, 1993. On aid in a complex world see Uphoff, 1992, final chapter.

Civil society, citizens networks and social movements

Looking at the grassroots see Schneider, 1988; Durning, 1989. For non-profit projections and speculations, see Salamon, 1989, 1994; James, 1989. For NGDO contracting see Smith and Lipsky, 1993. For analysis of renewing civil society and its relationship to global development, see: Blaney and Pasha, 1993; Oliviera and Tandon, 1994; Schearer, 1995; James and Caliguire, 1996. On social movements and the evolution of transnational networks in world politics, see: Dalton and Kuechler, 1990; Lipschutz, 1992; Waltzer, 1992; Smith, Pagnucco and Romeril, 1994; Smolar, 1996. On the Internet, see Okada, 1994.

Index

Printed in the USA/Agawam, MA
August 8, 2013

578731.103